LEAN LIFE SOLUTION (LLS)

Lean Life Solution (LLS)

Ibrahim Issaka Lucky

Contents

Introduction

In life, it can be challenging to find balance and achieve personal and professional success. We often find ourselves overwhelmed with numerous tasks, commitments, and responsibilities, leading to a life filled with stress and dissatisfaction. "Lean Life Solutions" is a book that offers a practical and sustainable approach to simplifying your life and maximizing your potential by applying the principles of lean thinking to every aspect of your daily routine.

The concept of lean thinking, which originated in the manufacturing industry, focuses on eliminating waste and increasing efficiency to create more value with fewer resources. In "Lean Life Solutions," we will explore how these principles can be adapted and applied to our personal lives to help us achieve a higher level of satisfaction, productivity, and overall well-being. By identifying and eliminating the non-value-added activities that consume our time and energy, we can create a more streamlined and purposeful life.

In this book, you will discover various tools and techniques for applying the leanness equation ($L = A - W$) to various aspects of your life. We will cover topics such as time management, goal setting, personal productivity, health and wellness, relationships, and financial management, among others. Through practical examples and real-life case studies, you will learn how to identify the activities that truly matter and eliminate the waste that prevents you from reaching your full potential.

As you progress through "Lean Life Solutions," you will begin to see that the concept of leanness is not just about doing more with less;

it is about living a more fulfilling and meaningful life. By focusing on what truly matters and eliminating distractions and waste, you will be able to create a life that aligns with your values, passions, and goals. This journey toward a leaner life is not a quick fix or a one-size-fits-all solution, but rather an ongoing process of self-discovery, reflection, and continuous improvement.

"Lean Life Solutions" is not just a book; it is a guide to a more balanced, purposeful, and efficient life. It is a call to action for individuals who are ready to take control of their lives and make the necessary changes to create a future filled with happiness, success, and personal fulfillment. Whether you are a busy professional looking for ways to improve your productivity, a parent striving for work-life balance, or someone seeking personal growth and a more meaningful existence, this book has something to offer you.

Embark on this transformative journey with "Lean Life Solutions" and discover the power of lean thinking in reshaping your life. Learn how to identify the activities that add value to your life and eliminate the waste that holds you back. With commitment, perseverance, and the insights gained from this book, you can create a leaner, more efficient, and ultimately more satisfying life. Join us on this path to self-improvement and unlock your true potential as you embrace the principles of lean thinking and apply them to your everyday life.

About the Author

As a certified Lean Six Sigma expert (holding qualifications up to the Black Belt level) and quality inspector with a diverse range of quality certifications, my life's focus has been on the relentless pursuit of operational excellence and ongoing enhancement.

My interest in Lean Six Sigma began during my studies in engineering, where I was introduced to the concepts of efficiency and process improvement. Intrigued by the potential impact of these methodologies on businesses, I decided to further explore the world of Lean Six Sigma and quality.

Over the years, I have had the opportunity to work across various industries, applying Lean Six Sigma methodologies to optimize processes and systems. By identifying problems and implementing solutions, I have helped organizations reduce waste, improve efficiency, and enhance the quality of their products and services. Currently, I serve in the combined capacity of a Lean Six Sigma expert and Quality Inspector. My daily tasks revolve around implementing process enhancements and maintaining the utmost quality standards for products and services. As a Quality Inspector, my responsibility is to guarantee that my clients products adhere to the strict quality criteria set by both the organization and industry regulators. This encompasses carrying out routine inspections and audits, overseeing production processes, and detecting any discrepancies from the established protocols.

Lean Six Sigma experts are skilled in accomplishing more with minimal resources and effort. The success of numerous industries can be credited to the principles of quality and Lean Six Sigma methodologies.

With this in mind, I realized that if I could assist industries in achieving more with reduced effort, I could also apply these principles to help modern individuals. This fundamental idea inspired me to write the "Lean Life Solution" book. I authored this book to guide individuals in realizing their dream life with less effort and limited resources available to them.

In the book "Lean Life Solution," I have demonstrated how to approach everyday activities (efforts to manifest a dream life) by incorporating the core principles of Lean Six Sigma and quality management. In addition to presenting existing methods, I have introduced new principles and tools that I have developed through my experience as a Lean Six Sigma and quality expert.

These novel tools and concepts presented in the book have been thoroughly tested and validated by my fellow experts and professors in the fields of Lean Six Sigma and quality management. By extending the principles of Lean Six Sigma beyond the industrial setting, I have adapted and customized these methodologies to suit the needs and challenges faced by individuals in their daily lives.

LEAN LIFE SOLUTION, SOLVING OUR PROBLEMS.

I appreciate your decision to join Lean Life Solution and extend my best wishes for success in all your endeavors. As you use this book as your guide to problem-solving, I hope you find it helpful and insightful.

I would like to remind you that our platform is always open for your queries and concerns. Feel free to reach out to me, and I will be glad to assist you. I believe that together, we can formulate solutions tailored to your specific needs on all facets of life.

Thank you again for choosing Lean Life Solution.

LEAN LIFE SOLUTION AND YOU RESPOND "SOLVING OUR PROBLEMS"

PLATFORM: leanmind.org

Why Read This Book

The "Lean Life Solution" aims to empower readers with the knowledge and tools required to transform their lives, achieve their goals, and live a more fulfilling and efficient life. Drawing from my extensive experience as a Lean Six Sigma and quality expert, I have crafted a comprehensive guide that bridges the gap between professional methodologies and personal development, enabling readers to benefit from the proven strategies that have driven success in various industries.

The "Lean Life Solution" serves as a practical manual designed to address and resolve a wide array of personal and professional challenges, ultimately guiding readers and practitioners towards the rewarding and fulfilling life they aspire to achieve. This book aims to make a positive impact by offering actionable insights and strategies rooted in Lean Six Sigma and quality management principles.

Some of the key aspects that make this book a valuable resource include:

1. Real-world examples: The "Lean Life Solution" features relatable real-life scenarios and case studies, illustrating how Lean Six Sigma principles can be applied to everyday situations and challenges.

2. Step-by-step guidance: The book provides clear, step-by-step instructions for implementing the various tools and methodologies, making it easy for readers to follow along and apply these concepts to their own lives.

3. Customized solutions: Recognizing that each individual's circumstances and goals are unique, the "Lean Life Solution" offers a flexible approach to personal and professional problem-solving, allowing readers to tailor the principles and strategies to their specific needs.

4. Comprehensive approach: This book covers a wide range of topics, from time management and goal setting to financial planning and interpersonal relationships, providing a holistic approach to personal development and problem-solving.

5. Proven techniques: The principles and methodologies presented in the "Lean Life Solution" are based on the well-established and widely-recognized Lean Six Sigma and quality management systems, ensuring their effectiveness and reliability.

By providing readers with practical, easy-to-understand, and proven techniques, the "Lean Life Solution" empowers individuals to take charge of their lives, overcome obstacles, and achieve their personal and professional goals. Through the application of these powerful methodologies, readers can unlock their full potential and pave the way to a more efficient, fruitful, and fulfilling life.

Chapter 1: Balancing Efforts for Success: Practical and Spiritual Approaches

The idea of success is intricate and multi-layered, and achieving it calls for a well-rounded strategy that takes into account both the material and the spiritual parts of one's life. To be successful, one must not only put in a lot of effort and have a lot of endurance, but one must also have a feeling of purpose and inner serenity. This chapter discusses the significance of striking a healthy balance between your material and spiritual endeavors as you work toward achieving your goals.

Practical Efforts for Success

By "practical efforts," I mean the actual, tangible steps you take to realize your dreams and better your life. Goal setting, habit-building, and lifelong learning and improvement are all examples of what may fall under this category.

Determining your goals and actively pursuing them is a vital pragmatic endeavor. To attain success, it's essential to delineate what success entails and recognize when you have accomplished it. Establishing beneficial habits and routines is another crucial step to undertake. Enhancing one's physical and mental well-being through consistent exercise, adequate rest, and a balanced diet can positively impact overall energy levels, focus, and efficiency.

Finally, making an effort to learn and develop both now and in the future is crucial to achieving your goals. Acquiring new information and abilities can help you see things in a broader context, grow in new areas of expertise, and improve your odds of success in all aspects of life.

Spiritual Efforts for Success

Spiritual endeavors are the introspective actions you take to strengthen your bond with your true self and discover your life's true calling. Meditation, conscious awareness, and prayer are all examples of ways to make these kinds of efforts.

Being present in the moment is a vital spiritual practice for fulfillment. Meditation can help you focus and motivate yourself by bringing your attention to the sensations, thoughts, and events occurring in the here and now. Spiritually, meditation is a potent tool for achievement. Meditation is a terrific way to calm the mind, reduce anxiety, and learn more about who you are and what you're here to do.

Finally, making a spiritual connection with a higher force can be an effective spiritual effort. A sense of calm, meaning, and purpose in life can be attained by a connection with something bigger than yourself, whether through religious or spiritual practice or simply by taking in the splendor of nature.

Striking a Balance Between Material and Ethereal Efforts

True and sustainable achievement requires a harmony between material and spiritual pursuits. Improve your chances of success and discover balance and happiness in your life by giving equal attention to both the outside world and the workings of your own mind.

Achievement is a process, not an endpoint. You can achieve greater personal development and happiness in all spheres of your life by integrating spiritual and material practices into your everyday routine.

The Nature of Reality: Is the World We Experience Really What It Seems?

For ages, thinkers in the fields of philosophy, science, and mysticism have attempted to unravel the mysteries surrounding the essence of reality. The crux of the reality problem is the inquiry into whether or not the world we perceive is exactly as it seems, or if there are other, unseen levels of meaning and comprehension.

This idea that reality itself is illusory is ancient and pervasive. According to this theory, the reality we see around us is not objectively real, but rather something we create in our own heads. Many Eastern systems, including Buddhism, hold that our sense of reality is an illusion based on our own preferences and biases.

But Western thought and science have long maintained that the world we inhabit is real and objective. For instance, the empiricist school of thought maintains that we learn about the world by our senses and that things are as they appear to us. Recent discoveries in physics and neurology, however, have shown that our understanding of the world is not as simple as we once thought.

For instance, quantum mechanics argues that subatomic reality functions differently from our macroscopic everyday reality. According to the theory of wave-particle duality, atomic particles can be in more than one state at once, and their actions are very unpredictable. As such, it conflicts with the idea of a static, objective world.

Likewise, studies in neuroscience have demonstrated that how we interpret the world is significantly influenced by our own mental processes. Our knowledge of the world is not passively transmitted to us via our senses, but rather is constructed by our brain, as recent studies have shown. Because of this, it's reasonable to conclude that the world we perceive is an illusion created by our own minds.

To sum up, the nature of reality is a varied and intricate topic that has been investigated by a wide range of academic fields. Despite the widespread assumption in Western thought that the world we see to be real and objective, advances in physics and neuroscience have shown that this is not necessarily the case. The belief that everything we see and experience is merely a mental creation is becoming increasingly mainstream in the modern world, making it an intriguing and fruitful field for research.

The Power of Perception

Our worldview is formed by the beliefs we have and the points of view we take, which in turn determines the reality we experience. The act of perceiving the world around us is not a passive one, but rather an active activity that requires the interpretation and organizing of information received from the senses. Our prior experiences, feelings, and expectations all have a role in how we perceive and organize this information, which in turn is influenced by those experiences.

The act of interpreting and arranging information gleaned from one's senses in order to construct a coherent mental representation of the external world is what we mean when we talk about perception. It is a complicated process that incorporates a number of different cognitive and physiological processes, including sensation, attention, memory, and emotion, among others.

The importance of prior knowledge, which may be defined as the information and experiences that we have amassed over the course of our lives, is widely regarded as one of the most essential components of perception. The way in which we interpret new information is influenced by our prior knowledge, and this in turn forms our expectations. For instance, if we have had a negative experience with a specific kind of food in the past, we may be less likely to enjoy it when we encounter it again.

The function of attention is another essential component of the perceptual process. The cognitive process of focusing one's attention on some features of one's surroundings while ignoring other aspects is referred to as attention. Our desires, aspirations, and feelings all have an impact on the way we direct our attention. For instance, if we are strolling through a bustling metropolis, we could pay more attention to the passing automobiles and people than we do to the structures or trees that surround us.

In addition, our feelings significantly contribute to the formation of our perceptions. Emotions are mental and physiological states that are related with certain thoughts, memories, and the stimulation received from the environment. They have the ability to shape how we see and react to information presented to us. For instance, if we are feeling nervous, iwe may be more prone to interpret a scenario as dangerous, even if it is not actually harmful in and of itself. This can happen even if the situation is not actually dangerous.

In a nutshell, perception is an active process that is formed by our beliefs, the viewpoint we take on things, and the experiences we have had in the past. It is a complicated process that incorporates a number of different cognitive and physiological processes, including sensation, attention, memory, and emotion, among others. When we have a greater understanding of the power of perception, we can have a better understanding of how we see the world around us and how our perceptions create the reality that we experience.

Mind, Body, Heart, and Soul

Life is complex, and it's important to understand how the mind, body, heart, and soul are connected to live fully and meaningfully. When all these parts of us work in harmony, we can reach our true potential. Each part plays a unique and important role in our overall health.

The mind serves as the nerve center for all our mental processes, including thoughts, beliefs, and perceptions. Our capacity to reason, comprehend, and make sense of the reality that surrounds us is directly attributable to its presence. On the other hand, the body is the physical vessel that houses our mind and gives us the ability to move around and engage in activities with the outside world. Sensations and emotions are felt and experienced by us in the world through our bodies.

The emotional center of our being, the heart, is the organ that is in charge of our sentiments as well as our desires. Love, compassion, and empathy all spring from this one wellspring. And finally, the soul is the spiritual part of who we are; it is the component of our being that links us to something that is more important than ourselves. It is the wellspring from which our intuition, creativity, and awareness of our life's mission flow.

However, in spite of the significance of each of these facets of who we are, it is not unusual to have the feeling that at least one of them is lacking or that there is an imbalance between them. It is possible for us to get caught up in negative thought patterns, become detached from our bodies, become numb to our feelings, or have a feeling of being lost and directionless.

The image of "forever does thy light illumine the darkness" comes into play at this point. This light is the light of our true selves, the part of ourselves that is whole and complete; it is the light that is being alluded to here. Even in the darkest of times, there is a ray of light that shines from within each one of us. And it is precisely this light that we need to conjure up and make manifest in order to shed some light on the shadows that have been put upon us.

Because we are so much more than the shadow that is in our heart, the bad ideas that are in our head, the suffering that is in our body, and the emptiness that is in our soul. The light that shines within us is who we are, and it is this light that will lead us out of the darkness and into a place where there is balance and harmony.

To regain a state of equilibrium in our lives, we need to engage in activities that promote well-being across all dimensions of our being, including our minds, bodies, hearts, and souls. These may involve practices such as mindfulness meditation, yoga, exercise, healthy eating, and adequate sleep. By taking care of our physical health and emotional well-being, we can cultivate a sense of inner harmony that allows us to function optimally in our daily lives.

At the same time, we also need to focus on unleashing our inner potential and bringing to light the talents, skills, and passions that reside within us. This involves a process of self-discovery and self-exploration, in which we tap into our unique strengths and abilities and use them to pursue our goals and aspirations. Through creative expression, learning, and personal growth, we can activate the light that lies dormant inside us and use it to illuminate our paths forward, dispelling the shadows of doubt, fear, and uncertainty that may hold us back.

Chapter 2: Your Body System is a Factory

The human body is an extraordinary machine, with many interconnected systems all working together to maintain our wellbeing. It's incredible to think of the human body as a factory, with all the parts working together to make one thing: a fully-functioning, healthy human being. The brain represents the company's chief executive officer, the various systems are the divisions, and the cells are the employees. We should dig deeper into this idea.

The Mind as the CEO

The brain acts as the body's CEO (mind) gadget. The brain acts as the body's master controller, deciding what has to be done and ordering the various systems to go to work. The brain and nervous system make sure everything is running well by communicating with each other and the rest of the organization.

Your mind is the CEO of your body. It is always sending out orders in the form of thoughts that shape how you think, what you believe, and what you do. Your mind is in charge of the overall success of your life, just like a CEO is in charge of the overall success of a company. Your thoughts can either help you reach your goals or stop you from getting there. If you know how powerful your thoughts are, you can take charge of your life and make a good future for yourself.

The Cardiovascular System - The Production Department

The cardiovascular system functions like the factory floor of the body. Its job is to pump blood throughout the body so that every cell may have the oxygen and nutrients it needs to function. The circulatory system consists of the cardiovascular system and the blood. When the heart beats, blood leaves the heart and travels through the body's blood vessels to the various organs and tissues where it carries oxygen and nutrients to the cells

The Respiratory System - The Quality Control Department

The respiratory system is like the factory's quality assurance division. It guarantees that the blood is removing carbon dioxide, which can be harmful if it builds up in the body, and that the body is receiving enough oxygen. The lungs, nasal passages, and breathing muscles all make up the respiratory system. The lungs process the air we breathe to pull out oxygen and release carbon dioxide.

The Digestive System - The Raw Materials/ processing Department

The digestive tract can be thought of as the raw materials department of the body. A healthy digestive system is essential because it converts food into the nutrients the body needs for things like growth and repair as well as sustained energy. The digestive system consists of the oral cavity, the esophagus, the stomach, the small intestine, the large intestine, the liver, and the pancreas. In the mouth, food is chewed and mixed with saliva before being swallowed and transported to the stomach and intestines, where it is further digested and broken down into its component nutrients.

The Nervous System - The Communication Department

The nervous system functions similarly to the "communications division" of a government agency. It acts as a messenger between the brain and the rest of the body, facilitating communication and coordination between the many bodily functions. The brain, spinal cord, and nerves all make up this system. The brain takes in data from the senses, analyzes it, and then communicates those conclusions to the rest of the body via nerve impulses.

The Skeletal System - The Support Department

One way to think of the skeletal system is as the support department of the manufacturing facility. It gives the body structure and support, helping to keep the internal organs safe while still enabling movement. This system is comprised of skeletal elements such as bones and joints, as well as connective tissues such as tendons and ligaments. Moreover, the bones are responsible for the production of blood cells and the storage of vital minerals.

The Immune System - The Security Department

The immune system is kind of like the body's security office. It keeps viruses and bacteria from getting into the body and repairs damaged tissues. White blood cells, lymph nodes, and the spleen are all parts of this system. White blood cells find and kill harmful invaders, while the lymph nodes and spleen filter out harmful substances from the blood.

The Endocrine System - The Regulating Department

The endocrine system is like the department in a factory that controls how things work. It controls how the body works by making and releasing hormones, which send messages to other parts of the body. This system includes glands like the pituitary, thyroid, and ad-renal glands, which make hormones that control metabolism, growth, and how the body reacts to stress.

The Cells as the Staff

The cells are like the factory's employees. They are the people who work in the factory and do specific jobs to keep things running smoothly. Cells do a lot of different things in the body, from making energy to fixing damaged tissues. Each worker in a factory has a specific job to do, and the same is true for each cell in the body.

Our Cells are Always in the Present

Our bodies are made up of trillions of cells, each one working in unison to keep us alive and functioning. While our minds may wander to the past or future, our cells are always in the present, carrying out their tasks in real-time.

Cells are the building blocks of life. They are responsible for carrying out all the functions necessary to keep us alive, such as producing energy, creating new cells, and repairing damage. Cells are constantly communicating with each other to ensure that our bodies are working correctly.

One of the fascinating things about cells is that they are always in the present moment. Unlike our minds, which can wander to the past or future, cells have no concept of time. They exist in the here and now, carrying out their functions in real-time.

This present-moment awareness of our cells is essential for our survival. For example, when we cut ourselves, our cells immediately spring into action, releasing clotting factors to stop the bleeding and beginning the process of repairing the damaged tissue. This process happens in real-time, with each cell playing its unique role in the healing process.

Even on a more basic level, the present-moment awareness of our cells is critical. Every second, our cells are taking in nutrients and oxygen and expelling waste products. They are constantly working to maintain a delicate balance of chemicals and ions in our bodies, keeping us in a state of homeostasis.

The present-moment awareness of our cells can also teach us something about mindfulness. Mindfulness is the practice of being fully present in the moment, without judgment. When we are mindful, we are fully engaged with our surroundings, noticing sensations, thoughts, and emotions without getting caught up in them.

Just as our cells are always in the present moment, we too can strive to be more present in our lives. By focusing on the present moment and letting go of worries about the past or future, we can reduce stress and increase our sense of well-being.

Our cells are always in the present moment, carrying out their vital functions in real-time. This present-moment awareness is essential for our survival, and it can also teach us something about mindfulness. By striving to be more present in our lives, we can reduce stress, increase well-being, and live more fulfilling lives.

The Power of Positive Thinking

One's life can be profoundly altered by adopting an optimistic mindset. Your self-esteem, drive, and toughness can all benefit from a shift in perspective toward the positive. In addition, keeping a growth mindset requires positive thinking, which allows you to see setbacks as learning experiences.

The mental command "I can" ranks among the most powerful you have. Your order reflects your confidence in your own abilities to bring about the desired results. Self-confidence is a prerequisite for taking the necessary steps toward achieving one's goals.

And someone may issue the order, "I can accomplish this," when confronted with a difficult assignment. An optimistic outlook like this can push you past self-doubt and into action, ultimately leading to success.

The Dangers of Negative Thinking

Having a negative outlook might have the opposite impact, slowing you down and making it harder to reach your objectives. Fear and self-doubt can paralyze you if you dwell on negative thoughts. The negative outlook that results from this type of thinking is called a "fixed mindset," and it causes people to see obstacles in their way as dangers and to feel helpless.

The thought "I can't" is one of the most harmful orders you can give yourself. You're sending a message of self-doubt and a lack of faith in your own abilities with this order. If you give yourself this order, you'll be more likely to stop trying to achieve your full potential and settle for less.

An individual may issue the order "I can't do this" when confronted with an impossible assignment. Feelings of hopelessness and inaction may follow from entertaining such a negative thought.

Taking Control of Your Thoughts

Realize the influence of your thoughts and learn to master them. A positive mentality that helps you achieve your goals and objectives can be developed via deliberate attention to positive thoughts and the rejection of negative ones.

The use of positive affirmations is one technique for mastering one's thoughts. Affirmations are phrases of encouragement that can be repeated to oneself over and over to foster growth in constructive thought patterns. If you want to convince yourself that you can succeed, you may say something like, "I am capable of reaching my goals" or "I am confident in my talents."

Mindfulness training is another method for mastering your thoughts. Being mindful entails paying attention to the here and now while suspending judgment about what you're thinking. By self-awareness, you may identify destructive thought habits and replace them with more productive ones.

Synchronizing Mind and Heart with Cells in the Present

Our cells are always in the present. They do their jobs in real time, with no side trips or distractions. If we could match the awareness of the present moment in our mind and heart with that of our cells, we could do amazing things in our lives.

Our minds are always moving quickly from one thought to the next, and our emotions can pull our hearts in different directions. Because of this, we often think about the past or worry about the future instead of living in the present. We lose touch with the present, which can make us feel stressed, anxious, and like life isn't worth living.

But if we could align our thoughts and feelings with the present-moment awareness of our cells, we could tap into a huge source of inner strength, creativity, and resilience. We could reach our full potential and do amazing things if we brought our minds and hearts into the present moment.

To get our mind and heart in sync with our cells' awareness of the present moment, we have to make a conscious effort to stay in the here and now. We can do this by practicing mindfulness, which means paying attention to our thoughts, feelings, and physical sensations without making any judgments about them.

Through mindfulness, we can learn to understand how we work on the inside and let go of things that keep us from being in the moment.

We can also learn to control our feelings and thoughts so that they don't take over or keep us from being in the present.

When we live in the present, we notice our surroundings and the people around us more. We can connect with others and understand what they need better, which helps us build stronger relationships and work together more effectively.

Also, we can use our intuition and creativity when our mind and heart are in sync with the present-moment awareness of our cells. We can come up with new ideas and ways to solve problems, which helps us grow both personally and professionally.

If we could synchronize our mind and heart with the awareness of our cells in the present moment, we could do amazing things in our lives. We can access our inner strength, creativity, and resilience by practicing mindfulness and staying in the moment. We can also connect with others better, build stronger relationships and teams, and grow both personally and professionally. Let's try to live in the here and now and use all of our abilities.

Chapter 3: Quantum Entanglement: Using Within to Impact Without

Quantum entanglement is an interesting idea in physics that has been getting more attention in recent years because it could be used in many different fields, such as psychology, spirituality, and personal growth. In this chapter, we'll look at the idea of quantum entanglement and how it relates to how the conscious and subconscious minds are connected, as well as the "As Within, So Without" principle.

Quantum Entanglement

The term "quantum entanglement" is used to describe the occurrence in quantum physics in which two distant particles can become coupled in such a way that the state of one particle is reliant on the state of the other. Two particles are said to be "entangled" if they have an instantaneous link that defies classical physics.

The idea that particles can be coupled in such a way that information can be conveyed immediately between them, regardless of their distance, is called "non-locality," and is sometimes compared to quantum entanglement.

Conscious Mind and Subconscious Mind

The conscious and unconscious parts of the mind can be viewed in a similar fashion, as though they were intertwined. The thoughts, feelings, and beliefs that we are consciously aware of are represented by the conscious mind, while the beliefs, patterns, and habits that we are not consciously aware of are represented by the subconscious mind.

Both minds rely on and contribute to the other. The behaviors and patterns we engage in on a subconscious level can influence our conscious beliefs and objectives, and vice versa.

AS WITHIN, SO WITHOUT

Quantum entanglement is related to the "As Within, So Without" principle, which argues that our interior experiences have an equivalent in the external world. According to this theory, the things we tell ourselves (such as our ideas, beliefs, and attitudes) have a significant effect on the world around us.

If we wish to alter the environment around us, we need to start by altering our own internal states. The state of our brains (both conscious and unconscious) on the inside is a major element in shaping our lives and the world around us.

AS ABOVE, SO BELOW

Both the "As Above, So Below" principle and the "As Within, So Without" principle can be understood to mean the same thing. This principle proposes that the patterns and relationships that are present in the universe are also present within us, and that the individual experiences we have are a reflection of the larger patterns that are present in the cosmos.

In this way, the principles of quantum entanglement and the interconnectedness of the conscious and subconscious mind can help us to understand the interplay between our internal and external worlds, as well as how we can use our thoughts, beliefs, and attitudes to shape both the experiences we have and the outcomes of those experiences.

The idea of quantum entanglement, along with the principles of "As Within, So Without" and "As Above, So Below," provide a powerful perspective on the interconnectedness of our internal and external worlds, as well as the impact that our thoughts, beliefs, and attitudes have on our experiences and the outcomes of those experiences. We may harness the potential of our minds to direct the course of our lives and make progress toward our objectives if we are willing to acknowledge and accept this reality.

Chapter 4: The Influence of Emotions

Emotions play a significant part in the formation of both our perspectives of the world and the ways in which we make decisions. They are mental and physiological states that are related to ideas, memories, and external stimuli. These states can be triggered by either internal or external factors. Emotions, even though they can be helpful guides for our conduct, can sometimes obscure our judgment and lead to judgments that aren't in our best interests.

There are many ways in which our feelings might sway our decisions. For instance, feelings of dread or anxiety might drive us to overestimate the possibility of undesirable consequences, which can then induce us to make judgments that are either excessively cautious or avoidant. In a similar vein, emotions such as rage or annoyance have the potential to make us grossly underestimate the potential repercussions of our actions, which in turn might force us to make choices that are hasty or irresponsible.

The phenomenon of emotional contagion is yet another manner in which our feelings might have an effect on the decisions that we make. Emotional contagion is the tendency for one person's feelings to be transmitted to another, most frequently through nonverbal signs such as body language or facial expressions. When we are in the company of others who are experiencing intense feelings, we are more likely to also feel those feelings and to make decisions that are impacted by them.

The ability to think clearly and make decisions that are reasonable can also be impacted by our emotional state. When we are going through intense feelings, our brains release hormones that might cloud our judgment and make it difficult for us to think properly. This can lead to a situation that is known as emotional reasoning, which is when we make conclusions based not on objective evidence but rather on how we feel at the time.

There are many approaches that can be taken to reduce the impact that our feelings have on the decisions that we make. Before making a choice, it can be helpful to take a step back and give yourself some space to think about the issue for a while. It is possible that doing so will assist us in regaining our emotional equilibrium and in arriving at a judgment that is more firmly based on logic and reason. In addition to this, it is essential for us to be conscious of our feelings and to be aware of the ways in which they may be affecting the choices we make. This can assist us in recognizing when our feelings are clouding our judgment and in making decisions that are more deliberate and reflective on our part.

In a nutshell, our feelings significantly contribute to the formation of both our perspectives on the world and the ways in which we make choices. Emotions, despite the fact that they can be helpful guides for our conduct, can sometimes obscure our judgment and lead to judgments that aren't in our best interests. It is possible for us to make decisions that are more deliberate and thought-out if we are conscious of the influence of our emotions and actively work to manage them.

Using the Forces That Are Already Within Us

Seeing and investigating the world around us through the lens of the four classical elements—water, air, earth, and fire—has been a practice that has persisted for many years. But were you aware that these components can also be found within each one of us? Because we all have these four components within us, we could reach our full potential and accomplish amazing things if we learn to harness them. Let's investigate how each of these innate qualities might be utilized to our advantage.

WATER

Emotion and instinct are associated with the element of water. There is a connection between it and the ebb and flow of life, the tides, and the cyclical aspect of the earth. To tap into the power of the water element that is within us, we need to develop the ability to communicate with our feelings and pay attention to our gut instincts. This requires us to set aside some time to consider our emotions, to recognize and accept them, and to look for constructive strategies of expressing them.

Meditation and other practices that cultivate mindfulness are two ways that one can connect with the water element. Getting in touch with the water element that resides inside us can also be accomplished by spending time beside a body of water or by taking a long, soothing bath. If we give ourselves permission to go with the flow of our feelings and intuition, we can gain a deeper understanding of who we are and our purpose in the world.

AIR

The ability to think and communicate is closely related to air. It is connected to the mind, logic, and the ability to express oneself through language. To tap into the power of the air element that resides within us, we need to develop our analytical thinking and interpersonal communication skills. This necessitates setting aside sufficient time for careful consideration of the material at hand, the formulation of thoughtful conclusions, and the eloquent presentation of those opinions.

Reading and writing are two activities that can help you establish a connection with the air element. Reading presents us with novel concepts and points of view, whereas writing gives us the opportunity to clarify our own ideas and articulate them in a manner that is both clear and succinct. Participating in discussions or giving speeches in public can also help us tap into the strength of the air element that resides inside us.

EARTH

Earth is the element that provides steadiness and a sense of anchoring. It is connected to the material world, the human body, and the natural environment that surrounds us. Learning how to connect with our bodies and the world around us is necessary if we want to tap into the potential of the earth element that is inside us. This requires us to not just take care of our bodies, but also to cultivate a sense of connection with the environment by spending time outside and engaging in outdoor activities.

Yoga, hiking, and gardening are all examples of physically active hobbies that can help people feel more connected to the earth element. These activities not only enable us to maintain our physical health and emotional stability, but they also provide us with the opportunity to connect with the natural world and cultivate an attitude of gratitude toward the land and the resources it provides.

FIRE

Fire is the element of transformation and the driving force behind passion. It is connected to vigor, the ability to exert one's will, and the capacity to effect transformation. To control the element of fire that resides within us, we need to acquire the ability to tap into our innate sense of drive and motivation. This entails the creation of objectives, the formulation of a strategy, and the execution of decisive moves in the direction of realizing our ambitions.

One method to connect with the fire element is through creative pursuits such as painting, music, or writing. These activities provide us with the opportunity to express ourselves and draw on the passion and creativity that lie dormant within us. Activating the power of the fire element that is within us can be facilitated through goal setting and the successful completion of those goals in both our personal and professional life.

We can liberate our full potential and do great things if we learn to utilize the elements that are already present within us. We can become the best versions of ourselves and have a positive influence on the world around us by developing a connection with our feelings and intuition (water), thinking critically and communicating effectively (air), taking care of our bodies and cultivating a sense of connection with the earth (earth), and tapping into our inner drive and motivation (fire). Each of these practices corresponds to one of the five elements of the compass.

Maintaining Positive Emotions and Feelings: Using the PDCA Cycle

Positive emotions and feelings are very important to our overall health, but it can be hard to stay positive in today's fast-paced world. But using the PDCA (Plan-Do-Check-Act) cycle, which is a way to keep getting better, can help people keep feeling good and improve their overall quality of life.

Step 1: Plan

The first step in utilizing the PDCA cycle to assist in maintaining a regular level of happy emotions and feelings is the process of planning. This may involve creating goals, determining areas of specialization, and developing a strategy for reaching these goals at some point in the future. An individual might, for instance, decide that they want to reduce their stress levels and then devise a strategy for doing so by engaging in activities such as physical activity, practicing mindfulness, and engaging in relaxation routines.

Step 2: Do

Under the methodology known as Plan-Do-Check-Act (PDCA), the next step in maintaining positive feelings and emotions is to take some kind of action. The following step is to put into action the strategy that was developed in the previous stage (step 1). In order to be better able to deal with stress, an individual, for instance, could begin engaging in regular physical activity, begin meditating, and learn how to relax.

Step 3: Check

Checking is the third step in the PDCA cycle, and it plays an important role in maintaining positive feelings and emotions. Now is the moment to evaluate the outcomes of step 2 and determine how close you are to achieving the objectives you set out with in the beginning. An individual may choose to monitor their own stress levels in order to evaluate the effectiveness of stress-reduction measures such as physical activity, mindfulness training, and deep breathing.

Step 4: Act

The conclusion of the PDCA cycle for maintaining positive emotions involves taking some kind of action. Considering the findings obtained in step 3, modifications are made to the original plan. If an individual observes that incorporating new mindfulness or relaxation techniques into their exercise routine or altering their exercise routine in some other way dramatically lowers their levels of stress, then it is possible that they will be driven to implement such adjustments.

People have the ability to maintain a positive attitude and improve their standard of living by utilizing the PDCA cycle. People are able to maintain their focus on the work at hand, which is to maintain a positive perspective and improve their well-being, by setting goals, taking action, reviewing their progress, and making modifications. By incorporating the PDCA cycle into their day-to-day activities, people can increase the likelihood of ongoing success and enhance their capacity to take full advantage of life.

Improving Positive Emotions and Feelings for Success: Using VSM

Feelings and emotions that are positive are necessary for success in one's personal life as well as one's professional life. Not only do they contribute to our overall well-being, but they also assist us in performing at a higher level and achieving our objectives. Individuals can improve their positive emotions and feelings using the Value Stream Mapping (VSM) tool, which is part of the Lean manufacturing methodology. This can lead to increased success in both their personal and professional lives.

Step 1: Identifying Value Streams

In order to use VSM to increase happiness, we must first determine which aspects of our life already have value. Work, family time, hobbies, and personal growth are all examples of value streams that contribute to a fulfilled life. Recognizing our value streams allows us to prioritize our efforts and put our energy where it will have the greatest impact

Step 2: Mapping the Process

The second step in using VSM to improve positive feelings and emotions is to map each value stream's process. This means breaking each task down into smaller steps, figuring out where the process isn't working well or where there are roadblocks, and looking for ways to make the process better. For example, a person might realize that their work value stream is causing them stress and look for ways to streamline the process and reduce stress.

Step 3: Eliminating Waste

Getting rid of unnecessary activities is the third stage in applying VSM to boost upbeat feelings. The term "waste" is used here to describe any action or series of actions that does not improve our quality of life. For instance, a person might find strategies to lessen stress at work or give up time-wasting habits like social media.

Step 4: Streamlining Processes

Streamlining operations is the fourth phase in adopting VSM to boost good moods. Here, we adjust the procedure to increase productivity while decreasing waste. In order to lessen the impact of stress in one's life, one strategy is to adjust one's work schedule, or to practice mindfulness and/or relaxation techniques regularly.

Step 5: Continuously Improving

The last step in using VSM to boost happy feelings is to keep getting better. To accomplish this, it is necessary to keep an eye on the procedure and adjust it as needed to keep the good vibes flowing. A person might, for instance, regularly evaluate their stress levels and, if necessary, adjust their daily routine in order to lower their stress levels.

Success in both one's personal and professional life can be boosted through the use of VSM to cultivate more positive emotions and feelings. Individuals can increase their chances of success and happiness by identifying value streams, mapping the process, eliminating waste, streamlining processes, and continuously improving.

Chapter 5: The Role of Ego

The ego is the part of the mind that creates and maintains our individual identities. It's what makes us unique as individuals and sets us apart from other organisms. The ego is a fundamental part of our personalities, but it has the potential to cloud our judgment.

Egocentrism is a way in which the ego distorts our perspective of the world. When we are egocentric, we view the world through the lens of our own experiences and beliefs and assume that everyone else does the same. This can cause us to place too much weight on our own thoughts and experiences while failing to recognize the value in those of others.

The ego can also distort our view of reality through a tendency known as self-serving bias. This leads to an exaggerated sense of our own worth. It becomes easy to take credit for everything and blame others when things go wrong. Moreover, this bias can make us overvalue our skills while undervaluing the abilities of others.

Self-justification is another way in which the ego can distort our perception of the world. The tendency to justify one's own behavior and choices, even when they are obviously inappropriate, is known as self-justification. This can cause us to refuse to change our minds despite mounting evidence to the contrary.

Realizing the existence and weight of one's ego is the first step toward mitigating its destructive effects. We can take a step back and try to see things from alternative angles, as well as take into account the viewpoints of those around us. Understanding the bounds of our own perceptions and being willing to admit that we could be wrong are also crucial. It's also crucial to be self-aware and humble enough to recognize and accept responsibility for our own mistakes.

The ego is an integral part of our psyche, but it also has the potential to cloud our judgment. Some of the ways in which the ego distorts our perceptions are through egocentrism, self-serving bias, and the need to justify our own actions. Recognizing its presence and impact, maintaining a sense of modesty, and being open to new ideas can all lead to a more complete picture of the world.

Using 5S to Minimize Adverse Consequences of Ego

The ego is a potent force that can shape our lives for the better or the worse. An inflated ego, on the other hand, can lead to negative emotions like anger, frustration, and disappointment rather than the confidence and drive that a healthy ego provides. Though it was designed for use in Lean manufacturing, the 5S framework can also be used to reduce the harmful effects of ego and boost well-being.

Step 1: Sort (Seiri)

Sorting through our thoughts, beliefs, and actions is the first step in using 5S to lessen the impact of the ego. We do this by picking apart our negative thought and action patterns, such as critical self-talk, from our more constructive ones. Sorting through our thoughts and actions can help us pinpoint the areas of our lives where our ego is causing us harm.

Step 2: Simplify or set in order (Seiton)

Getting rid of unnecessary complexity is the second step in using 5S to lessen the impact of the ego. De-cluttering one's life means giving attention to the things that matter most rather than the many, less essential ones. Stress, anxiety, and the influence of the ego can all be mitigated by streamlining our daily routines.

Step 3: Sweep (Seiso)

The next stage in adopting 5S to lessen the detrimental effects of the ego is to go through our lives and get rid of any negative thought patterns and actions that we may have. This entails making a concerted effort to alter our negative thought patterns and actions, and then actively striving to replace them with positive thought patterns and behaviors. For instance, a person could replace negative self-talk with positive affirmations, or they could participate in mindfulness or meditation in order to lower their levels of stress and anxiety.

Step 4: Standardize (Seiketsu)

The standardization of our good ideas and behaviors is the fourth step in employing 5S to offset the negative consequences of the ego. Creating a habit of a routine that includes good thoughts and actions requires first developing the routine, and then turning the routine into a habit. For instance, a person could create time in their schedule every day to practice mindfulness or meditation, or they could incorporate positive affirmations into their typical activities.

Step 5: Sustain (Shitsuke)

Keeping up our good mental and behavioral habits is the fifth and last step in the 5S method of minimizing the destructive effects of the ego. This requires always keeping a close watch on our thoughts and actions and being willing to adjust as required in order to keep a good and healthy ego. For instance, a person may routinely evaluate their thought patterns and adjust their daily routine in order to lower their levels of stress and anxiety. They could also participate in self-reflection in order to make sure that their ego is kept in control.

Individuals can improve their general well-being and boost their chances of success in both their personal and professional lives by utilizing 5S to reduce the negative impacts of the ego. This can be done in both their personal and professional lives. Individuals can keep their egos in control, which will lead to increased levels of happiness and success, by sorting through their ideas and behaviors, simplifying their life, clearing out bad patterns, standardizing positive thoughts and behaviors, and maintaining these positive habits.

The Impact of Societal Expectations

Societal expectations are the unspoken rules and norms that tell us how to act in a certain culture or society. These expectations can have a big effect on what we choose to do and how we think about what is normal or okay.

Conformist behavior is one way that societal expectations can affect the choices we make. Conformist behavior is when people tend to act and believe like the people around them. This can lead us to make choices that align with societal norms, even if those choices conflict with our personal values or beliefs.

The "social comparison" is another way that what other people expect of us can affect the choices we make. Social comparison is when we judge ourselves and what we do based on what other people do and what they think about us. This can make us choose things we think other people will like or respect more than things that are in line with our own values or beliefs.

Societal expectations can also be imposed in the form of stereotypes and biases, which can limit the options and opportunities for certain groups of people, like gender, race, or sexual orientation. For example, the idea that men should be assertive and in charge can make men hide their feelings and avoid showing that they are weak. In the same way, the idea that women should be nurturing and submissive can make women downplay their own accomplishments and put them in second place in their careers and personal lives.

To lessen the bad effects of social expectations, it's important to know what they are and how they affect you. It's also important to question and challenge societal norms and expectations when they go against our own values or beliefs. Also, it's important to be aware of the stereotypes and biases that might be put on us and to work against them.

In a nutshell, societal expectations are the unwritten rules and norms that tell us how to act in a certain culture or society. These expectations can have a big effect on what we choose to do and how we think about what is normal or okay. Being aware of societal expectations, questioning and challenging them, and being aware of stereotypes and biases can help us make decisions that are in line with our own values and beliefs.

Mitigating Societal Expectation Using SWOT Analysis

Expectations from society can have a big effect on both individuals and groups. They can put people under pressure and make them act in ways that might not fit with their own values or goals. To lessen the effects of societal expectations, you can do a SWOT analysis to learn more about the situation and come up with ways to deal with it.

SWOT analysis is a way to look at a situation and figure out what its strengths, weaknesses, opportunities, and threats are. In this situation, a SWOT analysis can help figure out the good and bad things about societal expectations, as well as the opportunities and problems that might arise from them.

Strengths:

People can be motivated by societal expectations, which give them a clear sense of direction and purpose. They can also help people feel like they belong by putting them in touch with people who have similar values and goals.

Weaknesses:

Society's expectations can also be limiting because they put people under pressure and stress, which can lead to burnout or less happiness with life. They may also make it hard for people to grow and be creative because they feel like they have to fit in with norms and expectations that have already been set.

Opportunities:

Expectations from society can be used to help you grow and develop as a person. By understanding and aligning with societal expectations, people can gain a stronger sense of purpose and direction, which can help them reach their goals.

Threats:

The pressures of society can be dangerous if they conflict with an individual's core beliefs and aspirations. A person may experience irritation, disappointment, and even resentment as a result of this. Anxiety, despair, and fatigue are just some of the negative health effects that can result from trying to live up to unrealistic cultural standards.

Through a SWOT analysis, individuals and organizations can gain a deeper understanding of the influence of societal expectations and develop plans to counteract the negative effects of such expectations. Whether it's maximizing the benefits of society expectations, overcoming their drawbacks, capitalizing on growth and development chances, or warding off threats to one's happiness and contentment, a SWOT analysis can help you navigate the obstacles posed by societal norms.

Mitigating Societal Expectation Using SELF

Societal expectations can have a big effect on people and organizations, shaping their thoughts, actions, and choices. The SELF framework is a tool for personal development and growth that can be used to lessen the effect of societal expectations.

Self-Awareness, Empathy, Logic, and Flexibility are the words that make up SELF. You can use these four things to understand and lessen the effects of societal expectations.

Self-awareness: To deal with societal expectations, the first step is to learn more about yourself. This means figuring out what your own beliefs, values, and actions are and how they might be affected by what other people expect of you. By becoming more self-aware, people can learn more about what drives them and what they want, and they can see where they might need to make changes to get closer to their own goals and dreams.

Empathy is the ability to understand and feel what other people feel. Empathy can help people understand why other people think or act the way they do in the context of societal expectations. This can help people understand and care about each other more, as well as find things they have in common with others and build stronger relationships.

Logic: Being able to reason and think critically is what logic is. When it comes to coping with societal expectations, logic can help people look at the evidence and arguments that support the expectations and decide if they fit with their own values and goals. This can help people decide how to meet the expectations in a more well-informed way.

Flexibility: Being flexible means being able to change with the times. When it comes to societal expectations, being flexible can help people keep an open mind and adjust to new information or changing situations. This can be very important when a person's own beliefs or values are at odds with what society expects of them. By being flexible and able to change, people can get through these situations more easily and effectively.

The SELF framework can be a useful tool for reducing the effects of societal expectations. By incorporating self-awareness, empathy, logic, and flexibility into their personal growth and development, people can learn more about themselves and the expectations that affect their lives and come up with ways to deal with these expectations and reach their goals.

Chapter 6: The Dangers of Attachment

The emotional tie we develop with other people, things, and concepts is called attachment. It's a key part of what makes us human, allowing us to bond with other people and derive satisfaction from our interactions with them. If it becomes excessive or unreasonable, though, attachment can also cause a person to make poor choices.

Loss aversion is one way that attachment can cause people to make poor choices. The term "loss aversion" describes the bias toward giving greater weight to possible drawbacks of a choice than to its potential upsides. We often make poor choices, such as holding on to a losing investment or a toxic relationship, because we are afraid of losing what we are attached to.

The sunk cost fallacy is another manner in which attachment might cause one to make a poor choice. The sunk cost fallacy is when a person makes a decision to keep putting money into something because of the time and effort they have already put into it, rather than considering the decision in light of the prospective future benefits. This might cause us to act irrationally, like keeping our money in a business that is clearly failing or continuing to work in a profession that no longer gives us satisfaction.

It's important to remember that attachment might cause you to make poor choices when it comes to other people, especially in romantic partnerships. When we feel strongly about someone, it's hard to take a step back and assess the situation objectively. Because of this, we may fail to see warning signs and continue to engage in destructive interactions.

Awareness of and inquiry into one's own attachment patterns might help lessen the potential harm associated with attachment. Think about what could go wrong and compare that to what could go right. It's also crucial to develop a healthy dose of emotional distance and learn to let go of attachments, whether to material possessions, relationships, or even memories.

Attachment is a key characteristic of human beings because it facilitates the development of deep relationships and the pursuit of purpose. But, if it becomes excessive or unreasonable, attachment can cause a person to make poor choices. We can improve our ability to assess situations rationally and make sound choices by increasing our awareness of, and ability to question, our own attachment patterns; by considering the impact of possible losses; and by developing and maintaining a healthy level of emotional distance.

Mitigating the Negative Effects of Attachment with the 5 Whys Technique

While attachment is a normal element of human interactions, it can lead to unhealthy outcomes including anxiety, reliance, and even co-dependence. The 5 Whys method is a problem-solving approach that can be used by individuals to lessen the severity of these results by identifying and addressing the underlying causes of the problem.

By asking "why" questions in a specific order, the 5 Whys method helps get to the bottom of any issue. The first step is to recognize a difficulty or concern, and then to ask "Why?" five times, or until the underlying cause is found. The principle underlying this method is that the symptoms of an issue are usually only the top of the iceberg, and that you need to look underneath the surface to uncover the real problem. Individuals can use the 5 Whys technique to determine the origin of their attachment problems and work toward resolving them. If someone is feeling uncomfortable when their significant other isn't around, they might first wonder why that is. As a result, they may start to wonder, "Why do I need my spouse to be with me all the time?" The conclusion that low sense of self-worth is at the heart of the attachment problem can become apparent as a result.

Once the source of an attachment problem has been discovered, the 5 Whys method can be used to arrive at a satisfactory resolution. The person in the previous scenario could wonder, "Why do I have so poor self-esteem and self-worth?" A person's low sense of self-worth may have its roots in traumatic experiences, false ideas, or destructive internal dialogue. A strategy for dealing with these challenges, such as counseling or practicing positive self-talk skills, can then be formulated.

To sum up, the 5 Whys methodology is a useful method for reducing the drawbacks of attachment. As people learn what triggers their attachment problems, they may create interventions that do more than just mask the symptoms. The 5 Whys method can help people improve their relationships, make better decisions, and live happier, healthier lives.

Below is a case study demonstrating how the 5 Whys Technique can be used to mitigate the negative effects of attachment.

Step	Problem/ Question	Why	Solution/ Realization
1	Jane feels stressed and unhappy at work.	Why does Jane feel stressed and unhappy at work?	Jane realizes she's become overly attached to a specific project outcome.
2	Jane is overly attached to a specific project outcome.	Why is Jane attached to this specific outcome?	She believes it will lead to a promotion and recognition.
3	Jane believes the project outcome will lead to a promotion and recognition.	Why does Jane think this project is the only way to achieve promotion and recognition?	She has not explored other opportunities for growth within the company.
4	Jane has not explored other opportunities for growth within the company.	Why hasn't Jane explored other opportunities?	She has been focused on this project and has not made time for professional development.

5	Jane has not made time for professional development.	Why hasn't Jane prioritized her professional development?	She has been overly attached to the idea of success through this specific project.

Solution/Realization: By using the 5 Whys Technique, Jane realizes that her stress and unhappiness at work are rooted in her attachment to a specific project outcome. She understands that diversifying her focus and prioritizing professional development can lead to growth and recognition through multiple avenues, thus mitigating the negative effects of attachment.

Chapter 7: The Importance of Mindfulness

The act of practicing mindfulness entails paying attention to one's present state of mind as well as one's thoughts, feelings, and the world around them. Mindfulness is a skill that may be fostered through meditation and other mindfulness activities, and it has been demonstrated to have a range of benefits, including the ability to make better decisions.

Increasing our awareness of our own thoughts and feelings is one of the ways in which practicing mindfulness can assist us in making more informed decisions. When we are mindful, we are better able to examine our own thoughts and feelings without becoming enmeshed in them. When we are not mindful, we are more likely to become caught up in them. This can assist us in making decisions that are founded on reason and logic rather than allowing our feelings to sway us in the decision-making process.

Mindfulness can also help us make better decisions by improving our capacity to focus, which is yet another benefit of practicing it. Our capacity to concentrate and give our full attention to the here and now can be improved via the practice of mindfulness, which includes activities such as meditation. This can assist us to make choices that are more considered and deliberate, rather than getting distracted by either the distractions that come from the outside or the thoughts that come from within ourselves.

The practice of mindfulness can also assist us in recognizing limiting beliefs and societal expectations that may play a role in our decision-making and assisting us in challenging those beliefs and expectations. We can become aware of the patterns and influences that may be impacting our perceptions and decisions if we pay attention to our thoughts and emotions, and then we can take measures to modify those patterns and influences.

There are many different techniques, such as meditation, yoga, or mindful breathing, that can be useful when trying to create mindfulness in oneself. In addition, it is essential to allot some time every day for the practice of mindfulness, even if it is only for a few minutes, and to make an effort to include mindfulness into activities that are performed on a daily basis, such as walking, eating, or performing housework.

In a nutshell, the practice of mindfulness refers to being fully present in the here and now while also being aware of our thoughts, feelings, and the world around us. By enhancing our awareness of our thoughts and emotions, our ability to focus, and our ability to identify and confront limiting beliefs and societal expectations, it can assist us in making more informed decisions and improve the quality of our lives. It is possible for us to become better able to make meaningful decisions by cultivating mindfulness through activities such as meditation, yoga, or mindful breathing, and then incorporating that attention into our day-to-day activities.

Improving Mindfulness with the PDCA Cycle

When it comes to bettering oneself in both professional and personal contexts, mindfulness cannot be overstated for its role in mitigating stress and fostering concentration and contentment. The PDCA (Plan-Do-Check-Act) cycle is an excellent way for enhancing mindfulness since it is a continual improvement method.

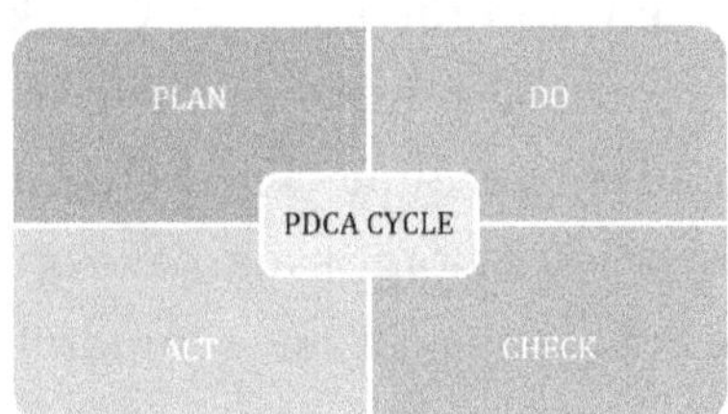

The PDCA cycle is a four-step method for planning, executing, and assessing the success of an improvement initiative.

The PDCA cycle is comprised of the following phases:

- Plan: Figure out what needs fixing and make a strategy to fix it.
- Do: Carry out the strategy and gather information.
- Check: Verify: Examine the information critically and judge the outcomes.
- Act: Take action: Based on the review, implement necessary adjustments to the plan.

Individuals can use the PDCA cycle to enhance their mindfulness practices by first determining what aspects of their practice they would like to change, such as their ability to deal with stress, maintain concentration, and feel good about themselves. They can then take steps toward betterment, such as beginning meditation or stress-reduction practice.

After planning, people can put it into action and track their outcomes. One way to do this is by keeping a mindfulness notebook or by asking for feedback on how they are doing.

Anyone can assess their own performance by reviewing obtained data in the check phase. They can evaluate how well their mindfulness practices are serving them.

Acting on the results of one's evaluation and revised plan is the final step in the evaluation-planning-action cycle. For instance, if they find that their mindfulness practice isn't relieving stress to the extent that they'd like, they could try combining other stress-relieving strategies.

Using the steps outlined in the Plan-Do-Check-Act (PDCA) cycle, practitioners can systematically increase their mindfulness practices and develop their abilities over time. The PDCA cycle is a useful tool for maintaining motivation, monitoring development, and deciding where and how to make changes in one's mindfulness practice. Using the PDCA cycle encourages introspection, which in turn can improve one's capacity for self-awareness and provide new perspectives on one's mindfulness training.

For these reasons, the PDCA cycle is a powerful tool for developing greater awareness. Individuals can attain their goals and experience the many advantages of mindfulness, such as decreased stress, increased attention, and greater well-being, by using the PDCA cycle to continuously refine and strengthen their mindfulness practices.

The Value of Seeking Wisdom

Seeking wisdom means actively looking for advice and information so you can make better decisions. It means being open to new ideas and points of view and actively looking for advice and direction from other people.

One of the best ways to gain knowledge is to ask experts for their advice. Experts know a lot about their field and have a lot of experience, so they can give valuable advice and tips. This is especially important when making decisions about things we don't know much about.

Reading and learning is another way to get wiser. Books, articles, and other kinds of information can teach us useful things and give us new perspectives that can help us make better decisions. It's also important to be curious and look for new information and points of view instead of just relying on what we already know and have done.

Seeking wisdom can also mean actively looking for advice from people you trust, like mentors or close friends. These people can give us helpful ideas and points of view, and they can help us see things we might not have seen on our own.

Lastly, seeking wisdom can mean thinking about yourself and looking inside yourself. It's important to take time to think about our own thoughts and feelings and how they might affect the choices we make. This can help us learn more about ourselves and make decisions that fit better with our values and beliefs.

In short, seeking wisdom means actively looking for advice and information so that you can make better decisions. It means getting advice from experts, learning and reading, asking for help from others, and taking time to think about yourself and look inside yourself. These habits can help us gain new points of view, knowledge, and understanding, which can help us make decisions that are more well-thought-out and well-informed.

Seeking Expert Advice for Success: the 5W2H Method

Getting professional help is crucial to your growth and development in any area of your life. The 5W2H technique (What, Why, Where, When, Who, How, and How Much) is useful when consulting specialists.

The 5W2H approach is a technique used to solve problems by breaking them down into their component parts and then figuring out the best way to tackle them. Here are the 5W2H steps:

- What: Point out the issue or goal.
- Find out why you need help and what you hope to accomplish by consulting an expert.
- If you need help, you need to find a place where you can get it.
- When is the best time to consult an expert?
- Where: Figure out where to find the professional help you need.
- How: Decide on a strategy for getting professional help (e.g., in-person, phone, email).
- Find out how much money or other resources you must spend on getting professional help.

One might start the 5W2H process of consulting an expert by determining what it is they want help with. Whether they want to learn something new, find a solution to an issue, or get some guidance on a tough choice, they can figure out why they need to consult an expert.

The next step is for them to establish when and where they'll go for professional guidance. If they need guidance, they'll know who to look to for it, whether it's a mentor, coach, or consultant.

Individuals can choose between in-person, over-the-phone, or online consultations with experts in the how phase. They are able to ascertain whether or not professional assistance is affordable.

Individuals can make well-informed decisions with the help of the 5W2H technique, which gives an organized approach to collecting information from experts. The 5W2H approach helps people find the most qualified advisor for their needs, select the most efficient means of consulting with them, and maximize their available assets. The 5W2H technique also encourages introspection, which can improve one's familiarity with one's own thoughts and feelings and lead to new understanding of one's problem or goal.

In conclusion, consulting experts via the 5W2H method is a fruitful strategy. The 5W2H technique provides users with access to professional guidance while they determine the best way to reach their objectives. An organized way to make the most of expert resources and succeed, the 5W2H method can be used for both personal and professional advice seeking.

The Role of Intuition

The term "intuition" is used to describe the mental process by which one gains quick knowledge of a topic without resorting to deliberate thought. It's something many people refer to as a "gut feeling" or "sixth sense" and it may be extremely helpful when making choices.

Intuition helps us make snap judgments when time is of the essence, which is one of its main advantages. When the stakes are high or time is of the essence, trusting our gut instincts can help us make the right choice fast.

When we use our intuition, we are more likely to make choices that are consistent with our core values and principles. Insight into what matters most to us can be gained through tapping into our intuitive senses, which are generally based on our past experiences and emotions. If we do this, we'll be better able to make choices that are genuine to who we are as individuals.

While weighing potential consequences, one's gut instinct may also prove useful. We may use our intuition to better gauge the level of danger in each situation and make judgments that are more in line with our comfort zone.

Yet, one's gut instincts aren't always correct; thus, they shouldn't be relied on as the sole basis for making choices. It's important to factor in your gut instincts alongside logic, expert opinion, and data while making important life choices. Therefore, before deciding based on intuition alone, we should check our assumptions and make sure we aren't being influenced by our prejudices or emotions.

Intuitive understanding is the capacity to grasp a concept without resorting to deliberate thought. It can be a useful resource for weighing risks, making quick decisions in line with our beliefs, and other aspects of decision-making. Decisions based solely on logic are risky, so it's important to use logic in conjunction with other methods and to keep in mind the role that prejudice and emotion might play in the decision-making process.

SHARPENING OUR INTUITION: TECHNIQUES FOR ENHANCING OUR INNER VOICE

We can rely on our intuition to help us with decision-making, problem-solving, and getting through the tough times in life. Many of us, however, depend too heavily on reason and analysis instead of trusting our gut instincts when making important life choices.

Intuition is the ability to make informed decisions without having all the information at hand. It's a manner of knowing that doesn't rely on reason or analysis so much as it does on a gut feeling. Intuition is a skill that may be cultivated and improved through experience; it is a vital aid in decision-making and overcoming obstacles.

TECHNIQUES FOR SHARPENING OUR INTUITION

Methods exist to help us listen more closely to our gut feelings and develop our intuitive faculties. The following are examples of such methods:

Intuition may be honed with the help of a wonderful tool: meditation. This practice helps us quiet our thoughts and listen to our inner wisdom. We may strengthen our connection to our intuition and learn to rely on it more while making decisions through consistent meditation practice.

In order to make good choices, it's important to tune into the cues and signals our bodies send us. We can learn more about our intuition by tuning in to the signals it sends to us through the feelings occurring in our bodies.

Writing in a journal is an excellent method for gaining insight into and strengthening your intuitive abilities. By recording our inner monologue, we can better understand and rely on our intuition.

Developing our intuition relies in large part on learning to trust our gut instincts. Trusting our first impressions allows us to forge a stronger bond with our intuition, which in turn allows us to depend on it more frequently when making choices.

THE BENEFITS OF SHARPENING OUR INTUITION

There are various reasons to work on honing our intuition.

- We can make better decisions with less information and greater trust in our gut instincts.
- Enhanced Creativity: Intuition can serve as a springboard to fresh ideas and innovative approaches.
- Gaining Insight into Oneself & One's Motivations by the Practice of Developing One's Intuition, One Might Have a Greater Knowledge of Both.

Instinct is a valuable resource for solving problems and making important choices in life. We may strengthen our intuition and listen to our inner voice through practices like meditation, body awareness, writing, and trusting our first impressions. Better judgments, more creative problem-solving, and a more satisfying existence are all possible when we tap into our own intuitive abilities.

The Dangers of Overthinking

Overthinking is the habit of giving too much thought to a problem, making it hard to choose a course of action or even to decide between several options. While making a choice, it's vital to think about all the potential outcomes and balance the benefits and disadvantages, but it's also crucial not to let this process go on indefinitely, as doing so can delay action and have unintended repercussions.

Overthinking can impair decision making by causing analysis paralysis. If you overthink your options to the point where you can't make a choice, you may be suffering from analysis paralysis. We may miss out on chances or be unable to take advantage of time-sensitive circumstances as a result.

Overthinking also increases the risk of having second thoughts after making a choice. When you feel regret or unhappiness after making a choice, you may be experiencing decision regret. When we give too much thought to a situation, we increase the likelihood of second-guessing ourselves and feeling regret over our choices.

It's possible that overthinking is contributing to your state of anxiety and stress. Overthinking and worrying can have negative effects on our health and happiness.

Setting a deadline for making a choice can help prevent the harmful impacts of deliberation. By doing so, we may narrow in on the most crucial factors of the decision and make a more informed choice.

Overcoming Overthinking: Using 5S for Mental Clarity

When we allow ourselves to engage in excessive mental processing, we open ourselves up to feelings of stress, anxiety, and general exhaustion in our daily lives. When we overthink, we become mired in our own thoughts to the detriment of our overall perspective. As a result, it may be challenging to focus on the here and now, make decisions, and take action.

The 5S technique is a straightforward approach to eliminating unnecessary thoughts and fostering focus. The 5S method is based on the tenets of cleanliness, orderliness, simplicity, standardization, and sustained effort.

S1 S2 S3 S4 S5

The first phase of the 5S method is to go through your ideas and determine which are helpful and which are not. The result is a clearer head and sharper concentration.

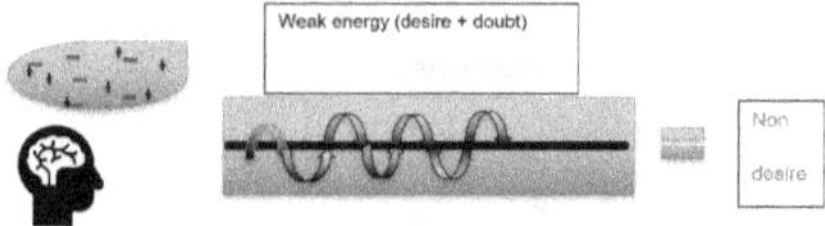

Next, simplify your ideas by eliminating unnecessary details. This implies distilling your ideas down to their barest essentials, which will make them more manageable and accessible.

Step three is to normalize your way of thinking. To do this, you must develop a logical and consistent thought process that will aid you in avoiding the trap of overthinking.

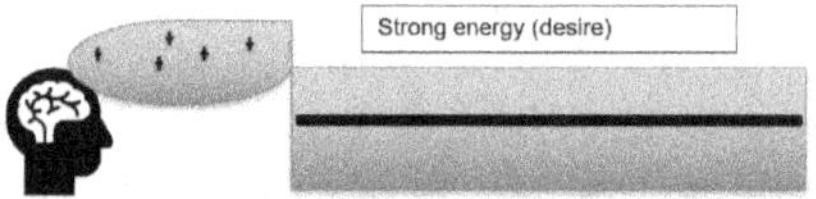

The fourth stage is to keep the progress you've made going strong. To do this successfully, you must fully embrace your altered perspective and initiate behavior changes that strengthen it.

Self-Discipline This final phase entails continuing to follow the 5S method and keeping a clear, concentrated mind.

THE BENEFITS OF OVERCOMING OVERTHINKING

The benefits of overcoming overthinking are numerous.

The 5S method has been shown to increase clarity of thought by helping people get rid of unnecessary distractions and refocus on what's truly important.

The ability to live in the moment and fully appreciate life is greatly enhanced when worry and stress are diminished through the practice of overcoming overthinking.

When you learn to control your overthinking, you'll gain confidence in your own judgment and actions.

To sum up, excessive mental processing can be a major source of stress, anxiety, and general feelings of being swamped by life's demands. The 5S approach is useful for preventing mental fog and improving focus. It will be easier to focus on the here and now, make sound decisions, and act with conviction if our minds are free of mental clutter.

According to the idea known as "the Law of Attraction," one can bring about in their lives whatever they give their full attention to. Depending on the predominant attitude, this might have a beneficial or bad effect. If people want to employ the Law of Attraction to stop overthinking, they need to replace their negative thoughts and feelings with more optimistic ones.

Counting one's blessings and dwelling on one's good fortune is one approach. Alternatively, you might imagine yourself successful and concentrate on how that will make you feel. Changing one's point of view in this way has been shown to have a positive effect on one's mental and emotional state, producing more joy and optimism.

Overcoming Negative Thinking using Metacognition and 5 Whys

Overcoming negative thinking can be achieved by using meta-cognition (thinking about one's thinking) and the 5 Whys technique, which are complementary approaches that promote self-awareness and critical thinking.

Metacognition:

Metacognition involves stepping back and examining your thought process, including self-reflection, awareness of cognitive biases, and evaluating the validity of your thoughts. This approach can help you recognize negative thinking patterns and develop more balanced, constructive thoughts.

Steps to use metacognition to overcome negative thinking:

a) Identify negative thoughts: Recognize when you're having negative thoughts or experiencing cognitive distortions (e.g., all-or-nothing thinking, overgeneralization, catastrophizing).

b) Reflect on the thought process: Analyze the underlying thought process and question the assumptions, beliefs, or evidence behind the negative thoughts.

c) Evaluate the validity of the thoughts: Assess the accuracy of the negative thoughts and consider alternative perspectives or explanations.

d) Replace negative thoughts with more balanced thoughts: Develop more constructive, rational thoughts that counteract the negative thinking patterns.

The 5 Whys technique:

The 5 Whys technique involves asking "why" repeatedly (usually five times) to uncover the root cause of a problem or an issue. By applying the 5 Whys to your negative thinking, you can identify underlying beliefs or assumptions that contribute to your negative thoughts and challenge them.

Top of Form

Steps	Description
1. Identify a negative thought	Recognize when you're having a negative thought that you want to explore further.
2. Ask "why" five times	For each negative thought, ask yourself "why" you think that way, and then ask "why" again for each subsequent answer until you've asked "why" five times. This process helps you dig deeper into the underlying beliefs or assumptions behind the negative thought.

3. Example	Negative thought: "I always mess up presentations." 1st Why: "Why do I think I always mess up presentations?" Answer: "Because I get nervous and forget what I want to say." 2nd Why: "Why do I get nervous and forget what I want to say?" Answer: "I'm afraid of being judged by my colleagues." 3rd Why: "Why am I afraid of being judged by my colleagues?" Answer: "I'm worried about not meeting their expectations and losing their respect." 4th Why: "Why am I worried about not meeting their expectations and losing their respect?" Answer: "I have a deep-seated fear of rejection and failure." 5th Why: "Why do I have a deep-seated fear of rejection and failure?" Answer: "Growing up, I was often criticized and never felt good enough."
4. Challenge underlying beliefs	Identify any irrational beliefs or assumptions you uncovered using the 5 Whys technique, and question their validity.
5. Develop alternative perspectives	Consider different perspectives or explanations.

For example, if your negative thought is "I'll never be successful in my career," the 5 Whys technique might look like this:

1. Why do I think I'll never be successful? (I feel like I'm not making progress in my current job.)
2. Why do I feel like I'm not making progress? (I've been in the same position for a while without a promotion.)
3. Why haven't I been promoted? (I haven't been proactive about seeking new opportunities or discussing my career goals with my manager.)
4. Why haven't I been proactive? (I'm afraid of rejection or failure.)
5. Why am I afraid of rejection or failure? (I have an underlying belief that I'm not good enough.)
6. Challenge and reframe the negative thought: Now that you've identified the root cause of your negative thinking, challenge the validity of the thought and reframe it into a more positive, constructive perspective. In the example above, you could reframe the thought as, "I can take control of my career by discussing my goals with my manager and seeking new opportunities for growth."
7. Develop an action plan: Create an action plan to address the root cause of your negative thinking. For instance, you might decide to set a meeting with your manager, research professional development courses, or network with colleagues to explore new opportunities.
8. Practice self-compassion: Finally, practice self-compassion and recognize that everyone experiences negative thoughts from time to time. Be kind to yourself and remind yourself that it's okay to feel negative emotions. The key is to acknowledge them, analyze them, and work towards a more positive mindset.

By using metacognition and the 5 Whys technique, you can identify the root causes of your negative thinking, challenge those thoughts, and develop a more positive mindset to overcome negativity.

Chapter 8: Attraction Theory, or the Law of Attraction

Mastering the law of attraction = desire + allowing (no doubt or limiting belief)

If we use the Law of Attraction effectively, we can bring our dreams into reality. Simply put, the Law of Attraction states that we manifest in our lives that which we give our attention and energy to. Many people, however, have difficulty bringing their dreams to fruition because they are plagued by self-doubt or self-limiting ideas. Let's discuss how to make better use of the Law of Attraction by examining the interplay between desire and allowing.

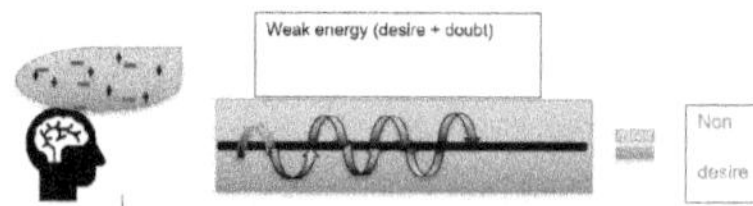

Figure Out What You Really Want

To start using the Law of Attraction, you must first determine what it is that you want. That's why it's important to have a crystal-clear picture of your end goal in mind. More specificity is always welcome.

What do I want, and why do I want it? are important questions to ask yourself.

Remove Self-Doubt and Self-Limiting Beliefs

Getting rid of self-doubt and stifling ideas is the next step. Negative thoughts prevent positive results from materializing. Your desire is less likely to come true when you send the universe mixed signals by doubting your ability to bring it into being. Your ability to bring your desires into reality can be hindered by limiting beliefs. Statements like "I'm not good enough," "I'm not worthy," and "It's not possible for me" are all examples of limiting beliefs.

Let the manifestation of your desire take place.

The last thing to do is open yourself up to the possibility of your dream coming true. By "allowing," means "letting go of control" and "having faith" that what we want will come to pass. The key to successful manifestation lies in this very phase. To receive what you want in life, you must first let go of the energy that has been keeping it from you.

Envision your success and affirm it to yourself.

Both positive visualization and affirmations are potent tools for bringing about the changes you seek in your life. To visualize is to form an image in one's mind of that which one seeks. The more intently you concentrate on your goal, the more likely it is to come to fruition. Affirmations are statements that encourage you to think positively and build faith in your ability to bring your desire into reality by using positive self-talk.

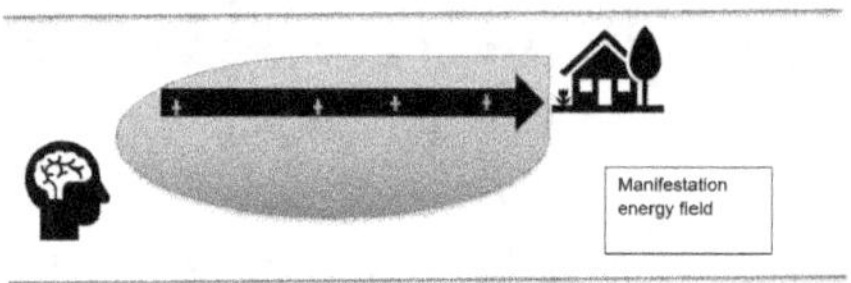

Take Action

Ultimately, you need to do something to fulfill your desire. This means that you ought to make every effort to realize your goal. In order to reach your objective, you must take the necessary steps to get there.

If we use the Law of Attraction effectively, we can bring our dreams into reality. Many people, however, have difficulty bringing their dreams to fruition because they are plagued by self-doubt or self-limiting ideas. An effective application of the Law of Attraction requires an appreciation for the part that desire plays in the manifestation process and the willingness to work with that desire. The power of manifestation can be amplified through the use of positive imagery, affirmations, and action.

Desire and Allowing

Desires	Allowing Statements
I want to earn a million per month	A lot of people like me are already making millions per month
I desire to travel the world	Countless individuals have traveled the world and enjoyed the journey
I want to create a successful business	Many entrepreneurs have started successful businesses from scratch
I aim to have a healthy and fit body	Plenty of people have achieved their fitness goals with dedication
I want to become an expert in my field	Others have mastered their field through hard work and perseverance
I desire to find the perfect life partner	Many people have found their ideal life partners and are happy together
I wish to have a beautiful, comfortable home	Numerous individuals have built their dream homes and enjoy living in them

The Law of Attraction is a powerful principle that can transform our lives when harnessed effectively. One of the most important aspects of this law is the use of "I Am" statements. These affirmations, when stated with conviction and without any disbelief or self-doubt, can help manifest our desires into reality. By consciously choosing empowering beliefs and focusing on positive thoughts, we can attract our dreams and create the life we've always imagined. Let's turn our allowing statements into "I Am" statements and learn how to use them to unlock the full potential of the Law of Attraction.

Category	I Am Statement
Financial Success	I am a successful, prosperous individual who is capable of earning millions per month
World Traveler	I am part of a community of people who have traveled the world and enjoyed the journey
Entrepreneurship	I am a driven entrepreneur who can start a successful business from scratch
Fitness and Health	I am dedicated to achieving my fitness goals through consistent hard work
Mastery in a Field	I am committed to mastering my field through hard work and perseverance
Relationships	I am among those who have found their ideal life partners and are happy together

Dream Home

I am capable of building my dream home and enjoying living in it

Case Study: Nancy's Journey to Great Business Success (desire + allowing)

Nancy, a 32-year-old woman with a passion for sustainable fashion, always dreamt of creating her own clothing line. With a strong desire to make a difference in the fashion industry, she decided to build a business that would promote environmentally friendly and ethically produced clothing.

Desire:

Nancy's primary desire was to establish a successful business that would not only provide her with financial security but also make a positive impact on the environment and society. She envisioned her brand becoming a leader in sustainable fashion, offering stylish and affordable clothing that customers would love.

Allowing:

Nancy recognized that many entrepreneurs had already achieved great success in their respective fields, and this inspired her to believe that she could do the same. She reminded herself that there were numerous successful sustainable fashion brands in the market, and there was room for her business to thrive as well.

Steps to Success:

1. Market Research: Nancy began by conducting thorough market research to identify her target audience, understand their needs, and study her competitors. This allowed her to create a unique selling proposition that set her brand apart from others.
2. Building the Brand: Nancy focused on developing a strong brand identity, incorporating her values of sustainability and ethical production into the brand's story. She designed a logo, selected a color palette, and created a consistent brand image across all marketing materials.
3. Sourcing Sustainable Materials: Nancy researched and partnered with eco-friendly suppliers to ensure her clothing line would use only sustainable materials. This also included working with ethical manufacturers to guarantee fair labor practices.
4. Developing a Business Plan: Nancy developed a comprehensive business plan that outlined her goals, strategies, and financial projections. This plan provided a roadmap for her business's growth and helped her secure funding from investors who shared her vision.
5. Marketing and Promotion: Nancy used a combination of digital marketing techniques, including social media, content marketing, and influencer partnerships, to create brand awareness and attract customers to her online store.
6. Constant Improvement: Nancy regularly sought feedback from her customers and made adjustments to her products and business strategies as needed. This commitment to continuous improvement allowed her business to grow and evolve.

Outcome:

Nancy's dedication and belief in her desire to create a successful sustainable fashion brand led her to great business success. Through strategic planning, effective marketing, and a strong commitment to her values, Nancy was able to grow her brand into a recognized leader in the sustainable fashion industry.

By allowing herself to believe in her ability to achieve success and embracing the idea that many entrepreneurs have built thriving businesses, Nancy turned her dreams into reality. Her journey serves as an inspiring example of how desire and allowing can lead to significant accomplishments.

5S and the law of attraction

5S, a systematic approach to workplace organization, can enhance the Law of Attraction by fostering clarity and focus. By maintaining a clean and orderly environment, individuals can reduce distractions, cultivate a positive mindset, and direct their energy towards manifesting their desires. In turn, this optimized setting amplifies the effectiveness of visualization and affirmation practices, thus accelerating the realization of personal goals.

Sort: The first step of the 5S method is to sort through your things and get rid of anything you don't need or that is making a mess. In the context of your spiritual journey, this means sorting through your beliefs, habits, and activities and getting rid of anything that doesn't fit with your spiritual goals. This could mean letting go of negative thoughts, spending less time on social media or other things that distract you, or ending relationships that don't help you.

Set in Order: Once you've gone through your things and found what you need, the next step is to set them up so they're easy to find and use. In the context of your spiritual journey, this means making a routine and schedule that lets you focus on your spiritual practices, like meditation or prayer, and setting aside time for self-reflection and learning.

Shine: The third step of 5S is to keep your workspace clean and well-maintained. In the context of your spiritual journey, this means taking care of your physical, emotional, and mental health, like by exercising, eating well, and learning how to deal with stress. It also means being aware of your thoughts and actions and trying to live in line with your values and beliefs.

Standardize: The fourth step of 5S is to set a standard for how your workspace should be kept clean and organized. In terms of your spiritual journey, this means setting up a regular practice or routine, like meditating every day or going to church once a week, and making sure you stick to it. It also means being consistent in what you do and trying to live in a way that is true to your values and beliefs.

Sustain: The last step of 5S is to keep the systems and processes in place to make sure the program continues to work well. In the context of your spiritual journey, this means that you should keep sorting through your beliefs, habits, and activities and make any changes you need to make to make sure you stay on track with your spiritual goals. It also means keeping track of your progress and making any changes to your routine or practice that you need to make to make sure it stays useful and helpful.

5S is a powerful method for keeping a workspace clean and organized, and it can also be used to help you on your spiritual journey. You can have a more focused and meaningful spiritual experience by sorting through your beliefs, habits, and activities and getting rid of anything that doesn't fit with your spiritual goals. You can also organize your routine and schedule, take care of your health, start a regular practice, and check in on your progress.

5W2H in the law of attraction

The Law of Attraction is a set of rules that says we can bring good things into our lives by thinking and feeling good things. The 5W2H method, which is a quality tool (an action plan), is a way to solve problems and make decisions that can be used in many areas of life, such as with the Law of Attraction. Using the 5W2H method and the Law of Attraction together, you can learn more about what you want to bring into your life and make a clear plan for how to get it. Let's look at how the 5W2H method can be used with the Law of Attraction.

What

"What?" is the first question of the 5W2H method. With this question, you figure out what you want to bring into your life. When you use the Law of Attraction, you should be clear about what you want to bring to you. This means that you should not only know what you want, but also how you want to feel when you get it. For example, instead of saying "I want to be rich," you could say "I want to be financially secure and feel confident in my ability to take care of myself and my loved ones."

Why

"Why?" is the second question in the 5W2H method. This question helps you figure out why you want something to come into your life. When using the Law of Attraction, it helps to know why you want something. This will keep you motivated and on track. For example, if you want to be financially secure, you might want to bring more money into your life so you can feel more secure, comfortable, and have more choices in life.

Who

"Who?" is the third question of the 5W2H method. This question helps you figure out who will help you bring what you want into your life. When using the Law of Attraction, it's important to figure out who can help you reach your goals and who might be getting in your way. For example, if you want to be financially stable, you might need to find a financial advisor or mentor who can help you make a plan to reach your goals.

Where

"Where?" is the fourth question of the 5W2H method. This question helps you figure out where you want to be physically to bring what you want into your life. When using the Law of Attraction, it's important to be clear about where you want to be and what you want your surroundings to look like. For example, if you want to be financially stable, you might want to attract a nice place to live, a stable job, and a safe and secure environment.

When

"When?" is the fifth question of the 5W2H method. This question helps you figure out how long you want to give yourself to get what you want. When using the Law of Attraction, you should know exactly when you want to reach your goals. This will help you stay focused and motivated, and it will also help you make a plan to reach your goals.

How

"How?" is the sixth question in the 5W2H method. You can use this question to figure out what you need to do to bring what you want into your life. When you use the Law of Attraction, it's important to know what you need to do to reach your goals. For example, if you want to be financially stable, you might need to make a budget, buy stocks, or start a business.

Manifestation MAP

To effectively chart our path towards the realization of our aspirations, it is crucial to have a clear and well-defined guide (map) that can help us navigate the journey. This is why I have developed, tested and evaluated to prove it beneficial the Manifestation MAP.

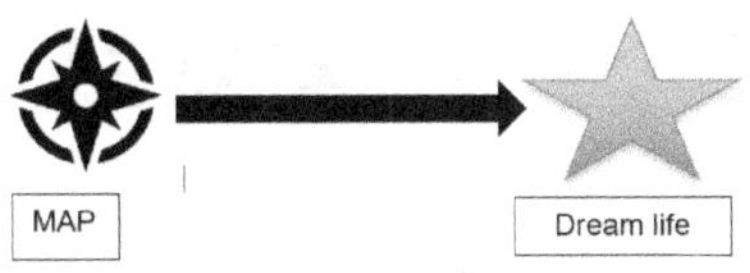

The MAP Process: Magnifying, Attracting, and Pursuing Your Goals

The MAP process is a simple yet powerful manifestation tool that helps individuals bring their desires to fruition. The process consists of three steps: Magnifying, Attracting, and Pursuing.

Magnifying: At this stage, it's important to visualize the final result in great detail. This method entails imagining the accomplishment in detail, recording your thoughts on paper, and acting as though the event has actually taken place. Be as detailed as you can and try to picture everything that goes into making your dream a reality, from the sounds to the smells to the way it makes you feel.

Attracting: Here, you imagine that your wish has already come true and center on emotions like joy and satisfaction. To encourage these feelings, try making a gratitude list, meditating, or using affirmations. By doing this, you'll be able to attract the outcome you're after by ensuring that your vibration is in sync with it.

Pursuing: At this stage, you'll begin making progress toward your objective. Achieving this requires developing a strategy, establishing manageable intermediate goals, and taking concrete actions. This is a critical stage because it demonstrates to the universe your determination and ownership in making your desired outcome a reality.

The MAP process can be applied to any goal, big or small. It is especially useful for manifesting financial prosperity, personal relationships, career advancement, and health and wellness. Whether you want to manifest a new job, a promotion, a better relationship, or a healthier body, the MAP process can help you achieve your desired outcome.

The benefits of using the MAP (Magnifying, Attracting, Pursuing) process for manifestation include:

By focusing on the finer points of your end goal, you may better visualize and conceptualize its actual manifestation.

Vibrational Alignment: Keeping a positive outlook and a heart full of appreciation and anticipation makes it simpler to draw success and happiness your way.

If you take concrete steps toward your goal, you'll send a message to the universe that you're serious about seeing it come to fruition and are willing to shoulder the burden of making it happen.

Boosted Belief and Self-Esteem: When you visualize achieving your goals and then take actionable steps to make it happen, you strengthen your faith in your own power to make it happen.

Improved and more satisfying outcomes can be achieved by integrating mental imagery, optimistic feelings, and concrete steps toward a goal.

Overall, the MAP process aids people in realizing their dreams by focusing their minds, hearts, and hands on achieving those dreams.

Case Study: Using the Manifestation MAP to Achieve Career Goals

Samantha is a recent college graduate who has just started her first job in the marketing department of a major corporation. She has a long-term goal of becoming the marketing director of her company, but she's not sure how to get there. After researching different manifestation tools, Samantha decides to use the MAP process to help her achieve her career goals.

Magnifying: Samantha starts by visualizing herself as the marketing director of her company. She imagines the feeling of accomplishment and pride she would have in achieving this goal. She writes down her vision in detail, including the tasks and responsibilities that come with the position, the colleagues she would work with, and the impact she would have on the company.

Attracting: Samantha focuses on the emotions associated with achieving her goal. She creates a gratitude list and meditates daily, expressing gratitude for the skills she has learned so far, the opportunity to work for a great company, and the support of her colleagues. She uses positive affirmations to reinforce her belief in herself and her ability to achieve her goal.

Pursuing: Samantha creates a plan to achieve her goal. She identifies intermediate goals, such as completing a certification program and developing strong relationships with her colleagues, that will help her achieve her long-term goal. She takes action by attending networking events, volunteering for new projects, and seeking out mentorship opportunities within the company. Samantha remains committed to her goal, and her actions demonstrate her determination and ownership in making her desired outcome a reality.

After several months of practicing the MAP process, Samantha notices positive changes in her career. She's made strong connections with colleagues and has been given additional responsibilities within her department. She feels more confident in her ability to achieve her long-term goal and is committed to the actions needed to make it a reality. The MAP process has helped her to stay focused, motivated, and on track towards achieving her career aspirations.

Personal "W.A.R" to Manifest

Every person has their own personal war within, where they fight against their own self-doubt and anxiety. They eventually triumph over this profound struggle within themselves as they make strides toward self-improvement and inner peace.

The Personal W.A.R framework is a simple yet effective tool for individuals seeking to manifest their dreams and desires. The framework consists of three steps: Wish, Act, and Receive.

Wish: In this step, you focus on defining your desires, dreams, and goals. This includes visualizing what you want to achieve and writing down your aspirations in clear and specific terms.

Act: In this step, you focus on taking action to make your wishes a reality. This includes doing everything in your power to achieve your goals, using your imagination to create a positive mindset, and taking practical steps to bring your desires to life.

Receive: In this step, you focus on assuming that you have already received what you desire. This includes visualizing yourself as already having achieved your goals, acting as if your desires have already come to fruition, and embracing gratitude for what you already have.

Implementing the Personal W.A.R framework requires a commitment to personal growth and a focus on manifestation. To get started, focus on defining your desires and goals, and taking action to make them a reality. During the manifestation process, focus on acting as if you have already received what you desire, and embracing gratitude for what you have.

The Personal W.A.R framework provides a simple yet effective tool for individuals seeking to manifest their dreams and desires. By following the steps of wishing, acting, and receiving, individuals can bring their aspirations to life and achieve their goals. Stay focused, stay committed, and never stop seeking ways to improve your manifestation process.

Step	Description	Practical Example
1. Wish	Define desires, dreams, and goals, visualizing achievements and writing them down in clear terms.	Goal: Write a 300-page novel within 12 months.
2. Act	Take action towards goals, maintain a positive mindset, and use practical steps to manifest desires.	Plan: - Create a writing schedule (5 pages per day). - Join a writing group for support and feedback. - Research and outline the novel's plot and characters.

3. Receive	Assume you have already achieved your goals, visualize success, and embrace gratitude for the present.	Visualization: See yourself holding the finished novel and receiving praise from readers. Gratitude: Appreciate the progress made and the ability to pursue your dream.

Case Study: Sarah's Personal W.A.R Journey

Sarah is a 35-year-old accountant who has always dreamed of starting her own business. However, she has struggled with self-doubt and anxiety, which has prevented her from taking the necessary steps towards achieving her goal.

Wish: Sarah began her Personal W.A.R journey by focusing on defining her desires and goals. She spent time visualizing her dream of owning her own business and wrote down her aspirations in clear and specific terms. She wanted to start a boutique bookstore and coffee shop that combined her love of books and coffee.

Act: In the next step, Sarah focused on taking action to make her wishes a reality. She started researching the process of starting a business, attending seminars and workshops, and connecting with other entrepreneurs. She also used her imagination to create a positive mindset, visualizing herself as a successful business owner and embracing affirmations that reinforced her belief in her own abilities.

Receive: Finally, Sarah focused on assuming that she had already received what she desired. She continued to visualize herself as a successful business owner, acting as if her dream had already come true. She also embraced gratitude for what she already had, including a supportive family, a stable job, and a comfortable home.

After months of hard work, Sarah was able to secure a loan and launch her boutique bookstore and coffee shop. Her business quickly gained a loyal following, and she was able to quit her accounting job and focus on her passion full-time. Sarah's journey with the Personal W.A.R framework helped her overcome her self-doubt and anxiety and allowed her to achieve her dream of starting her own business.

The SATS Science (State Akin to Sleep)

The State Akin to Sleep (SATS), attributed to Neville Goddard is a powerful and transformative mental state that lies at the threshold between wakefulness and sleep. It is a state of deep relaxation, where the conscious mind is at rest, and the subconscious mind becomes more receptive. SATS offers a unique opportunity to tap into the immense potential of our subconscious mind, enabling us to manifest desired outcomes and achieve personal growth.

State Akin to Sleep (SATS) is a type of deep relaxation and rejuvenation that shares certain characteristics with sleep but is otherwise unique. The truth is, we all go through this every day, whether we recognize it or not. Let's delve into the research behind SATS to find out what it is, how it functions, and how it might improve our health.

SATS...what is it?

Natural and separate from sleep, SATS is a state of deep relaxation. It's a mental state characterized by lessened mental and physical activity and a sense of peace and tranquility. Both SATS and meditation/hypnosis share the same goal of generating a profoundly relaxed state.

The "fight or flight" response, which is controlled by the sympathetic nervous system, is dampened by SATS. The parasympathetic nervous system takes control when we reach SATS because we are deeply relaxed. Our "relax and digest" response, which helps to reduce heart rate, blood pressure, and digestive issues, is mediated by the parasympathetic nervous system.

The sympathetic nervous system's activity is lowered and the brain's alpha waves are stimulated by SATS. While we are daydreaming or meditating, our brain waves typically display a pattern known as alpha, which is connected with a state of calm alertness. Focus, tension, and well-being can all benefit from SATS's ability to boost alpha wave activity.

Positive Effects of SATS

It has been established that SATS is beneficial to our health and well-being in a variety of ways. Some of the most significant gains from SATS include:

- SATS is a proven method for alleviating stress and anxious feelings. Naturally occurring painkillers and mood-boosters called endorphins are produced by the body when we enter a state of SATS.
- Since muscle tension is relieved and the mind is calmed, the quality of our night's sleep is enhanced thanks to SATS.
- The right hemisphere of the brain, which is responsible for creative thinking, becomes more active after SATS training.
- Alpha wave activity in the brain is increased with SATS, which in turn improves our ability to learn and retain knowledge.
- SATS has been demonstrated to improve immune function by increasing the activity of natural killer cells. These cells are a type of white blood cell that helps the body fight off infections and other diseases.

Tips for Doing Well on the SATS

- Meditation, hypnosis, and guided relaxation are just a few of the methods that can be used to enter a SATS state. How to do well on the SATS tests is discussed below.
- Choose an undisturbed area that is both relaxing and silent.

- Try shutting out the world and concentrating on your breathing by closing your eyes. Breathe in through your nose and out through your mouth, slowly and deeply.
- Get rid of everything that might be bothering you mentally. If your thoughts wander, softly return them to your breathing.
- Deep relaxation can be attained using guided relaxation techniques, such as progressive muscle relaxation or visualization.

Understanding the Four Types of Intelligence

The concept of intelligence is quite complicated, and research on it dates back hundreds of years. Researchers have come to acknowledge that there are various dimensions of intelligence, in contrast to the traditional definitions of intelligence which have primarily focused on cognitive abilities such as logical reasoning and problem-solving. The four primary forms of intelligence: emotional intelligence (EQ), intellectual intelligence (IQ), spiritual intelligence (SQ), and adaptive intelligence (AI).

Emotional Intelligence (EQ)

The capacity to comprehend and control one's own feelings and behaviors, as well as those of other people, is referred to as emotional intelligence (EQ). Individuals who have a high EQ are able to identify and control their own emotions, as well as empathize with and understand the feelings of others, which enables them to form healthy relationships. EQ is essential for success in both personal and professional relationships, and it also has the potential to assist individuals in more efficiently managing stress and difficult situations.

Intellectual Intelligence (IQ)

Intellectual Intelligence is the standard definition of intelligence, which places an emphasis on cognitive abilities such as logical reasoning, problem-solving, and remembering. Another definition of intelligence, Emotional Intelligence, places less of an emphasis on cognitive abilities. Standardized tests are commonly used to determine a person's

IQ; however, it is crucial to keep in mind that these exams only provide a snapshot of a person's talents, and they do not take into consideration the individual's emotional or social intelligence.

Spiritual Intelligence (SQ)

The ability to connect with a higher power or purpose, as well as the comprehension of the meaning and purpose of life, are both components of spiritual intelligence. Individuals who have a high SQ are able to find meaning and fulfillment in their life, as well as overcome difficulties and challenges while maintaining a sense of perspective. Meditation and mindfulness are two techniques that can assist individuals in developing their sensitivity intelligence (SQ), which is typically associated with these disciplines.

Adaptive Intelligence (AQ)

The ability to adjust one's behavior and flourish in different environments while also being able to solve novel and difficult challenges is what's meant by the term "adaptive intelligence." Individuals that have a high AQ are able to think creatively and flexibly, as well as come up with original solutions to issues and ways to get around difficulties. In a world that is evolving at such a quick rate, where conventional modes of thinking may no longer be successful, AQ is absolutely necessary for success.

The four subtypes of intelligence paint a more comprehensive picture of a person's capabilities, strengths, and the likelihood of their achieving their goals. Individuals can become more well-rounded and capable of reaching their objectives in their personal as well as professional lives if they work on cultivating all four categories of intelligence. These goals can be in any aspect of life.

The Application of Pareto Analysis to the Promotion of the Four Forms of Intelligence

There are a lot of different ways to get smarter and better at each sort of intelligence, which is helpful because intelligence is an essential component of both personal and professional growth. The Pareto Analysis is one method that is useful since it enables people to concentrate their efforts on the most important aspects of their lives that need to be improved.

Increasing Intellectual Intelligence (IQ)

It is possible to increase one's intellectual intelligence through practice that is both concentrated and purposeful. In order to utilize Pareto Analysis, individuals can conduct an evaluation of their existing skills and pinpoint the areas in which they feel they could make improvements. The 80/20 rule, also known as the Pareto Principle, allows them to then prioritize their efforts on the areas that will have the greatest impact by concentrating on the 20% of activities that will generate 80% of the results. They can do this by directing their attention to the 20% of activities that will generate 80% of the results. For instance, rather than striving to enhance their IQ in all areas at once, a person may choose to focus on improving their logic and memory skills as well as their critical thinking abilities through the practice of various activities.

Enhancing One's Capacity for Emotional Intelligence (EQ)

Self-reflection, empathy, and the ability to control one's emotions are three ways that one might work to enhance their emotional intelligence. Individuals can evaluate their current capacities to comprehend and control not just their own but also the emotions of others when using Pareto Analysis because it allows them to do so. They are then in a position to prioritize their efforts on the areas that will have the biggest impact, such as cultivating emotional self-awareness, practicing active listening, and learning coping skills for stress and anxiety.

Developing Spiritual Intelligence (SQ)

It is possible to increase one's Spiritual Intelligence by engaging in spiritual activities, cultivating mindfulness, and cultivating a connection to a greater purpose. Individuals can evaluate their existing level of spiritual fulfillment and connection and pinpoint the aspects of their practice in which they feel they could make improvements by employing the Pareto Analysis technique. They are then in a position to focus their attention and energy on the activities that will have the most significant effect, such as meditating on a regular basis, spending time in nature, and investigating their core values and beliefs.

Enhancing One's Capacity for Adaptive Intelligence (AQ)

Thinking creatively, being flexible, and being innovative are all ways in which one might increase one's adaptive intelligence. Individuals can do a self-assessment of their current ability to adapt and solve difficult situations, and then pick areas in which they feel they could improve. This is the first step in using Pareto Analysis. They are therefore able to prioritize their efforts on the areas that will have the greatest impact, such as practicing brainstorming, learning new skills, and seeking out new challenges and experiences.

The Pareto Analysis is an effective method that can be used to improve all four categories of intelligence. Individuals are able to accomplish their objectives and live up to their full potential in their personal and professional lives if they direct their efforts toward those aspects of their lives that will have the biggest impact on the world.

Chapter 9: Balance

Balance refers to a state of harmony or equilibrium. It is essential to seek balance in all parts of our lives, including our decisions and selections. When we seek balance, we can create a life that is more satisfying.

Prioritizing our values is one strategy to strike a balance in our decision-making. By recognizing what is genuinely important to us and aligning our decisions with our values, we may create balance and satisfaction in our lives.

Another strategy to establish equilibrium is to evaluate the long-term effects of our decisions. Short-term benefits or pleasures can be enticing, but they frequently result in discontent or regret in the long run. We can make decisions that will lead to a more balanced and meaningful existence if we examine the long-term effects of our decisions.

Additionally, seeking balance in our judgments necessitates evaluating how our decisions affect others. By considering how our decisions may affect those around us, we can make decisions that are not only beneficial for ourselves but also for the community and individuals around us.

Obtaining equilibrium also requires taking care of ourselves physically and mentally. Self-compassion and self-care can assist us in achieving a sense of balance and contentment in our lives.

Balance is the state of being in equilibrium or concord. It is essential to pursue equilibrium in all parts of our lives, including our decisions and selections. We may create a more fulfilling existence by prioritizing our beliefs, contemplating long-term repercussions, being sensitive of how our decisions may influence others, and taking care of ourselves.

Attaining Balance: The Importance of Balance and Using Pareto Analysis

In the fast-paced world we live in now, it can be easy to get caught up in our daily tasks and forget about our own health. To live a healthy, happy life, it's important to find a good balance between work, rest, and play.

How important of balance

Balance is important for the health of your body, mind, and emotions. A well-balanced life means taking care of our bodies, doing work that matters, caring for our relationships, and making time for fun things. When we have balance, we feel like we have more control over our lives and are happier.

Pareto Analysis

The Pareto Analysis is a tool that can help us figure out which parts of our lives need the most work. It means figuring out which 20% of activities or tasks cause 80% of the results. We can improve our overall balance and well-being if we pay attention to these key areas.

Using Pareto Analysis, you can reach a state of balance by taking the following steps:

- Find the most important parts of your life: Write down everything you want to change in your life, such as your work, your relationships, your health, and the things you do for fun.
- Think about the effects of each area: Check how each area affects your balance and health as a whole. Think about how much time and effort you put into each area and what results you are getting.
- Use the Pareto Principle: Using the Pareto Principle, find the 20% of areas that cause 80% of the results. First, work on getting better in these key areas.

Once you've figured out what the key areas are, you can make changes to improve your overall balance. This could mean spending more time on fun things, taking better care of your body, or changing the way you work.

The Benefits of Attaining Balance

Finding balance has many advantages, such as:

- Better physical and mental health: When our lives are in balance, we can take care of our physical and mental health, which gives us more energy and a better sense of well-being as a whole.
- Better Relationships: When our lives are in balance, we have more time and energy to spend with the people we care about.
- Increased Productivity: If we focus on the most important parts of our lives, we can be more productive and get better results in all areas.

Balance is important for the health of your body, mind, and heart. By finding the 20% of areas that are responsible for 80% of the results, Pareto Analysis can be used to find a good balance. By putting our attention on these important areas, we can improve our overall balance and well-being, which will lead to a healthier, more satisfying life.

The 8+8+8 Rule: A Guide to a Fulfilling Life

Life is all about balance. We often get so caught up in our daily routine that we forget to take care of ourselves and our loved ones. We focus so much on work that we neglect other important aspects of our lives. That's where the 8+8+8 rule comes in. This rule is a simple guide to living a fulfilling life that balances work, rest, relationships, health, and personal growth. Let's explore the three components of the 8+8+8 rule.

8 Hours of Hard Work

Work is an essential part of our lives. It gives us a sense of purpose, financial security, and personal growth. However, too much work can lead to burnout and stress. That's why it's important to work smart and not just hard. It's not about the number of hours you work, but about the quality of work you produce.

To make the most of your workday, prioritize your tasks and focus on the most important ones. Take breaks throughout the day to recharge your mind and body. Use technology to automate repetitive tasks and free up your time. And most importantly, leave work at work. When you're off the clock, focus on your personal life and hobbies.

8 Hours of Sound Sleep

Sleep is essential for our physical and mental health. It's the time when our body repairs itself and our brain processes information. Lack of sleep can lead to a host of health problems, including depression, obesity, and heart disease. That's why it's important to prioritize sleep and aim for 8 hours of uninterrupted sleep every night. To improve the quality of your sleep, create a sleep-friendly environment. Keep your bedroom dark, cool, and quiet. Avoid using electronic devices before bedtime as the blue light can interfere with your circadian rhythm. Stick to a sleep schedule and avoid napping during the day. And if you have trouble sleeping, try relaxation techniques like meditation or deep breathing exercises.

8 hours on (3Fs, 3Hs, and 3Ss)

The 8-hour balance of 3Fs, 3Hs, and 3Ss is the key to a fulfilled life. By dedicating time to Family, Friends, and Faith, we nurture our relationships and beliefs. The 3Hs, Health, Hygiene, and Hobby, focus on personal well-being and self-care. Lastly, the 3Ss, Soul, Service, and Smile, emphasize inner growth, giving back to the community, and fostering positivity. Integrating these elements into our daily lives paves the way for a harmonious and purposeful existence.

3Fs (Family, Friends, and Faith)

Relationships are an important part of our lives. They give us a sense of belonging, support, and love. Spending time with family and friends can improve our mental health and reduce stress. And having faith can provide us with a sense of purpose and meaning in life.

To prioritize your relationships, schedule time for family, friends, and faith. Plan regular activities like dinner parties, game nights, or outdoor adventures. Attend religious services or volunteer for a cause you believe in. And most importantly, be present in the moment and enjoy the time spent with your loved ones.

3 Hs (Health, Hygiene, and Hobby)

Health is wealth. Taking care of our physical and mental health is crucial for a fulfilling life. Good hygiene habits can prevent the spread of diseases and improve our self-esteem. And having a hobby can provide us with a creative outlet and a sense of accomplishment.

To prioritize your health, make time for exercise and physical activity. Choose nutritious foods and limit unhealthy ones. Practice good hygiene habits like washing your hands regularly and brushing your teeth twice a day. And find a hobby that you enjoy, whether it's painting, dancing, or gardening.

3 SS (Soul, Service, and Smile)

Personal growth is important for a fulfilling life. Nurturing our soul, serving others, and finding joy in life can improve our mental health and overall well-being.

To prioritize your personal growth, spend time alone to reflect and meditate. Serve others by volunteering, donating to a charity, or helping a neighbor. And find joy in life by practicing gratitude, laughing, and engaging in activities that bring you happiness.

The Power of Forgiveness

To forgive is to release oneself from bitterness and hostility towards one who has mistreated them. It's a potent resource for helping us boost our health and well-being through better decision-making.

Forgiveness has been shown to have a positive effect on mental health by lowering levels of stress and other unpleasant feelings. Keeping a grudge or being bitter towards someone is bad for your health since it causes you to feel angry, frustrated, and bitter. The act of forgiving helps us let go of these painful feelings and eases the mental strain that comes with them.

To put it another way, forgiving others can help us have better personal connections. Keeping a grudge or being resentful can put a burden on our relationships because it fosters distrust and distance. Through forgiveness, broken relationships can be repaired.

Making better choices is another way in which forgiveness aids us. Keeping a grudge or harboring resentment can make it hard to see things clearly and cause you to act counter to your own best interests. Forgiving frees up mental space, allowing us to think clearly and make judgments based on facts rather than emotions.

Understanding that forgiveness is a process that requires patience is the first step toward practicing forgiveness. Forgiveness is not ignoring or dismissing cruel behavior; rather, it is letting go of resentment and wrath. Understanding the other person's feelings and trying to put yourself in their shoes are equally crucial.

Forgiveness is the decision to stop harboring bitter feelings toward a person who has mistreated us. It's a potent resource for easing anxiety and depression, strengthening bonds with loved ones, and making wiser life choices. Recognizing our emotions, accepting that forgiveness is a procedure, showing empathy, and realizing that forgiveness does not imply forgetting or condoning wrongdoing are all necessary steps in achieving true reconciliation.

Forgiveness Using the PDCA Cycle

Being able to forgive others is essential to your own development and mental health. To release painful feelings and move on with our lives. Let's discuss the value of forgiveness and how the PDCA (Plan-Do-Check-Act) Cycle can aid in the healing process.

The ability to forgive others is a potent weapon that can assist in the healing of emotional scars and liberate us from destructive ideas and emotions. Keeping resentment, wrath, and bitterness inside causes nothing but harm to ourselves and can have a negative effect on the connections we have with other people. We are able to let go of these bad feelings and move forward in a more positive direction when we are able to forgive.

Self-forgiveness is a crucial component of any healthy personal development plan. Sometimes we are too hard on ourselves for the mistakes we've made in the past, but it's crucial to remember that we're only human and that everyone makes mistakes. We are able to let go of negative self-talk and embrace a more optimistic perspective on life if we are able to forgive ourselves.

It is equally vital to forgive other people. When we forgive people, we are not excusing the behavior of the person we have forgiven; rather, we are letting go of our resentment and anger toward the person we have forgiven. Because of this, we are able to heal and make progress in a constructive way.

The PDCA Cycle is a way to solve problems that can be used to help people forgive each other. To use the PDCA Cycle to give forgiveness, you can do the following:

Plan: Figure out why it is hard for you to forgive yourself or others. Think about the specific things you need to do to be forgiven.

Do: Do something to show forgiveness. You could do this by being kind to yourself, writing a letter of forgiveness, or talking to the person you need to forgive.

Check: Think about how far you've come in forgiving others. Think about how you feel and if the things you have done have helped.

Act: Make any changes you need to your plan. If you are still having trouble forgiving someone, you might want to talk to a therapist or counselor.

The Benefits of Granting Forgiveness

Better mental health: Letting go of bad feelings when we forgive can improve our mental health and make anxiety and depression symptoms less severe.

Stronger Relationships: Forgiving others can make our relationships stronger by reducing arguments and making it easier to talk to each other.

Increased Emotional Resilience: Being able to forgive ourselves and others can help us be better able to deal with problems in the future.

It's important for personal growth and emotional health to be able to forgive. By using the PDCA Cycle, we can try to forgive ourselves and others, let go of bad feelings, and move forward in a good way. There are many benefits to forgiving someone, such as better mental health, stronger relationships, and more emotional strength.

The Dangers of Impulsivity

Impulsivity is the propensity for taking action or making a choice without giving it much consideration. It might lead to thrilling and unexpected adventures, but it can also cause you to act in ways you'll later come to regret.

Poor fiscal judgment is an unfortunate risk that comes with impulsivity. There are long-term monetary repercussions to buying on impulse, spending too much, and other forms of impulsive behavior.

Being impulsive can also cause people to act in ways that are harmful to themselves or others. Sinister outcomes may result from impulsive actions, such as substance misuse or dangerous sexual conduct.

Relationship missteps are another potential consequence of impulsivity. Hasty decisions, like jumping into a relationship or terminating one without giving it enough thought, are common results of acting on impulse.

Mindfulness and self-awareness training can help reduce the harm caused by impulsivity. Recognizing our emotional triggers allows us to take a step back and consider all of our options before acting. It's also helpful to have a strategy for dealing with temptations, including taking a break or consulting a reliable friend or family member.

Impulsivity is the propensity to act or make decisions without giving them much consideration. It might lead to thrilling and unexpected adventures, but it can also cause problems with money management, bad health choices, and relationship missteps. Reducing the harmful effects of impulsivity can be accomplished through the cultivation of mindfulness, self-awareness, and an action plan for dealing with impulses.

Overcoming Impulsivity: Utilizing the VSM and 5S Methodologies

Being impulsive is a common problem that can hurt our personal and professional lives. It can cause people to make bad decisions, have money problems, and have trouble getting along with others. Here, we'll talk about what makes people act on impulse and how the VSM (Value Stream Mapping) and 5S methods can help them stop.

How to Understand Being Hasty

Impulsivity is when someone does something without thinking or caring about the results. It can be caused by a number of things, like not being able to control your emotions or impulses or having it in your genes. It's important to know what makes someone impulsive in order to deal with it effectively.

The method of VSM

The VSM methodology is a tool for lean manufacturing that can help improve efficiency and cut down on waste. The VSM method can be used to stop being impulsive by doing the following:

Identify the Current State: Figure out what makes you so impulsive and how that affects your daily life.

Map the Present Situation: Map out the steps you take to make a decision and look for places where you tend to act on impulse.

Analyze the Current Situation: Look at the situation as it is now and find ways to make it better.

Improve the Current State: Change the way you make decisions to stop acting on impulse. This could involve using tools like mindfulness, self-reflection, and ways to deal with stress.

Standardize the Improved State: Make a routine that includes the changes you made to stop being so impulsive.

The Five S Method

The 5S method is a way to organize a workplace in order to make it more efficient and cut down on waste. The 5S method can be used to stop acting on impulses in the following ways:

Sort: Sort your thoughts and actions to figure out which ones are rash.

Simplify or set in order: Make it easier to make decisions by cutting out steps you don't need and focusing on what's important.

Sweep: Get rid of impulsive thoughts and actions by concentrating on the present and practicing mindfulness.

Standardize: Make your way of making decisions more consistent by forming habits and routines that make you less impulsive.

Sustain: Keep moving forward by keeping an eye on your progress and making changes as needed.

THE BENEFITS OF OVERCOMING IMPULSIVITY

Getting control of your impulses has various advantages, including the following:

Reduced Impulsivity Allows for Better Decision-Making. When we lower our levels of impulsivity, we are better able to make decisions that are based on thoughtful consideration and reflection.

Stability in Financial Matters Overcoming impulsivity can assist us in improving our financial decision-making, hence decreasing the likelihood of experiencing financial difficulties and boosting our level of stability.

Stronger Relationships: We may strengthen our relationships and decrease the amount of conflict that we experience by simply making better decisions.

Being impulsive can have unfavorable effects on both our personal and professional lives. Both the VSM and the 5S techniques can be utilized to reduce impulsivity by enhancing the decision-making process and decreasing the amount of impulsive thinking and behavior, respectively. Conquering impulsivity has many advantages, including enhanced decision-making, increased financial stability, and strengthened interpersonal connections.

120 | IBRAHIM ISSAKA LUCKY

The Importance of Self-Care

The term "self-care" refers to the activities that we carry out in order to safeguard our mental, emotional, and physiological health. Empathy is an important part of our life, and it can assist us in reaching superior conclusions, both for ourselves and for the people around us.

Self-care has many benefits, and one of those benefits is the ability to help us become more present and focused. When we take care of ourselves, we are able to make better decisions because we are better able to concentrate, be more productive, and spend our time more wisely.

One further advantage of practicing self-care is that it can assist us in becoming more resilient. By taking care of ourselves, we may improve our ability to manage stress and reduce the likelihood that we will get overwhelmed by challenging circumstances. Because of this, we will be able to make decisions that are better thought out and more logical.

Taking care of ourselves can also make us more compassionate and understanding toward other people. When we are well-rested, both mentally and physically, we could put ourselves in the shoes of others and come to decisions that are beneficial to all parties concerned.

Self-care can be practiced in a variety of ways, including engaging in physical activity, maintaining a nutritious diet, getting an adequate amount of sleep, socializing with friends and family, and participating in hobbies. Self-care should be a top priority, and we should arrange time for it in the same way that we would organize time for other key responsibilities and activities.

In a nutshell, self-care refers to the activities that we engage in to ensure that our mental, emotional, and physical health are maintained. It is essential to place a high priority on self-care because doing so can assist us in being more present, focused, resilient, and empathic, as well as in coming to better decisions for both ourselves and others. It is necessary to schedule time for it, just as we would schedule time for other important duties, because it can manifest itself in a variety of ways.

SELF-CARE: UTILIZING THE 5S METHODOLOGY

Self-care is important for your overall health and is a key part of living a healthy, balanced life. In this section, we'll talk about how important self-care is and how the 5S method can help make it better.

Self-care is a term for actions and habits that aim to keep or improve a person's physical, mental, and emotional health. Self-care should be a top priority if you want to stay healthy and happy in general.

The 5S method is a way to organize a workplace in order to make it more efficient and cut down on waste. The 5S method can be used to help with self-care in the following ways:

Sort: Look at the things you do to take care of yourself and figure out which ones are most important to you.

Simplify: Make your self-care routine easier by getting rid of things that don't work or aren't necessary.

Sweep: Get rid of distractions and bad thoughts by concentrating on the present and practicing mindfulness.

Standardize: Make your self-care routine more consistent by adding habits and routines that are good for your health.

Sustain: Keep up your self-care routine by keeping track of your progress and making changes as needed.

THE BENEFITS OF IMPROVED SELF-CARE

The advantages of better self-care are numerous.

Physical well-being can be enhanced via regular exercise, nutritious nutrition, and sufficient rest.

Benefits to Mental Health: Activities like meditation, counseling, and stress reduction have been shown to have positive effects on people's emotional and psychological health.

Happier and healthier people often practice better self-care since doing so improves their overall happiness and sense of well-being.

Taking care of oneself is vital to one's health and happiness and plays a significant role in achieving a harmonious balance in one's life. By the application of the 5S paradigm, we may simplify and standardize our self-care routine, leading to better physical and mental health and greater enjoyment.

The Value of Diversity

The term "diversity" refers to the fact that individuals can be distinguished from one another in a number of ways, including their racial or ethnic background, gender, sexual orientation, age, abilities, and points of view. It is a necessary component of the decision-making process, and it has the potential to improve the quality of the choices we make by exposing us to a wider variety of points of view.

One of the primary advantages of variety is that it often results in more original and original thinking when decisions are being made. When we actively seek out the viewpoints of a variety of people, we are presented with a greater number of ideas and options. Because of this, we may be able to come up with answers that are more creative and original as a result of our expanded thinking.

One further advantage of variety is that it can help to discourage people from engaging in groupthink. A phenomenon known as "group thinking" is the tendency of people to conform to the beliefs and decisions of the group, despite the fact that such opinions and conclusions may be erroneous. We can ensure that a variety of viewpoints, opinions, and ideas are heard and taken into consideration if we actively seek out varied perspectives.

Also, diversity can assist us in making decisions that are more equal and inclusive for all parties involved. When we actively seek out other points of view, we increase the likelihood that we will take into account the requirements and points of view of underrepresented or marginalized groups. This can assist us in making decisions that are more equal and inclusive for all parties involved.

In order to increase diversity, it is essential to actively seek out and engage with individuals who come from a variety of different backgrounds, experiences, and points of view. Creating a culture of inclusiveness, aggressively recruiting and promoting employees from varied backgrounds, and supporting a variety of thinking and ideas are some of the ways in which this can be accomplished.

To summarize, diversity refers to the presence of variances among persons, such as disparities in race, ethnicity, gender, sexual orientation, age, abilities, and perspectives. Diversity also includes differences in geographical origin. It is an essential part of the decision-making process, and it can help us make better decisions by providing us with a wider range of perspectives, leading to more creative and innovative decision making, preventing us from falling into the trap of groupthink, and allowing us to make decisions that are more inclusive and equitable. In order to increase diversity, it is necessary to actively seek out and engage with individuals who come from a variety of different backgrounds, perspectives, and experiences, as well as to cultivate a culture that is accepting of all people.

The Role of Values

The views, ideals, and standards that are significant to us are referred to as our values. They serve as the basis for our decision-making and ensuring that our behaviors are congruent with our values can assist us in arriving at choices that are genuine to who we are as individuals.

It is much more probable that we will have a sense of fulfillment and contentment with the decisions that we make when those actions are consistent with our beliefs. This is because our core values are a manifestation of our deepest aspirations, and when we live in line with those desires by adhering to our values, we are living in accordance with who we truly are.

When our behaviors are in harmony with the principles that guide us, we are better able to make choices that are true to ourselves and our beliefs. When we are authentic to who we are, we are less likely to be swayed by the expectations of others or the pressures that come from the outside world.

The decisions that we make in terms of our ethics and morals might also be guided by our values. They help us to grasp what is important to us and what we stand for, which enables us to make judgments that are in line with our own personal ethics and morals, which is a benefit.

To ensure that our behaviors are congruent with our values, it is essential that we first take the time to recognize and comprehend those values. This can be accomplished by engaging in self-reflection, keeping a journal, or having an honest conversation with a reliable person. Once we have gained an understanding of our core values, we will be able to use those values as a guide when making decisions.

In a nutshell, our values can be defined as the views, concepts, or standards that we hold to be the most essential. Our activities should be aligned with our values so that we may make decisions that are true to who we are, fulfilling, real, genuine, ethical, and moral. Our values serve as the basis for our decision-making, and we should ensure that our actions reflect our beliefs. It is important to take the time to identify and understand our values through self-reflection, journaling, or talking to someone we trust, and to use them as a guide in decision making in order to align our actions with our values. Taking this time is the first step in aligning our actions with our values.

Chapter 10: Money

To promote trade, settle debts, and accumulate riches, humans use money as a means of exchange, a measure of value, and a store of value. It's crucial to any functioning economy since it facilitates the buying and selling of products and services between private entities at a much higher volume and lower cost than barter.

Understanding the Energy of Money

People frequently think of money as a tangible item, something that can be held in the hand and traded for other things like goods and services. Yet, money is also a type of energy, and just like any other form of energy, it can be attracted, loved, and cared for in the same ways that other forms of energy may. In this section, together we will investigate the idea that money is a form of energy and talk about how having this understanding can lead to having a relationship with money that is more positive and abundant.

The first thing you need to do in order to comprehend the power of money is to acknowledge the fact that money is merely a medium of trade. It is a means by which we can trade our time, energy, and skills for the things that we require and desire in our lives. The accumulation of wealth is not an end in and of itself; rather, it serves as a tool that enables us to lead the life styles we envision for ourselves.

When we realize that money is nothing more than a tool, we can start to change our relationship with it and how we use it. We might start to think of money not as a limited resource but as an abundant and ever-flowing energy rather than a limited resource. We have the ability to learn to attract, cherish, and take care of this energy in a manner that is comparable to how we would treat any other energy that we encounter in our lives.

Visualization and positive affirmations are two techniques that can be used to attract the energy of money. We can begin to shift our subconscious beliefs and attract more money into our lives if we begin by envisioning ourselves in a state of wealth and affirming that we are worthy and deserving of financial abundance. By doing this, we can begin to bring more money into our lives.

Gratitude is another method that can be used to attract the energy of money. When we are grateful for the money that we already have, we give out a positive frequency that attracts more money to us. When we are not appreciative, we send out a negative energy. It is essential that we have a healthy appreciation for the worth of money and the positive changes it can make in our lives.

Because you love money, you should handle it with care and respect. It implies using sound judgment regarding our money matters and acting responsibly with regard to our resources. When we have a healthy relationship with money, we are better able to bring more of it into our lives. It also implies taking pleasure in the act of earning money rather than concentrating solely on reaching the destination.

Being frugal also entails being conscious of our spending patterns and employing a strategic approach to the management of our financial resources. That entails making an investment in both our present selves and our future selves, as well as being mindful of how the way we spend our money matches both our core beliefs and our long-term objectives.

Money is a sort of energy that may be drawn, loved, and cared for by the person who possesses it. We can transform our connection with money and begin to develop a more positive and plentiful experience with it if we realize that it is really a tool. This understanding enables us to do this. When we cultivate an attitude that attracts, loves, and takes care of money, we pave the way for more financial wealth and prosperity in our lives.

Healing Money Wounds

Money is a multifaceted force that can affect many facets of our life. Many people's happiness, contentment, and even feeling of self-worth are directly related to their financial situation. Nonetheless, for other people, their feelings towards and interactions with money are complicated.

To put it simply, money wounds are long-held, unfavorable attitudes and perceptions about money that operate below the conscious level. These scars may have been inflicted by early exposure to poverty, trial with finances, or the inculcation of bad attitudes toward monetary matters. Social indoctrination linking wealth to avarice, tyranny, and control can also play a role.

Feelings of guilt, humiliation, or inadequacy in relation to financial matters are all possible outcomes of financial trauma. A person may start to think things like, "I'll never have enough money," or "I'm not worthy of financial prosperity." Having these thoughts and feelings running in the background might sabotage our efforts to build wealth and create the life we want.

To mend financial wounds, one must first gain insight into the thoughts and feelings that are fueling them. This typically entails thinking critically about our upbringing and the financial advice we were given as children. It also necessitates the rejection of self-defeating ideas in favor of more optimistic and uplifting ones.

Financial scars can be healed through writing. Putting our money-related attitudes and emotions on paper can help us better understand and deal with them. It also helps us deal with and let go of any resentment or guilt we may feel about monetary matters.

Visualization and positive affirmations are another method that has proven useful. We can begin to alter our underlying assumptions and bring more money into our lives by seeing ourselves in a position of material prosperity and asserting that we are worthy and deserving of such a situation.

Developing a healthy and affectionate perspective on money is an integral part of recovering from financial trauma. This includes keeping one's financial affairs in order, being responsible with one's money, and making sound choices with one's money. Rather than merely focusing on the result, you should learn to take pleasure in the steps along the way to financial success.

To sum up, money wounds are unfavorable attitudes and emotions toward money that have been ingrained from a young age and are unconscious. To mend these wounds, one must first grasp the thoughts and feelings that are at their core. A more positive and abundant relationship with money can be cultivated via introspective thinking, the examination of limiting ideas, and the development of a caring and supportive attitude toward financial matters.

Universal Currency: Time, Money, and Knowledge

These days, we tend to view monetary value as the ultimate measure of worth. Other forms of exchange, however, are not less significant or beneficial. Learn how to get one using the other two by understanding the concept of global currency.

Time is an irreplaceable resource that can never be repaid. It's important to be frugal with such a precious commodity. Money can't buy happiness, but time spent wisely can. Working for a living allows us to put our earnings toward our long-term goals, such as retiring, starting a business, or getting a better education.

We are all familiar with money as a medium of exchange. It's the means by which we can acquire the things we require and desire. It's not just that we need money to stay alive, but that it's crucial to our development and progress as well. It enables us to put money back into our lives, our households, and our neighborhoods.

The value of knowledge exceeds that of both time and money. Knowledge is the sum of all one's experiences and the knowledge one has gleaned from them, and it's what one uses to make better choices, find better solutions, and accomplish one's goals. For the sake of one's own development and progress, knowledge is a valuable commodity.

Either of the other two currencies can be used to purchase the third. The time we spend working can be used to generate money, and that money can be used to further our education and get more insight. Or we can use what we've learned to launch a business or hone a skill, both of which can lead to monetary gain. As an added bonus, we can put our spare time toward expanding our knowledge base, which in turn will help us spend our resources more wisely.

In sum, the currencies of time, money, and knowledge are all crucial to our progress and development. A more satisfying and plentiful existence can be achieved by learning the value of each money and how to exchange one for another. Bear in mind that these currencies are intertwined and that it is impossible to have one without the other. It is possible to live in peace and prosperity if we learn to properly balance and employ these currencies.

Understanding Money EQ and Money IQ

In terms of our emotional connection to and mastery over monetary resources, "Money EQ" and "Money IQ" are two key notions. Money EQ, also known as financial emotional intelligence, is the degree to which an individual is aware of and in control of their feelings and attitudes in relation to financial matters. Our "money IQ," also known as our "financial intelligence," reflects how well we are versed in and able to put into practice a variety of financial principles. These two ideas are the cornerstones on which sound financial judgment and prosperity are built.

We need to cultivate our "money EQ" since our feelings and beliefs about money strongly influence our actual money habits. For instance, if we view money negatively, we may be less likely to set financial goals, stick to a budget, and build savings. But if we see money with optimism and know the worth of saving and investing, we are more inclined to act prudently with our resources.

Understanding and making use of financial concepts and instruments requires a certain level of "money IQ," which is why this concept is so crucial. Understanding the benefits of compound interest and starting an investment portfolio at a young age, for instance, can guide our retirement planning selections. Knowing the ins and outs of the tax code can also help us make the most of our money and pay the least amount of tax possible.

Learning about money, budgeting, saving, investing, and tax regulations can help you develop a higher level of emotional intelligence and increase your financial literacy. You can equip yourself with the knowledge and skills to make sound financial decisions by reading books, articles, and attending seminars and workshops on the subject. You can get more out of life and closer to your financial goals by consulting with a financial counselor or specialist.

Budgeting, saving, investing, and keeping up to date with financial news are all vitally important financial habits to cultivate. Maintaining control of your finances and making sure you are on track to reach your financial goals can be done by the careful monitoring of your spending, the establishment of realistic financial goals, and the periodic evaluation of your progress toward those goals.

Both financial intelligence (Money IQ) and emotional intelligence (Money EQ) are crucial for success in the financial realm. Smart financial judgments and mastery of one's financial future are within one's reach through an appreciation for and management of one's emotional and mental state in relation to money, as well as through familiarity with relevant financial concepts and instruments.

Money Mantra

A money mantra is a meaningful phrase or remark that serves as a constant reminder to keep our financial priorities in order and to adopt a more optimistic outlook on wealth. Simple words like "I am financially secure" or "I am in charge of my finances" can serve as effective mantras. Consistent use of these mantras can assist us in altering our perceptions of wealth and reorienting our attention toward more fruitful areas of life.

CREATING AND USING MONEY MANTRAS

Mantras about money are positive affirmations meant to alter how we think and feel about money, so attracting more of it into our lives. We may retrain our subconscious mind, overcome limiting beliefs, and attract money and prosperity by repeatedly saying these affirming phrases to ourselves.

Examples of money mantras include:

"Money comes to me effortlessly and with ease."

"I am a money magnet who attracts prosperity and fortune."

"I am financially independent and enjoy a life of plenty."

"I am deserving of riches and money."

"My income continues to increase."

To employ money mantras effectively, repeat them frequently with conviction and feeling. Imagine the desired financial outcome and have faith in your abilities to attain it. These habits will transform your financial situation over time, opening the way to abundance and prosperity.

The Pareto Principle in Money-Making

The Pareto Principle argues that roughly eighty percent of outcomes result from twenty percent of inputs; this holds true in many contexts, including financial success. The top 20% of your clientele may account for 80% of your revenue. Similarly, perhaps only 20% of your offerings are responsible for 80% of your revenue. If you know where your money is coming from, you can put your efforts there and increase your profits.

Profit maximization can be improved by using the Pareto Principle, which suggests putting the majority of effort into keeping and expanding relationships with the top 20 percent of customers. By putting your attention on this group of customers, you can boost your earnings without investing in advertising or a larger customer base. To a similar extent, you can ascertain which of your offerings brings in the most money, then devote more resources to marketing and selling that item while cutting back or doing away with the others.

The Pareto Principle can also be used to financial success by zeroing down on the top 20% of revenue generators. If you find that 80 percent of your revenue comes from online sales, for instance, you should prioritize developing your online presence and increasing online sales.

IMPLEMENTING THE PARETO RULE

Before you can apply the Pareto Principle to your efforts to make more money, you must first determine which aspects of your business are currently bringing in the greatest revenue for you. This can be accomplished by conducting a thorough examination of your income and expenditures and determining the source of the majority of your financial resources. Once you have discovered these areas, you will be able to place your attention there and thereby increase your financial gain.

After that, you need to concentrate your efforts on the revenue-producing strategies that have proven to be the most successful in the past. For instance, if you discover that making sales online is the most profitable technique of producing cash for your business, you should prioritize growing your online presence and elevating the volume of your online sales. You can accomplish this by making investments in internet marketing, enhancing the quality of your website, and expanding your presence on social media.

The last step in using the Pareto Principle to your attempts to make money is to actually do something about it. This can be accomplished by concentrating on the clients or customers who bring in the most revenue for your business, marketing and selling the goods or services that bring in the most revenue, and concentrating on the strategies that bring in the most money.

The 80/20 rule, often known as the Pareto principle, is a powerful principle that may be applied to many different aspects of life, including the generation of income. You can improve your financial situation and increase your income by gaining an awareness of the sources from where the majority of your funds originate and concentrating your efforts on the activities that are the most productive in terms of bringing in cash. You can meet your financial objectives, as well as enhance your income and profits, by applying the 80/20 rule to the activities that lead to the generation of revenue. It is important to keep in mind that the Pareto Rule is not a money-making magic trick; rather, it is a straightforward theory that, if applied appropriately, can assist you in concentrating on the most vital aspects of your company or personal finances.

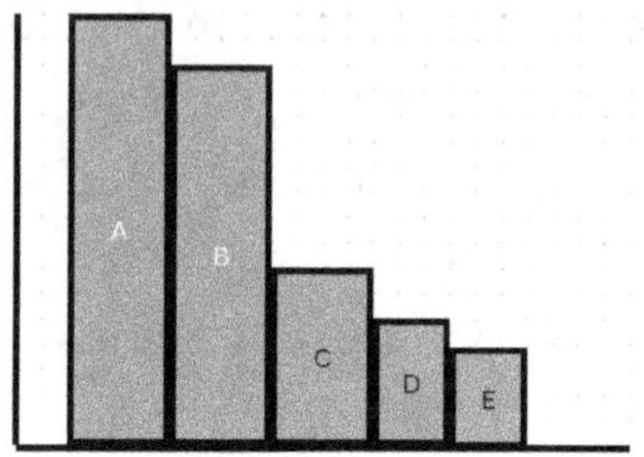

Money CAKE to become Rich

Imagine a cake that, once consumed, bestows unimaginable wealth upon the person who tastes it. While it may sound like a far-fetched fantasy, the money cake has long been a subject of intrigue and curiosity, persisting in urban legends and folktales. But is there any truth to this fascinating concept? Let's delve into the mystery of the money cake.

THE MONEY CAKE FRAMEWORK

The Money Cake framework is a tool designed to help individuals achieve financial abundance and stability. The framework consists of four steps: Confess, Attract, Keep, and Extend.

Confess: In this step, you focus on confessing your love for money and admiration for the rich. This includes affirmations, visualization exercises, and other methods of reinforcing your positive relationship with money.

Attract: In this step, you focus on assuming that you are already rich and have financial abundance. This includes visualizing yourself as already having the financial stability you desire, and acting as if you already have everything you need.

Keep: In this step, you focus on maintaining your faith and commitment to financial abundance. This includes staying focused on your goals, and avoiding negative thoughts and beliefs that may undermine your progress.

Extend: In this step, you focus on extending a helping hand to others. This includes using your financial stability and abundance to support others and making a positive impact in your community and the world.

Implementing the Money Cake framework requires a commitment to financial growth and a focus on attracting abundance. To get started, focus on confessing your love for money, and assuming that you are already rich and have financial stability. During the manifestation process, focus on maintaining your faith and commitment to financial abundance, and extending a helping hand to others.

The Money Cake framework provides a simple yet effective tool for individuals seeking to achieve financial abundance and stability. By following the steps of confessing, attracting, keeping, and extending, individuals can bring financial abundance into their lives and reach their goals. Stay focused, stay committed, and never stop seeking ways to improve your financial situation.

C	A	K	E
Confess	Attract	Keep	Extend
I love money Money is good for me I love the rich	I attract/ command £2000,000 into my account I gain a million-dollar idea I deserve unlimited amount of money	I am working towards my desire amount I am in the process of receiving £2000,000	I donate to help fellow humans I patronage to help feed other family (when buying)

Case Study: Laura James and the Money Cake Framework

Laura James, a 32-year-old woman from a small town, had always dreamt of becoming financially stable and wealthy. Despite having a stable job, she found herself struggling to make ends meet and was unable to create a life of abundance for herself and her family. After learning about the Money Cake framework, she decided to give it a try and transform her financial life.

Step 1: Confess

Laura started by confessing her love for money and admiration for the rich. She began writing daily affirmations in a journal, such as "I am worthy of wealth and abundance" and "I respect and admire those who have achieved financial success." She also visualized herself in the company of successful people, attending high-profile events, and living in her dream home. By doing this, Laura reinforced her positive relationship with money and started to change her mindset.

Step 2: Attract

Laura then moved on to the Attract phase, where she focused on assuming the identity of someone who was already wealthy. She visualized herself living a life of financial abundance, wearing designer clothes, and driving a luxury car. She began to act as if she already had everything she desired – making financial decisions with confidence and surrounding herself with positive, success-oriented people.

She also started investing in her personal development by attending financial seminars, reading books on wealth-building, and seeking advice from successful mentors. These actions helped her to develop a deeper understanding of money management and investment strategies.

Step 3: Keep

During the Keep phase, Laura concentrated on maintaining her faith and commitment to financial abundance. She set clear, measurable financial goals for herself and regularly reviewed her progress. Whenever she faced setbacks or felt discouraged, Laura reminded herself of her affirmations and visualizations to maintain her motivation and stay focused on her objectives.

Laura also cut ties with negative influences in her life, including friends who constantly complained about money or had poor financial habits. Instead, she sought out a support network of like-minded individuals who shared her commitment to financial success.

Step 4: Extend

After achieving a significant level of financial stability, Laura entered the Extend phase. She began using her newfound wealth to support others in her community by donating to local charities, sponsoring educational programs, and offering financial advice to those in need. Laura also started a blog where she shared her journey and the lessons she learned along the way, inspiring others to pursue their own financial goals.

Result

Through the Money Cake framework, Laura was able to transform her financial life, achieve her goals, and create a lasting impact in her community. By confessing her love for money, attracting abundance, keeping her faith, and extending help to others, Laura not only built a life of wealth and stability for herself but also inspired others to follow in her footsteps.

5W2H Application to personal life and money making

The 5W2H technique, or the 7QC Tools as they are sometimes referred to, is a useful strategy for resolving issues and making important decisions in many different areas of one's life, including one's private life and one's financial standing. The 5W2H technique consists of the following questions: What, Why, Who, Where, When, How, and How Much. With the answers to these questions in hand, you'll be better equipped to analyze the situation and develop workable solutions. Applying the 5W2H approach to your own life and financial situation is the focus of this section.

The 5W2H approach can be used in everyday life to pinpoint issues and generate workable answers. To determine the origin of your tension and anxiety, for instance, the 5W2H technique might be used.

The 5W2H method can also be applied to the process of producing money, which will assist you in recognizing issues and conceiving of efficient solutions. You can utilize the 5W2H method, for instance, to figure out why you aren't producing enough money by determining the factors that are contributing to the issue.

Question	Answer
Who	Identify your target audience or potential customers. Who will benefit from your product or service?
What	Determine the product or service you will provide. What problem does it solve or need does it fulfill?
Where	Decide on the location or platform for your business. Where will you sell or provide your service?
When	Establish the timeline for starting and growing your business. When is the ideal time to launch?

Why	Understand the purpose and motivation behind your business. Why do you want to make money this way?
How	Outline the steps and strategies for building and promoting your business. How will you achieve success?
How Much	Calculate the costs and potential profits of your business. How much will it take to start and maintain the business, and how much can you expect to earn?

The 5W2H method is a powerful problem-solving and decision-making tool that can be applied to various areas of life, including personal life and money-making. By asking the questions of What, Why, Who, Where, When, How, and How Much, you can gain a deeper understanding of a problem or situation and come up with effective solutions. By applying the 5W2H method to your personal life and money-making efforts, you can identify problems and come up with effective solutions to improve your overall well-being and financial success.

Chapter 11: Wealth

The term "wealth" is used to describe a person's or a group's financial and material well-being. It's a way to compare how financially stable different people or organizations are. Income, investments, inheritance, and property ownership are just a few of the ways that one can amass wealth.

Building Wealth Using DMAIC, 5S, Pareto Analysis, and 5 Whys

Wealth building is a process that requires a systematic approach in order to be successful. One such approach is to use a combination of DMAIC, 5S, Pareto Analysis, and 5 Whys. These tools are widely used in the field of quality management and can also be applied to personal finance and wealth building.

BUILDING WEALTH WITH THE 5 WHYS: UNCOVERING THE ROOT OF FINANCIAL SUCCESS

The 5 Whys is a powerful problem-solving technique that involves asking "why" five times to identify the root cause of a problem. By applying this method to wealth-building, we can uncover the fundamental principles that contribute to financial success.

Why do I want to build wealth?

Understanding your motivation for building wealth will help clarify your financial goals and create a roadmap to achieve them.

Why do some people accumulate wealth while others struggle?

Identifying the habits and mindset of financially successful individuals can help you adopt these practices and avoid common pitfalls.

Why is financial literacy important?

By comprehending the importance of financial literacy, you will be more likely to invest time and energy in educating yourself about money management, investments, and wealth-building strategies.

Why should I diversify my income sources?

Recognizing the value of multiple income streams will encourage you to explore various opportunities, reducing financial risk and enhancing overall wealth.

Why is it essential to have a long-term perspective?

Understanding that building wealth takes time and patience will help you develop a long-term mindset, making it easier to stay committed to your financial goals and overcome setbacks.

By examining the 5 Whys of wealth-building, you can gain insights into the core principles of financial success and create a solid foundation for achieving your financial aspirations.

PARETO ANALYSIS:

The Pareto Analysis is a technique that can be utilized to determine which aspects of a challenge or objective are the most significant contributors. The Pareto principle, which asserts that 80% of the effects arise from 20% of the causes, serves as the foundation for this idea. When it is applied to personal finance and the accumulation of wealth, it can assist individuals in determining which aspects of their financial plans should receive the greatest attention in order for them to realize their desired level of economic success.

For instance, a study of spending using Pareto Analysis could disclose that the majority of expenditures are going toward housing and transportation, while just a small fraction of expenditures are going toward entertainment. This could be the case if the Pareto Analysis was used. This would imply that these are the areas in which the individual's financial condition may be improved by making the most significant changes, as shown by the previous sentence.

DMAIC:

Define, Measure, Analyze, Improve, and Control is what the acronym DMAIC stands for. It is an approach for the improvement of processes that is frequently utilized in Six Sigma initiatives. When it is applied to personal finance and the accumulation of wealth, it can assist individuals in identifying areas in which they can better their financial status and in taking steps to reach the goals that they have set for themselves.

The first thing that has to be done in order to move forward with the DMAIC process is to define the problem or the goal. This could be a specific monetary objective, such as putting money down for a down payment on a house or paying off all of one's credit card debt. After the objective has been outlined, the subsequent step is to evaluate the present circumstance. Creating a budget, keeping track of costs, and performing an income analysis are all potential steps in this process.

The objective of the third stage, which is to examine the situation, is to isolate the fundamental reasons that the problem or goal exists. This may involve determining areas in which you have unnecessary spending or places in which you have opportunities to boost your revenue. After determining the primary reason for the issue, the next stage is to devise means of solving the problem. Among the possible steps in this process is the formulation of a strategy to either cut costs or raise revenues.

Controlling the situation is the fifth and last step in the process. Taking this step could entail establishing a budget and keeping track of your expenditures to ensure that you remain on track to achieve your monetary objectives.

5S:

Sort, simplify, sweep, standardize, and sustain are the five steps that make up the 5S methodology. It is a strategy that is implemented in workplaces in order to maintain a tidy and well-organized setting. When it is applied to the management of personal money and the accumulation of wealth, it can assist individuals in organizing their financial affairs, clearing away unnecessary paperwork, and developing a long-term financial strategy.

The first thing you need to do to get started with the 5S process is to organize your funds and get rid of anything that isn't absolutely necessary. This could involve canceling subscriptions that aren't needed, shutting credit card accounts that aren't being utilized, and getting rid of assets that aren't required.

The second stage is to reduce the complexity of your financial situation. Consolidating your several bank accounts, developing a spending plan, and streamlining your investment portfolio are all potential steps in this direction.

The next stage is to take a thorough look at your financial situation and make sure everything is in order. This can require matching up bank records, looking over credit reports, and making sure that all bills are paid on time.

The standardization of your financial operations is the fourth step to take. Setting up automatic payments for bills, coming up with a regular savings strategy, and evaluating your insurance coverage are all examples of things that could fall under this category.

The very last thing you need to do is stick to your financial strategy. In this context, "frequently evaluating" can mean assessing your financial strategy and budget on a regular basis and making adjustments as required.

Profiting from a Liability

A standard definition of a liability is something that results in monetary loss and the diversion of other valuable resources. The fact of the matter is, however, that a liability can in fact be transformed into a lucrative opportunity with the application of the appropriate plan and approach. This section will discuss a variety of strategies for making a profit from a liability, and it will also demonstrate how to transform your liabilities into assets.

Refinance Your Responsibility If you want to turn a liability into a profit, one of the most straightforward ways to do so is to refinance the liability. If you have a loan or debt with a high interest rate, one option for you to consider is refinancing it so that the rate can be lowered and your monthly payments can be reduced. This will not only save you money on interest costs throughout the course of the loan's duration, but it will also free up cash flow that can be spent in other areas to make profits.

Leverage Your Liability for Income: Another option is to harness your liability to generate income, a process called "monetizing" your liability. For example, if you have a property that's burdensome due to considerable maintenance expenses, consider renting it out to earn passive income. This approach not only helps cover some of the property's costs but also, over time, transforms it into a profit-generating asset.

Make Use of Your Liability as Collateral If you have a liability that has a high value, you may use it to acquire loans by using it as collateral. Because of this, you will have access to additional funds, which you may then use to make investments in other opportunities and create income from those investments. Be sure to conduct exhaustive study on the potential dangers, and carefully examine how taking out a loan may affect the amount of responsibility you have.

Sell Your Liability: It is possible that in certain circumstances it might be more beneficial to just sell your liability. This is especially the case if the liability is no longer helpful or important to achieving the goals and objectives you have set for yourself. You will not only be able to cut your costs by selling the responsibility, but you will also be able to create a profit from the sale, which you can then put toward the pursuit of other prospects.

A liability may represent a significant burden for an organization, but with the appropriate strategy, it may also represent an opportunity for financial gain. You can transform a liability that is costing you money into an asset that is working for you to produce revenue and profits if you refinance it, monetize it, use it as collateral, or sell it. To guarantee that you achieve your goals, you should carefully analyze your options and, if required, seek the counsel of professionals.

Achieving Financial Stability through Budgeting, 5S, and VSM

Financial stability is an essential aspect of life that can provide a foundation for reaching personal and financial goals. The three tools of budgeting, 5S, and VSM are effective in helping individuals achieve financial stability.

Budgeting is the process of creating a plan for managing income and expenses. It involves tracking spending, determining where money is going, and making changes to spending habits to meet financial goals. A budget should include both fixed expenses (such as rent or mortgage payments) and variable expenses (such as food and entertainment).

Steps to create a budget:

- Track spending: Keep track of all expenses for one month to get an idea of where money is being spent.
- Determine income: Establish a clear understanding of the monthly income, including all sources of income.
- Categorize expenses: Divide expenses into categories, such as housing, food, transportation, entertainment, and so on.
- Set financial goals: Identify the financial goals, such as paying off debt, saving for a down payment on a house, or building an emergency fund.

- Allocate funds: Based on financial goals, allocate funds to different categories.
- Review and adjust: Regularly review the budget and make adjustments as needed.

The 5S approach is a Lean Six Sigma tool that facilitates workplace organization and increases efficiency. Sort, simplify, sweep, standardize, and sustain are the five steps.

Steps to implement 5S in personal finance:

Sort: Identify and remove items that are not needed. This step can be applied to bank statements, credit card bills, and other financial documents.

Simplify: Streamline processes and simplify information to make it easier to understand. This can be applied to tracking expenses, creating a budget, and organizing financial documents.

Sweep: Regularly clean up and reorganize the workspace. This step can be applied to cleaning up a cluttered desk or computer desktop and keeping financial documents organized.

Standardize: Establish standard procedures for organizing, tracking, and managing finances.

Sustain: Maintain the system and continue to improve processes.

Value Stream Mapping (VSM) is a Lean Six Sigma tool that assists individuals in comprehending the flow of value throughout a process. By outlining the procedures required in managing finances, it can be utilized to discover opportunities for improvement in personal finance.

Steps to create a VSM for personal finance:

Identify the process: Define the process of managing finances.

Map out the process: Draw a map of the process, including the steps involved and the flow of value.

Analyze the process: Look for areas for improvement, such as ways to reduce waste or increase efficiency.

Improve the process: Implement changes to improve the process and achieve financial stability.

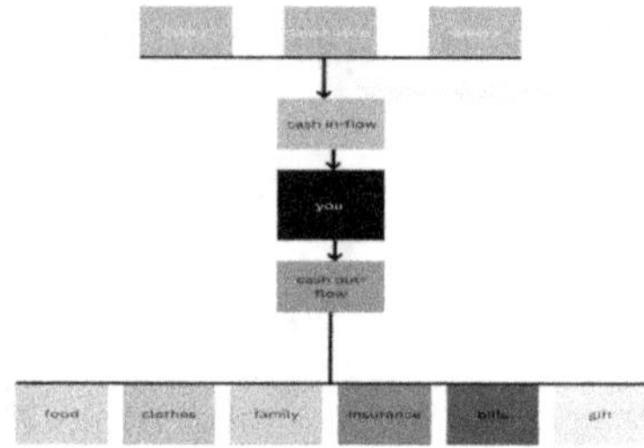

Money at hand = total (cash in-flow)-total (cash out-flow)

Plan, organize, and strive for constant improvement to achieve financial security. When used together, budgeting, 5S, and VSM provide a framework for controlling income and expenses, arranging financial documentation, and enhancing processes, all of which contribute to monetary stability. One can gain financial independence and stability by employing these methods.

Personal Break-Even Point

A personal break-even point refers to the financial situation where an individual's income is just enough to cover their basic living expenses, such as rent or mortgage, utilities, food, transportation, and healthcare, without incurring debt or accumulating savings. It's often considered a state of financial stagnation because the individual is not progressing towards financial goals or building wealth.

To calculate your personal break-even point, follow these steps:

1. Identify your monthly income: Determine your total monthly income, including your salary, any freelance or side gig income, and any other sources of regular income.
2. List your monthly expenses: Make a list of all your essential monthly expenses, such as rent or mortgage, utilities, groceries, insurance, and transportation costs. Be sure to include any recurring expenses, like loan payments or subscriptions.
3. Calculate your total monthly expenses: Add up all your monthly expenses to determine the total amount you spend each month on essential living costs.
4. Compare your income to your expenses: Compare your total monthly income to your total monthly expenses. If your income is equal to or slightly above your expenses, you have reached your personal break-even point.

To move beyond financial stagnation and start building wealth, you may need to either increase your income, decrease your expenses, or both. Some strategies to consider include:

1. Increase your income: Look for opportunities to earn more money, such as negotiating a raise, finding a higher-paying job, or starting a side hustle.
2. Decrease your expenses: Review your expenses and identify areas where you can cut back, such as reducing discretionary spending, negotiating better rates for services like insurance, or downsizing your living situation.
3. Create a budget: A detailed budget can help you track your income and expenses more effectively, identify areas for potential savings, and allocate funds towards savings and investments.
4. Build an emergency fund: Save a portion of your income in an emergency fund to cover unexpected expenses, so you don't end up in debt during difficult times.
5. Prioritize savings and investments: Make saving and investing a priority by automating savings and investment contributions or treating them as non-negotiable expenses in your budget.

By taking control of your finances and working towards increasing your income or reducing your expenses, you can move beyond the break-even point and achieve financial growth.

A case study to overcome personal break-even using the 5W2H method

Who	What	When	Where	Why	How	How Much
John, a 28-year-old graphic designer	Increase income	Within the next six months	Both at his current job and through freelance work	To move beyond his break-even point and start saving for a down payment on a house	Asking for a raise at his current job, taking on freelance projects, and enhancing his skills to qualify for higher-paying projects	Aim to increase his monthly income by 20%

John	Reduce expenses	Ongoing, starting immediately	In various areas of his spending, including housing, utilities, and discretionary spending	To free up more of his income for savings and investments	Negotiating better rates for services, cutting back on non-essential expenses, and considering more affordable living situation	Aim to reduce his monthly expenses by 10%
John	Create and follow a budget	Starting immediately and reviewed monthly	Using a budgeting app or spreadsheet	To have a clear understanding of his income and expenses, and to allocate funds effectively	Categorizing his income and expenses, setting spending limits, and tracking his spending regularly	Allocate at least 10% of his income towards savings and investments

John	Build an emergency fund	Over the next 12 months	In a high-yield savings account	To cover unexpected expenses and avoid going into debt	Automating a monthly transfer from his checking account to his emergency fund	Aim to save three to six months' worth of living expenses
John	Prioritize savings and investments	Starting immediately with ongoing contributions	Using a mix of savings accounts, retirement accounts, and investment platforms	To build long-term wealth and achieve his financial goals	Automating monthly contributions, treating savings and investments as non-negotiable expenses, and regularly reviewing his financial goals	Allocate a minimum of 10% of his income towards savings and investments

In this case study, John uses the 5W2H method to identify action-able steps to overcome his personal break-even point. By increasing his income, reducing his expenses, and prioritizing savings and invest-ments, he can move beyond financial stagnation and work towards achieving his financial goals.

Applying the PDCA Cycle to Benefit from Inflation

Inflation, the general increase in prices and decrease in the purchasing power of money, is often seen as a challenge for individuals and businesses alike. However, it is possible to turn this economic phenomenon into an opportunity by employing a systematic approach.

Inflation, often seen as a financial challenge, can be turned into an opportunity with a strategic approach. The Plan-Do-Check-Act (PDCA) cycle provides a systematic method for continuous improvement and learning. Let's explore how to benefit from inflation using the PDCA cycle;

The PDCA cycle involves four stages:

1. Plan: Identify a problem or opportunity and create a plan to address it.
2. Do: Implement the proposed changes or actions.
3. Check: Measure the results and compare them to the desired outcomes.
4. Act: Based on the analysis, make adjustments, refine the plan, and repeat the cycle.

The table below provides examples of how the PDCA cycle can be applied to benefit from inflation.

Stage	Action	Example
Plan	Analyze the impact of inflation	Assess how inflation affects your expenses, income, investments, and financial goals.
	Identify opportunities	Determine sectors that experience growth during inflationary periods or investments that benefit from rising prices.
	Develop a strategy	Create a plan outlining the steps to capitalize on the identified opportunities and mitigate inflation-related risks.
Do	Adjust spending and saving habits	Cut back on discretionary expenses and increase savings to maintain purchasing power.
	Diversify investments	Invest in assets that outpace inflation, such as stocks, real estate, or inflation-protected securities.

	Implement cost-control measures	Reduce costs and increase efficiency to maintain profitability in an inflationary environment (for business owners).
Check	Monitor economic indicators	Stay informed about inflationary trends by tracking the Consumer Price Index (CPI) and interest rates.
	Evaluate financial performance	Periodically review financial statements and investment portfolios to assess the effectiveness of your inflation-benefiting strategy.

	Assess progress	Determine whether your actions are helping you achieve your financial goals and adjust your strategy as needed.
Act	Refine your strategy	Make necessary adjustments to your plan based on the results of your evaluations.

	Implement changes	Execute the revised plan and continue monitoring your progress.
	Repeat the cycle	Continuously iterate through the PDCA cycle to identify new opportunities and refine your approach as the economic environment changes.

Case Study: Jane's Small Business and the PDCA Cycle

Jane runs a small coffee shop that offers specialty beverages, fresh pastries, and artisanal sandwiches. As inflation rises, the prices of her supplies and operating costs increase. Jane decides to use the PDCA (Plan, Do, Check, Act) cycle to help her business not only survive but benefit from inflation.

1. Plan: Jane starts by analyzing the current state of her business and how inflation is affecting her costs. She identifies areas where higher costs are impacting her profits, such as increasing prices for raw materials, rent, and wages. Jane then sets a goal to increase revenues and optimize expenses to maintain profitability.

To achieve this goal, she develops a plan with the following actions:

- Increase menu prices to pass some of the increased costs onto customers.
- Find alternative suppliers that offer better prices or negotiate with current suppliers.
- Implement cost-saving measures like reducing food waste and optimizing energy usage.

- Offer promotions and loyalty programs to retain customers and attract new ones.
- Diversify her product offerings, such as adding high-margin items or catering services.

1. Do: Jane starts implementing her plan. She raises menu prices by a reasonable amount, ensuring that the price increase won't drive customers away. She researches new suppliers and negotiates with her current ones to get better deals. Jane also trains her staff on cost-saving measures and introduces energy-efficient appliances. She launches a loyalty program and runs promotions to keep customers coming back.

2. Check: After a few months, Jane reviews her financial statements and customer feedback to evaluate the effectiveness of her plan. She compares the revenue, expenses, and profit margins before and after implementing the changes. Jane also analyzes customer feedback and sales data to understand how her actions affected customer behavior, satisfaction, and loyalty.

3. Act: Based on her analysis, Jane finds that her plan has been successful in increasing revenue and maintaining profitability despite inflation. However, she notices that some menu items have lower sales than before, and certain cost-saving measures are not as effective as she had hoped. Jane decides to make necessary adjustments, such as:

- Further refining her menu by removing low-selling items and adding more popular, high-margin options
- Identifying more effective cost-saving measures and training her staff accordingly
- Considering other revenue-generating opportunities, such as hosting events or partnering with local businesses for cross-promotion

Jane then loops back to the planning stage and continuously applies the PDCA cycle to adapt her business to the changing economic landscape and ensure its success amidst inflation.

Managing money with the Budget Square

To help you save more money, the Budget Square Technique recommends categorizing your income, savings, emergencies, and expenditures into four separate boxes.

The Budget Square Method is a visual method of budgeting in which a square is used to represent a person's income, savings, and emergency fund. You can readily spot problem areas, establish reasonable savings targets, and track your progress by dividing your financial data into these four broad buckets.

Income	Expenses
Saving	Emergency fund

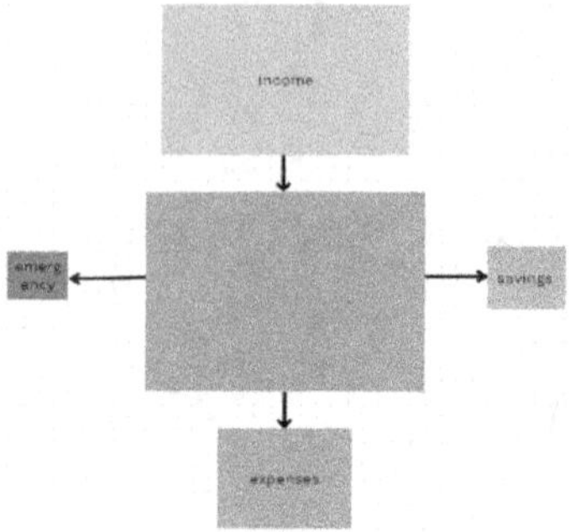

The benefits of using the Budget Square Method include:

- The four-box method of structured budgeting streamlines the planning process and shows you where you are financially in an instant.
- The method raises consciousness by prompting a thorough analysis of one's spending patterns in order to locate areas where money might be saved.
- The Budget Square Method is adaptable, so you may make it work for your specific needs and objectives.
- The strategy encourages you to stick to your financial goals by helping you define specific, attainable ones.

USING THE FOUR-SQUARE BUDGETING METHOD

To get started, tally up all the money coming in from various sources including a regular job, side gigs, and investments (Inflow). The next step is to detail your present emergency fund and savings. Finally, detail your outgoing cash flow by itemizing your monthly rent, utilities, food, and entertainment costs. Provide as much information as you can to help others gain a full grasp of your financial condition.

MAKE A BUDGET SQUARE

Create four equal quadrants on a sheet of paper or a digital canvas to track your income, savings, emergencies, and expenditures. The square can be adjusted in size and design to better fit your needs.

Plan out how your money will be spent, earned, and saved for unexpected events.

Put the amounts you earn, the amount you save, the amount you have set aside for an emergency, and the amount you spend in their respective quadrants.

Make the distinction between the four groups clear with the help of color or symbols. If you want to give a clear picture of your financial status, you need to include the quantities for each area.

Check the Budget square

Check the Inflow and Outflow quadrants of your completed Budget Square for a sense of equilibrium. Find ways to save money or earn more money, then use that information to calculate how much you can put into your "Savings" and "Emergency" categories.

Create a Savings and Rainy-Day Fund Plan

Create sensible and workable plans for your savings and emergency fund based on your findings. Saving for a trip is an example of a short-term goal, whereas retirement or a six-month emergency fund are examples of long-term goals. Put your goals in writing on the Budget Square to keep you motivated and on track.

Continuously Assess and Modify

Keep your Budget Square up-to-date and read it so often to monitor your progress toward your savings and emergency fund objectives. To keep on track, make any necessary adjustments, such as cutting costs or looking for new ways to earn money.

Focusing on four primary categories—Inflow, Savings, Emergencies, and Outflow—the Budget Square Technique is a practical and successful approach to managing your finances and saving more money. By categorizing your money-related data in this way, you'll be able to spot problem areas, establish achievable savings and emergency fund targets, and better manage your finances overall.

Linear Programming Model

Linear Programming (LP) is a mathematical optimization technique that is used to maximize or minimize a linear objective function, subject to linear equality and inequality constraints. It is widely used in various fields such as finance, engineering, transportation, and manufacturing, among others.

The LP model is represented by a set of linear equations and inequalities that define the constraints and the objective function. The decision variables in the model represent the quantities of different products or services that need to be produced or consumed.

The LP model can be expressed as follows:

Maximize or Minimize: $Z = c_1x_1 + c_2x_2 + c_3x_3 + ... + c_nx_n$

Subject to: $a_{11}x_1 + a_{12}x_2 + a_{13}x_3 + ... + a_{1n}x_n \leq b_1$ $a_{21}x_1 + a_{22}x_2 + a_{23}x_3 + ... + a_{2n}x_n \leq b_2$ ... $a_{m1}x_1 + a_{m2}x_2 + a_{m3}x_3 + ... + a_{mn}x_n \leq b_m$

Where Z is the objective function to be maximized or minimized, $x_1, x_2, x_3, ..., x_n$ are the decision variables, $c_1, c_2, c_3, ..., c_n$ are the coefficients of the objective function, $a_{11}, a_{12}, a_{13}, ..., a_{1n}, a_{21}, a_{22}, a_{23}, ..., a_{2n}, ..., a_{m1}, a_{m2}, a_{m3}, ..., a_{mn}$ are the coefficients of the constraints, and $b_1, b_2, ..., b_m$ are the constraints' limits.

The LP model's objective function can be either to maximize or minimize, depending on the problem's requirements. The constraints represent the limitations or restrictions in the problem, which must be satisfied while optimizing the objective function.

There are two main types of LP problems: the maximization problem and the minimization problem. In a maximization problem, the objective is to find the maximum value of the objective function, subject to the constraints. In a minimization problem, the objective is to find the minimum value of the objective function, subject to the constraints.

The LP model is often used in solving optimization problems in various industries. For example, in the manufacturing industry, the LP model can be used to determine the optimal production levels of different products, subject to constraints such as production capacity and demand.

In the transportation industry, the LP model can be used to determine the optimal distribution of goods and services, subject to constraints such as transportation costs, delivery time, and capacity limitations.

In the finance industry, the LP model can be used to determine the optimal investment portfolio, subject to constraints such as risk tolerance, expected returns, and investment limitations.

In summary, the LP model is a powerful optimization tool that can be used in various fields to maximize or minimize a linear objective function, subject to linear equality and inequality constraints. Its applications are numerous, and it is widely used in industry and academia to solve complex optimization problems.

Case Study: Minimizing Household Expenses Using Linear Programming

Problem Description: The Smith family is trying to minimize their monthly household expenses. They have identified four major expense categories: groceries, utilities, transportation, and entertainment. They want to allocate their budget in a way that minimizes their total expenses while meeting specific constraints and requirements.

Objective: Minimize the total monthly household expenses for the Smith family.

Decision Variables: Let x1 = amount spent on groceries (in dollars) Let x2 = amount spent on utilities (in dollars) Let x3 = amount spent on transportation (in dollars) Let x4 = amount spent on entertainment (in dollars)

Objective Function: Minimize Z = x1 + x2 + x3 + x4

Constraints:

1. The family needs to spend at least $400 on groceries to meet their nutritional needs. x1 ≥ 400
2. Utilities (electricity, water, and gas) have a minimum fixed cost of $200 per month. x2 ≥ 200
3. The family must spend at least $300 on transportation (fuel, public transport, and vehicle maintenance) to meet their commuting needs. x3 ≥ 300
4. For mental well-being, they want to allocate at least $100 per month for entertainment. x4 ≥ 100
5. The family has a total budget of $1,500 per month for these four expense categories. x1 + x2 + x3 + x4 ≤ 1500
6. Non-negativity constraint: x1, x2, x3, x4 ≥ 0

Linear Programming Model: Minimize Z = x1 + x2 + x3 + x4 Subject to: x1 ≥ 400 x2 ≥ 200 x3 ≥ 300 x4 ≥ 100 x1 + x2 + x3 + x4 ≤ 1500 x1, x2, x3, x4 ≥ 0

By solving this linear programming model, the Smith family can determine the optimal allocation of their budget to minimize their total monthly household expenses while meeting their specific constraints and requirements.

Problem: Maximizing Investment Returns

Suppose you have $10,000 to invest in two different investment options, Investment A and Investment B. Your goal is to maximize your annual returns while considering constraints such as risk levels and investment limits.

Let x1 be the amount invested in Investment A, and x2 be the amount invested in Investment B. Investment A has an expected annual return of 8%, while Investment B has an expected annual return of 12%.

Objective function: Maximize: R = 0.08x1 + 0.12x2

where, R = Total annual returns x1 = Amount invested in Investment A x2 = Amount invested in Investment B

Constraints:

1. Investment budget: You have a total of $10,000 to invest. x1 + x2 ≤ 10,000
2. Investment A limit: You can invest a maximum of $6,000 in Investment A. x1 ≤ 6,000
3. Investment B limit: You can invest a maximum of $5,000 in Investment B. x2 ≤ 5,000
4. Risk constraint: To limit risk, at least 40% of the total investment must be in Investment A. x1 ≥ 0.4(x1 + x2)

In matrix form, the linear program model can be represented as:

Maximize: R = [0.08, 0.12] * [x1, x2]

Subject to: [1, 1] * [x1, x2] ≤ [10,000] [1, 0] * [x1, x2] ≤ [6,000] [0, 1] * [x1, x2] ≤ [5,000] [-0.6, 0.4] * [x1, x2] ≤ [0]

By solving this linear program model, you will obtain the optimal allocation of your investment budget to maximize your annual returns while adhering to the given constraints.

To solve the linear programming model, we can use the Simplex Method or any other linear programming algorithm. In this example, we'll use Python and the PuLP library to solve the problem.

First, install the PuLP library:

pip install pulp

Next, create a Python script to solve the linear program:Top of Form

import pulp

Define the problem

problem   =   pulp.LpProblem("Maximize_Investment_Returns", pulp.LpMaximize)

```python
# Variables
x1 = pulp.LpVariable("x1", lowBound=0, cat="Continuous")
x2 = pulp.LpVariable("x2", lowBound=0, cat="Continuous")
# Objective function
problem += 0.08 * x1 + 0.12 * x2, "Total Annual Returns"
# Constraints
problem += x1 + x2 <= 10000, "Investment Budget"
problem += x1 <= 6000, "Investment A Limit"
problem += x2 <= 5000, "Investment B Limit"
problem += x1 >= 0.4 * (x1 + x2), "Risk Constraint"
# Solve the problem
problem.solve()
# Print the results
print("Status:", pulp.LpStatus[problem.status])
print("Optimal Allocation:")
print(f"Investment A: ${x1.varValue:.2f}")
print(f"Investment B: ${x2.varValue:.2f}")
print(f"Total Annual Returns: ${pulp.value(problem.objective):.2f}")
```

Status: Optimal

Optimal Allocation:

Investment A: $6000.00

Investment B: $4000.00

Total Annual Returns: $720.00

OPM AND PDCA Cycle

Using the Other People's Money (OPM) strategy in conjunction with the Plan-Do-Check-Act (PDCA) cycle can indeed help individuals amass wealth, but it's important to approach this combination with a clear understanding of both strategies and a focus on risk management.

The OPM strategy involves using borrowed capital, such as loans, credit lines, or investor funding, to finance investments. This allows investors to leverage other people's resources to increase their investment power and potential returns. However, it also means taking on additional risk, as borrowed capital must be repaid with interest or dividends.

The PDCA cycle is a continuous improvement process that consists of four steps:

1. Plan: Identify the investment opportunity and develop a strategy, including how to use OPM effectively and manage risk.
2. Do: Implement the plan by acquiring the necessary capital and making the investment.
3. Check: Monitor the investment's performance, comparing actual results with expected outcomes.
4. Act: Analyze the results, identify areas for improvement, and adjust the strategy as needed before repeating the cycle.

Combining OPM and PDCA can help maximize returns and mitigate risk in the following ways:

1. Improved decision-making: The PDCA cycle encourages thorough planning, research, and analysis before making investment decisions, which can lead to better-informed choices and a higher likelihood of success.
2. Continuous monitoring: By regularly reviewing investment performance and comparing it to expectations, investors can identify issues early on and take corrective action, preventing potential losses.
3. Risk management: The PDCA cycle's emphasis on analysis and adjustment helps investors identify and address risks associated with using OPM, such as over-leveraging or failing to meet repayment obligations.
4. Flexibility: The iterative nature of the PDCA cycle allows investors to adapt their strategies based on new information or changing market conditions, increasing the chances of long-term success.

OPM and PDCA strategies applied to a real estate investment

Step	Description	OPM & PDCA Application
Plan	Identify a real estate property with potential for growth	Research properties, neighborhoods, and market trends; develop a financial plan including OPM sources and risk management
Do	Acquire funding and purchase the property	Estimate costs, potential returns, and repayment schedules for borrowed capital Secure loans, credit lines, or investor capital; negotiate and close the property deal
Check	Monitor the property's performance	Regularly assess property value, rental income, and expenses; track actual results against projections

Act	Analyze results and adjust strategy as needed	Identify areas for improvement, such as cost reduction or increasing rental income; consider refinancing or adjusting repayment terms if needed
Repeat	Apply lessons learned to new investment opportunities	Use insights from previous investments to refine strategy, improve risk management, and identify new OPM sources

In this example, an investor plans to use the OPM strategy to purchase a real estate property with potential for growth. They follow the PDCA cycle to develop a plan, secure funding, monitor the investment's performance, and make adjustments as necessary. By continually applying the PDCA cycle, the investor can maximize their returns and mitigate risks associated with using OPM.

Case Study: Jessica Martinez and Building Wealth through Property Sales Using Other People's Money (OPM)

Jessica Martinez, a 35-year-old dreamer from a modest background, had always been fascinated by the world of real estate. She believed that selling properties could be her ticket to financial success, but she lacked the initial capital required to start her own real estate business. After learning about the concept of using Other People's Money (OPM), Jessica decided to leverage this strategy to build her wealth through property sales.

Step 1: Education and Networking

To succeed in the competitive real estate industry, Jessica knew she needed to gain comprehensive knowledge and build a strong network of contacts. She enrolled in real estate courses and attended industry events, seminars, and workshops. Through these activities, she met experienced real estate agents, brokers, investors, and other professionals who provided valuable insights and guidance on using OPM effectively in the property market.

Step 2: Obtaining a Real Estate License

Jessica understood that to sell properties on behalf of others, she needed to become a licensed real estate agent. After completing her real estate education, she passed the required exams and obtained her license, allowing her to legally represent property owners in the sale of their homes.

Step 3: Partnering with Property Owners

Jessica began to approach property owners, offering her services as a real estate agent to sell their properties. By working on a commission basis, she was able to leverage the property owners' assets (their homes) to generate income for herself without investing her own money. This strategy allowed her to enter the real estate market using OPM.

Step 4: Building a Reputation and Client Base

As Jessica gained experience and completed successful property sales, she started building a reputation as a knowledgeable and trustworthy real estate agent. She focused on providing excellent customer service, conducting thorough market research, and utilizing effective marketing strategies to attract potential buyers. Satisfied clients began referring her to their friends and family members, allowing her to grow her client base and increase her earnings.

Step 5: Expanding into Property Investment

With her growing income from property sales, Jessica decided to expand into property investment. She used OPM in the form of bank loans to purchase rental properties, which generated a steady stream of passive income. As her property portfolio grew, she began to attract the attention of other investors who were interested in partnering with her on real estate deals, further increasing her access to OPM.

Step 6: Giving Back to the Community

After achieving a high level of financial success, Jessica decided to give back to her community. She started a mentorship program to help aspiring real estate agents learn the ropes of the industry and offered free workshops on property investment strategies. She also donated a portion of her earnings to support local housing initiatives and charities.

Result

By leveraging the power of Other People's Money, Jessica Martinez turned her dream of becoming wealthy through property sales into a reality. Her journey demonstrates the potential for success in the real estate industry by utilizing OPM, building a strong network, and providing exceptional service to clients.

Quality Value

Quality Value refers to a product or service that offers significant benefits to customers, which they recognize and are willing to pay for. It implies that the product or service meets or exceeds customer expectations in terms of performance, reliability, durability, and overall satisfaction. In essence, quality value is achieved when the benefits provided by a product or service justify its price.

Here's an example of a product with quality value:

Product: High-Performance Electric Bicycle

Features and Benefits:

1. Powerful Motor: The electric bicycle is equipped with a high-quality motor, providing a smooth and efficient riding experience, enabling riders to easily tackle hills and other challenging terrains.
2. Long-Lasting Battery: The bicycle features a durable and reliable battery, allowing riders to travel long distances on a single charge, reducing the need for frequent recharging.
3. Lightweight Frame: The bicycle is designed with a lightweight, yet sturdy frame that is easy to handle and maneuver, enhancing the overall riding experience.
4. Comfortable and Ergonomic Design: The electric bicycle is designed with user comfort in mind, featuring an ergonomic saddle, adjustable handlebars, and a well-balanced frame that ensures a comfortable riding experience.

5. Advanced Safety Features: The bicycle is equipped with integrated LED lights, reflective elements, and high-quality brakes to ensure rider safety in various riding conditions.

6. Low Maintenance: The electric bicycle is designed for easy maintenance, with minimal moving parts and high-quality components that are built to last, reducing the need for frequent repairs or replacements.

7. Environmentally Friendly: The electric bicycle is a sustainable transportation option, producing zero emissions and reducing the rider's carbon footprint.

Customers are willing to pay for this high-performance electric bicycle because it offers a range of benefits that enhance their riding experience, promote safety, and contribute to environmental sustainability. The product's quality value lies in its combination of performance, durability, comfort, and eco-friendliness, which customers recognize as worth the investment.

Wealth Equation

Wealth refers to the abundance of valuable assets, resources, or possessions that an individual, family, or organization has accumulated over time. It is a measure of financial well-being and can be seen as a store of value that can be used to meet future needs, achieve financial goals, and improve one's quality of life.

Wealth can be generated by creating products or services with high quality value and leveraging resources and opportunities to maximize returns.

*Wealth = Quality Value * Leverage*

1. Quality Value: This refers to the benefits a product or service provides to customers, which they recognize and are willing to pay for. The higher the quality value, the more likely customers will be satisfied and become repeat customers, generating increased revenue and profits.

2. Leverage: This refers to using resources and opportunities to amplify returns on investment. Leverage can come from different sources, such as financial leverage (using borrowed funds), operational leverage (maximizing efficiency and productivity), or network leverage (utilizing connections and partnerships).

By multiplying quality value with leverage, the wealth formula suggests that to generate wealth, one should focus on creating products or services that provide significant benefits to customers and effectively leverage resources and opportunities to maximize returns.

For example, consider a software development company that creates a high-quality project management tool (Quality Value) and leverages its resources (financial, human, and technological) and marketing channels (Leverage) to reach many potential customers. The company's wealth will grow as it successfully combines the quality value of its product with effective leveraging strategies.

The wealth formula emphasizes the importance of both creating value for customers through quality products and services and leveraging resources and opportunities to maximize returns and achieve financial growth.

Case study of wealth equation

Let's consider a physiotherapy clinic that offers services to patients. We will use the Wealth = Quality Value * Leverage equation to demonstrate how the clinic can generate wealth by improving the quality value of its services and leveraging its resources and opportunities. Here's a numerical example:

Suppose the clinic currently serves 20 patients per day and charges $100 per session. The clinic earns a daily revenue of $2,000 (20 patients * $100 per session).

1. Quality Value: The clinic decides to improve the quality value of its services by investing in advanced physiotherapy equipment and providing additional training to its therapists. As a result, the patient satisfaction rate increases, and the clinic can now charge $120 per session due to the enhanced quality of its services.
2. Leverage: The clinic decides to increase its leverage in three ways:
   1. Financial Leverage: The clinic borrows $10,000 to expand its facilities, allowing it to accommodate more patients.
   2. Operational Leverage: The clinic optimizes its scheduling system, enabling therapists to increase their productivity by serving 30% more patients.
   3. Network Leverage: The clinic forms partnerships with local hospitals and sports clubs to receive patient referrals, increasing the number of new patients by 25%.

Now let's calculate the new wealth generated by the clinic:

1. After improving Quality Value, the clinic now charges $120 per session.
2. With increased Leverage:
    1. The clinic serves 20 patients * 1.30 (operational leverage) = 26 patients per day.
    2. The number of new patients grows by 25% (network leverage), so 26 patients * 1.25 = 32.5, which we'll round to 33 patients per day.

The clinic's new daily revenue is 33 patients * $120 per session = $3,960.

Therefore, the Wealth generated by the clinic after improving Quality Value and utilizing Leverage is: Wealth = $3,960 (new daily revenue) - $2,000 (original daily revenue) = $1,960

This numerical example illustrates how a physiotherapy clinic can generate increased wealth by focusing on improving the quality value of its services and leveraging its resources and opportunities effectively.

PDCA and Wealth Equation

The PDCA (Plan-Do-Check-Act) cycle is a four-step iterative management method used for continuous improvement and problem-solving. Applying the PDCA cycle to the wealth equation (Wealth = Quality Value * Leverage) can help individuals and businesses continuously improve their strategies for generating wealth. Here's a breakdown of the PDCA cycle applied to the wealth formula in a table format:

Phase	Action	Description

Plan	Identify opportunities for increasing Quality Value and Leverage	Analyze your current financial situation, products, services, and resources. Identify areas where you can increase quality value (improve products or services) and leverage (utilize resources more effectively). Set specific, measurable, achievable, relevant, and time-bound (SMART) goals for wealth generation. Develop a strategy to reach these goals.
Do	Implement the strategies to improve Quality Value and Leverage	Execute the strategies and plans to increase quality value and leverage. This might involve enhancing product features, improving customer service, streamlining operations, expanding marketing efforts, or optimizing resource allocation. Monitor progress and document any changes or results during the implementation phase.

| Check | Evaluate the effectiveness of the improvements made | Review the results of your efforts to improve quality value and leverage. Measure the outcomes against your SMART goals and analyze the data to determine the effectiveness of your strategies. Identify any discrepancies, successes, and areas that need further improvement. |
| Act | Adjust and refine strategies based on the evaluation | Based on the insights gained from the Check phase, make adjustments to your strategies and plans to improve quality value and leverage further. Refine your approach to enhance results and continuously work towards generating wealth. |

By following the PDCA cycle, individuals and businesses can systematically identify opportunities, implement strategies, evaluate results, and make adjustments to continuously improve their wealth generation efforts through quality value and leverage. This iterative process fosters growth and progress towards financial goals.

Case Study: Tom Johnson's Journey to Extreme Wealth through Fish Farming Business

Tom Johnson, a 42-year-old entrepreneur with a passion for sustainable agriculture, saw an opportunity in the growing demand for healthy and environmentally friendly food sources. With a vision to create a successful fish farming business, Tom decided to utilize the "Wealth = Quality Value * Leverage" formula to achieve his goal of becoming extremely wealthy.

Step 1: Creating High-Quality Value Products

Tom began by conducting extensive research on fish species that were in high demand, sustainable, and could be farmed efficiently. He decided to focus on tilapia, a fast-growing and protein-rich fish known for its adaptability and relatively low environmental impact.

To ensure that his fish farming operation provided the highest quality value to customers, Tom invested in advanced aquaculture technologies, such as recirculating aquaculture systems (RAS), to maintain optimal water quality and reduce waste. He also implemented stringent quality control measures and followed sustainable practices, which ultimately resulted in a premium product that customers recognized and were willing to pay for.

Step 2: Leveraging Financial Resources

To fund the initial setup of his fish farm, Tom approached several banks and secured a business loan at a competitive interest rate. This financial leverage allowed him to establish his operation and begin producing high-quality fish without depleting his personal savings.

Step 3: Operational Leverage through Efficiency and Productivity

Tom understood that maximizing efficiency and productivity was crucial for the success of his business. He invested in automated feeding systems and water quality monitoring devices to optimize the growth of his fish while minimizing labor costs. Additionally, he implemented best practices in fish farm management, which further improved his operational leverage and increased profitability.

Step 4: Network Leverage through Partnerships and Connections

To expand his market reach and create additional revenue streams, Tom formed strategic partnerships with local restaurants, grocery stores, and food distribution companies. These partnerships allowed him to access a larger customer base and increase the demand for his premium fish products. He also networked with other fish farming experts, industry leaders, and government agencies to stay informed about new opportunities, regulations, and best practices.

Step 5: Scaling the Business and Diversifying Revenue Streams

As Tom's fish farming business grew, he continued to reinvest his profits into expanding his operation. He acquired additional land and set up new fish farms, further increasing his production capacity. To diversify his revenue streams, Tom started producing value-added products, such as smoked fish and fish-based pet food. This diversification not only increased his overall revenue but also reduced his dependence on a single product line.

Step 6: Giving Back to the Community

With his newfound wealth, Tom became actively involved in philanthropic activities. He contributed to local environmental initiatives, supported educational programs, and provided financial assistance to aspiring entrepreneurs in the sustainable agriculture sector.

Outcome

By focusing on creating high-quality value products and leveraging resources and opportunities, Tom Johnson achieved extreme wealth through his fish farming business. His journey exemplifies the effectiveness of the "Wealth = Quality Value * Leverage" formula in generating wealth and success in the world of sustainable agriculture.

Return on Investment (ROI)

Return on Investment (ROI) is a financial metric that is widely used to measure the probability of gaining a return from an investment. It is a ratio that compares the gain or loss from an investment relative to its cost. The formula for ROI is:

ROI = (Net Profit / Cost of Investment) × 100

Where:

- Net Profit = Total returns (or gains) - Cost of Investment
- Cost of Investment = Initial amount invested

In the context of the previous example, we can calculate the ROI for each investment option as follows:

1. Investment A:
1. Cost of Investment: $6,000
2. Total returns: 8% of $6,000 = $480
3. Net Profit: $480
4. ROI = (Net Profit / Cost of Investment) × 100 = ($480 / $6,000) × 100 = 8%
1. Investment B:

- Cost of Investment: $4,000
- Total returns: 12% of $4,000 = $480

- Net Profit: $480
- ROI = (Net Profit / Cost of Investment) × 100 = ($480 / $4,000) × 100 = 12%

So, the ROI for Investment A is 8% and for Investment B is 12%.

Internal Rate of Return (IRR)

Is a financial metric used to evaluate the attractiveness of an investment opportunity. It is the discount rate at which the net present value (NPV) of an investment equals zero. In other words, IRR is the rate at which an investment breaks even in terms of NPV.

The IRR is typically used for capital budgeting decisions and helps investors compare different investment opportunities by estimating the potential profitability of each investment.

The IRR can be calculated using the following formula:

$$0 = NPV = \Sigma\ [C_t / (1 + IRR)^t]$$

Where:

- NPV = Net Present Value
- C_t = Net cash inflow (or outflow) during the period t
- IRR = Internal Rate of Return
- t = Time period (e.g., year, quarter, month)

Calculating the IRR requires an iterative process or a financial calculator, as it involves finding the root of a polynomial equation.

Here's an example of an investment project with a series of cash flows over a five-year period. We will calculate the IRR for this investment using Microsoft Excel.

Year	Cash Flow
0	-10000
1	3000
2	4000
3	2000
4	5000
5	6000

To calculate the IRR using Microsoft Excel, follow these steps:

1. Open a new Excel spreadsheet.
2. Create a table with the years (0 to 5) in column A and the corresponding cash flows in column B. Make sure to input the initial investment as a negative value (e.g., -10000).
3. In any empty cell, type the formula **=IRR(B1:B6)**, where B1:B6 is the range of cells containing the cash flows.
4. Press Enter.

Excel will calculate the IRR for the given cash flows. In this example, the IRR is approximately 26.8%.

Net Present Value (NPV)

Is a financial metric used to evaluate the profitability of an investment. NPV calculates the difference between the present value of cash inflows and the present value of cash outflows over the life of an investment. It helps to determine the value of an investment today, taking into account the time value of money.

The formula for NPV is:

$$NPV = \Sigma \left[C_t / (1 + r)^t \right] - I_0$$

Where:

- NPV = Net Present Value
- C_t = Net cash inflow (or outflow) during the period t
- r = Discount rate
- t = Time period (e.g., year, quarter, month)
- I_0 = Initial investment cost

A positive NPV indicates that the investment is expected to generate more cash than its cost, making it a profitable venture. A negative NPV suggests that the investment may not generate enough returns to cover its cost, making it less attractive.

Using the previous cash flow example, let's calculate the NPV with a discount rate of 10%.

Year	Cash Flow

0	-10000
1	3000
2	4000
3	2000
4	5000
5	6000

To calculate the NPV using Microsoft Excel, follow these steps:

1. Open a new Excel spreadsheet.
2. Create a table with the years (0 to 5) in column A and the corresponding cash flows in column B. Make sure to input the initial investment as a negative value (e.g., -10000).
3. In any empty cell, type the formula =NPV(0.1, B2:B6) + B1, where B1:B6 is the range of cells containing the cash flows, and 0.1 is the discount rate (10%).
4. Press Enter.

Excel will calculate the NPV for the given cash flows and discount rate. In this example, the NPV is approximately $3,684.54. Since the NPV is positive, the investment project is expected to generate more returns than its cost, making it a profitable venture.

Chapter 12: Relationship and Communication

The ability to connect with others and convey your ideas effectively is crucial in all facets of life. They're the bedrock of productive teamwork, creative problem-solving, and individual development. Building meaningful connections with others and refining one's communication abilities can have far-reaching effects on one's happiness and success in all walks of life.

The Importance of Communication

The practice of exchanging information, ideas, and thoughts with another person verbally, in writing, or through the use of any other media can be referred to as communication. It is vital to the process of decision making since it enables us to properly articulate our thoughts and ideas as well as to listen to and comprehend the viewpoints of others.

Good communication can lead to increased levels of collaboration, which in turn can lead to more satisfying decision making. When we are able to communicate clearly, we are able to work together to collect information, comprehend various points of view, and arrive at a conclusion that is in everyone's best interest.

Good communication also enables us to articulate our requirements and worries in a manner that is transparent and forthright, which can play a role in reducing the likelihood of misunderstandings and disagreements. It also enables us to understand the wants and worries of other people, which can lead to decisions that are more empathic and sensitive of other people's feelings.

The ability to actively listen, to articulate oneself clearly, and to recognize nonverbal signs are all essential components of effective communication abilities. In addition to this, you need to have an open mind and be willing to take into account the viewpoints of others.

Establishing clear lines of communication, establishing ground rules, and encouraging open and honest communication are all critical things to do in order to increase communication during the decision-making process. In addition to this, it is essential to engage in the practice of active listening and to provide people the opportunity to express themselves.

Communication can be defined as the process of exchanging information, ideas, and thoughts through the use of spoken language, written language, or any other media. It is vital to the process of decision making since it enables us to properly articulate our thoughts and ideas as well as to listen to and comprehend the viewpoints of others. Good communication can lead to more collaborative and satisfying decision making, as well as the prevention of misunderstandings and disputes, as well as the making of decisions that are more compassionate and sensitive of others. Establishing clear lines of communication, establishing ground rules, encouraging open and honest communication, practicing active listening, and giving people an opportunity to express themselves are all key steps to take in order to improve communication during the decision-making process.

Building Relationships Using 5W2H

The 5W2H method is an effective problem-solving and decision-making tool that involves answering seven key questions: Who, What, Where, When, Why, How, and How Much. By applying the 5W2H method to building relationships at work, you can create a strategic plan for fostering strong connections with your colleagues, which can contribute to a positive work environment and professional success.

Question	Answer
Who	Identify the colleagues or stakeholders you need to build relationships with, including teammates, managers, and other departments.
What	Determine what types of relationships you want to develop (e.g., professional, mentoring, or collaborative) and what shared goals or interests can help strengthen these connections.

Where	Decide on the most suitable settings or platforms for relationship-building, such as team meetings, workshops, or social events, and consider digital platforms like internal communication channels or video conferences.
When	Establish the timeline for building and maintaining relationships, identifying key opportunities to connect and interact with others, and develop a consistent plan for ongoing communication.
Why	Understand the importance of building relationships at work, such as improving teamwork, increasing job satisfaction, and fostering a supportive work environment.
How	Outline strategies for building relationships, including active listening, empathy, offering support, and engaging in open communication.
How Much	Assess the time and effort required to invest in relationship-building activities and balance these with other professional responsibilities.

By using the 5W2H method to guide your approach to building relationships at work, you can create a targeted plan that addresses the key aspects of relationship development, helping you forge strong connections that contribute to a positive work environment and professional success.

The Importance of Networking

Establishing and maintaining meaningful connections is essential for both professional and personal development. Networking with other professionals in your field might open doors to new learning experiences and business expansion possibilities.

Forming Connections through Questioning

Building your network might be facilitated by inquiring about others' work and offering assistance. This strategy will help you meet like-minded people who are interested in lending a helping hand.

How to Ask the Right Questions

To get the most out of a "what do you do/how can I help you?" conversation, show genuine curiosity about the other person's line of work and give them your whole attention. Doing so will help you appreciate their efforts and lay the groundwork for a deep friendship.

Adding Worth

As soon as you have a firmer grasp of someone's role, you may start considering ways to pitch in and lend a hand. Make yourself available to help in any way you see fit by offering introductions, referrals, or support. Doing so demonstrates a desire to assist and encourage one another in professional endeavors.

Fostering Connections

A network is not something you build in a day; rather, it is something you work at constantly. Maintain contact and keep the conversation going after the initial meeting. One way to do this is to invite them to connect on LinkedIn, write them an email, or invite them out for coffee or lunch. You can make a new contact more useful to your network by following these procedures.

THE VALUE OF A SOLID SUPPORT SYSTEM

Some of the advantages that can be gained through a solid network are as follows:

Job possibilities and promotions can be found through one's network, making it essential for professional success.

The expansion of a company's sphere of influence, the acquisition of new clients, and the forging of productive business relationships are all possible through strategic networking.

Meeting new people, expanding one's knowledge base, and forming new connections are all ways in which networking can help one develop personally.

A great way to advance in your career is to start conversations with complete strangers about what they do and how you might lend a hand. Building solid connections with other professionals in your field can open doors to new professional, financial, and personal prospects.

Case Study: Building a Mutually Beneficial Business Relationship

Mr. A, a skilled marketer, attends Mr. C's son's birthday party, where he meets Mr. B, cosmetics shop retailer. To establish a meaningful connection and explore potential collaboration, Mr. A uses the "How could I help with your business?" technique to learn more about Mr. B's needs and challenges. This approach leads to a strong professional network where both the marketer and the retailer benefit from their partnership, going beyond mere pleasantries.

1. The Encounter: At the birthday party, Mr. A and Mr. B strike up a conversation about their respective professions. Instead of focusing solely on his own achievements or business, Mr. A tactfully asks Mr. B about his cosmetics shop and any current challenges he faces. By doing so, Mr. A demonstrates genuine interest in Mr. B's business and an eagerness to provide support.

2. Identifying Opportunities for Collaboration: As Mr. B opens up about his business struggles, including limited foot traffic, low brand awareness, and stiff competition, Mr. A listens attentively and identifies areas where his marketing expertise could be beneficial. He suggests implementing targeted marketing campaigns, utilizing social media platforms, and hosting in-store events to

increase customer engagement and generate buzz around Mr. B's shop.

3. Establishing a Business Relationship: With Mr. A's help, Mr. B's cosmetics shop experiences a noticeable increase in foot traffic and sales. In return, Mr. B offers to promote Mr. A's marketing services through in-store signage, referrals, and word-of-mouth recommendations to his network of fellow retailers. This collaboration creates a win-win situation for both parties, as Mr. A's marketing services gain exposure, and Mr. B's cosmetics shop experiences growth.

4. The Power of the "How could I help with your business?" Technique: By employing the "How could I help with your business?" technique, Mr. A demonstrates the effectiveness of genuine interest and a willingness to provide support. This approach fosters trust, encourages open communication, and helps establish long-lasting professional relationships that go beyond superficial connections. Both Mr. A and Mr. B benefit from their partnership, proving the value of this technique in building strong networks and fostering collaborative opportunities.

This case study highlights the importance of a sincere, proactive approach when networking and building business relationships. By using the "How could I help with your business?" technique, professionals can uncover opportunities for collaboration, establish strong connections, and create mutually beneficial partnerships that contribute to their success.

How to Be a Good Receiver for Success

Mastering the art of receiving is crucial to achieving success in relationships and careers of all kinds. The ability to receive and make good use of resources, assistance, and direction, as well as an openness to new experiences and possibilities, are all part of this trait.

One of the best methods to improve as a receiver is to train your thoughts to be optimistic and receptive. To adopt this mindset, one must be open to learning and interested in exploring new possibilities, rather than skeptical or resistant. Recognizing that success typically necessitates the contributions of multiple individuals or groups is also essential.

Gaining fluency in communicating well is another crucial component of receiving well. In addition to being able to articulate what you want; you must also be a good listener and show empathy for other people's experiences and viewpoints.

Being a good receiver involves a positive attitude, the ability to communicate clearly, and the willingness to put in the work and make things happen. This requires an attitude of initiative and the taking of measures to convert possibilities into outcomes. Furthermore, it necessitates taking personal ownership for one's actions and choices and a readiness to reflect on and improve upon one's shortcomings.

Ultimately, a receiver needs to learn thanks and appreciation in order to be effective. It's important to show gratitude for the people and things that help you along the journey, as well as the experiences and opportunities that come your way.

So, it's clear that the ability to effectively receive information is crucial to success. Individuals can become more successful receivers by developing traits like an optimistic and open outlook, good communication abilities, a diligent work ethic, and an attitude of gratitude.

Chapter 13: Health

The concept of "health" encompasses a comprehensive state of mental, emotional, and physical well-being, which together contribute to the overall fitness of an individual. This holistic notion of health is crucial to a person's overall sense of well-being, as it directly impacts their ability to navigate the complexities of day-to-day life effectively and with ease. By fostering each of these dimensions of health, individuals can experience a greater sense of balance, satisfaction, and vitality as they engage in their daily activities and pursue their goals.

Improving Personal Health with Kaizen

Maintaining physical and mental health is essential to living a happy and fulfilling life. The Kaizen approach, from the Japanese for "improvement" or "change for the better," is an effective strategy for bettering one's health. Though this technique is typically employed in corporate settings, it is just as applicable to the improvement of one's own health and well-being.

The Kaizen philosophy is based on the idea that consistent, incremental changes can accumulate to yield significant outcomes. This approach emphasizes the importance of continuous fine-tuning and gradual progress towards a goal, rather than relying on drastic or sudden transformations.

First, Determine Your Objectives

Step one in applying the Kaizen approach to bettering one's health is settling on a target. This could be anything from a general goal of better health to a more specific one, such as a desire to change one's weight, handle stress better, or lower one's risk of a certain disease. Goals should be SMART (specific, measurable, attainable, relevant, and time-bound).

The Second Step: Assess the Present Condition

After settling on a target, it's time to take stock of where things stand. Keeping a food journal or keeping track of your activity level are just two examples of ways to monitor your health and wellness. If you take stock of the current state of affairs, you may pinpoint problem spots and develop strategies to fix them.

Assess the Current State of Affairs

The third phase entails investigating the matter to find its origin. If you want to reduce weight, you could, for instance, look at your food diary and realize that you're not getting enough exercise or that you eat too many processed foods. Finding the cause of the issue will allow you to fix it once and for all.

Stage 4: Make Things Better

Repairing the current state is the fourth action to do. Making a plan to eat less processed food and exercise more, as well as establishing other concrete, measurable goals, would fall under this rubric.

Applying Value Stream Mapping to Better One's Health (VSM)

VSM has typically been used in settings like manufacturing, but it can also be used to great effect on an individual's health. Your personal health journey can be analyzed and improved using VSM.

Taking Individual Health Seriously as a Dynamic Process; You can apply VSM to your own health by first thinking of it as a process, with inputs (such as food, exercise, sleep, and stress management), outputs (such as weight, energy levels, and overall well-being), and stages in between. You can learn more about the interplay between these factors and your health by breaking down your experience into their constituent parts.

Make a plan for your health right now by listing everything you do, such as:

- Inputs: Make a list of everything that has an effect on your health, including food, exercise, rest, stress management, and medication (e.g., medications or therapies).
- Procedures: Make a list of the things you do on a regular basis (daily, weekly, or monthly) that have an effect on your health (e.g., meal planning, grocery shopping, exercise routines, relaxation techniques, and doctor appointments).

- What is Produced? Set goals for your health process, such as a stable weight, increased stamina, less anxiety, and better rest.

Performing a Value Stream Analysis on Your Own Health

Once your map is complete, you can examine its parts and the connections between them to spot waste, ineffective steps, and other problem areas. Consider the following questions:

Can any of your health care procedures be simplified or done away with altogether?

Is there anything you could do to improve your health, either by adding something new or changing something you're already doing?

Could your time, money, or the help of others be used more effectively to improve your health in some way?

Methods for Making Adjustments and Checking Performance

Create a strategy to enhance your own health value stream based on your findings. This could entail:

Starting a new routine or behavior, like eating more healthily or exercising regularly. Changing the time of day, you work out or getting professional help managing stress are examples.

Using a health journal, fitness tracker, or routine visits with a healthcare professional to track your progress and make necessary adjustments.

Value Stream Mapping is a useful technique for bettering one's health because it offers a graphical representation of the steps you take to maintain or restore wellness. To improve your health, it is helpful to dissect your routine into its constituent parts, pinpoint areas of inefficiency, and then make specific adjustments.

5W2H Technique for Health improvement

What, Why, Where, When, Who, How, and How Much is an acronym for a method that can be used to solve problems. This method is known as the 5W2H method. The 5W2H method has the potential to be a useful tool for improving one's personal health since it provides an organized way to identifying and treating issues that are related to one's health.

Recognizing Concerns About One's Own Health

To get started, take some time to evaluate your present state of health and think about any issues or areas in which you would like to see improvements. This may involve the control of weight, improvement of physical fitness and fitness overall, decrease of stress, and enhancement of sleep quality. Take some time to jot down the precise concerns that you want to address.

Apply the 5W2H method to each problem that has been discovered in order to investigate the variables that are contributing to the problem and generate focused solutions:

Question	Answer

Who	You, as the individual, are responsible for taking charge of your own health, with support from healthcare professionals, friends, and family.
What	Identify areas of improvement in your physical, mental, and emotional health, and implement consistent and sustainable habits, such as a balanced diet, regular exercise, stress management, and social interaction.
When	Start immediately and incorporate health-promoting habits into your daily routine, making adjustments as needed based on progress and well-being.
Where	Health improvement can take place in various settings, such as at home, work, the gym, or outdoors, depending on the activities and lifestyle changes you choose to adopt.
Why	Improving your health is crucial for overall well-being, longevity, and the ability to effectively engage in daily activities and accomplish personal goals.

How	Develop a personalized plan that addresses your unique health needs, incorporating activities and habits that you enjoy and can sustain long-term. Seek guidance from healthcare professionals, as needed, and make use of available resources, such as books, apps, and online tools.
How Much	Monitor your progress and adjust your efforts based on your health goals, capabilities, and preferences. Remember, consistency and gradual improvement are key to long-lasting change, so focus on incremental steps rather than drastic measures.

a. What: Fully state the issue or problem that you are currently dealing with. For instance, if you are having trouble controlling your weight, you can say something along the lines of "I am having trouble keeping a healthy weight."

b. Why: Determine the underlying factors that are contributing to the issue. In the context of the management of one's weight, this may refer to things such as making poor dietary choices, leading a sedentary lifestyle, or not getting enough sleep.

c. In Which: Find the precise places or situations where the issue occurs and investigate them. This could refer to your house, place of employment, or even social surroundings. You might, for instance, discover that you have a hard time maintaining proper portion control when you eat at restaurants.

d. When: Determine the different timeframes or patterns that are connected to the issue. Is there a particular time of day, a certain day of the week, or a particular season in which the problem becomes more apparent? For instance, you may find that you are more prone to overeat in the evenings or on the weekends. This may be something that you have noticed about yourself.

a. Who: Think about the people or groups that are involved in the issue, including yourself and others who may have an impact on the decisions you make on your health. Are there people in your life, such as friends, family members, or coworkers, who encourage you to make decisions that aren't good for your health, or who, on the other hand, could help you achieve your health goals?

f. How: Conceive of potential methods for dealing with the issue by taking into account the primary contributors, the places, and the people who are engaged. In the context of effective weight control, this can entail making a dietary plan, enrolling in a fitness center or class, or seeking support from friends and family.

f. How Much: Find out what resources, such as time, money, or support from other people, will be required to put the solutions you've chosen into action. Have goals and expectations that are attainable, keeping in mind that making changes may involve taking baby steps one at a time.

Putting Solutions into Action While Keeping an Eye on Progress

After finishing your 5W2H analysis, the next step is to devise a strategy for putting your chosen answers into action. This may involve the defining of precise goals, the creation of a timeframe for change, and the identification of any resources or assistance that may be required.

Maintain a consistent monitoring of your advancement and be prepared to make necessary adjustments in order to stay on track toward achieving your health objectives. You might want to think about utilizing tools to help you istay accountable and monitor your performance, such as keeping a health journal, wearing a fitness tracker, or scheduling regular check-ins with a healthcare expert.

The 5W2H technique is an organized and all-encompassing strategy to improving one's own health by determining the underlying causes of health-related problems and generating remedies that are specifically geared toward addressing those causes. You will be able to develop an individualized strategy for reaching your health objectives and improving your general well-being if you apply the 5W2H method to your personal health journey and see how it works for you.

Case Study: 5W2H for Personal Health

John employs the 5W2H technique (Who, What, Where, When, Why, How, and How Much) to improve his health and well-being. John modifies his unhealthy lifestyle to improve his health.

Aspect	Description
Who	John takes charge of his health. He realizes that friends, family, and healthcare experts can help him reach his goals.
What	John prioritizes nutrition, exercise, and mental wellness. He wants to eat better, exercise more, and reduce stress.
Where	John will adjust his lifestyle at home, work, the gym, and outdoors. He wants to continue his good habits everywhere.

When	John plans his implementation and progress. He will gradually introduce new habits by setting weekly and quarterly targets. John can track and adapt his progress with a timetable.
Why	John wants to improve his health to minimize chronic illness risk, boost energy, and improve his quality of life. He thinks focusing on his health will improve his life.
How	John makes a detailed health plan: -Nutrition: John will eat more fruits, vegetables, whole grains, lean protein, and healthy fats. He reduces his processed food and added sugar intake. -Physical Activity: John adds aerobic, strength, and flexibility activities to his routine. He exercises five days a week for 30 minutes. -Mental Health: John will practice mindfulness meditation, do hobbies, and seek help from friends, family, and professionals to reduce stress and improve his mental health.

How Much	John sets goals and measures results for each health aspect: -Nutrition: John aspires to eat five servings of fruits and vegetables, cut processed food by 50%, and drink eight glasses of water everyday. -Physical Activity: John wants 150 minutes of moderate-intensity exercise each week, including two strength-training sessions. - Mental Health: John commits to 10 minutes of mindfulness meditation and one hour of leisure time per week.

John organizes his health using the 5W2H technique. This systematic approach helps him plan, create goals, and track progress. John improves his nutrition, physical exercise, and mental health, improving his overall health and quality of life.

The Health T.R.E.E. System

The HEALTH T.R.E.E. (Trace, Reflect, Examine, and Employ) methodology is a method for systematically mapping, reflecting on, analyzing, and acting on health-related concerns in order to improve one's own health. In this section, we'll discuss how to tailor the HEALTH T.R.E.E. framework to your own health goals.

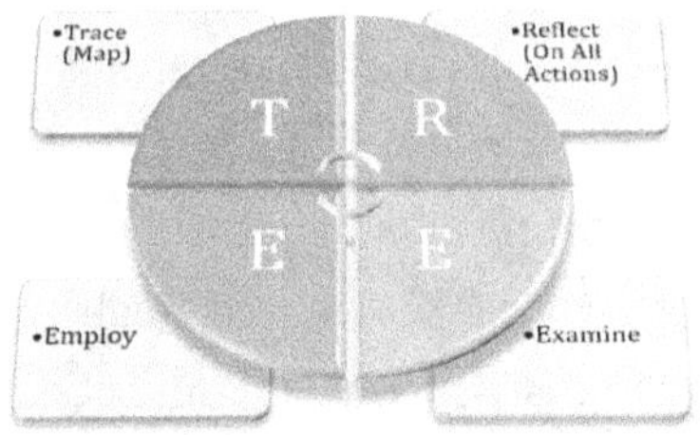

Trace (Map)

To kick off your HEALTH T.R.E.E. analysis, it's helpful to draw a diagram of your existing health-related routines and routine activities. Things to think about could include:

a. Diet: What do you generally eat, and how much of it?

a. Physical activity: What kinds of exercise do you perform, and how often do you do them?

b. Sleep: How long do you sleep for, and how good is it?

d. coping mechanisms; how do you deal with stress and what methods of relaxation do you employ?

g. Health and medicine: How often and for what do you see doctors?

Reflect (On All Actions)

Take a moment to think about the following in light of your health map:

a. What do you do well and what are you good at when it comes to your current health routine?

b. In what ways do you think your health could use some work?

c. Have you seen any tendencies or patterns in your health-related behavior that might be influencing certain health issues?

Examine (Identify Where Health Issues Occur)

Look at your health map for each problem area to see what might be causing it. Take the following into account:

Are there any particular behaviors that add to the problem?

a.Is the issue being made worse by reasons that are not immediately obvious?

b. Could the problem be made worse by environmental or social influences?

c. Have we exhausted all possible avenues of improvement and answers?

Employ (Put Action to Enhance Health)

Formulate a strategy to deal with the health problems you've discovered based on your investigation, paying special attention to:

In order to improve your health, you can make a few changes to your current routine.

a. Identifying which components of your current health routine can be modified. You might, for instance, make it a priority to cut back on serving sizes, ramp up your exercise, and stick to a regular bedtime routine.

b) Using novel tactics: Explore other options for how you might improve your health and use those to your advantage. Some examples of such measures are learning new methods of dealing with stress, consulting a nutritionist, or signing up for a support group.

Goal setting that can be measured and tracked: Create a health improvement plan with measurable, attainable, and time-bound objectives. Check in on your progress toward your goals frequently, and make any necessary adjustments to your approach.

By tracking, reflecting on, analyzing, and implementing specific approaches to health-related challenges, the Health T.R.E.E. method provides a holistic, systematic approach to enhancing individual health. Using the Health T.R.E.E. framework to one's own health journey enables one to develop a unique strategy for boosting healthy behaviors, fixing specific problems, and generally bettering one's health.

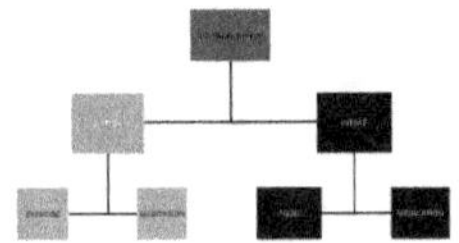

Case Study: Using the HEALTH T.R.E.E. Methodology to Improve Health

Mary, a 42-year-old woman, has been struggling with frequent illnesses such as asthma, migraines, and gastrointestinal issues, along with persistent fatigue and weight gain. Frustrated with her health issues, Mary discovered the HEALTH T.R.E.E. methodology.

The HEALTH T.R.E.E. methodology is a systematic approach to mapping, reflecting on, analyzing, and acting on health-related concerns. Mary worked with a health coach to create a personalized plan using the following steps:

1. Trace: Mary traced her health history and identified patterns in her illnesses, symptoms, and triggers. She discovered that stress, lack of sleep, and certain foods were common triggers for her health issues.

2. Reflect: Mary reflected on her current lifestyle and habits and how they may be contributing to her health problems. She realized that her diet was high in processed foods, she wasn't getting enough exercise, and her sleep was often disrupted.

3. Examine: Mary examined her health goals and developed a plan to achieve them. She set goals to improve her diet, increase physical activity, reduce stress, and improve her sleep quality.
4. Employ: Mary employed her plan by making lifestyle changes and tracking her progress. She started eating more whole foods, incorporated regular exercise into her routine, practiced stress-reducing activities like meditation and yoga, and implemented a sleep hygiene routine.

After a few months of using the HEALTH T.R.E.E. methodology, Mary experienced significant improvements in her health. She lost weight, her asthma symptoms decreased, and her migraines and gastro-intestinal issues became less frequent. She also felt more energized and better equipped to manage her stress.

PDCA Technique to Improve Health

The PDCA (Plan-Do-Check-Act) method is a problem-solving strategy that is utilized in a variety of industries to improve both the processes and the results. This iterative cycle can also be applied to personal health, offering a structured framework for identifying health-related issues, developing solutions, and monitoring progress. This can be done through the iterative process of identifying health-related problems, developing solutions, and tracking progress. Together, we will discuss how you can use the PDCA approach into your own personal health journey in order to achieve better results.

Plan

To begin, it is important to pinpoint the exact health problems or areas in which you would like to see improvements. This may involve the control of weight, improvement of physical fitness and fitness overall, decrease of stress, and enhancement of sleep quality. Create a strategy that takes into account the following for each problem:

a. Creating goals that are SMART, which stands for specific, measurable, achievable, relevant, and time bound.

b. Figuring out the plans, resources, or actions you need to take in order to accomplish your objectives.

c. Creating a timeline and a series of milestones for the purpose of monitoring your progress.

Do

Now that you have a strategy, you can start putting the many tactics and tasks you've selected into action. This may entail the following:

a. Changing habits or routines that are already in place, such as modifying your diet, increasing the amount of physical activity you get, or learning new methods for dealing with stress.

b. Incorporating new practices or resources, such as getting advice from a medical practitioner, becoming a member of a support group, or making use of digital tools to track your health.

c. Participating in consistent acts of self-evaluation and reflection in order to guarantee that your actions are in line with your goals and plan.

Check

Evaluate how well you are doing in meeting your health objectives on a regular basis as you put your strategy into action. Examples of this could be:

a. Monitoring your progress in relation to the milestones and the schedule that you specified during the planning phase.

b. Assessing the efficacy of the tactics and actions you've taken, taking into consideration whether or not they are achieving the results that are desired.

c. Recognizing any difficulties or challenges that may be keeping you from attaining your goals, and thinking about potential solutions or adjustments that could be made to overcome these issues and barriers.

Act

Determine, on the basis of your assessment of your progress, whether or not any alterations or modifications are required to improve your health results. This may entail the following:

a. Improving the efficacy of your current strategies or actions by making necessary adjustments to them.

b. Revising your goals or timeframe in the event that the conditions have altered or if you have come across problems that were not anticipated.

c. Putting into action novel approaches or activities in order to overcome specified barriers or difficulties.

Repeat the PDCA cycle once you've made any necessary modifications, continually improving your strategy and methods to maximize your health journey. Once you've made any necessary adjustments,

Facilitating goal setting, action planning, progress assessment, and continuous improvement are the four pillars of the PDCA technique, which offers a disciplined, iterative approach to improving one's personal health. You will be able to develop an individualized strategy for resolving health-related concerns, reaching your objectives, and improving your overall health and well-being if you apply the PDCA approach to your own health journey and follow its steps.

The Power of Positive Thinking

The term "positive thinking" is used to describe the mental attitude of looking for the best in any circumstance. It's a potent resource for helping us solve problems and improve our decision-making.

The ability to have an optimistic and hopeful perspective is one of the greatest strengths of positive thinking. Fear, wrath, and despair are less likely to completely take over when we keep a positive frame of mind. We can use this information to make better, more educated choices.

The ability to maintain a positive outlook through difficult times is another benefit of positive thinking. One's ability to come up with novel solutions and recover quickly from failures increases when one maintains an optimistic frame of mind. This can make it easier for us to deal with difficult situations.

Positivity has the added bonus of boosting our chances of success. Positivity increases the likelihood of goal-setting, goal-attainment, and productivity.

Focusing on the here and now and seeing the silver lining in seemingly hopeless situations are two of the cornerstones of positive thinking. It's also crucial that we spend time doing things that we enjoy and that make us happy.

Positive thinking, in a nutshell, is the process of seeking out the positive aspects of a given circumstance and making the most of them. It's a potent instrument that can help us keep a positive frame of mind, persevere in the face of adversity, and achieve our goals. You may train your mind to be more optimistic by doing things like meditating, reading inspirational books, spending time with supportive friends, and doing things that make you happy.

Using PDCA to Enhance Positive Vibes for Success

Stage	Description	Example
Plan	Define your objectives and identify areas for improvement in cultivating positive vibes.	Set a goal to create a more positive work environment for yourself and others.
	Assess the current situation, brainstorm potential solutions, and develop a detailed plan for improvement.	Identify factors contributing to negativity and outline strategies to address them.
Do	Execute the plan by implementing the proposed solutions.	Implement changes, such as improving communication, offering recognition, and encouraging collaboration.
Check	Evaluate the results of your actions by measuring progress and assessing outcomes.	Monitor the overall atmosphere and track improvements in morale and productivity.

Act	Analyze the results and make necessary adjustments to refine your plan.	If the initial strategies are not effective, revise your approach and test new methods.
	Iterate through the PDCA cycle until the desired level of positive vibes is achieved.	Continue the cycle of improvement to maintain and enhance positive vibes for ongoing success.

This table provides an overview of using the PDCA cycle to enhance positive vibes for success, illustrating each stage with relevant examples. By applying this iterative approach, you can create a more uplifting environment that supports personal and professional growth.

Chapter 14: Start-Up

Starting a Business with Desire, No Limiting Beliefs, and a Lean Six Sigma Approach

Establishing a firm from scratch is no easy feat, but with the right motivation, outlook, and methodology (such as Lean Six Sigma), it can be a rewarding and fruitful experience.

Prioritize your enthusiasm for the venture. This requires knowing exactly what you want out of life and being enthusiastic about getting there. Your enthusiasm will propel you to put in the long hours and hard work necessary to launch and build your firm.

The next step is to release any self-doubt or negative outlook that has been holding you back. The likes of "I'm not good enough" and "I don't have enough experience" are examples of such negative beliefs. You can move on with optimism and assurance in your abilities once you identify and reject these self-defeating attitudes.

Starting a firm with the mentality that it is already successful is an excellent strategy. Imagine that your company is already thriving and operating at full capacity. You'll be able to bring in the right people, funding, and possibilities as a result.

Ultimately, implementing Lean Six Sigma can help your organization run more smoothly, more efficiently, and more profitably. Lean Six Sigma is a process management strategy that merges the ideals of Lean production with those of Six Sigma quality assurance to boost productivity and efficiency.

In order to ensure your startup is successful from the get-go, it's important to approach it with the right mindset from the outset. This includes having the drive to succeed, not letting fear or doubt get in the way, and adopting a Lean Six Sigma strategy.

Starting a Business with the DMEDI Lean Six Sigma Ideology

Establishing a company from scratch might be difficult, but the DMEDI (Define, Measure, Explore, Develop, Implement) philosophy of Lean Six Sigma can make the process much more manageable.

The DMEDI process begins with defining the issue or possibility at hand. This involves pinpointing the exact goals of the company and the problems that need fixing.

Examining how well the company is doing right now is the next stage. As part of this process, you will need to gather and analyze data to ascertain the current state of the company.

Solution Exploration follows the defining and quantifying of an issue or opportunity. Thinking creatively about how to respond to a challenge or seize an opportunity entail doing some preliminary study.

Having identified potential avenues of attack, the next stage is to formulate an approach. Specifically, it entails making comprehensive plans and schedules for putting the selected remedy into action.

The final phase is carrying out the strategy and monitoring its effectiveness. This involves carrying out the strategy and keeping tabs on its development to make sure the goals are met.

If business owners follow the DMEDI approach, they can guarantee that their efforts will be directed toward the right issues and that any solutions they implement will be grounded in evidence.

The DMAIC (Define, Measure, Analyze, Improve, and Control) process forms the backbone of Lean Six Sigma; it is a process improvement methodology that aids firms in cutting down on waste, minimizing defects, and maximizing output.

The DMEDI Lean Six Sigma philosophy helps business owners zero in on the root causes of issues and create lasting fixes after carefully analyzing relevant data. This will aid in standardizing processes, boosting productivity, and producing better results for the company as a whole.

Lean Six Sigma isn't just a collection of tools; it's a philosophy that can be used to every part of a company's operations and fosters a culture of constant improvement, not only production or assembly.

It's a good beginning, however it lacks specifics on each topic and could be expanded upon. Send me a message with your inquiries, and I'll do my best to provide answers.

Example

Starting a cleaning company using the DMEDI (Define, Measure, Explore, Develop, Implement) Lean Six Sigma methodology involves a structured approach to launch and manage your business effectively. Here's a table outlining the steps:

Stage	Description
Define	Identify the niche for your cleaning company (residential, commercial, or specialized). Define project objectives, scope, and key stakeholders. Establish customer requirements and expectations. Develop your business plan, including market analysis and financial projections.

Measure	Determine key performance indicators (KPIs) for your cleaning company, such as customer satisfaction, employee productivity, and service quality. Set up systems to collect and analyze data on an ongoing basis.
Explore	Research best practices in the cleaning industry and identify potential improvements. Explore innovative cleaning techniques, products, and tools that can enhance your service offerings. Investigate potential partnerships and suppliers for your business.
Develop	Design your cleaning company's processes, procedures, and systems, incorporating identified improvements and innovations. Develop a marketing strategy to attract customers and build your brand. Train employees on new processes, customer service, and Lean Six Sigma principles.
Implement	Launch your cleaning company and implement the new processes and procedures. Continuously monitor and adjust as needed. Measure the impact of changes on KPIs and customer satisfaction. Establish a system for ongoing improvement and growth.

By following the DMEDI Lean Six Sigma methodology, you can ensure a well-structured approach to starting your cleaning company and continuously improve its operations to stay competitive in the market.

Case Study: Starting a Fish Supplying Business with DMEDI

John, an entrepreneur, is passionate about the fishing industry and wants to start a fish supplying business to cater to local restaurants, grocery stores, and individual consumers. He decides to use the DMEDI (Define, Measure, Explore, Develop, Implement) methodology to ensure a systematic approach to launching his business.

Define:

John begins by defining the scope and objectives of his fish supplying business. He identifies the key stakeholders, including local fishermen, customers, and regulatory authorities. He sets a target to supply at least 500 pounds of fish daily within the first year of operation and achieve a 20% market share in the local fish supply market within three years.

Measure:

To better understand the market, John conducts market research and gathers data on the demand for different fish species, the existing competition, and the target customers' preferences. He collects information on the prices, quantities, and quality standards of fish supplied by his competitors. He also gathers data on the fishing industry's regulations, licenses, and guidelines that his business needs to follow.

Explore:

John identifies areas where he can differentiate his fish supplying business from competitors. He considers offering a wider variety of fish species, providing eco-friendly packaging, and promoting sustainable fishing practices. He explores partnerships with local fishermen and fish farms to ensure a steady supply of high-quality fish. John also investigates the possibility of using advanced cold storage and transportation facilities to ensure the freshness of the fish he supplies.

Develop:

Based on his research, John develops a business plan and a marketing strategy. He decides to collaborate with local fishermen and fish farms to obtain a reliable supply of fish. He invests in state-of-the-art cold storage and transportation facilities to maintain fish quality. John also designs a unique, eco-friendly packaging for his fish products and launches a website to showcase his sustainable fishing practices and commitment to the environment. He finalizes the pricing, promotional activities, and distribution channels for his fish supplying business.

Implement:

John registers his business and obtains the necessary licenses and permits. He establishes relationships with local fishermen and fish farms, finalizing agreements on fish supply, quality, and prices. He sets up the cold storage and transportation systems and trains his staff on handling and delivering fresh fish. John starts marketing his fish supplying business to potential customers, emphasizing the freshness, variety, and sustainability of his products. He closely monitors customer feedback and adjusts his marketing strategy accordingly.

Outcome:

Within the first year, John's fish supplying business successfully reaches its target of supplying 500 pounds of fish daily. The unique selling points of his business, such as the eco-friendly packaging and commitment to sustainability, attract a loyal customer base. By the end of the third year, John achieves his goal of capturing a 20% market share in the local fish supply market.

This case study illustrates how the DMEDI methodology can help an entrepreneur like John systematically start a fish supplying business, identify opportunities for differentiation, and achieve his business goals.

The Startup Triangle

The Startup Triangle is a Model for Getting New Businesses Off the Ground Successfully.

The Startup Triangle is a pragmatic structure that was developed to assist aspiring business owners in successfully launching their enterprises and growing them over time. This section will give you with actionable insights to help you develop a successful business from the ground up by introducing the Startup Triangle, explaining its major components, and providing an introduction to the Startup Triangle.

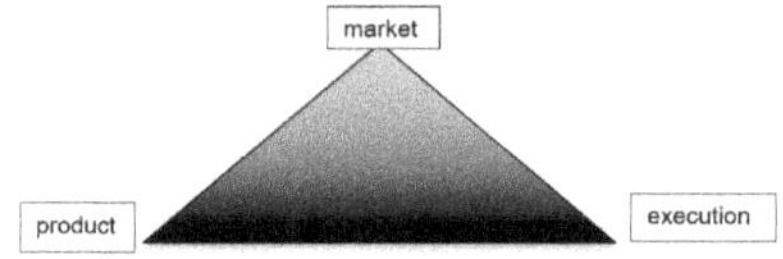

The Market, the Product, and the Execution make up the three critical components that make up the Startup Triangle. To ensure the success of a startup, these aspects need to collaborate effectively with one another. The ability of entrepreneurs to strike a balance between these factors enables them to more successfully discover opportunities, develop new solutions, and carry out their plans.

Constituents of the Entrepreneurial Triangle

In order to comprehend and make use of the Startup Triangle, it is essential to investigate its three primary components, which are as follows:

Market: A new business must respond to a large void or opportunity in the existing market. In order to determine the potential for success, it is essential to have a solid understanding of the dynamics of the market, the challenges faced by customers, and the nature of the competition.

Product: The company's goods or services should be cutting edge, distinct from those of competitors, and able to meet the requirements of the target market in order to be successful. The product also needs to be able to scale and be flexible enough to react to changing market conditions.

The term "execution" refers to the process of putting a plan into action. A successful execution requires the creation of a powerful team, the establishment of efficient operations, and the development of a well-crafted go-to-market strategy. To be successful, new businesses need to be nimble and resilient, with the ability to adapt quickly to changing circumstances and overcome obstacles.

PUTTING THE STARTUP TRIANGLE INTO PRACTICE

Research and Evaluation of the Market

Determine the segments of the target market and the types of customers: Find out the size of the market, the growth possibilities, and the demographics of the audience you want to attract. Learn the aches and pains of your customers: To gain a deeper understanding of the requirements and preferences of the target audience, you can gather information by conducting interviews, surveys, or focus groups. Examine the nature of the existing competition: Do a thorough analysis of the present competition and determine the potential dangers and possibilities posed by the market.

Development of the Product

Create a unique value proposition: Provide an explanation of the primary advantages and selling points of your product or service.

Experiment and improve: Construct prototypes, minimum viable products (MVPs), or beta versions of your offering so that you may collect input from users and improve it.

Prepare for expansion in scale: Be sure that your product or service can develop and evolve to satisfy the ever-increasing demand and changing conditions of the market.

Execution

Create a powerful team by: To ensure the success of your startup, put together a well-rounded team consisting of knowledgeable experts whose areas of expertise compliment one another.

Develop effective business practices: Create reliable methods and systems for handling your finances, as well as your product development, sales, and marketing.

Develop a strategy for entering the market: Create a detailed strategy for the debut of your product or service, taking into account aspects like as pricing, distribution, and promotional activities.

Monitoring and Adjusting

The path taken by a startup is rarely one that is linear, thus its founders need to be ready to modify their strategy in reaction to new knowledge or shifts in the company's environment. Always keep a close eye on the performance of your startup, the trends in the industry, and the comments from your customers, and be ready to adjust your strategy or make adjustments as necessary.

The Startup Triangle is a powerful framework that helps aid entrepreneurs in the process of creating successful enterprises by focusing on three crucial components: the market, the product, and the execution of the plan. Startups have the potential to boost their prospects of success and long-term growth if they take the time to have a comprehensive understanding of the industry, create a compelling product or service, and effectively carry out their plans. You can optimize your potential to develop a thriving business in today's competitive environment by implementing the concepts of the Startup Triangle. This will allow you to maximize your potential.

Start-Up BIBLE

Welcome to the ultimate entrepreneurial adventure! The Start-Up Bible: Building, Improving, Branding, Learning, and Enhancing. Your Business is your trusty compass to navigate the exhilarating and unpredictable world of entrepreneurship. This comprehensive guide will equip you with the tools, insights, and wisdom to transform your ambitious vision into a thriving empire. Whether you're a first-time founder or a seasoned business owner seeking to revamp your venture, this technique got you covered. Prepare to embark on the journey of a lifetime as this method reveals the secrets of successful startups, explore the art of branding, and unveil strategies for continuous growth and improvement. So, buckle up, trailblazers – it's time to turn your dreams into reality!"

The START-UP BIBLE is a practical guide for entrepreneurs and business owners who want to build, improve, brand, learn, and enhance their business. The process consists of five steps: Build, Improve, Brand, Learn, and Enhance.

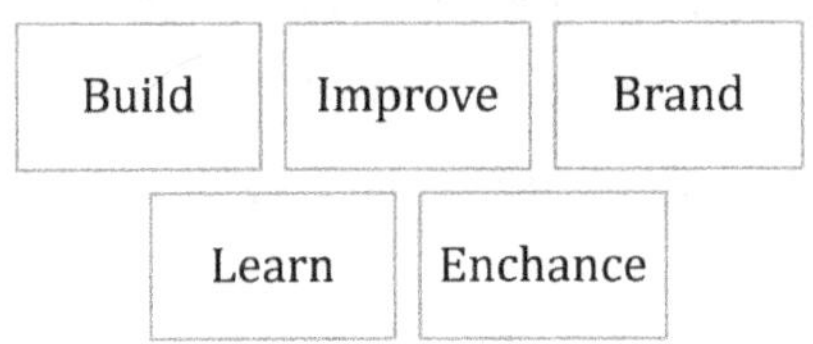

Build: This level focuses on laying the groundwork for your business. This comprises the creation of a strong business plan, the development of a product or service, and the establishment of systems and procedures.

Improve: In this phase, you concentrate on enhancing your business. This involves optimizing operations, boosting efficiency, and implementing modifications to enhance the client experience.

Brand: In this phase, you concentrate on branding and marketing your company. This includes establishing a brand identity, creating a website, and promoting your firm via multiple media.

Learn: This level focuses on constant learning and improvement. This includes soliciting client feedback, staying abreast of industry developments, and consistently enhancing your skills and expertise.

Enhance: This level involves allowing positive changes to occur and focusing on business growth. This includes growing your product or service offerings, pursuing new prospects, and investing in your company's expansion.

Applying the advice in the START-UP BIBLE is an ongoing task that needs your whole attention and effort. Before beginning, it is important to determine what needs to be done and how to do it. Plan out your progress with reasonable checkpoints and evaluate it frequently. Seek out experienced business people as guides, build lasting connections with other businesses, and keep your mind open to new ideas. Always keep in mind that achieving company success calls for thoughtful planning, consistent effort, and a growth mindset.

If you're an entrepreneur or business owner looking to create, improve, brand, learn, and enhance your firm, The START-UP BIBLE is must-read. If you follow the five phases in this procedure, you'll have a far better chance of reaching your business objectives. Maintain your will and optimism, and never give up on your goal of creating a prosperous business.

Here's a table illustrating key aspects of the Start-Up Bible (Build, Improve, Brand, Learn, and Enhance) for building a marketing consultancy business:

Stage	Description
Build	Develop a solid business plan, identify your target market, define your services, and establish a strong foundation for your marketing consultancy business.
Improve	Continuously analyze your processes and workflows, identify areas for improvement, and optimize your services to deliver better results for clients.
Brand	Create a distinctive brand identity, including a memorable name, logo, and tagline that reflect your company's values and expertise. Build a strong online presence through a professional website and engaging content.
Learn	Stay updated on the latest marketing trends, tools, and best practices. Attend industry events, network with peers, and invest in ongoing professional development for yourself and your team.
Enhance	Expand your service offerings, explore new markets, and develop strategic partnerships to grow your business. Focus on maintaining high-quality services and excellent customer relationships to foster long-term success.

By following the stages outlined in the Start-Up Bible, you can create a thriving marketing consultancy business that continuously evolves and adapts to the dynamic marketing landscape.

Case Study: Launching a New Tea Product Using the START-UP BIBLE Methodology

Jane, a tea enthusiast, decides to launch a new tea product that combines unique flavors and health benefits. She aims to target health-conscious consumers who are seeking premium, innovative tea blends. Jane decides to use The START-UP BIBLE methodology to ensure a comprehensive approach to launching her new tea product.

Build:

Jane starts by building her business foundation. She conducts extensive market research to understand the preferences and expectations of her target audience. She identifies gaps in the market and decides to focus on organic, ethically sourced ingredients to create her unique tea blends. Jane develops a detailed business plan, including her mission, vision, target market, product offerings, and financial projections.

Improve:

To improve her product offerings, Jane experiments with various tea blend recipes, using organic and sustainably sourced ingredients. She gathers feedback from friends, family, and potential customers to refine the taste and health benefits of her tea blends. Jane also researches packaging options, aiming to use eco-friendly materials that protect the tea's flavor and freshness while minimizing environmental impact.

Brand:

Jane focuses on creating a strong brand identity for her new tea product. She chooses a memorable name and designs a logo that reflects her commitment to sustainability and wellness. Jane develops a unique selling proposition (USP) that emphasizes the health benefits, exceptional taste, and ethical sourcing of her tea blends. She crafts a compelling brand story that resonates with her target audience and sets her product apart from competitors.

Learn:

Jane continually learns about the tea industry, her competitors, and her customers' evolving preferences. She attends tea industry events, networks with other tea entrepreneurs, and subscribes to industry newsletters to stay informed. Jane closely monitors customer feedback and sales data to identify trends and opportunities for growth. She also explores new tea blend ideas, marketing strategies, and potential partnerships to expand her business.

Enhance:

With a solid foundation, an improved product offering, and a strong brand identity, Jane focuses on enhancing her business. She invests in marketing efforts, including social media campaigns, influencer partnerships, and in-store sampling events, to create buzz around her new tea product. Jane optimizes her website to provide an engaging, user-friendly shopping experience and implements a customer loyalty program to encourage repeat purchases. As her business grows, Jane continuously looks for ways to improve her operations, expand her product line, and exceed customer expectations.

Outcome:

Jane successfully launches her new tea product using The START-UP BIBLE methodology. Her unique tea blends, compelling brand story, and commitment to sustainability resonate with health-conscious consumers, resulting in strong initial sales and positive customer feedback. By consistently learning and enhancing her business, Jane positions her tea product for long-term success and growth in the competitive tea market.

Start-Up SHOE for quality

The START-UP SHOE is a simple, yet effective framework for businesses looking to increase efficiency and achieve success. The process consists of four steps: Standardize, Honor, Operate, and Evaluate.

Standardize: In this step, you focus on establishing standards and procedures for your business. This includes creating a standard operating procedure manual, establishing guidelines for employees, and setting performance expectations.

Honor: In this step, you focus on honoring the standards and procedures that you have established. This includes consistently following the established procedures and holding employees accountable for meeting performance expectations.

Operate: In this step, you focus on producing results by operating your business effectively. This includes implementing the established procedures, working with employees to improve performance, and continuously seeking ways to improve efficiency.

Evaluate: In this step, you focus on evaluating the results of your efforts. This includes regularly tracking performance metrics, seeking feedback from employees and customers, and using the information gathered to make informed decisions about the future of your business.

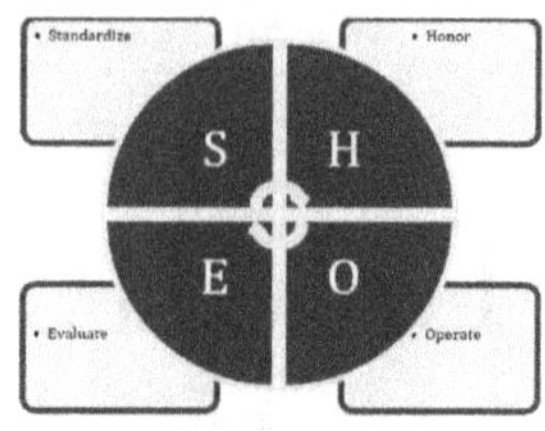

Step	Description
Standardize	Establish standards and procedures for your business. Create a standard operating procedure manual, guidelines for employees, and set performance expectations.
Honor	Consistently follow the established procedures and hold employees accountable for meeting performance expectations. Ensure that everyone in the organization is committed to honoring the standards.
Operate	Implement the established procedures and work with employees to improve performance. Focus on producing results and continuously seek ways to improve efficiency.

Evaluate	Regularly track performance metrics, seek feedback from employees and customers, and use the information gathered to make informed decisions about the future of your business. Identify areas for improvement and adjust your procedures and strategies accordingly.

Implementing the Start-Up SHOE requires a commitment to excellence and a focus on continuous improvement. To get started, begin by establishing clear standards and procedures for your business. Then, consistently follow and enforce these standards, while operating your business effectively and efficiently. Finally, evaluate the results of your efforts and make necessary changes to improve performance.

The Start-Up Shoe is a simple and effective framework for businesses looking to increase efficiency and achieve success. By standardizing, honoring, operating, and evaluating, businesses can improve their processes, increase performance, and achieve their goals. Stay focused, stay committed, and never stop seeking ways to improve your business.

Case Study: Yusuf's Shirt Printing Business Using the START-UP SHOE Methodology

Yusuf owns a small shirt printing business that creates custom designs for individuals and organizations. He wants to increase efficiency and achieve success in his business. Yusuf decides to use The START-UP SHOE methodology, which consists of four steps: Standardize, Honor, Operate, and Evaluate.

Standardize:

Yusuf begins by standardizing his shirt printing processes to ensure consistency in quality and customer satisfaction. He develops detailed guidelines for creating and printing designs, specifying the types of materials, printing techniques, and quality control measures. Yusuf documents these processes in a comprehensive operation manual and trains his employees to follow these standardized procedures.

Honor:

Yusuf recognizes the importance of honoring his commitments to customers, suppliers, and employees. He strives to build trust and credibility by delivering on his promises and maintaining transparency in his business dealings. Yusuf establishes clear communication channels with his customers, providing regular updates on order progress and addressing any concerns promptly. He also maintains strong relationships with his suppliers, ensuring timely delivery of materials and negotiating favorable terms.

Operate:

With standardized processes in place and a commitment to honoring his obligations, Yusuf focuses on operating his shirt printing business efficiently. He invests in high-quality printing equipment, enabling his team to produce more shirts with fewer errors and faster turnaround times. Yusuf also optimizes his inventory management system to reduce waste and improve cash flow. He streamlines his order fulfillment process, ensuring that completed shirts are packaged and shipped promptly to customers.

Evaluate:

Yusuf continuously evaluates the performance of his shirt printing business, using key performance indicators (KPIs) such as order volume, customer satisfaction, and profitability. He closely monitors these KPIs and compares them to industry benchmarks to identify areas for improvement. Yusuf conducts regular employee performance reviews, providing constructive feedback and recognizing outstanding work. He also seeks feedback from customers, using their insights to refine his processes and enhance the overall customer experience.

Outcome:

By implementing The START-UP SHOE methodology, Yusuf successfully improves the efficiency and performance of his shirt printing business. The standardized processes lead to higher quality products, and his commitment to honoring his obligations fosters trust and loyalty among customers and suppliers. Yusuf's focus on efficient operations results in reduced costs and faster order fulfillment, while continuous evaluation enables him to identify and address potential issues proactively. As a result, Yusuf's shirt printing business experiences increased customer satisfaction, repeat business, and sustained growth.

The 4 Ps of Marketing: A Comprehensive Guide for Startup Success

The 4 Ps of marketing, also known as the marketing mix, is a fundamental framework for any business, especially startups. This framework consists of product, promotion, price, and place. By understanding and applying the 4 Ps, startups can create a comprehensive strategy for growth and long-term success. In this chapter, we will delve deeper into each component, providing insights, best practices, and real-life examples.

Product: Creating a Winning Solution for Your Target Market

- Identifying Customer Needs and Preferences To develop a successful product or service, startups must first understand their target market's needs and preferences. This can be achieved through market research, surveys, interviews, and studying consumer behavior. Businesses should analyze demographic data, buying habits, pain points, and competitive landscape.
- Product Differentiation Once startups understand their target market's needs, they should differentiate their product or service from competitors. Differentiation can be achieved through unique features, superior quality, innovative design, or exceptional customer service. Startups should focus on creating a

unique selling proposition (USP) that sets them apart from the competition.

- Continuous Improvement and Innovation A successful startup must continuously iterate and improve its product or service based on customer feedback, market trends, and technological advancements. This will ensure that the product remains relevant, valuable, and competitive.

Promotion: Effectively Communicating Your Value Proposition

- Developing a Comprehensive Marketing Plan Startups need a well-rounded marketing plan that encompasses social media, email marketing, content marketing, and advertising. This plan should target the ideal audience and be tailored to their preferences. For example, if the target audience is millennials, focusing on social media marketing may be more effective.
- Leveraging Influencers and Networking Opportunities Influencers can help startups reach a wider audience and build credibility. By identifying and building relationships with key influencers in their industry, startups can expand their reach and brand awareness. Attending conferences, events, and trade shows can also provide networking opportunities to build relationships with potential customers, investors, and partners.

Price: Setting the Right Value for Your Product or Service

- Determining the Target Audience and Willingness to Pay Pricing should be based on the target audience's willingness to pay, which can be determined through market research, surveys, and competitor analysis. Startups should consider their costs, value proposition, and competitive pricing strategies when setting prices.
- Pricing Strategies There are several pricing strategies to choose from, such as cost-plus pricing, value-based pricing, and

competitive pricing. The choice depends on the startup's objectives, target audience, and market conditions. Startups may need to adjust their pricing over time as they gain more data about customer preferences and buying habits.

Place: Choosing the Right Distribution Channels for Success

- Analyzing the Target Audience and their Buying Preferences Startups must consider where their target audience is and how they prefer to buy. Will they sell directly to consumers or through a retail partner? Will they use e-commerce or brick and mortar stores?
- Distribution Channel Factors When choosing distribution channels, startups should consider factors such as target audience, cost of distribution, competitor distribution, and scalability. The right distribution channels will ensure that the product or service reaches the target audience effectively and efficiently.

The 4 Ps of marketing is a powerful framework that can guide startups toward growth and success. By focusing on product, promotion, price, and place, startups can create a comprehensive strategy that meets customer needs, effectively communicates their value proposition, sets the right price, and ensures the product or service reaches.

Case Study: Murphy's Sustainable Clothing Startup and the 4 Ps of Marketing

Murphy, an eco-conscious entrepreneur, decided to launch a sustainable clothing startup. His aim was to provide environmentally friendly, fashionable, and affordable clothing options to environmentally conscious customers. To achieve success, Murphy applied the 4 Ps of marketing to his startup. This case study will examine how he utilized the product, promotion, price, and place components of the marketing mix to grow his business.

Product: Eco-friendly and Stylish Clothing

Identifying Customer Needs and Preferences Murphy conducted extensive market research to understand the preferences and needs of environmentally conscious consumers. He discovered that his target market valued sustainable production methods, ethical labor practices, and high-quality materials. Customers were also concerned about the environmental impact of fast fashion and sought long-lasting, versatile clothing items.

Product Differentiation Based on his research, Murphy designed a clothing line that used eco-friendly materials such as organic cotton, recycled polyester, and Tencel. He ensured that the manufacturing process was sustainable and ethical by partnering with Fair Trade

Certified factories. To differentiate his brand further, he focused on creating timeless, versatile designs that could be easily integrated into customers' existing wardrobes.

Continuous Improvement and Innovation Murphy constantly sought customer feedback and kept abreast of sustainable fashion trends. He continually improved his product line by incorporating new eco-friendly materials and production methods, ensuring his brand remained at the forefront of sustainable fashion.

Promotion: Building Brand Awareness and a Loyal Community

Developing a Comprehensive Marketing Plan Murphy created a marketing plan that emphasized his brand's eco-friendly values and high-quality products. He utilized social media platforms, email marketing, content marketing (such as blog posts and educational articles), and targeted advertising. He focused on visually appealing content and storytelling to engage his audience and communicate his brand's values.

Leveraging Influencers and Networking Opportunities Murphy collaborated with eco-conscious influencers to promote his brand and expand his reach. He also attended sustainable fashion events and conferences to network with industry leaders, potential customers, and like-minded entrepreneurs.

Price: Affordability and Value for Environmentally Conscious Consumers

Determining the Target Audience and Willingness to Pay Murphy understood that environmentally conscious consumers were willing to pay a premium for sustainable products but also sought value for their money. Through market research and competitor analysis, he determined an appropriate price range that reflected the value and quality of his products.

Pricing Strategies Murphy adopted a value-based pricing strategy, setting prices that reflected the high-quality materials, ethical production methods, and overall value of his clothing. He also offered occasional discounts and loyalty rewards to incentivize repeat purchases and customer loyalty.

Place: Convenient and Eco-friendly Distribution Channels

Analyzing the Target Audience and their Buying Preferences Murphy's market research revealed that his target audience preferred online shopping for its convenience and accessibility. He also recognized the importance of minimizing the environmental impact of shipping and packaging.

Distribution Channel Factors Murphy decided to sell his products primarily through an e-commerce platform. He implemented eco-friendly packaging and carbon-neutral shipping options to further align with his brand's values. Additionally, he partnered with a select number of sustainable fashion boutiques to provide customers with a brick-and-mortar shopping experience.

By applying the 4 Ps of marketing to his sustainable clothing startup, Murphy successfully created a differentiated product, effectively promoted his brand, priced his products appropriately, and chose the right distribution channels. As a result, his startup experienced significant growth and attracted a loyal customer base that shared his eco-friendly values.

The START UP FISH Framework: Fixer, Innovator, Seller, Hacker

The START UP FISH framework is an acronym representing the four key roles that every successful startup needs: Fixer, Innovator, Seller, and Hacker. Each role brings unique strengths and expertise, fostering a dynamic environment where creativity, efficiency, and growth flourish. When these roles come together, they form a powerful synergy that propels the startup to new heights.

Embrace the START UP FISH framework and embark on an unforgettable entrepreneurial adventure. Dive into the exciting world of business creation, where your passion and drive, combined with the talents of your team, will lead to the realization of your dreams. Get ready to make a lasting impact and leave a legacy for generations to come.

The START UP FISH framework is a model that identifies four key roles necessary for a successful startup: Fixer, Innovator, Seller, and Hacker. Each role brings a unique set of skills and expertise that, when combined, can drive a startup towards growth and success. In this guide, we will explore each role in detail and explain their importance in the startup ecosystem.

1. Fixer: Problem Solver and Operations Expert

The Fixer is a critical thinker and problem solver who ensures the smooth operation of the startup. They excel at identifying and resolving issues, both internally and externally. The Fixer's responsibilities may include:

- Managing day-to-day operations and logistics
- Developing and implementing efficient processes and systems
- Identifying and resolving bottlenecks in the workflow
- Ensuring compliance with legal and regulatory requirements

A successful Fixer can adapt to changing circumstances and quickly implement solutions that keep the startup running smoothly.

1. Innovator: Creative Visionary and Product Developer

The Innovator is the creative force behind the startup, driving product development and innovation. They possess the ability to envision new ideas and transform them into marketable products or services. The Innovator's responsibilities may include:

- Identifying customer needs and market gaps
- Developing innovative product or service concepts
- Collaborating with the Hacker to bring ideas to life
- Continuously improving and iterating on the product or service based on feedback and market trends

A successful Innovator can balance creative thinking with a practical approach to product development, ensuring that the startup's offerings meet customer needs and stand out in the marketplace.

1. Seller: Sales and Marketing Strategist

The Seller is the driving force behind the startup's revenue generation, responsible for marketing and sales efforts. They possess excellent communication skills and the ability to persuade potential customers and investors. The Seller's responsibilities may include:

- Developing and implementing a comprehensive marketing strategy
- Establishing and maintaining relationships with customers, partners, and investors
- Identifying and pursuing new business opportunities
- Setting and achieving sales targets

A successful Seller can effectively communicate the value proposition of the startup's products or services and build long-lasting relationships that contribute to the company's growth.

1. Hacker: Technical Expert and Developer

The Hacker is the technical expert in the startup, responsible for developing and maintaining the company's products, services, and infrastructure. They possess strong coding and technical skills, as well as the ability to quickly learn and adapt to new technologies. The Hacker's responsibilities may include:

- Developing and maintaining the startup's products, services, and systems
- Ensuring the security and reliability of the technical infrastructure
- Collaborating with the Innovator to turn ideas into functional products or services
- Researching and implementing new technologies to improve the startup's offerings

A successful Hacker can efficiently develop and maintain the technical aspects of the startup, ensuring that the products and services are reliable, secure, and up-to-date.

The START UP FISH framework highlights the importance of having a diverse team with complementary skills and expertise. By combining the strengths of the Fixer, Innovator, Seller, and Hacker, a startup can effectively navigate the challenges of product development, marketing, sales, and technical infrastructure. Building a well-rounded team that embodies these roles is a key factor in achieving startup success and growth.

Case Study: GreenSolutions, a Sustainable Energy Startup and the START UP FISH Framework

Role	Description and Background	Key Contributions
Fixer	Linda, the Fixer, had a background in operations management and was responsible for overseeing the day-to-day operations of GreenSolutions. She ensured that the company adhered to industry regulations and maintained a streamlined workflow.	- Established efficient processes for order fulfillment and customer support - Coordinated with suppliers and logistics partners to optimize supply chain operations - Identified and resolved potential issues, maintaining smooth company operations

Innovator	Alex, the Innovator, was an expert in sustainable energy with a vision to create a solar panel system that was efficient, affordable, and easy to install. He led the research and development team, ensuring that GreenSolutions' products were innovative and met customer needs.	- Conducted market research to identify customer pain points and preferences - Designed a modular solar panel system that simplified installation and reduced costs - Collaborated with the Hacker to integrate smart monitoring technology into the product
Seller	Mia, the Seller, had a background in marketing and sales, focusing on promoting GreenSolutions' products and driving revenue growth. She created a comprehensive marketing strategy that targeted eco-conscious homeowners and businesses.	- Developed marketing campaigns that emphasized the environmental and financial benefits of GreenSolutions' solar panels - Built strong relationships with potential customers, partners, and investors - Successfully negotiated and closed deals with large commercial clients

Hacker	John, the Hacker, was a software engineer with experience in renewable energy systems. He was responsible for developing the technical aspects of GreenSolutions' solar panel systems and ensuring that the products were reliable and secure.	-Developed the smart monitoring software for GreenSolutions' solar panels - Collaborated with the Innovator to integrate new technologies into the product - Maintained the company's technical infrastructure and ensured system security

5W2H for Job-Seeking Graduates and Aspiring Entrepreneurs

It can be difficult for recent college grads to find work, especially during periods of high unemployment. The 5W2H technique (What, Why, Where, Who, When, How, and How much) can help recent grads streamline their job search and improve their odds of success.

The 5W2H technique is a useful problem-solving method that involves writing down and categorizing the five most important aspects of a given scenario. It's a useful tool for organizing and carrying out activities related to looking for work or launching a new business.

Fresh grads need to start by asking themselves what it is they are hoping to find in their first professional or entrepreneurial role. What they want to accomplish professionally, the field they hope to enter, and the abilities they hope to hone all go into this decision.

The next step is to figure out why they want this career or business. Their inspirations, aims, and hopes all fall under this category.

The location of the available work or business opportunity is the "Where" component of the 5W2H strategy. Consider where the graduate is located and what kind of business or organization would be a good fit.

Graduates can benefit from the connections made through the Who component of the 5W2H technique. Everyone from close relatives and buddies to role models and experts in their chosen industry counts.

The 5W2H approach When component addresses the feasibility of the job hunt or company initiative. This includes when people should reasonably expect to find work or launch a business, and when they should look for jobs.

The "How" component of the 5W2H approach refers to the actions that must be completed in order to get a job or launch a business. Among these activities are drafting a business strategy and seeking for jobs or internships.

How much, the final component, refers to the time, energy, and money that will be expended in order to accomplish the objective.

Graduates can take a methodical approach to their job search or business startup by adopting the 5W2H strategy to manage their efforts. This will improve their prospects for success and keep them fired up and concentrated throughout the procedure.

It's worth noting that this approach isn't just useful for recent grads looking for work or entrepreneurs sizing up prospective challenges and opportunities; it's a straightforward but powerful technique that may benefit anyone in these situations.

It's a good beginning, however it lacks specifics on each topic and could be expanded upon. Send me a message with your inquiries, and I'll do my best to provide answers.

Boosting Business with Law of Attraction, SWOT, VSM & DMAIC

Achieving long-term business success requires a well-rounded approach that encompasses various strategies and methodologies. In this article, we will explore how to boost your business by combining the power of the Law of Attraction, SWOT analysis, Value Stream Mapping (VSM), and DMAIC. By understanding and implementing these methods, you can unlock your business's full potential and ensure sustainable growth.

Law of Attraction:

The Law of Attraction is a metaphysical principle that suggests that positive thoughts attract positive experiences, while negative thoughts attract negative experiences. When applied to business, this principle emphasizes the importance of maintaining a positive mindset, setting clear goals, and visualizing success.

How to apply the Law of Attraction in business

Step	Description

Set Goals	Establish clear, specific, and achievable goals for your business. Write them down and review them regularly.
Visualize	Create a vivid mental image of your business achieving its goals. Practice this visualization daily to reinforce your intentions.
Affirm	Use positive affirmations to reframe negative thoughts and beliefs. Repeat them daily to maintain a positive mindset.
Take Action	Act on opportunities and ideas that align with your goals. Stay persistent and maintain a proactive attitude.
Gratitude	Practice gratitude by acknowledging and appreciating the progress and successes in your business.

SWOT Analysis:

SWOT analysis is a strategic planning tool used to identify a business's internal strengths and weaknesses, as well as external opportunities and threats. This analysis can provide valuable insights to inform decision-making and help you develop a competitive advantage.

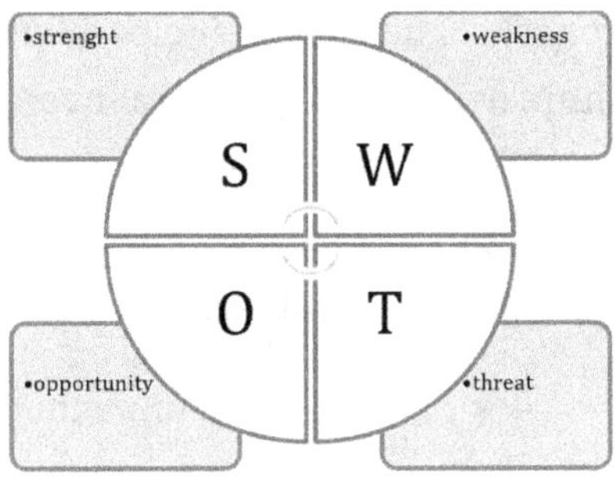

Components of a SWOT analysis

Component	Description
Strengths	Identify your business's internal strengths, such as skilled employees, unique products, or a strong brand.
Weaknesses	Determine internal weaknesses, such as limited resources, outdated technology, or poor management.
Opportunities	Recognize external opportunities for growth, such as new markets, partnerships, or technological advancements.
Threats	Identify external threats to your business, such as competition, economic downturns, or regulatory changes.

Value Stream Mapping (VSM):

VSM is a Lean management tool used to analyze and optimize the flow of materials and information through a business's processes. By creating a visual representation of your entire value stream, you can identify waste, bottlenecks, and inefficiencies, allowing you to streamline operations and improve overall performance.

Steps in creating a Value Stream Map

Step	Description
Define Scope	Determine the process or value stream you want to analyze and improve.
Map Current State	Create a visual representation of the current state of the process, identifying all steps, delays, and information flows.
Identify Waste	Locate areas of waste, such as excessive inventory, waiting times, or overproduction.
Map Future State	Develop an optimized version of the value stream, incorporating improvements and waste reduction strategies.
Implement Changes	Execute the necessary changes and monitor progress, adjusting as needed to achieve the desired future state.

DMAIC:

DMAIC is a structured problem-solving methodology used in Six Sigma, consisting of five phases: Define, Measure, Analyze, Improve, and Control. This approach provides a systematic way to identify and address the root causes of problems, ultimately leading to improved business performance.

Overview of the DMAIC methodology

Phase	Description
Define	Clearly define the problem or opportunity, establish project goals, and identify key stakeholders and project scope.
Measure	Determine key performance indicators (KPIs) and collect baseline data on the current process performance.
Analyze	Analyze the data to identify the root causes of the problem or inefficiencies, using tools such as cause-and-effect diagrams, Pareto charts, or process maps.
Improve	Develop and implement solutions to address the identified root causes, test their effectiveness, and make necessary adjustments.
Control	Monitor and maintain the improved process, ensuring that it remains stable and continues to meet performance goals. Establish control mechanisms to prevent the recurrence of the problem.

By combining the Law of Attraction, SWOT analysis, Value Stream Mapping, and DMAIC, you can develop a comprehensive approach to boosting your business. These methodologies can help you maintain a positive mindset, make informed strategic decisions, optimize processes, and solve problems effectively. Implementing these techniques can lead to increased efficiency, improved performance, and long-term business success.

Chapter 15: Growth and Business Development

In an increasingly competitive world, businesses must be agile, adaptive, and ever evolving to survive and thrive. Growth and business development are no longer optional, but rather essential ingredients for long-term success.

Growth and business development are closely intertwined. While growth represents the overarching goal, business development serves as the vehicle for achieving growth objectives. Effective business development strategies facilitate the identification and pursuit of growth opportunities, creating a symbiotic relationship that fuels organizational success. By understanding the synergy between growth and business development, you can maximize your chances of achieving sustainable and accelerated growth.

GROWTH Framework for Business Expansion

The GROWTH framework is designed to guide businesses through a structured process for sustainable expansion and success. By incorporating different aspects of business development, the GROWTH framework provides a comprehensive approach to achieving long-term growth.

G - Goals R - Resources O - Opportunities W - Workflows T - Team H - Holistic Evaluation

Table: GROWTH Framework

Stage	Description
Goals	Set clear, measurable, and achievable goals for your business. Align short-term objectives with long-term growth strategies.
Resources	Assess and optimize the allocation of resources, including financial, human, and technological assets, to support growth.
Opportunities	Identify and capitalize on new market opportunities, such as untapped customer segments, emerging trends, or technological advancements.

Workflows	Streamline and improve internal processes and workflows, eliminating inefficiencies and waste, to enhance productivity and support growth.
Team	Develop a strong and skilled team, invest in employee development, and maintain a positive company culture to drive performance.
Holistic Evaluation	Regularly evaluate overall business performance, analyze the impact of growth strategies, and adjust as needed to maintain a sustainable and successful trajectory.

The GROWTH framework offers a balanced and holistic approach to business growth, addressing multiple aspects of development. By following this framework, businesses can create a solid foundation for expansion, improve internal processes, and foster a strong team culture that supports long-term success.

Case Study: Reviving a Struggling Cleaning Company Using the GROWTH Framework

CleanCo, a residential and commercial cleaning company, has been struggling with stagnant growth, declining customer satisfaction, and low employee morale. The company's management decides to use the GROWTH framework to address these issues and put the business back on track for sustainable expansion and success.

Goals:

CleanCo's management starts by setting clear, specific, and measurable goals for the company. They aim to increase revenue by 25% within a year, improve customer satisfaction rates by 15%, and reduce employee turnover by 10%. The management communicates these goals to the entire team, ensuring everyone understands the company's objectives and the importance of working towards them.

Resources:

To achieve these goals, CleanCo identifies and allocates the necessary resources. The company invests in new cleaning equipment and technology to improve efficiency and service quality. They allocate funds for marketing campaigns and employee training programs, focusing on skill development and customer service improvement.

Opportunities:

CleanCo explores new business opportunities to expand its services and reach a wider customer base. The company adds specialized cleaning services, such as carpet and upholstery cleaning, to its portfolio. They also tap into the growing market for eco-friendly cleaning solutions by offering green cleaning services to environmentally conscious clients.

Workflows:

To improve operational efficiency, CleanCo revisits its workflows and processes. The company implements a centralized scheduling system to optimize job assignments and minimize travel time for cleaning crews. They also introduce quality control measures and performance metrics to monitor service quality and ensure consistency across all teams.

Team:

CleanCo recognizes that employee morale and engagement play a critical role in the company's success. They invest in team-building activities and implement a rewards and recognition program to acknowledge employees' hard work and dedication. The company also provides opportunities for career advancement and professional development, encouraging employees to grow within the organization.

Holistic Evaluation:

CleanCo's management regularly evaluates the company's performance using a holistic approach. They track key performance indicators (KPIs) related to revenue, customer satisfaction, and employee turnover to measure progress towards their goals. The management also solicits feedback from customers and employees to identify areas for improvement and implement necessary changes.

Outcome:

By adopting the GROWTH framework, CleanCo successfully addresses its challenges and revives its struggling business. The company achieves its revenue growth target, experiences a significant improvement in customer satisfaction, and reduces employee turnover. CleanCo's renewed focus on efficient workflows, employee engagement, and a diverse range of services leads to sustainable expansion and long-term success.

VSM for Personal Growth & Business Development

Value Stream Mapping (VSM) is a powerful tool that can be used to discover and eliminate non-value-added tasks in a person's daily routine as well as in a business process. VSM can also be used to identify and eliminate activities that offer no value to the overall process. Individuals and businesses are able to increase their efficiency, cut their waste, and ultimately nurture both personal growth and the success of their businesses when they use VSM.

The first thing to do when utilizing VSM is to create a map of the process in its current state. This can be done for a personal routine or for a company procedure. This requires determining all of the activities and steps that are involved, as well as the amount of time and resources that are required for each phase.

Identifying the activities that do not add any value to the final product or service is the next step that needs to be taken. Non-value-added activities include things like procrastination, spending an excessive amount of time on social media, and in a business process, things like unnecessary paperwork or delays in approvals.

After determining which activities do not contribute to the creation of value, the following step is to get rid of those activities. This can be accomplished through the use of a range of strategies, including automation, outsourcing, or the redesign of processes.

The following phase, which comes after getting rid of the activities that didn't offer any value, is to create a map of the process's future state. This requires determining the new and enhanced processes and activities that will be used, as well as the amount of time and resources that are required for each phase.

In conclusion, it is essential to put the new procedure into action and keep an eye on it to check whether or not it is performing as anticipated and to make any necessary modifications.

Individuals and enterprises alike have the potential to enhance their efficiency and cut their waste by employing VSM, which, in turn, can lead to increased opportunities for both parties. In addition to this, it can assist in the identification of potential for growth and innovation, and it can also help to promote a culture of continuous improvement.

It is essential to point out that VSM is not a one-time procedure; rather, it is a method for continuous improvement. Because of this, it is essential to do the method on a regular basis in order to continue improving the process and locating new chances for expansion.

In one's personal life, VSM can be used to optimize daily routines, increase productivity, and accomplish one's personal goals. In one's professional life, VSM can be used to optimize business processes, decrease expenses, and increase customer satisfaction.

Cultivating a Savings Habit to Create Wealth

In order to become financially secure, it is essential to start saving money. There is no way to prepare for the future, save for emergencies, or reach financial goals without a savings strategy. Thankfully, learning to save regularly requires little more than effort and self-control.

Starting with a budget is the first step in learning to save money regularly. If you want to know where your money is going each month, you need a budget. Expenses and income must be itemized before a budget can be created. So, at the conclusion of each month, you may compare the two lists to see whether you have any spare cash. There should be some room for cutting costs if there is no spare change.

Create a savings target after you've established a budget. A SMART objective is one that is clear, realistic, attainable, and time-bound. Try setting a goal of saving 10% of your monthly income, or $500 each month, for the following six months.

The next step is to allocate a significant portion of your income toward savings. Don't just throw money at your savings account every month; set aside a particular amount. Monthly transfers from your checking account to your savings account can be automated using a one-click transfer service.

In addition to setting aside money regularly, maintaining your motivation is crucial. Rewarding yourself for small victories along the way is one strategy. One tactic is to give oneself a token incentive at certain points in your savings strategy, such as when you reach your goal amount. To keep yourself motivated, it might be helpful to picture yourself achieving your long-term financial goals, such as purchasing a home or paying off debt.

Being adaptable is also crucial. Having the financial flexibility to respond quickly to unforeseen circumstances is essential. To keep your spending under control, for instance, if your income suddenly drops, you may need to revise your budget. But, make it a point to save money regularly and only use funds for emergencies.

Last but not least, remember to keep tabs on your development. Always remember to track your financial progress and to evaluate your progress frequently. You can then change your course of action if necessary to ensure you reach your desired outcome.

Creating a practice of saving money is crucial to increasing one's net worth and securing one's financial future. You can take charge of your finances and reach your goals if you make a budget, set a savings target, make saving a priority, remain motivated, remain flexible, and track your progress. Keep in mind that the secret to financial success is to save money on a regular and deliberate basis. You may train yourself to save money regularly, and that will serve you well in the future.

Minimizing Waste and Enhancing Savings with Law of Attraction, 5S, and VSM

The careless use of resources can result in considerable monetary losses and have a detrimental effect on the quality of our lives. In our day-to-day lives, we may lessen the amount of waste we produce and increase the amount of money we save by implementing the 5S system, the Law of Attraction, and Value Stream Mapping (VSM).

Create a "saving mindset" through the use of the law of attraction.

Using the Law of Attraction, the first thing you need to do to avoid being wasteful and start saving more money is to cultivate an attitude of saving. Put all of your attention and effort into working toward the goal of reducing waste and increasing your savings. Repeat positive affirmations that support the goal you want to achieve and keep an optimistic view on life.

Use the 5S Approach in your work.

The second phase is to implement the 5S Methodology in your day-to-day activities with the goal of reducing waste. The 5S Technique consists of five steps: sorting, simplifying, sweeping, standardizing, and maintaining the system. To get started, clear the clutter from your house and workstation and get rid of anything that isn't necessary. Your life will become less complicated and messy as a result of this.

Implement Value Stream Mapping (VSM)

The third stage is to put in place Value Stream Mapping (VSM), which will help you comprehend and improve the flow of your day-to-day costs. Make use of value stream mapping (VSM) to locate aspects of your day-to-day life in which you are spending money unnecessarily. The flow of your spending should be analyzed, and you should search for opportunities to streamline and improve it. Make adjustments to the routines and activities in your life that are contributing to wastefulness and inefficiency.

Track the progress being made and rejoice in the victories.

The fourth stage is to keep track of your advancement and acknowledge the victories you achieve along the route. Maintain an accurate record of your savings and make modifications as required. You should reward yourself for making progress and keep your mind on the end goal, which is to reduce your waste and save more money.

Creating a mentality of saving, reducing waste, and making the most of one's resources are the three components of the recipe for increased savings and less frivolous spending. You may improve your financial condition and bring about good change in your day-to-day life by making use of the Law of Attraction, the 5S Method, and the VSM. You will be able to feel the satisfaction and fulfillment that come along with having financial stability and independence if you keep your attention on your intended objective and celebrate your success along the way.

Value Stream Mapping to Fight the Diderot Effect (VSM)

The Diderot Effect is the unforeseen chain reaction of further purchases that often follows the acquisition of a single new item, trapping the buyer in a never-ending cycle of consumerism and overspending. Value Stream Mapping is a method for combating the Diderot Effect and regaining control of one's spending habits.

VSM is a tool of lean management used to map out and examine the information and resources that go into making and delivering a product or providing a service to a client. We may make better judgments and move toward a more sustainable way of life by applying VSM to our purchasing habits and pinpointing the wasteful and inefficient parts.

Explaining the Diderot Effect by Tracing Its Origins

To counteract the Diderot Effect, one must first recognize the impulses that lead to frivolous purchasing.

a) Go back on your acquisitions and do a cost-benefit analysis to ascertain whether circumstances or feelings contributed to your tendency toward impulse buys.

b) Keep an eye out for repetitions: consider the possible influences on your spending, such as peer pressure, advertising, or unmet emotional needs.

Improve your self-awareness by learning more about yourself and what you value most in order to spot instances where your spending isn't supporting your long-term objectives.

Making Your Own Value Stream Diagram

Make a Value Stream Map of your own finances to investigate your spending habits and spot any unnecessary expenditures.

Create a spending journey map, detailing everything from first wanting something to its eventual disposal.

It's important to separate value-adding from non-value-adding tasks. Figure out which parts of your spending adventure are truly worthwhile.

Find garbage dumps: The causes of wasteful purchasing and accumulation of unneeded items, such as impulse buys and procrastination, can be isolated if one takes the time to reflect on their habits.

Using Lean Concepts to Cut Down on Waste

After spotting inefficiencies in your spending habits, you can use lean concepts to cut back on wasteful activities and boost productivity.

Reduce or eliminate non-value-adding activities, such as impulsive shopping, unused things, and hoarding.

Spend your money wisely by giving priority to events and possessions that reflect your values and help you flourish as a person.

Maintaining alignment between your spending patterns and your values and priorities through regular evaluation and revision of your own Value Stream Map.

Acquiring More Ethical Consumption Practices

Focus on long-term financial, emotional, and environmental health through developing sustainable consumption patterns.

a) Spend with intention, taking into account the item's genuine value and potential impact on your life before making a purchase.

b) Adopt a minimalist lifestyle, prioritizing quality over quantity by spending money on things that will last a long time and provide you joy.

c) Think about how your purchases will affect the environment and choose sustainable options and waste less when possible.

If we apply the methods of Value Stream Mapping to our own purchasing patterns, we can better understand what causes the Diderot Effect and how to counteract it. We can break the consumerist cycle and live healthier, happier lives if we learn to recognize areas of waste, maximize value, and adopt sustainable consumption practices. Keep in mind that, just like any lean process, overcoming the Diderot Effect calls for constant refinement and introspection so that we can develop and expand in accordance with our changing needs and goals.

Avoiding Repetitive Mistakes in Building a Business

Starting and growing a successful business is a hard journey that requires careful planning, hard work, and dedication. Many business owners make the same mistakes over and over, which can cause them to fail and be disappointed. Together, we'll talk about how to use the Law of Attraction, SWOT Analysis, and the 5 Whys Method to avoid making the same mistakes over and over again when building a business.

The Law of Attraction: The Law of Attraction is a universal rule that says that like attracts like. This means that what we think, feel, and believe has a big effect on what we experience and what happens to us. By thinking and feeling positively, we can bring more good things into our lives, such as the success of our business.

Step	Description
Set Goals	Establish clear, specific, and attainable objectives for your business to minimize the risk of making repetitive mistakes.

Visualize	Regularly visualize your business overcoming challenges and avoiding past errors, fostering a proactive and adaptive mindset.
Affirm	Use positive affirmations to reinforce a growth-oriented mindset and a commitment to learning from past mistakes.
Reflect	Periodically assess past errors and identify their root causes. Use this understanding to inform your decision-making process.
Take Action	Implement measures to prevent recurring mistakes, such as enhanced training, improved communication, or updated processes.
Gratitude	Acknowledge and appreciate the lessons learned from past mistakes, fostering a resilient and growth-focused business culture.

By applying the Law of Attraction in these steps, you can create a business environment that actively avoids repetitive mistakes, promotes continuous improvement, and fosters long-term success.

SWOT Analysis is a tool used to find out what a business's strengths, weaknesses, opportunities, and threats are and to evaluate them. It gives you a structured way to think about yourself and can be used to figure out where you can grow and improve. In the context of building a business and avoiding making the same mistakes over and over, a SWOT analysis (with monitor and review) can help find areas that are likely to fail and help come up with plans to fix them.

Step	Description
Strengths	Identify your business's strengths that can help prevent repetitive mistakes, such as effective management or strong teamwork.
Weaknesses	Recognize internal weaknesses that contribute to recurring errors and develop strategies to address them.
Opportunities	Seek opportunities to improve your business processes, invest in employee training, or implement new tools to avoid past mistakes.
Threats	Identify external factors that may contribute to repetitive mistakes, such as market changes or competition, and devise strategies to mitigate them.
Monitor	Continuously track your progress in avoiding past errors, adjusting your strategies as needed to ensure ongoing improvement.
Review	Regularly reassess your SWOT analysis to keep it up to date and relevant, enabling you to stay proactive in preventing mistakes.

The 5 Whys Method: The 5 Whys Method is a way to solve problems by asking "Why?" five times to get to the bottom of the problem. This method can be used to figure out why a business mistake happened and to come up with ways to stop it from happening again.

Step	Description
Identify	Recognize the repetitive mistakes that are negatively impacting your business.
First Why	Ask "Why?" to uncover the immediate cause of the mistake. Document the cause and its contributing factors.
Second Why	Ask "Why?" again to dig deeper into the underlying issues that led to the immediate cause. Continue documenting your findings.
Third Why	Repeat the process, asking "Why?" to discover the root causes of the problem. Record all information gathered.
Fourth & Fifth Whys	Continue asking "Why?" until you reach the core reasons for the repetitive mistakes. Document all findings.
Implement Solutions	Address the root causes identified through the 5 Whys analysis. Implement corrective actions and preventative measures to avoid future repetitions.

Monitor & Review	Regularly track progress in avoiding past errors, adjusting your strategies as needed, and reassess the effectiveness of implemented solutions to ensure ongoing improvement.

Using the 5 Whys technique, you can systematically identify and address the root causes of repetitive mistakes in your business, fostering a culture of continuous improvement and long-term success.

Conquering Addiction with Law of Attraction, Mental Discipline, and SWOT Analysis

Those who struggle with addiction can lose everything and have their lives changed by it. But with the right mind-set and tools, it is possible to beat addiction. Let's explore how the Law of Attraction, mental discipline, and SWOT analysis can be used to help someone stop an addiction.

The Law of Attraction is a very powerful tool that can help people bring good things into their lives. To use the Law of Attraction to get rid of an addiction, a person must think about what they want, which is to be free from their addiction. They have to see themselves living without their addiction and feel the feelings that come with that. Over time, these good thoughts and feelings will bring them more of the same, which will help them beat their addiction.

Another important tool for getting over an addiction is mental discipline. People who want to be free of their addiction must learn to control their thoughts and feelings and focus on what they want. This takes practice and a lot of patience, but with time and work, people can learn the mental discipline they need to beat their addiction.

Lastly, SWOT analysis can be used to help people figure out what their addiction's strengths, weaknesses, opportunities, and threats are.

By looking at these factors, people can come up with a plan to beat their addiction and get the result they want.

Table: Conquering Addiction Using SWOT Analysis

Component	Description
Strengths	Identify personal strengths that can support your recovery journey, such as determination, resilience, or a strong support network.
Weaknesses	Recognize personal weaknesses that may hinder your recovery, such as triggers, lack of self-discipline, or negative influences.
Opportunities	Seek opportunities to strengthen your recovery, including new coping strategies, support groups, or therapeutic interventions.
Threats	Identify external factors that could jeopardize your recovery, such as stressors, high-risk environments, or unsupportive relationships.
Action Plan	Develop a recovery plan based on your SWOT analysis. Prioritize addressing weaknesses and threats while leveraging your strengths and opportunities for growth.

Monitor & Review	Regularly reassess your progress and the effectiveness of your recovery plan. Make adjustments as needed to maintain and enhance your recovery journey.

By applying a SWOT analysis to your addiction recovery, you can develop a comprehensive understanding of your personal strengths, weaknesses, opportunities, and threats. This information can guide you in creating a tailored action plan that supports your recovery and long-term well-being.

Top of Form

In the end, getting over an addiction requires having the right mindset, tools, and plans. People can get over their addictions and live happier, healthier lives by using the Law of Attraction, mental discipline, and the SWOT analysis. Anything is possible if you have patience, stick with it, and are determined.

Sale Power

Techniques and approaches that can assist sales professionals in achieving success in their chosen area are referred to as sales power tactics. If you put these methods into action, you may be able to boost your sales performance, establish solid relationships with customers, and propel the growth of your company. Consider some of these powerful sales methods that are now available:

Understand your target market:

Learn your target audience's wants, preferences, and pain spots so you may better serve them. With this information, you will be able to modify your sales pitch and provide solutions that are tailored to the individual customer's requirements.

Create a unique value proposition:

Provide a concise explanation of the distinctive advantages that your company's product or service possesses in comparison to those offered by rivals. Concentrate on the features that set your product or service apart from others on the market and highlight the benefits it bestows on clients.

Building trust and rapport with customers is critical to achieving success in sales. Develop strong relationships. Pay attention to what your clients have to say, display empathy for them, and show that you are genuinely interested in meeting their requirements. The likelihood of receiving repeat business and recommendations will increase if good ties are developed.

Active listening skills should be utilized: When engaging in sales conversations, it is important to utilize active listening skills by fully focusing on the client, asking clarifying questions, and summarizing the customer's main points. This will assist you in better comprehending their requirements and in establishing your product or service as the best possible answer.

Learn to tell compelling tales:

Not only do stories connect with people on an emotional level, but they are also strong tools in the sales process. Telling a story is a great way to construct a clear picture of how a customer's problem can be solved by your product or service, or how their life may be improved.

Use social proof to showcase the value of your product or service by showcasing customer testimonials, case studies, and favorable reviews. The use of social evidence in interactions with prospective clients helps to create credibility and trust.

Develop your abilities as a negotiator:

Construct effective strategies for handling objections and concluding deals during negotiations. Always be ready to give alternate solutions or concessions while still preserving the necessary profit margins for your business.

Establish crystal-clear objectives, and monitor your progress:

Your sales efforts should include SMART targets, which means that they should be specific, measurable, achievable, relevant, and time-bound. Maintain a consistent monitoring of your progress and be prepared to make necessary adjustments to your approach in order to stay on track.

Maintain a high level of proficiency in sales by:

Have an up-to-date knowledge of the most recent sales strategies, tools, and trends in the business. Participating in activities such as workshops, seminars, and conferences will allow you to hone your abilities and pick up valuable insights from industry professionals.

Utilize technology and tools: Make use of Customer Relationship Management (CRM) software, sales enablement tools, and other technology solutions to help you optimize your sales process, manage customer interactions, and analyze data in search of insights and ways to improve.

You will be able to improve your sales performance, establish solid relationships with your customers, and drive growth in your company if you put these sales power methods into action. Always keep in mind that in order to be successful in sales, you need to continuously learn, adapt, and grow. In order to achieve success in the cutthroat world of sales, you must maintain your focus on your objectives and be willing to make adjustments to your methods whenever necessary.

Selling More using Law of Attraction, SWOT and VSM

In order to succeed, sales must be approached from multiple angles using a wide range of methods. In order to boost sales and accomplish objectives, organizations can use the Law of Attraction, SWOT Analysis, and Value Stream Mapping. This section will delve into the ways in which these resources might be applied to the sales process to propel expansion and success.

Using the Law of Attraction in Selling

When two things are similar, they are naturally drawn to one another. This means that firms can attract more clients and boost revenue by maintaining a happy frame of mind. Using the principles of the Law of Attraction can help businesses attract more customers by painting a good picture of their brand, building trust with existing clients, and highlighting the benefits of their products and services.

SWOT Analysis for Sales

The SWOT Analysis is a method for assessing the advantages, disadvantages, opportunities, and threats facing a company. With this method, you can see where your company has room for growth and how you can best leverage your existing skills in the sales department. A company's sales strategy can benefit from a SWOT Analysis if the company's inadequate sales procedures or lack of market distinction are revealed. Opportunities for expansion, like entering new markets or taking advantage of emerging technologies, can also be spotted by these experts.

Value Stream Mapping and Selling

Businesses can gain insight into the full life cycle of their products and services with the aid of Value Stream Mapping. When applied to the world of sales, this instrument can help pinpoint inefficiencies and help improve workflow. Creating a flowchart of the sales process helps companies detect bottlenecks and inefficiencies in the sales cycle, as well as approaches to boost conversion rates.

Using the Law of Attraction, SWOT Analysis, and Value Stream Mapping in sales can help businesses make more money and reach their goals. By using these three powerful tools together, businesses can create a positive and attractive brand image, build strong relationships with customers, and streamline their sales process to drive growth and success. Businesses can reach their sales goals and grow if they follow these steps and constantly monitor and improve their sales process.

G.A.P Method for Career Growth

The GAP method is a proven and effective approach to achieving career growth and success. By following these three steps, you can turn your career aspirations into reality and reach your full potential.

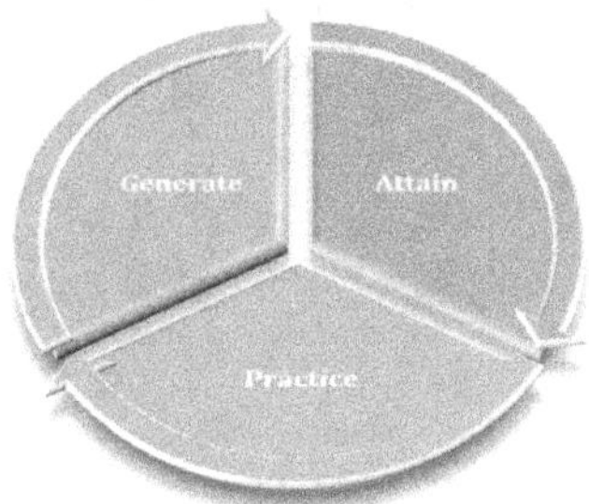

G - Generate

The first step in the GAP method is to generate new ideas and opportunities. This means that you need to stay open to new ideas, take calculated risks, and actively seek out new challenges and opportunities for growth. This may involve exploring new industries, acquiring new skills, or taking on new responsibilities in your current role.

A - Attain

Next, it's time to attain the skills and knowledge you need to grow in your career. This involves setting specific and measurable goals for your career, and taking the necessary steps to reach them. This may include further education, attending training programs, or seeking out mentorship and guidance from experienced professionals.

P - Practice

The final step in the GAP method is to practice what you have learned. This means that you need to apply your newfound skills and knowledge in real-world situations, and continuously seek out new challenges and opportunities to grow. This will help you build your confidence, gain experience, and demonstrate your value to your current and future employers.

The GAP method provides a straightforward and effective approach to career growth and success. By following these three steps, you can turn your career aspirations into reality and reach your full potential. So, generate new ideas, attain the skills you need, and practice what you have learned.

Jane's career growth with the GAP Approach

Criteria	The GAP Method Case Study
Background	Professional Jane has been in her current role for several years and feels stuck in her career progression. She discovers the GAP method and decides to apply it to her career journey.
Objective	To achieve career growth and success using the GAP method, by generating new opportunities, attaining the necessary skills, and practicing the acquired skills in real-world situations.
Step 1: Generate	Jane attends networking events, explores potential industries, and takes on new responsibilities at work. This expands her professional network and exposes her to new opportunities.

Step 2: Attain	Jane sets specific goals to improve her skills, enrolls in a part-time course, attends training programs, and seeks mentorship from experienced professionals in her field.
Step 3: Practice	Jane applies her newfound skills in her current role and embraces challenging projects. She continuously seeks new opportunities to grow and demonstrate her value to her employer.
Results	Jane's expanded network leads to a new job offer in her desired industry. Her improved skills and experience make her a valuable asset, resulting in a promotion and increased salary.
Conclusion	The GAP method helped Jane to turn her career aspirations into reality by generating new opportunities, attaining essential skills, and practicing them in real-world situations.

The GROWTH Framework - A Personal Growth Tool

Personal growth is essential for both personal and professional success. Developing new skills, expanding knowledge, and improving self-awareness can lead to increased confidence and a more fulfilling life. The GROWTH framework is a personal growth tool designed to help individuals identify areas for improvement and create a structured plan for development.

The GROWTH Framework

GROWTH stands for Goals, Reflect, Observe, Work, Track, and Harvest. This framework guides individuals through a systematic process of personal growth, fostering continuous improvement and self-discovery.

Goals

Set specific, measurable, achievable, relevant, and time-bound (SMART) goals for your personal growth. These goals should be aligned with your values, interests, and desired outcomes. Clearly defined goals provide direction and motivation for your personal growth journey.

Reflect

Reflect on your current strengths, weaknesses, opportunities, and threats (SWOT analysis). This self-assessment helps you identify areas for improvement and provides insights into your unique skills, talents, and areas of expertise.

Observe

Observe and learn from others, including mentors, role models, and peers. Seek out opportunities to gain new knowledge and skills through workshops, online courses, books, podcasts, or networking events. Stay up-to-date with industry trends and best practices.

Work

Take action to work on your personal growth goals. Create a structured plan that includes specific steps, milestones, and deadlines. Allocate time and resources for learning, skill development, and self-improvement activities.

Track

Monitor your progress towards your personal growth goals regularly. Keep a journal or use digital tools to track your achievements, setbacks, and lessons learned. This tracking process helps you stay accountable, motivated, and focused on your growth journey.

Harvest

Celebrate your achievements and recognize the progress you've made in your personal growth journey. Reflect on the knowledge, skills, and experiences you've gained and consider how they can be applied to other areas of your life. Use this newfound growth to fuel further personal development and success.

Implementing the GROWTH Framework

To implement the GROWTH framework, individuals can follow these steps:

1. Set SMART goals for personal growth.
2. Reflect on strengths, weaknesses, opportunities, and threats.
3. Observe and learn from others and stay informed about industry trends.
4. Work on your personal growth goals with a structured plan and dedicated resources.
5. Track your progress and achievements regularly.
6. Harvest the benefits of your personal growth journey, applying the insights and skills gained in other areas of your life.

The GROWTH framework offers a structured approach to personal growth, helping individuals identify areas for improvement and create a plan for development. By following the GROWTH framework, individuals can enhance their skills, knowledge, and self-awareness, leading to increased confidence, personal fulfillment, and professional success.

Case Study: Mark's Personal Growth Journey Using the GROWTH Framework

Mark is an electrical engineer who has been feeling unfulfilled and unhappy in his career. He decides to use the GROWTH framework to reevaluate his personal and professional goals, foster continuous improvement, and embark on a journey of self-discovery.

Goals:

Mark begins by setting clear, specific, and achievable goals for his personal and professional growth. He aims to improve his work-life balance, expand his technical skills, and cultivate a more positive mindset. Mark creates a detailed action plan to achieve these goals, outlining the steps he needs to take and the timeline for each goal.

Reflect:

Mark spends time reflecting on his current situation, assessing his strengths, weaknesses, and areas for improvement. He identifies the factors contributing to his unhappiness, such as a lack of job satisfaction, limited opportunities for career advancement, and a high-stress work environment. Mark also recognizes his need for more fulfilling personal relationships and hobbies outside of work.

Observe:

Mark actively observes and learns from others around him. He seeks out colleagues who have successfully navigated career transitions or achieved a better work-life balance. Mark also attends professional workshops and conferences to gain insights into industry trends and potential career paths. On a personal level, he attends social events and joins local clubs to expand his social circle and discover new interests.

Work:

With a clearer understanding of his goals and the steps needed to achieve them, Mark puts in the work to make changes in his life. He enrolls in technical courses to expand his skills, networks with professionals in other fields, and applies for job opportunities that align with his new goals. Mark also dedicates time to developing new hobbies and nurturing personal relationships.

Track:

Mark regularly tracks his progress towards achieving his goals. He sets up a journal to document his thoughts, feelings, and accomplishments, helping him stay accountable and motivated. Mark also establishes milestones and checkpoints to measure his progress and adjust his action plan as needed.

Harvest:

As Mark implements the GROWTH framework, he begins to see the positive outcomes of his efforts. He successfully transitions to a more fulfilling job with better work-life balance and a more supportive work environment. Mark's expanded skill set and professional network open up new career opportunities for him. He also enjoys a more balanced life, with stronger personal relationships and engaging hobbies.

Outcome:

By using the GROWTH framework, Mark transforms his life, overcoming unhappiness and fostering personal and professional growth. He gains a deeper understanding of his needs and aspirations, paving the way for a more satisfying and fulfilling life. Mark's journey demonstrates the power of the GROWTH framework as a tool for continuous improvement and self-discovery.

Business Growth Using the Pareto Principle and DMAIC Methodology

Business growth is essential for long-term success, and organizations must continuously identify and prioritize opportunities for improvement. The Pareto Principle, also known as the 80/20 rule, combined with the DMAIC methodology, can provide a powerful framework for driving business growth and optimizing processes.

The Pareto Principle

The Pareto Principle states that roughly 80% of the effects come from 20% of the causes. In a business context, this implies that a small number of factors or actions will have a significant impact on results. By identifying and focusing on these high-impact areas, organizations can effectively drive growth and improvement.

The DMAIC Methodology

DMAIC is a structured, data-driven process improvement methodology that stands for Define, Measure, Analyze, Improve, and Control. It provides a systematic approach to identifying and resolving issues within processes or systems, leading to enhanced efficiency, effectiveness, and quality.

Business Growth Using the Pareto Principle and DMAIC

1. Define: Clearly define the business growth objectives and the scope of the improvement project. Identify the key performance

indicators (KPIs) and metrics that will be used to measure success.

2. Measure: Collect data on the current state of the business and its processes. Use the Pareto Principle to identify the most significant areas for improvement, focusing on the 20% of factors or actions that will have the greatest impact on the desired outcomes.

3. Analyze: Analyze the collected data to identify root causes and patterns related to the high-impact areas. Use statistical analysis and other problem-solving techniques to validate the identified issues and determine the best course of action.

4. Improve: Develop and implement solutions to address the identified issues and optimize the high-impact areas. This may involve process redesign, the introduction of new technologies, or changes in organizational structure. Monitor the results and make adjustments as needed to achieve the desired business growth objectives.

5. Control: Implement controls to maintain the improvements and ensure the processes continue to deliver the desired outcomes. This may include establishing standard operating procedures, ongoing monitoring and reporting, or the development of a continuous improvement culture.

Implementing the Pareto Principle and DMAIC for Business Growth
To implement the Pareto Principle and DMAIC methodology for business growth, organizations can follow these steps:

1. Define the business growth objectives and scope of the improvement project.

2. Measure the current state of the business and its processes.

3. Apply the Pareto Principle to identify high-impact areas for improvement.

4. Analyze the data and identify root causes related to the high-impact areas.

5. Develop and implement solutions to address the identified issues.
6. Monitor the results and adjust as needed to achieve the desired outcomes.
7. Implement controls to maintain the improvements and ensure ongoing success.

Combining the Pareto Principle with the DMAIC methodology provides a powerful framework for driving business growth and optimizing processes. By focusing on the high-impact areas and using a data-driven, structured approach, organizations can effectively address issues, enhance efficiency, and achieve their business growth objectives.

Chapter 16: Strategic Plan

A strategic plan is like a map that helps a company figure out what they want to do and how they will do it. It shows the way to grow and become better while making important decisions. A good strategic plan helps a company succeed and take advantage of new opportunities.

Here are the main parts of a strategic plan:

1. Vision Statement: This tells what a company wants to be in the future. It helps everyone feel excited and know what direction to go in.
2. Mission Statement: This explains why a company exists and what it wants to give to customers and the world. It should be easy to remember and match the company's values.
3. Core Values: These are the important ideas that guide how a company makes decisions. They should show the right way to act and do business.
4. SWOT Analysis: This helps a company understand what they are good at, what they need to work on, and what chances they must do better or face problems. SWOT stands for Strengths, Weaknesses, Opportunities, and Threats.
5. Goals and Objectives: Based on the vision, mission, and SWOT analysis, a company should create clear and specific goals. These goals should be both short-term and long-term, and should match the overall plan of the business.
6. Strategies: These are the big ideas a company will use to reach its goals. They should be based on the SWOT analysis and help the

company use its strengths, fix its weaknesses, make the most of opportunities, and avoid threats.

7. Action Plans and Tactics: For each strategy, a company should create a detailed plan that lists the steps, resources, and time needed to reach the goals. These plans should be given to specific people or teams to make sure they are responsible for getting them done.

8. Performance Metrics and Monitoring: To see how well a company is doing, they should set up ways to measure success and check their progress regularly. This helps them make better decisions and change their plans if needed.

9. Review and Update: A strategic plan should be updated regularly to make sure it stays useful and helps the company reach its goals. Having a schedule for reviewing and updating the plan can keep it working well.

Strategic Tools for Organizational Success - SWOT, PEST, and Hoshin Kanri

In today's dynamic and ever-changing business environment, organizations need to adapt and develop strategies that will enable them to achieve their goals and objectives effectively. The use of strategic tools is crucial for organizations to analyze and plan for their internal and external environment. This section will discuss three popular strategic tools: SWOT analysis, PEST analysis, and Hoshin Kanri.

SWOT Analysis

SWOT analysis is a widely used strategic tool that stands for Strengths, Weaknesses, Opportunities, and Threats. It provides a simple and effective framework for organizations to assess their internal and external factors, enabling them to make informed decisions and develop strategies for growth and success.

Strengths and Weaknesses

Strengths and weaknesses are internal factors within an organization. Strengths refer to the core competencies, resources, and capabilities that give an organization a competitive advantage. Weaknesses, on the other hand, are limitations or deficiencies that hinder an organization's ability to achieve its goals and objectives.

Opportunities and Threats

Opportunities and threats are external factors that can affect an organization's performance. Opportunities are favorable conditions or situations in the external environment that an organization can exploit for growth or improvement. Threats, conversely, are unfavorable conditions or situations that can harm an organization's performance or existence.

PEST Analysis

PEST analysis is another strategic tool used to examine the macro-environmental factors that may impact an organization's performance. PEST stands for Political, Economic, Sociocultural, and Technological factors.

Political Factors

Political factors refer to government policies, regulations, and political stability that can impact an organization's operations. Organizations must consider the political environment of the countries they operate in and adapt their strategies accordingly.

Economic Factors

Economic factors include inflation rates, interest rates, economic growth, and exchange rates, among others. These factors influence an organization's financial performance, investment decisions, and overall operations.

Sociocultural Factors

Sociocultural factors encompass demographic trends, cultural values, and social attitudes that can impact an organization's market and customer base. Understanding these factors is crucial for organizations to develop products and services that cater to the needs and preferences of their target audience.

Technological Factors

Technological factors include technological advancements, innovations, and the rate of technological change. Organizations must stay updated with technological trends and invest in research and development to remain competitive and relevant in their respective industries.

Hoshin Kanri

Hoshin Kanri, also known as Policy Deployment or Hoshin Planning, is a strategic planning tool that originated in Japan. It focuses on aligning an organization's goals and objectives with its daily operations and activities.

The Hoshin Planning Process

The Hoshin Planning process consists of seven steps:

1. Establish organizational vision and mission
2. Develop long-term strategic objectives
3. Identify annual objectives and priorities
4. Deploy annual objectives to departments and teams
5. Develop action plans and performance metrics
6. Implement action plans and monitor progress
7. Review and adjust plans based on performance feedback

Benefits of Hoshin Kanri

Hoshin Kanri provides several benefits to organizations, including improved communication, better alignment of resources and efforts, enhanced employee engagement, and a clear focus on strategic priorities.

SWOT, PEST, and Hoshin Kanri serve as potent strategic instruments, enabling organizations to traverse the intricate business landscape, pinpoint opportunities, and align their objectives with their overarching mission and vision.

The COMPASS Framework - A New Strategic Tool to Outperform Competitors

The ever-evolving business landscape demands that organizations continuously innovate and adapt their strategies to remain competitive. While traditional strategic tools like SWOT and PEST provide valuable insights, they may not be enough to stay ahead of competitors. The COMPASS framework is a new strategic tool that focuses on understanding and exploiting competitive advantages to outperform competitors.

The COMPASS Framework

COMPASS stands for Customer, Operations, Market, Profitability, Assets, Skills, and Synergy. This framework enables organizations to analyze their business environment, identify key competitive advantages, and develop strategies to leverage these advantages for sustained growth and success.

Customer

Understanding your customers' needs, preferences, and behaviors is crucial for creating value and establishing a competitive advantage. Analyze your customer segments, their pain points, and the factors influencing their purchasing decisions. Develop strategies to attract, retain, and delight your customers.

Operations

Efficient and effective operations are the backbone of any successful organization. Assess your operational processes, identify areas of improvement, and implement strategies to enhance efficiency, productivity, and quality. Streamlining operations can lead to reduced costs and increased competitiveness.

Market

Analyze the market landscape, including industry trends, competitor activities, and potential disruptors. Identify market opportunities and threats and develop strategies to capitalize on opportunities and mitigate risks.

Profitability

To outperform competitors, organizations must focus on profitability. Assess your organization's financial performance, identify key profit drivers, and develop strategies to maximize profits while minimizing costs.

Assets

Organizations must effectively manage and optimize their tangible and intangible assets, such as physical resources, intellectual property, and human capital. Evaluate your assets and determine how they contribute to your competitive advantage. Develop strategies to enhance, protect, and leverage your assets for improved performance.

Skills

An organization's skills and capabilities are essential for maintaining a competitive edge. Identify your organization's core competencies and unique capabilities, and invest in developing and nurturing these skills. Foster a culture of continuous learning and development to maintain a skilled and adaptable workforce.

Synergy

Synergy refers to the collaborative efforts of various organizational units and functions that contribute to overall performance. Assess how different departments, teams, and individuals work together to achieve organizational goals. Implement strategies that foster collaboration, communication, and coordination across the organization.

Implementing the COMPASS Framework

To implement the COMPASS framework, organizations can follow these steps:

1. Perform a comprehensive analysis of each COMPASS component.
2. Identify key competitive advantages and areas of improvement.
3. Develop strategies to exploit competitive advantages and address weaknesses.
4. Communicate the strategies to all stakeholders and ensure alignment.
5. Monitor progress, review performance, and make adjustments as needed.

The COMPASS framework offers organizations a comprehensive approach to analyze their competitive landscape and develop strategies to outperform competitors. By focusing on key components like customer, operations, market, profitability, assets, skills, and synergy, organizations can gain a deeper understanding of their competitive advantages and leverage them for sustained growth and success.

Top of Form

Below is a summary of the COMPASS framework in a table format. The first column lists the components of the COMPASS framework, and the second column provides examples of actions or initiatives related to each component.

Component	Actions / Initiatives

Customer	- Segment and analyze customer profiles - Identify customer needs and preferences - Develop targeted marketing strategies - Enhance customer engagement and retention initiatives
Operations	- Assess and optimize operational processes - Implement lean methodologies - Enhance supply chain management- Improve quality control systems
Market	- Analyze industry trends and competitor activities - Identify market opportunities and threats - Develop market penetration and expansion strategies - Monitor potential disruptors
Profitability	- Analyze financial performance and key profit drivers- Implement cost reduction initiatives - Optimize pricing strategies - Evaluate investment opportunities
Assets	- Evaluate tangible and intangible assets - Enhance asset utilization and management - Protect intellectual property rights - Develop strategies to acquire or leverage assets

Skills	- Identify core competencies and unique capabilities - Invest in employee training and development - Foster a culture of continuous learning - Attract and retain top talent
Synergy	- Assess collaboration and communication within the organization - Implement cross-functional projects and initiatives - Encourage knowledge sharing - Align organizational goals and objectives across all levels

By implementing these actions or initiatives, organizations can ensure they are effectively addressing each component of the COMPASS framework, leading to improved competitive advantage and sustained growth and success.

Below is an example of a table for an ads consultant business using the COMPASS framework:

Category	Description	Example (Ads Consultant Business)
Customer	Understanding customer needs, preferences, and motivations to provide tailored advertising solutions and services.	Conducting client research to develop targeted ad campaigns that resonate with their audience.

Operations	Ensuring efficient processes, systems, and service delivery to provide high-quality advertising solutions.	Implementing project management methodologies to streamline ad campaign creation and improve client satisfaction.
Market	Analyzing market trends, competition, and opportunities to position the business strategically.	Conducting a competitive analysis to identify market gaps and differentiate the advertising consultancy services.
Profitability	Monitoring financial performance and managing costs to maximize revenue and ensure business sustainability.	Regularly analyzing profit margins, cost structures, and ROI to optimize pricing strategies and operational efficiency.
Assets	Effectively utilizing and managing tangible and intangible assets to support business growth and value creation.	Leveraging industry partnerships, technology platforms, and data analytics to create a competitive advantage in the advertising market.

Skills	Developing and nurturing the skills and capabilities of the workforce to support innovation and business success.	Implementing training programs and investing in talent development to enhance team expertise in advertising strategy and execution.
Synergy	Encouraging collaboration, communication, and alignment between departments and teams to achieve common goals.	Establishing cross-functional teams and promoting knowledge sharing to improve collaboration and drive innovation in ad campaign strategies.

Case Study: M5's Cleaning Product Business Using the COMPASS Framework

Aspect	Analysis
Customer	M5 identifies its target customers as homeowners, small businesses, and larger commercial establishments. The company focuses on understanding customer needs and preferences, emphasizing product innovation, and providing exceptional customer service.
Operations	M5 continuously improves its manufacturing processes, ensuring efficient production and high-quality products. The company invests in advanced equipment and technology, implements lean manufacturing principles, and optimizes its supply chain.

Market	M5's market research reveals a growing demand for eco-friendly cleaning products. The company adapts its product line to cater to this trend, differentiating itself from competitors and capturing a niche market segment.
Profitability	M5 closely monitors its financial performance, aiming to achieve sustainable profitability. The company focuses on cost reduction, pricing strategies, and revenue growth initiatives to maintain a healthy bottom line.
Assets	M5 leverages its assets, such as intellectual property, manufacturing facilities, and distribution network, to create a competitive advantage. The company invests in R&D, expanding its product portfolio and maintaining an edge in the market.
Skills	M5 recognizes the importance of a skilled workforce, investing in employee training and development. The company promotes a culture of continuous learning, ensuring its team is equipped with the latest industry knowledge and expertise.

Synergy	M5 fosters synergy between its various business functions, ensuring alignment with its overall strategy. The company encourages cross-functional collaboration, leveraging the combined strengths of its team to drive growth and success.

Outcome:

By utilizing the COMPASS framework, M5 effectively analyzes its business environment, identifies key competitive advantages, and develops strategies to leverage these advantages for sustained growth and success. The company's focus on customer needs, operational efficiency, and product innovation allows it to thrive in a competitive market. M5's commitment to employee development, synergy, and financial sustainability ensures its long-term success in the cleaning product industry.

The CLARITY Framework - A New Strategic Tool for Ensuring Quality and Customer Satisfaction

Today's business climate is more competitive than ever, making it crucial to stand out from the crowd by offering superior service and goods. To help businesses evaluate and enhance quality and customer satisfaction, the CLARITY framework was created.

The CLARITY Framework

CLARITY stands for Customer insights, Leadership, Adaptability, Responsiveness, Innovation, Teamwork, and Yield. This framework helps organizations examine their internal processes, customer interactions, and team dynamics to ensure quality and customer satisfaction.

Customer Insights

Understanding your customers and their needs is the foundation of delivering quality and satisfying experiences. Collect and analyze customer feedback, preferences, and behavior to gain insights into their expectations and perceptions of your products and services.

Leadership

Strong leadership is essential for fostering a culture of quality and customer satisfaction. Leaders should set clear expectations, provide guidance, and empower employees to make decisions that prioritize quality and customer satisfaction.

Adaptability

Organizations must be adaptable to respond effectively to changing customer needs, preferences, and market conditions. Encourage flexibility and agility in processes and decision-making to maintain quality and customer satisfaction in a dynamic environment.

Responsiveness

Prompt and effective response to customer inquiries, complaints, and feedback is crucial for maintaining customer satisfaction. Develop processes and systems that facilitate timely communication and resolution of customer issues.

Innovation

Innovation is key to improving quality and customer satisfaction. Encourage a culture of continuous improvement and invest in research and development to create new products, services, and solutions that meet or exceed customer expectations.

Teamwork

Fostering teamwork and collaboration among employees is essential for delivering quality and satisfying customer experiences. Encourage open communication, knowledge sharing, and cross-functional collaboration to achieve common goals related to quality and customer satisfaction.

Yield

Yield refers to the measurable outcomes of your organization's efforts to ensure quality and customer satisfaction. Establish key performance indicators (KPIs) to track and monitor the effectiveness of your quality and customer satisfaction initiatives. Use data-driven insights to make informed decisions and improvements.

Implementing the CLARITY Framework

To implement the CLARITY framework, organizations can follow these steps:

1. Conduct a comprehensive analysis of each CLARITY component.

2. Identify areas of strength and opportunities for improvement.

3. Develop and implement strategies to enhance quality and customer satisfaction.

4. Communicate the strategies and expectations to all stakeholders.

5. Monitor progress, evaluate performance, and make adjustments as needed.

The CLARITY framework offers a holistic approach to ensuring quality and customer satisfaction in organizations. By focusing on customer insights, leadership, adaptability, responsiveness, innovation, teamwork, and yield, organizations can create a culture of continuous improvement and deliver exceptional products and services that meet or exceed customer expectations. This strategic tool can help organizations differentiate themselves in a competitive market and foster long-term success.Top of Form

Below is a table example of the CLARITY framework. The first column lists the components of the CLARITY framework, and the second column provides examples of actions or initiatives related to each component.

Component	Actions / Initiatives
Customer Insights	- Conduct regular customer surveys and interviews - Analyze customer feedback and reviews - Monitor social media and online forums for customer opinions - Create customer personas to better understand needs and preferences

Leadership	- Set clear expectations for quality and customer satisfaction - Provide regular training and coaching to employees - Empower employees to make customer-centric decisions - Recognize and reward employees who prioritize quality and customer satisfaction
Adaptability	- Implement agile methodologies in product and service development- Encourage a culture of experimentation and learning from failures- Regularly review and update processes to align with changing customer needs- Train employees in change management
Responsiveness	- Establish a dedicated customer support team - Implement a customer relationship management (CRM) system - Set response time targets and monitor performance - Provide training on effective communication and problem-solving skills
Innovation	- Allocate resources for research and development - Launch a company-wide idea generation platform - Collaborate with external partners, such as startups or research institutions - Regularly review and update product and service offerings

Teamwork	- Organize cross-functional workshops and team-building activities - Establish clear communication channels and protocols - Encourage knowledge sharing and collaborative problem-solving - Recognize and reward teamwork and collaboration
Yield	- Establish KPIs for quality and customer satisfaction - Monitor and analyze performance data regularly - Conduct periodic reviews of quality and customer satisfaction initiatives - Use data-driven insights to make informed decisions and improvements

By implementing these actions or initiatives, organizations can ensure they are effectively addressing each component of the CLARITY framework, leading to improved quality and customer satisfaction.

Below is an example of a table for a cleaning product business using the CLARITY framework:

Category	Description	Example (Cleaning Product Business)

Customer insights	Understanding customer needs, preferences, and pain points to serve them better.	Conducting market research to identify customers' preferences and needs for eco-friendly cleaning products.
Leadership	Establishing strong leaders who communicate the vision, set goals, and support the team.	Hiring experienced leaders in the cleaning product industry to drive the vision of sustainable, effective cleaning solutions.
Adaptability	The ability to pivot and change in response to market trends, customer needs, and internal challenges.	Adapting the product line to include new, innovative cleaning solutions based on emerging trends and customer feedback.
Responsiveness	Quickly reacting to customer feedback, market changes, and other external factors.	Implementing a robust customer support system to address customer inquiries, feedback, and complaints promptly.
Innovation	Encouraging a culture of creativity and continuous improvement in products, services, and processes.	Investing in research and development to create new, eco-friendly cleaning solutions that outperform competitors.

Teamwork	Fostering collaboration, open communication, and support among team members to achieve common goals.	Implementing regular team meetings, cross-functional collaboration, and team-building activities to promote a healthy work culture.
Yield	Measuring and tracking business performance, focusing on financial results and customer satisfaction metrics.	Monitoring key performance indicators such as sales, profits, and customer satisfaction ratings to ensure continuous growth and improvement.

This table provides an overview of how the CLARITY framework can be applied to a cleaning product business to optimize internal processes, improve customer interactions, and drive growth.

Strategizing for a Successful Venture using Law of Attraction, SWOT, and PEST Analysis

To achieve success in starting and growing a venture, strategic planning and effective decision-making are essential. This chapter will explore the use of Law of Attraction, SWOT Analysis, and PEST Analysis as tools for strategizing efforts to ensure success.

The Law of Attraction is a concept that emphasizes the power of positive thinking and visualization in shaping one's reality. It can be used in the context of starting and growing a venture to align efforts with desired outcomes, attract success and abundance, and overcome obstacles.

To use the Law of Attraction for success, individuals should focus on their desired outcomes, visualize themselves as already being successful, and maintain positive thoughts and emotions.

SWOT Analysis is a method of evaluating a venture's Strengths, Weaknesses, Opportunities, and Threats. This analysis can help identify key factors that may impact the success of a venture, and develop a strategic plan to address them.

To conduct a SWOT Analysis, individuals must identify the strengths, weaknesses, opportunities, and threats of their venture. For instance, a strength could be a unique product or service offering, while a weakness could be a lack of experience in a particular market.

PEST Analysis is a method of assessing the Political, Economic, Sociocultural, and Technological factors that may impact a venture. This analysis can help identify external factors that may impact the success of a venture and develop a strategic plan to address them.

To conduct a PEST Analysis, individuals must identify the political, economic, sociocultural, and technological factors that may impact their venture. For example, political factors could be changes in regulations, while technological factors could be advancements in automation.

Using the Law of Attraction, SWOT Analysis, and PEST Analysis as tools for strategizing efforts can help individuals align their efforts with desired outcomes, identify key factors that may impact their venture, and develop a strategic plan to overcome obstacles and achieve success.

Clarifying Ideas using the Law of Attraction, 5 Whys, and 5W2H

The process of starting a business can be overwhelming, particularly when it comes to defining and clarifying an idea. This chapter will explore the use of the Law of Attraction, 5 Whys, and 5W2H as tools for clarifying ideas in the early stages of starting a business.

The Law of Attraction

The Law of Attraction is the idea that like attracts like, and that individuals can attract positive experiences and outcomes into their lives through their thoughts, beliefs, and emotions. To use the Law of Attraction to clarify an idea, it is important to focus on positive thoughts and feelings towards the idea, and to cultivate a positive and supportive attitude towards it.

By focusing on positive thoughts and emotions towards the idea, individuals can attract positive outcomes and experiences in the development of the idea, leading to increased clarity and success. Additionally, a positive and supportive attitude can help individuals to effectively communicate the idea and to build support for it.

5 Whys

The 5 Whys is a problem-solving technique that involves asking "why" questions in order to uncover the root cause of a problem. In the context of clarifying an idea, the 5 Whys can be used to uncover the underlying motivations, goals, and objectives that drive the idea.

To use the 5 Whys to clarify an idea, individuals must start by defining the idea, and then ask "why" questions in order to uncover its underlying motivations, goals, and objectives. This process can be repeated several times, until the individual has a clear understanding of the idea and what it seeks to achieve.

5W2H

5W2H is a structured problem-solving method that involves answering seven questions in order to clearly define a problem or objective. In the context of clarifying an idea, 5W2H can be used to define the idea and to identify its key components.

The seven questions in the 5W2H method are: What, Why, Who, Where, When, How, and How Much. By answering these questions, individuals can gain a clearer understanding of the idea and what it seeks to achieve, and can use this information to develop a plan for bringing the idea to life.

Clarifying ideas is an essential step in the process of starting a business, and the Law of Attraction, 5 Whys, and 5W2H are powerful tools that can help individuals to do so. By using these tools and techniques, individuals can increase clarity, build support for their ideas, and achieve long-term success in their business endeavors.

PIN: A New Strategic Tool for Decision-Making

PIN is a groundbreaking strategic tool designed to aid organizations and individuals in making superior decisions while optimizing their planning processes. The acronym PIN represents the three fundamental stages of the decision-making process: Prioritize, Investigate, and Navigate. By employing the PIN framework, users can efficiently address intricate problems and accomplish their desired objectives.

The PIN Framework:

Prioritize (P): The initial step in the PIN process involves identifying and ranking the most urgent issues or goals. By evaluating these items based on importance, urgency, and potential impact, users can effectively allocate resources and concentrate their efforts. Key factors to consider during prioritization include:

- Importance: How vital is this issue or goal to the overall success of the project or organization?
- Urgency: How quickly must this issue be addressed or goal be attained?
- Impact: What are the potential positive or negative consequences of tackling this issue or achieving this goal?

Investigate (I): With priorities established, the next stage is to collect and analyze pertinent information for each priority. This may entail researching market trends, performing a SWOT analysis, assessing internal capabilities, or obtaining feedback from stakeholders. The objective is to gather sufficient data to facilitate informed decision-making. Key factors to consider during investigation include:

- Data collection: What information sources are available, and how can they be accessed?
- Analysis: How can the data be consolidated and interpreted to better comprehend the situation and make well-informed decisions?
- Stakeholder input: How can insights from relevant individuals be integrated into the decision-making process?

Navigate (N): Upon compiling and analyzing information, the final stage requires developing and executing a strategic plan to address each priority. This includes establishing clear objectives, pinpointing potential challenges, and effectively allocating resources. Monitoring progress and adapting the plan as necessary ensures success in achieving the desired outcomes. Key factors to consider during navigation include:

- Objectives: What are the specific goals and milestones for each priority?
- Challenges: What hurdles might be faced, and how can they be surmounted or mitigated?
- Resource allocation: How can resources (time, money, personnel) be efficiently allocated to achieve objectives?

The PIN framework provides a systematic and organized approach to decision-making, empowering organizations and individuals to prioritize issues, examine relevant information, and overcome challenges in the pursuit of success. By integrating the PIN tool into their strategic planning processes, users can augment their capacity to make well-informed decisions and enhance overall performance.

Implementing PIN for Strategic Decision-Making: A Case Study of TechCo

Section	Description
Introduction	The case study examines how TechCo used the PIN framework to streamline decision-making and optimize growth strategy.
Background	TechCo, an AI-driven start-up, faced challenges in resource allocation, product development, and market penetration.
Application	Describes the application of the PIN framework in three stages: Prioritize, Investigate, and Navigate.
- Prioritize (P)	TechCo identified and ranked key priorities, enabling effective resource allocation and focused efforts.

- Investigate (I)	TechCo gathered and analyzed relevant information to better understand their situation and identify growth opportunities.
- Navigate (N)	TechCo developed a strategic plan to address priorities, monitored progress, and adjusted plans as needed.
Results	TechCo saw significant improvements in decision-making and performance, leading to a stronger market position.
Conclusion	The case study highlights the effectiveness of the PIN framework for enhancing strategic planning and decision-making.

Chapter 17: Generating Capital

One of the most crucial aspects of starting or growing a business is raising capital. Adequate funding is essential for success, and entrepreneurs must explore various sources to secure the necessary funds. This chapter will discuss the seven primary sources of generating capital and offer guidance on how to leverage them effectively.

1. Personal Savings

The first and most common source of capital is an entrepreneur's personal savings. Self-funding demonstrates commitment and confidence in the business idea, making it easier to attract additional investors. To leverage personal savings, entrepreneurs should:

- Establish a separate account for business expenses.
- Create a budget and financial plan for the business.
- Maintain financial discipline and avoid dipping into savings unnecessarily.

1. Friends and Family

Friends and family members can provide valuable financial support, especially during a business's early stages. To tap into this source of capital, entrepreneurs should:

- Approach loved ones with a well-prepared business plan.
- Offer them equity or debt investment options.
- Clearly communicate the risks and potential rewards

1. Crowdfunding

Crowdfunding platforms, such as Kickstarter and Indiegogo, enable entrepreneurs to raise capital from the public. To successfully generate funds through crowdfunding, entrepreneurs should:

- Develop a compelling pitch and video presentation.
- Offer attractive rewards for different contribution levels.
- Promote the campaign extensively on social media and other channels.

1. Angel Investors

Angel investors are affluent individuals who invest in early-stage startups in exchange for equity or convertible debt. To attract angel investors, entrepreneurs should:

- Network extensively and attend industry events.
- Prepare a comprehensive business plan and financial projections.
- Highlight the business's unique selling points and growth potential.

1. Venture Capital

Venture capital firms invest in high-growth startups in exchange for significant equity stakes. To secure venture capital funding, entrepreneurs should:

- Research and target VC firms that invest in their industry.
- Create a robust pitch deck and financial model.

- Demonstrate a strong management team and market traction.

1. Bank Loans

Traditional bank loans offer entrepreneurs access to capital with repayment terms and interest rates based on creditworthiness. To obtain a bank loan, entrepreneurs should:

- Have a solid credit score and collateral.
- Prepare a detailed business plan with financial projections.
- Explore various loan options, such as SBA loans and term loans.

1. Grants and Competitions

Government grants and business competitions provide non-dilutive funding to eligible businesses. To secure capital through grants and competitions, entrepreneurs should:

- Research and apply for relevant grants or competitions in their industry.
- Meet eligibility requirements and adhere to application guidelines.

Present a strong business case and demonstrate the impact of their solution.

Raising Capital for Business Using the Law of Attraction and 5W2H

Raising capital for your business can be a challenging and time-consuming process. However, by leveraging the principles of the Law of Attraction and the 5W2H method, you can attract the right investors and funding opportunities for your business. Let's explore the Law of Attraction, the 5W2H method, and how to apply these techniques to raise capital effectively.

The Law of Attraction

The Law of Attraction is based on the principle that like attracts like. In the context of raising capital, this means that if you maintain a positive mindset and focus on your desired outcomes, you are more likely to attract the resources and opportunities you need to achieve your goals.

Applying the Law of Attraction to raising capital involves visualizing your desired outcomes, maintaining a positive attitude, and taking inspired action towards your goals.

The 5W2H Method

The 5W2H method is a problem-solving framework that focuses on answering seven key questions: Who, What, When, Where, Why, How, and How Much. By answering these questions, you can develop a clear and actionable plan for raising capital for your business.

Here's how the 5W2H method can be applied to the process of raising capital:

1. Who: Identify your target investors.
2. What: Determine the type of funding you need.
3. When: Set a timeline for securing funding.
4. Where: Locate the best sources and platforms for raising capital.
5. Why: Clearly articulate the purpose and goals of your funding request.
6. How: Develop a strategic approach to attracting investors.
7. How Much: Establish a target amount of capital to raise.

Combining the Law of Attraction and 5W2H for Raising Capital

The following table demonstrates how to combine the Law of Attraction and the 5W2H method to raise capital for your business effectively:

5W2H Question	Description	Law of Attraction Application
Who	Identifying target investors	Visualize the ideal investors who share your vision and values, and maintain a positive mindset to attract them.
What	Determining the type of funding needed	Focus on the desired funding type (e.g., equity, debt, grants) and believe in your ability to secure it.

When	Setting a timeline for securing funding	Trust in the timing of the funding process and remain optimistic about achieving your funding goals within the timeframe.
Where	Locating the best sources and platforms for raising capital	Envision the most suitable platforms and funding sources that will provide the necessary capital.
Why	Articulating the purpose and goals of the funding request	Believe in the importance of your funding goals and the positive impact they will have on your business.
How	Developing a strategic approach to attracting investors	Take inspired action by creating a compelling pitch, networking, and showcasing your business's strengths and potential.
How Much	Establishing a target amount of capital to raise	Visualize the desired amount of capital and trust in your ability to attract it.

Generating Capital Using PDCA

Generating capital is crucial for the success of any business, whether it's a startup or an established enterprise looking to expand. The PDCA (Plan-Do-Check-Act) model, a popular continuous improvement methodology, can be a valuable tool in the capital-raising process. This section will discuss how to use the PDCA approach to effectively generate capital and ensure financial stability.

1. Plan: Develop a Capital Generation Strategy

Before attempting to raise capital, entrepreneurs must have a well-defined strategy that outlines their funding goals and requirements. To create a capital generation plan, consider the following:

- Identify funding sources most suited to your business and its growth stage.
- Assess the amount of capital required and its intended use.
- Set realistic timelines and milestones for raising capital.
- Determine the best approach for approaching investors, lenders, or grant providers.

1. Do: Execute the Capital Generation Plan

Once a plan is in place, it's time to take action and start generating capital. Entrepreneurs should:

- Prepare necessary documentation, such as a business plan, pitch deck, and financial projections.
- Reach out to potential investors or lenders, leveraging networks and industry events.
- Apply for grants and competitions, ensuring compliance with eligibility requirements.
- Launch crowdfunding campaigns, if applicable, and promote them extensively

1. Check: Monitor Progress and Evaluate Results

Throughout the capital-raising process, it's essential to track progress and evaluate results. This step helps identify any shortcomings or bottlenecks that need to be addressed. To monitor and evaluate the capital generation efforts, entrepreneurs should:

- Review the success of funding applications or investor meetings.
- Track the amount of capital raised against set goals and milestones.
- Analyze the effectiveness of different funding sources and strategies.
- Gather feedback from investors or lenders to identify areas for improvement.

1. Act: Adjust and Improve the Capital Generation Strategy

Based on the insights gained during the Check stage, entrepreneurs must make adjustments to their capital generation strategy. This step aims to optimize the process, address any issues, and increase the likelihood of securing funding. To make improvements, entrepreneurs should:

- Refine their pitch or presentation based on feedback from investors or lenders.
- Adjust their funding goals or requirements, if necessary
- Explore alternative funding sources or strategies that may yield better results.
- Develop contingency plans to address potential obstacles or setbacks.

The PDCA methodology provides a structured approach to generating capital, ensuring that entrepreneurs continuously learn from their experiences and optimize their strategies. By following the Plan-Do-Check-Act cycle, business owners can increase their chances of securing the necessary funding to grow and succeed in their ventures. This iterative process promotes ongoing improvement and adaptation, allowing entrepreneurs to navigate the often-challenging capital-raising journey effectively.

Capital Creation Matrix (CCM)

The "Capital Creation Matrix" (CCM), a new and innovative tool designed to help you generate capital for your business venture. The CCM combines different capital generation strategies and opportunities to create a tailored action plan for your business. The matrix is divided into four quadrants: Traditional, Alternative, Network-based, and Creative.

1. Traditional: This quadrant focuses on conventional methods of raising capital, such as:

- Bank loans: Securing financing from a financial institution based on your credit history and business plan.
- Angel investors: Attracting wealthy individuals who provide capital in exchange for equity or debt in your business.
- Venture capital: Raising funds from venture capital firms that invest in high-growth potential startups.

1. Alternative: This quadrant explores non-traditional financing options, including:

- Crowdfunding: Raising capital through online platforms by offering products, services, or equity to a large group of people.

- Peer-to-peer lending: Borrowing money from individuals or groups of investors through online lending platforms.
- Grants and competitions: Applying for grants or participating in business competitions that offer cash prizes.

1. Network-based: This quadrant emphasizes the importance of leveraging your personal and professional network to access capital:

- Friends and family: Borrowing money or receiving investments from people you know and trust.
- Strategic partnerships: Collaborating with other businesses or organizations that can provide financial support or resources.
- Business incubators and accelerators: Joining programs that offer mentorship, resources, and sometimes funding for startups.

1. Creative: This quadrant encourages you to think outside the box and explore innovative ways to generate capital:

- Bootstrapping: Self-funding your business by minimizing expenses and using personal savings or revenue generated by the business.
- Bartering: Exchanging goods or services with other businesses or individuals without using money.
- Pre-sales: Generating capital by offering customers the opportunity to purchase products or services in advance, before they are produced or released.

To use the Capital Creation Matrix, assess your business needs and capabilities, and then identify the most suitable strategies within each quadrant. Create a tailored action plan by selecting the best combination of methods from each quadrant, considering factors such as your industry, target market, and risk tolerance. By diversifying your capital generation approach, you increase the likelihood of securing the necessary funds to launch and grow your business.

Here's an example of the Capital Creation Matrix (CCM) for a technology startup focusing on developing a mobile app for health and fitness:

Quadrant 1: Traditional

- Bank loans: Apply for a small business loan from a local bank, targeting those with favorable terms for tech startups.
- Angel investors: Research and pitch to angel investors interested in health and fitness or technology sectors.
- Venture capital: Create a list of venture capital firms specializing in health-tech and mobile apps and prepare a compelling pitch for potential meetings.

Quadrant 2: Alternative

- Crowdfunding: Launch a Kickstarter campaign offering early access, exclusive features, or merchandise to backers.
- Peer-to-peer lending: Research and choose a suitable P2P lending platform to raise funds from individual investors.
- Grants and competitions: Identify and participate in startup competitions or apply for grants related to health and fitness or technology.

Quadrant 3: Network-based

- Friends and family: Present a well-prepared pitch to friends and family, offering them an opportunity to invest in the business.
- Strategic partnerships: Approach health and fitness influencers, gyms, or wellness centers to form partnerships that may provide financial support or resources.

- Business incubators and accelerators: Apply to health-tech or mobile app-focused incubators and accelerators that offer mentorship, resources, and funding opportunities.

Quadrant 4: Creative

- Bootstrapping: Use personal savings, minimize expenses, and reinvest any revenue generated from early customers to fund the business.
- Bartering: Offer app development or marketing services to other businesses in exchange for their services, such as office space or legal counsel.
- Pre-sales: Generate capital by offering customers a pre-order discount or special features for purchasing the app before its official release.

After identifying suitable strategies in each quadrant, the technology startup can develop a tailored action plan by combining the best methods based on their specific needs, resources, and goals. This approach provides multiple avenues for capital generation, increasing the chances of securing the necessary funds to successfully launch and grow their business.

Chapter 18: Fear

Overcoming Fear using the Law of Attraction and SWOT Analysis

Fear is a frequent emotion that affects individuals differently. It can hinder our ability to take risks, follow our ambitions, and live a fulfilled life. With the correct tools and tactics, it is possible to conquer fear and enjoy a life of prosperity, happiness, and success. This chapter will examine the Law of Attraction and how it can be utilized in conjunction with SWOT (Strengths, Weaknesses, Opportunities, and Threats) analysis along with other techniques to overcome fear.

The Law of Attraction is a universal principle that maintains that similar things attract like things. This implies that our thoughts, emotions, and beliefs have a significant influence on our experiences and outcomes. By focusing on positive ideas and emotions, it is possible to attract positive experiences into one's life. Inversely, we can attract unpleasant experiences by focusing on negative thoughts and emotions.

Strengths, Weaknesses, Opportunities, and Threats (SWOT) analysis is a tool used to identify and analyze a person's Strengths, Weaknesses, Opportunities, and Threats. It offers a structured method to self-reflection and can be utilized to find growth and development opportunities. In the context of conquering fear, a SWOT analysis can assist us in identifying our strengths and weaknesses and developing plans for overcoming any potential hurdles that may hinder us from overcoming our anxieties.

Below is a SWOT (Strengths, Weaknesses, Opportunities, and Threats) analysis to help overcome fear.

	Internal Factors	
	Strengths	Weaknesses
Positive	1. Self-awareness: Recognizing fear and its triggers.	1. Lack of self-confidence: Doubting personal abilities to face fear.
	2. Coping skills: Previously developed strategies to manage fear.	2. Anxiety: Exacerbating fear due to constant worry.
	3. Resilience: Ability to recover from setbacks.	3. Negative thinking patterns: Focusing on worst-case scenarios.
	4. Support network: Friends and family to rely on.	4. Avoidance: Escaping from fearful situations.

	External Factors	
	Opportunities	Threats
Negative	1. Personal growth: Facing fear leads to increased self-confidence and personal development.	1. Unsupportive environment: People or situations that increase fear.

2. Professional help: Access to therapists, counselors, or support groups.	2. Overwhelming stress: Situations that exacerbate fear and hinder progress.
3. Skill development: Learning new techniques to manage fear (e.g., meditation, breathing exercises).	3. Negative reinforcement: Patterns that inadvertently reinforce fear (e.g., avoiding situations).
4. Positive role models: Observing and learning from others who have overcome similar	

Using the Law of Attraction and the SWOT Analysis to Conquer Fear: We may employ the Law of Attraction and SWOT analysis together to conquer fear. By envisioning ourselves overcoming our worries and focusing on our strengths and opportunities, we can attract great events and outcomes into our life. In addition, by recognizing and addressing our weaknesses and threats, we can proactively remove any impediments that may impede our ability to overcome our concerns.

First, determine your strengths and weaknesses: Take some time to consider your skills and shortcomings to get started. Examine your unique qualities, your strengths, and your interests. Then, consider any areas where you may have difficulties or struggle. Honestly record your ideas and observations in a journal.

Identifying opportunities and threats is the second step. Secondly, consider development and improvement opportunities, as well as any potential risks that may hinder you from overcoming your anxieties.

Identify any resources, relationships, or experiences that can aid you on your trip, as well as any potential hurdles you may encounter.

Focusing on your strengths and opportunities: After identifying your strengths and opportunities, prioritize them. Imagine yourself effectively overcoming your worries and achieving your goals. Repeat positive mantras to promote a positive frame of mind, and surround oneself with helpful individuals.

Fourth Step: Addressing Weaknesses and Dangers: Next, address any flaws and risks that may impede your ability to overcome your concerns. Consider modifying your habits, actions, or relationships, and if required, get assistance. By addressing these areas, you will be able to proactively address any potential barriers along the path.

Fear is a journey that demands concentration, commitment, and perseverance. Nonetheless, it is possible to attain a life of prosperity, joy, and success with the proper tools and techniques. You may conquer your worries and live the life you wish by utilizing the Law of Attraction and SWOT analysis. Remember to concentrate on your strengths, possibilities, and positive thoughts, as well as to address any potential flaws and threats. With perseverance and an optimistic outlook, anything is possible.

FEAR FRAMEWORK

Fear is a normal feeling that everyone has at some point in their lives. But when fear gets too big and starts to run our lives, it can stop us from reaching our goals and living a happy life. In this method, we'll talk about four key steps to help you get over your fears: facing them, acting on them, keeping track of them, and looking back on them.

Face your fear.

Face your fear head-on. That's the first step to getting rid of it. Avoiding or ignoring your fear may provide temporary relief, but it can also prolong your fear and make it even stronger. Instead, try to confront your fear by gradually exposing yourself to the things that make you afraid. If you're afraid of heights, for example, you could start by standing on a chair or climbing a small hill. As you get better at these small steps, you can gradually move on to more difficult situations.

Execute an Action Plan

The next thing to do is to make a plan of action to help you get over your fear. This plan should give you specific steps you can take to gradually face the things that scare you. For example, if you're afraid of public speaking, your plan could include practicing in front of a mirror, joining a public speaking group, or taking a public speaking course.

Make sure that your plan of action is doable and that you break it down into smaller, more manageable steps.

Account for Your Progress

It's important to keep track of your progress and hold yourself accountable as you work on your action plan. This can keep you going and on track with your goals. Keep a log or journal of your progress, and give yourself a reward when you reach a major goal. For example, if your goal is to get over your fear of speaking in front of a group, you could give yourself a favorite meal or fun activity every time you speak in front of a group without getting nervous.

Review Your Results

Lastly, it's important to look at your progress and figure out how well your plan is working. Take some time to think about what went well and what could be done better, and then change your plan as needed. For instance, if practicing in front of a mirror doesn't help you get over your fear of public speaking, you might need to try something else, like working with a public speaking coach or finding a helpful mentor.

In the end, facing your fear is a brave step toward getting rid of it. You can get over your fears and reach your goals by slowly putting yourself in situations that scare you, following an action plan, holding yourself accountable, and reviewing your progress. Remember that the journey may not always be easy, but in the end it will be worth it.

Fear Elimination Toolkit" (FET)

The "Fear Elimination Toolkit" (FET), an innovative approach designed to help individuals overcome fear and anxiety in various aspects of life. The FET incorporates five core components to address fear from different angles, allowing users to create a personalized strategy for conquering their fears.

1. Self-Assessment: The first step in overcoming fear is understanding its root cause. Use the Fear Analysis Worksheet to identify the specific fears you're facing, the situations that trigger them, and the underlying beliefs or experiences contributing to their development.

2. Mindfulness & Relaxation Techniques: Fear often arises due to a lack of control over our thoughts and emotions. The FET includes a selection of mindfulness practices, such as meditation, deep breathing exercises, and progressive muscle relaxation, to help users regain control over their mental and emotional state.

3. Cognitive Reframing: The way we perceive a situation plays a significant role in how we respond to it. The FET's Cognitive Reframing Guide teaches users how to reframe negative thoughts and beliefs associated with their fears, replacing them with more realistic and positive perspectives.

4. Exposure & Desensitization: Gradually facing your fears in a controlled manner can be an effective way to overcome them.

The FET's Exposure Ladder helps users create a step-by-step plan for confronting their fears, starting with less intimidating scenarios and progressing toward more challenging situations.

5. Support & Accountability: Having a support system can greatly improve the likelihood of overcoming fears. The FET's Accountability Partner Guide provides tips on selecting an accountability partner and outlines how to create a structured plan for mutual support and encouragement.

To use the Fear Elimination Toolkit:

1. Complete the Fear Analysis Worksheet to identify your fears and their root causes.
2. Choose and practice one or more mindfulness techniques regularly to help manage anxiety and stress.
3. Use the Cognitive Reframing Guide to challenge and replace negative thoughts related to your fears.
4. Develop an Exposure Ladder to gradually confront and conquer your fears in a controlled manner.
5. Find an Accountability Partner who can offer support, encouragement, and motivation throughout the process.

By following these steps and utilizing the Fear Elimination Toolkit, individuals can develop a comprehensive strategy to overcome their fears and enhance their overall well-being.

An example of the Fear Elimination Toolkit (FET) applied to overcoming the fear of public speaking:

1. Self-Assessment: Using the Fear Analysis Worksheet, identify that the fear of public speaking is primarily driven by the fear of judgment, the pressure to perform well, and past negative experiences.

2. Mindfulness & Relaxation Techniques: Choose deep breathing exercises and guided meditation as regular practices to help manage anxiety and stress related to public speaking.

- Deep breathing exercises: Practice taking slow, deep breaths before and during public speaking engagements to help calm nerves and reduce anxiety.
- Guided meditation: Dedicate 10-15 minutes daily to follow a guided meditation focused on relaxation and self-confidence.

1. Cognitive Reframing: Use the Cognitive Reframing Guide to challenge negative thoughts about public speaking:

- Negative thought: "I'm going to mess up and everyone will laugh at me."
- Reframed thought: "Everyone makes mistakes, and people are generally understanding. I'll focus on doing my best and learn from any mistakes I make."

1. Exposure & Desensitization: Develop an Exposure Ladder for gradually facing the fear of public speaking:

- Step 1: Practice speaking in front of a mirror.
- Step 2: Record a video of yourself giving a speech and watch it to identify areas for improvement.
- Step 3: Present a speech to a small group of friends or family members.
- Step 4: Volunteer to give a presentation at a local community group or club.
- Step 5: Present at a larger event or conference.

1. Support & Accountability: Find an Accountability Partner who also wants to improve their public speaking skills. Create a

structured plan for meeting regularly, practicing together, and providing feedback and encouragement.

By using the Fear Elimination Toolkit, the individual creates a comprehensive and personalized plan to overcome their fear of public speaking. This approach combines self-assessment, mindfulness techniques, cognitive reframing, exposure therapy, and social support to help build confidence and resilience in public speaking situations.

Chapter 19: Time Management

Mastering Parkinson's Law for Time Management

According to Parkinson's Law, "work expands to occupy the time available for its completion." This widely acknowledged law of time management emphasizes the significance of setting reasonable deadlines and avoiding procrastination. In this chapter, we will examine how to master Parkinson's Law in order to become more effective and productive at time management.

Set Realistic Deadlines:

Setting reasonable deadlines is one of the most crucial methods for mastering Parkinson's Law. By setting strict deadlines, you are forced to prioritize your work and concentrate on the most important tasks. This will assist you in avoiding procrastinating and enhancing your productivity. Yet, it is essential to remember to be realistic and not to establish targets that are impossible to accomplish.

Break Down Tasks into Smaller Pieces:

Learning to break down large work into smaller, more manageable chunks is another important step in managing Parkinson's Law. A huge work can be completed in less time and with greater enthusiasm if its components are broken down into smaller, more manageable tasks.

Eliminate Distractions:

Distractions can be a serious hindrance to getting work done. In order to fully grasp Parkinson's Law, it is crucial to remove any potential sources of distraction. In order to concentrate, you can silence your phone, exit your inbox, or put on noise-canceling headphones.

Use a Timer:

If you're having trouble keeping track of time or maintaining concentration, setting a timer may help. Limiting the amount of time spent on an activity and increasing productivity can be achieved by setting a timer for a predetermined period of time. You can stay on track with your priorities and get more done if you do this.

Prioritize Tasks:

Prioritizing work is crucial for succeeding under Parkinson's Law. This implies prioritizing the most critical activities and setting aside the less pressing ones. Organizing your work in terms of priority can help you get more done in less time.

The concept of Parkinson's Law is well-known in the field of time management, and it emphasizes the significance of not putting off tasks until the last minute. Having a firm grasp on Parkinson's Law will allow you to maximize your time and efforts. You can get more done in less time if you focus, eliminate distractions, divide activities into manageable chunks, use a timer, and prioritize your work.

You Have More Time Than You Think

Do you ever feel like you just don't have enough time? That's an easy out we often give ourselves when we don't want to work toward our goals or try something new. We use it as an excuse to put off doing things because they seem too difficult or to run away from the stress of trying to live up to other people's expectations. However, there is actually more time than we think. Actually, each week we have 167 hours to use however we like.

Let's break it down:

We work roughly 40 hours per week and require approximately 56 hours of sleep each week (assuming 8 hours a day)

Humans devote approximately 21 hours per week on eating, preparation and consumption.

Around 10 hours per week are required for personal hygiene tasks such as showering and grooming.

We may devote 5 to 10 hours each week to housework, such as cleaning and laundry.

We may spend five to ten hours per week commuting or performing errands.

All of these activities are essential to our health, yet they still leave us 30 to 40 hours each week for pleasure, personal development, and pursuing our goals. Even after deducting the time we spend on other obligations, we still have sufficient time to accomplish something extra for our development.

Example

Activity	work	sleep	eating	hygiene	Chores	errands	Family/pleasure	Faith/spirituality	health
Hours/wk.	40	56	21	10	5	5	21	3	3

TOTAL =164

Even after this tight schedule, we still manage to have 3 hrs. to read and advance in our field. You need to develop your own and allocate your personal activities and time required in your situation.

Then why do we still feel as though we lack sufficient time? Because we frequently waste time on irrelevant or useless tasks. We become engrossed in social media, binge-watching television, and other types of entertainment that bring little value to our lives. We may also put off vital chores or devote an excessive amount of time to pointless pastimes.

Effective strategies to manage time:

Determine your priorities: Take some time to consider what is significant to you. What are your aspirations and objectives? What activities give you a sense of fulfillment or purpose? Create a list of your priorities and use it to guide your time management decisions.

Time your activities: Build an agenda that reflects your top priorities. Schedule time for work, sleep, and other essential activities, but also set aside time for pleasure, personal development, and goal pursuit.

Be conscious of how you spend your time and avoid distractions that can divert your attention from your priorities. When you need to focus on critical tasks, disable your phone and notifications. Use apps or other time-management aids to better manage your time.

If you have a dauntingly large objective, break it down into smaller, more doable steps. Even if you feel like you don't have much time, this can make it simpler to get started and make progress.

Learn to say "no" to activities or obligations that do not line with your priorities. This can be challenging if you are accustomed to saying "yes" to everything. But, by saying "no," you will have more time for the things that are most important to you.

The common but mistaken belief that there isn't enough time to reach our goals or grow as individuals is at the heart of procrastination. The realization that we have more time than we give ourselves credit for and the application of that time wisely may help us overcome this excuse and realize our full potential. Keep in mind that time is limited, and make the most of it.

ABC Tasking Method

Discover the secret to accomplishing more with less time on your hands! Introducing the incredible ABC Tasking System - your ultimate productivity booster. This user-friendly and efficient method is designed to supercharge your progress while elevating the quality of your results. Say goodbye to sluggish performance and embrace the fast track to achieving your goals. Experience the transformative power of the ABC Tasking System and unlock your full potential today!

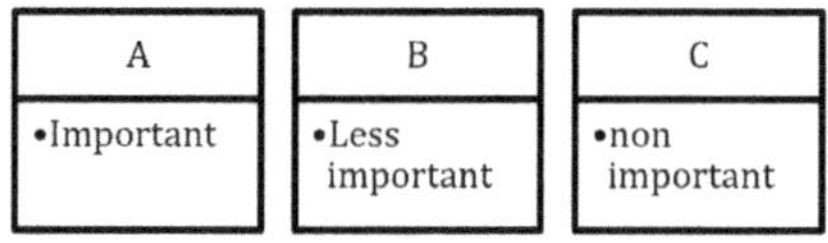

Priorities for tasks are determined using the ABC Tasking System, which takes into account both the importance and the urgency of each job. There are three tiers of assignments: "A" assignments, "B" assignments, and "C" assignments.

An A-list task is one that has to be done right away because it's crucial and time-sensitive. These are the things that can make or break your timelines and objectives.

The work in the B category is critical, but it is not as pressing as the work in the A category. Even though they come second to the A-list, these tasks nevertheless need to be finished before the C-list.

Things that need to be done, but aren't a priority, get a "C" grade. This work can be put off or given to another person.

The ABC Tasking Method can be put into action by following these steps:

Make a list of everything you have to do. Jot down everything that needs to be done. If you do this, you'll have a good grasp on what has to be accomplished.

Prioritize: Using the ABC framework, rank the order of importance of each assignment.

Prioritize the A-list items first. These are the top priorities that need to be addressed right away.

Take care of B-level duties after wrapping up A-level ones. They should be prioritized above C-level tasks because of their significance.

C chores can be put off till later or given to an assistant. Some errands aren't as critical or time-sensitive and can wait.

TIPS FOR USING THE ABC TASKING METHOD

Use the ABC Tasking Technique effectively with these pointers.

Tasks should be reviewed on a regular basis, and priorities should be adjusted as needed. You can prioritize your work and avoid falling behind if you use this method.

Use a task tracking system, such as a to-do list or software, to keep tabs on everything you need to get done. Having everything in one place like this will help you avoid forgetting anything.

Don't set your priorities in stone; be adaptable and willing to shift with the situation. There are occasions when a B-level task becomes an A-level priority.

Tasks should be delegated to other people whenever possible. This will allow you to devote more time to the most pressing matters at hand.

If you're having trouble keeping track of everything you need to get done, the ABC Tasking System is a straightforward approach that can help you prioritize your work. You can speed up the process and improve the quality of your results by using this strategy.

EXAMPLE: always develop your **ABC tasking (for the day)** as soon as you get to the workplace or start your day

DATE	TASK A LIST
TASK C LIST	TASK B LIST

Personal Work Scheduling

In order to effectively manage one's time, it is necessary to create a schedule for one's own work. It aids in prioritizing work, keeping track of due dates, and striking a balance between work and personal life. Scheduling one's own work can be done in a number of ways, each with its own set of benefits and drawbacks. Four of the most common methods are discussed here: FCFS (first come, first served), SPT (shortest processing time), EDD (earliest due date) and Weighted Shortest Processing Time (WSPT).

First Come First Serve (FCFS)

A straightforward method of scheduling first-in-first-out (FCFS) ensures that jobs are completed in the order in which they are received. As a result, the order in which tasks are received determines the order in which they are done. FCFS works well when there aren't any deadlines or the deadlines aren't really important. It's a no-nonsense strategy that's simple to grasp and put into practice.

Shortest Processing Time (SPT)

In SPT, tasks are scheduled in accordance with their projected processing times. Short-running jobs are finished first, then longer-running ones. When time is of the essence and you need to get the most out of your day, this strategy is the way to go. You can get more done in less time if you give higher priority to tasks that need less mental processing power.

Earliest Due Date (EDD)

EDD is a method of scheduling in which jobs are completed in accordance with their actual due dates. The order of priority for completing tasks is determined by their due dates, starting with the ones that are due first. When time is of the essence and you must meet strict deadlines, this method is your best bet. If you want to avoid falling behind or having to start over, give higher priority to jobs with earlier due dates.

Weighted Shortest Processing Time (WSPT)

It is an approach to scheduling that merges SPT with priority scheduling. In weighted shortest path to completion (WSPT), activities are given a value that reflects how important or urgent they are. Priority is given to tasks having a greater weight over those with a lower weight.

The WSPT algorithm considers the expected processing time and the weight of each task when determining the weighted processing time. Each task's estimated processing time is then factored into the scheduling process, with the lowest-weighted task being performed first. The ability to efficiently complete tasks while giving priority to those that are most important is made possible by this.

When there are many tasks to complete, or when competing priorities must be balanced, weighted score task prioritization (WSPT) can help. With WSPT, you can prioritize the high-priority project while still getting the low-priority chores done in a timely way, for instance if you have a deadline for both the high- and low-priority projects.

Making a schedule for your workday is an effective method of controlling your time and increasing your output. The three methods of prioritization—First Come First Serve (FCFS), Shortest Processing Time (SPT), Weighted Shortest Processing Time (WSPT), and Earliest Due Date (EDD)—discussed in this chapter are applicable in different contexts and can be combined in different ways to create an efficient individual work schedule. Your goals, deadlines, and available time will all play a role in determining the scheduling method that will work best for you.

Example 1

job	A	B	C	D	E

Processing time(mins)	30	20	55	40	25

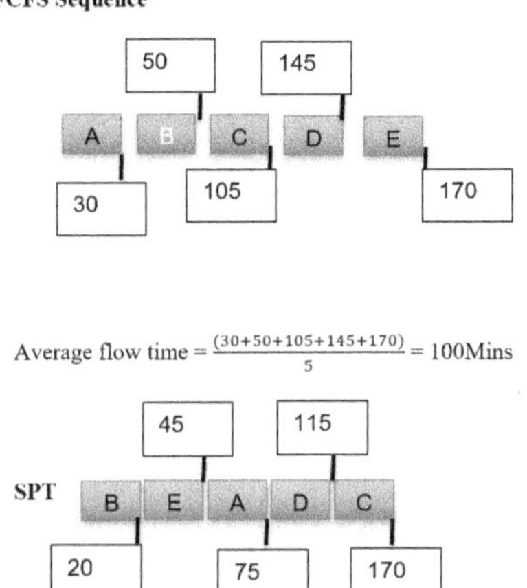

Average flow time $= \dfrac{(30+50+105+145+170)}{5} = 100\text{Mins}$

Average flow time $= \dfrac{(20+45+75+115+170)}{5} = 85\text{Mins}$

Job	Processing Time (in minutes)
A	5
B	3
C	8
D	2

In this example, we have four jobs (A, B, C, and D) and their respective processing times in minutes. To apply the shortest processing time method, we prioritize jobs with the shortest processing times first. This means that we would start by processing job D (which has a processing time of 2), followed by job B (processing time of 3), job A (processing time of 5), and finally job C (processing time of 8). By following this order, we can minimize the total processing time and improve efficiency in completing these jobs.

Top of Form

Using the SPT method and the FCFS method.

Using the SPT method, we prioritize jobs with the shortest process-ing times first, resulting in the following order:

Job	D	B	A	C
Processing time	2	3	5	8
End time	2	5	10	18

Average flow time = = 8.75Mins

FCFS

job	A	B	C	D
Processing time	5	3	8	2
End time	5	8	16	18

Average flow time = = 11.75Mins

John's Manufacturing Workshop Using Earliest Due Date (EDD) and First-Come, First-Served (FCFS)

John runs a small manufacturing workshop and has received four orders with different due dates and processing times. To ensure timely delivery and maintain customer satisfaction, John decides to compare First-Come, First-Served (FCFS) and Earliest Due Date (EDD) scheduling methods.

Scenario:

John has the following four orders:

Order	Processing Time (days)	Due Date (days from now)
A	3	8
B	2	5
C	4	11
D	1	4

FCFS Sequence:

John schedules the orders according to the order in which they were received (FCFS):

1. Order A
2. Order B
3. Order C
4. Order D

EDD Prioritization:

Using the EDD method, John prioritizes the orders based on their due dates:

1. Order D: Due in 4 days
2. Order B: Due in 5 days
3. Order A: Due in 8 days
4. Order C: Due in 11 days

Outcome:

By comparing the First-Come, First-Served (FCFS) sequence and the Earliest Due Date (EDD) prioritization, John can see the difference in scheduling. While the FCFS sequence follows the order in which tasks were received, the EDD prioritization focuses on due dates to ensure timely completion.

The EDD prioritization appears to be a more effective scheduling method, as it helps John avoid falling behind on orders with earlier due dates, such as Order D. Using the EDD method, John can ensure that his workshop meets strict deadlines, maintains customer satisfaction, and keeps his business running smoothly.

let's calculate the flow time for both First-Come, First-Served (FCFS) and Earliest Due Date (EDD) scheduling methods. Flow time is the time taken for an order to be completed from the moment it enters the system until it is finished.

Scenario:

Order	Processing Time (days)	Due Date (days from now)
A	3	8
B	2	5
C	4	11
D	1	4

FCFS Sequence:

1. Order A
2. Order B
3. Order C
4. Order D

Flow time for FCFS:

- Order A: 3 days (0 + 3)
- Order B: 5 days (3 + 2)
- Order C: 9 days (5 + 4)
- Order D: 10 days (9 + 1)

Total flow time for FCFS: 3 + 5 + 9 + 10 = 27 days

EDD Prioritization:

1. Order D
2. Order B
3. Order A
4. Order C

Flow time for EDD:

- Order D: 1 day (0 + 1)
- Order B: 3 days (1 + 2)
- Order A: 6 days (3 + 3)
- Order C: 10 days (6 + 4)

Total flow time for EDD: 1 + 3 + 6 + 10 = 20 days

Comparison:

The total flow time for FCFS is 27 days, while the total flow time for EDD is 20 days. The Earliest Due Date (EDD) scheduling method results in a shorter flow time compared to First-Come, First-Served (FCFS), leading to more efficient order processing and better utilization of resources.

Case Study: Minimizing Job Completion Time Using Weighted Shortest Processing Time (WSPT) in a Print Shop

Problem Description: A local print shop has received five orders with different processing times and priorities. The shop wants to minimize the total weighted completion time by scheduling the orders using the Weighted Shortest Processing Time (WSPT) rule. The print shop can only work on one order at a time.

Objective: Minimize the total weighted completion time using the WSPT rule.

Job Information:

Job	Processing Time (hours)	Priority (weight)
A	4	2
B	2	1
C	6	3

D	3	1
E	5	2

Calculating WSPT:

To calculate the WSPT values for each job, we divide the priority (weight) by the processing time:

WSPT = Priority / Processing Time

Job	Processing Time (hours)	Priority (weight)	WSPT
A	4	2	2 / 4 = 0.5
B	2	1	1 / 2 = 0.5
C	6	3	3 / 6 = 0.5
D	3	1	1 / 3 ≈ 0.333
E	5	2	2 / 5 = 0.4

Scheduling Jobs: To minimize the total weighted completion time, we schedule the jobs in descending order of their WSPT values. In case of a tie, we can choose any of the tied jobs. Here, we'll prioritize the job that came first.

1. Job C: WSPT = 0.5
2. Job A: WSPT = 0.5
3. Job B: WSPT = 0.5
4. Job E: WSPT = 0.4
5. Job D: WSPT ≈ 0.333

Calculating Weighted Completion Time:

Job	Processing Time (hours)	Priority (weight)	Start Time (hours)	Completion Time (hours)	Weighted Completion Time (hours)
C	6	3	0	6	3 * 6 = 18
A	4	2	6	10	2 * 10 = 20
B	2	1	10	12	1 * 12 = 12
E	5	2	12	17	2 * 17 = 34
D	3	1	17	20	1 * 20 = 20

Total Weighted Completion Time = 18 + 20 + 12 + 34 + 20 = 104

By using the WSPT rule, the print shop can minimize the total weighted completion time to 104 hours. The optimal schedule for processing the orders is C, A, B, E, D.Top of Form

PERT (Program Evaluation and Review Technique)

The Program Evaluation and Review Technique (PERT) is a technique for managing projects that is used to create and maintain a schedule for complex endeavors. The PERT system has widespread application in many industries, including construction, engineering, and software development.

PERT consists of three main components: the activity list, the network diagram, and the critical path analysis.

Activity list: This is a list of all the tasks or activities that need to be completed in a project.

Network diagram: This is a graphical representation of the project activities and their interdependencies. It shows the order in which the activities need to be completed and the relationships between them.

Critical path analysis: This is a technique used to determine the critical path, which is the sequence of activities that have the longest duration and must be completed on time for the project to be completed on schedule.

BENEFITS OF USING PERT FOR TIME MANAGEMENT

- In order to better plan and manage the project's schedule, PERT provides a more all-encompassing and accurate picture of the project.

- Reducing the possibility of delays and enhancing the likelihood of success, PERT facilitates greater coordination between the many departments and teams participating in a project.
- Efficient and productive results are achieved through the use of PERT, which helps to locate and eliminate potential sources of delay.
- PERT's visual representation of the project and its dependencies facilitates better risk management.

Implementing PERT for Time Management

Here are the steps for implementing PERT for time management:

- Define the project scope: Clearly define the scope of the project, including its goals, objectives, and deliverables.
- Identify the activities: Identify all the activities that need to be completed in the project.
- Determine the interdependencies: Determine the relationships between the activities and how they are interdependent.
- Create a network diagram: Create a network diagram to visually represent the project and its dependencies.
- Determine the critical path: Determine the critical path by identifying the longest path of activities that must be completed on time for the project to be completed on schedule.
- Monitor progress: Regularly monitor the progress of the project and adjust the schedule as needed.

PERT is a valuable tool for time management in complex projects. By using PERT, you can improve planning, coordination, efficiency, and risk management, ultimately increasing the chances of success for your project.

Example of a PERT chart for a project to develop a new software application:

Task	Optimistic Time	Most Likely Time	Pessimistic Time	Expected Time	Predecessors
A	4 days	7 days	10 days	7 days	None
B	2 days	3 days	5 days	3 days	A
C	6 days	8 days	12 days	8 days	A
D	3 days	5 days	6 days	5 days	B, C
E	2 days	4 days	6 days	4 days	D
F	1 day	2 days	4 days	2 days	D
G	4 days	6 days	8 days	6 days	E
H	3 days	4 days	6 days	4 days	F, G

In this example, we have eight tasks (A, B, C, D, E, F, G, and H) required to develop a new software application. For each task, we have estimated the optimistic, most likely, and pessimistic completion times, and calculated the expected completion time using the PERT formula: Expected Time = (Optimistic Time + 4 x Most Likely Time + Pessimistic Time) / 6.

We have also identified the predecessors for each task, which represent the tasks that must be completed before each task can begin.

USE EXCEL TO DRAW

Using this PERT chart, we can calculate the critical path, which represents the sequence of tasks that must be completed on time in order to complete the project on schedule. In this example, the critical path is A-C-D-E-G-H, which has a total expected completion time of 35 days. Any delays in these tasks would result in a delay in the overall project completion time.

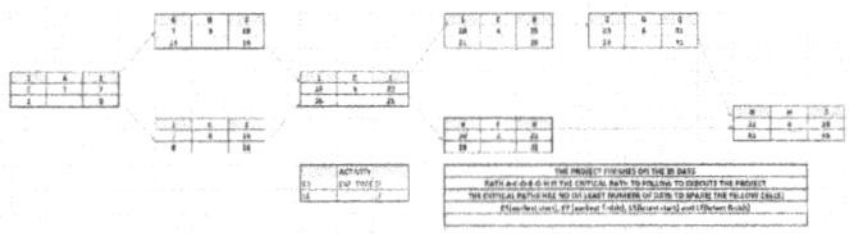

By using a PERT chart to map out the tasks required for a project, we can more accurately estimate the expected completion time, identify potential bottlenecks and critical tasks, and make informed decisions about how to manage the project to ensure timely completion.

Personal Kanban

One way to increase efficiency and better manage one's time is with the help of Personal Kanban, a visual task management system. It was modeled after the Kanban technique, which is popular in the fields of both manufacturing and computer programming. Effective work management and time allocation can be achieved with the use of Personal Kanban, a simple and adaptable solution.

Personal Kanban consists of three main components: the task board, the sticky notes, and the visual indicators.

Task board: This is a board or a whiteboard where you will list your tasks.

Sticky notes: These are small pieces of paper or notepads that you will use to write down your tasks.

Visual indicators: These are symbols or color codes that you will use to indicate the status of your tasks, such as to-do, in progress, and done.

Benefits of Using Personal Kanban

Personal Kanban helps you identify what you need to do and set priorities by providing a visual depiction of your work.

Improved concentration: Instead of switching back and forth between different tasks, which can reduce efficiency, you can use Personal Kanban to focus on only one at a time.

The ability to see what needs to be done and when makes Personal Kanban an invaluable tool for time management.

Personal Kanban is a flexible and user-friendly tool for organizing your work and keeping track of your progress.

Here are the steps for implementing Personal Kanban:

Have your task board ready by installing it in an easily accessible area.

Put your to-dos on paper by pasting them onto sticky notes and posting them on a task board.

Set priorities by bringing critical jobs to the top of the task board.

Assign visual indications: Use to-do, in-progress, and completed checklists and other visual indicators to keep track of your work.

Evaluate how far you've come: Check in on your progress at regular intervals and make any necessary changes to your to-do list.

For effective time and task management on an individual level, try Personal Kanban. It's easy to use and adaptable. Personal Kanban can help you achieve more mental clarity, attention, time management, and organizational efficiency, all of which will boost your professional and personal accomplishments.

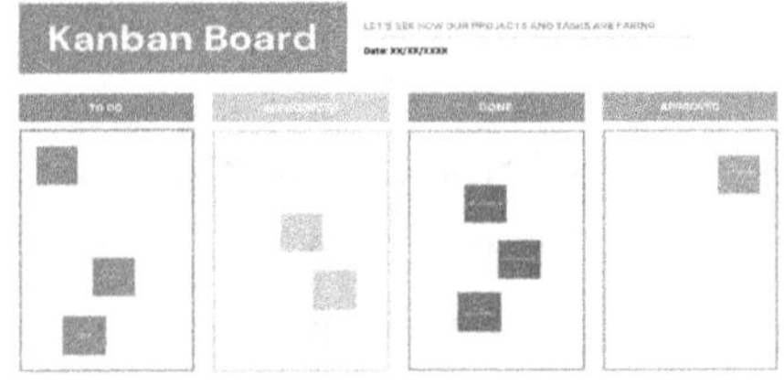

Prioritization in Life using the Law of Attraction and Pareto Analysis

It can be difficult to focus on what really matters in today's fast-paced environment. The Law of Attraction and the Pareto Analysis are two methods that can be used to zero in on what is most important to a person.

By putting one's attention on pleasant mental and emotional states, one can bring about those states in one's life, according to the Law of Attraction. The Law of Attraction is a powerful tool for bringing one's thoughts and behaviors into harmony with one's deepest values and life ambitions.

Steps to apply the Law of Attraction:

Choose which of your values and beliefs are the most significant to you.

See yourself acting in a way that is consistent with your ideals and enjoying the benefits of that.

Use affirmations to remind yourself of the good qualities and values you hold most dear.

Do something: Act in a way that is both consistent and congruent with your values and objectives.

Maintain an optimistic outlook by letting go of any limiting assumptions, behaviors, or feelings.

Pareto Analysis

Pareto Analysis is a method used to prioritize tasks based on their impact and importance. In personal development, this method can be used to identify the most important things in life and focus on them first.

Steps for Pareto Analysis:

Write down everything that matters to you: Compile a long list of your life's priorities.

Impose weights: give each item on the list a numerical value between 0 and 1 to show how important it is.

Arrange the elements in order of importance and start with the heaviest.

Concentrate on what really matters and drop the rest.

Repeatedly assess: Always ask yourself if you're putting your energy where it counts most, and if not, make the appropriate adjustments.

It takes insight, concentration, and action to determine what matters most in life and put them first. Individuals can use the principles of the Law of Attraction and Pareto Analysis as a guide for bringing their thoughts, feelings, and deeds into harmony with their values and objectives. With these methods, people can center their attention on what matters most to them and find more harmony and satisfaction in their life.

Chapter 20: Customer Focus

Prioritizing Clients using the Law of Attraction, Voice of Customers, and Kaizen Application

In order to keep customers happy, boost sales, and secure your company's long-term success, you must put them first. In this chapter, we'll look at how to prioritize customers using the Law of Attraction, customer feedback, and the Kaizen method.

One's ideas, beliefs, and emotions can bring about desirable experiences and events in life, according to the Law of Attraction. Focusing on good thoughts and feelings toward clients and cultivating a pleasant and helpful attitude towards them is essential for using the Law of Attraction to prioritize clients.

Customer satisfaction and loyalty can be boosted by maintaining a pleasant mental attitude toward those who make up a business' clientele. An upbeat and encouraging demeanor also facilitates clear communication and fruitful partnerships with customers.

Gathering and evaluating consumer input to better understand customer requirements, wants, and expectations is the goal of Voice of Customers (VOC) research. Prioritizing customers through the use of VOC requires individuals to actively seek out and listen to customer input, then utilize this feedback to guide their own decisions and actions.

Individuals can better serve their clients by prioritizing their interactions with them based on the insights gained from collecting and analyzing customer feedback. In this way, you can better serve your customers and earn their loyalty.

The Japanese term kaizen describes the practice of steadily bettering operational mechanisms. Kaizen can be used to continuously improve interactions with customers, which in turn increases customer satisfaction and loyalty in an environment where customers are prioritized.

If you want to apply Kaizen to customer service, you need to constantly assess your contacts with customers, look for ways to enhance their experience, and make adjustments accordingly. This can include trying out different methods of communicating with customers and learning from the results.

Putting customers first is critical for the health of your business, your bottom line, and your future prospects. Tools like the Law of Attraction, Voice of the Customer, and the Kaizen Application can help individuals prioritize customers and enhance their relationships with them. Increased customer satisfaction, solid client connections, and sustained professional success are all possible outcomes of employing these strategies.

Business SPINE to win more Clients

In today's competitive business landscape, having a strong foundation is essential for sustainable growth and long-term success. The Business SPINE, an acronym that stands for Specifying Your Target Client, Planning, Inspecting, Negotiating, and Excelling, serves as a blueprint to guide entrepreneurs and business owners in building a resilient and thriving enterprise.

The Business SPINE is a proven framework for businesses looking to succeed by focusing on their target client. The process consists of five steps: Specify, Plan, Inspect, Negotiate, and Excel.

Specify: In this step, you focus on identifying and specifying your target client. This includes researching your target market, understanding their needs, and creating a customer profile.

Plan: In this step, you focus on creating a plan to reach your target client. This includes developing a marketing strategy, creating a sales plan, and determining the best channels to reach your target client.

Inspect: In this step, you focus on inspecting the accuracy of your plan. This includes regularly reviewing your marketing and sales metrics, seeking feedback from customers, and making necessary adjustments to your plan.

Negotiate: In this step, you focus on persuading your target client to do business with you. This includes making offers, negotiating deals, and closing sales.

Excel: In this step, you focus on delivering excellence to your target client. This includes providing high-quality products or services, exceeding their expectations, and creating a positive customer experience.

Implementing the Business SPINE requires a focus on your target client and a commitment to excellence. To get started, begin by specifying your target client and creating a plan to reach them. Then, inspect the accuracy of your plan, negotiate deals, and deliver excellence to your target client. Remember, success in business requires a focus on your target client and a commitment to providing them with the best possible experience.

The Business SPINE is a proven framework for businesses looking to succeed by focusing on their target client. By specifying, planning, inspecting, negotiating, and excelling, businesses can improve their processes, increase performance, and achieve their goals. Stay focused, stay committed, and never stop seeking ways to provide excellence to your target client.

Case Study: Jeanne's Restaurant Using the Business SPINE Framework

Jeanne is a passionate restaurant owner who wants to expand her business and remain competitive in the challenging food industry. She decides to implement the Business SPINE framework to strengthen her enterprise's foundation and achieve long-term success.

Specify Your Target Client:

Jeanne begins by identifying her target clients. She conducts market research and discovers that her restaurant appeals to families and young professionals seeking quality food made from fresh, locally-sourced ingredients. Jeanne decides to focus her marketing and menu development efforts on catering to these specific customer segments.

Plan:

Jeanne creates a comprehensive business plan outlining her short-term and long-term objectives. She sets clear goals for revenue growth, customer satisfaction, and brand recognition. Jeanne also devises strategies to achieve these goals, such as investing in marketing, expanding her menu, and improving the overall dining experience.

Inspect:

To ensure the restaurant's continuous improvement, Jeanne regularly inspects her business operations. She gathers feedback from customers and employees, monitors key performance indicators, and conducts regular financial audits. Jeanne uses this information to identify areas for improvement and implement necessary changes.

Negotiate:

Jeanne recognizes the importance of strong relationships with suppliers, employees, and other stakeholders. She hones her negotiation skills to secure favorable deals with suppliers, ensuring high-quality ingredients at competitive prices. Jeanne also negotiates favorable terms with her employees, providing them with competitive wages and benefits in exchange for their dedication and hard work.

Excel:

Jeanne is committed to excellence in every aspect of her restaurant. She invests in employee training and development, ensuring her team is well-equipped to deliver exceptional service. Jeanne also stays updated on industry trends, continuously refining her menu and introducing innovative dishes to keep her customers engaged and coming back for more.

Outcome:

By implementing the Business SPINE framework, Jeanne strengthens her restaurant's foundation and drives sustainable growth. Her focus on target clients, planning, inspection, negotiation, and excellence helps her build a resilient and thriving enterprise. As a result, Jeanne's restaurant enjoys increased customer satisfaction, a growing customer base, and improved profitability, ensuring its long-term success in the competitive food industry.

Customer focus Optimization

Customer focus optimization refers to improving a business's performance by placing the customers' needs, preferences, and satisfaction at the center of its decision-making process. This approach helps organizations to enhance customer retention, increase revenue, and achieve long-term success. We will consider a simple example of optimizing customer focus in a restaurant setting.

Let's assume a restaurant wants to optimize its menu items and the quality of service to maximize customer satisfaction. The restaurant collects data on customers' preferences, ratings, and feedback for various menu items, as well as their experience with the restaurant's service quality.

Here, we will define a few key parameters and decision variables:
Parameters:

1. N: The number of menu items.
2. M: The number of service quality factors.
3. P_i: The profit generated by menu item i (i = 1, 2, ..., N).
4. R_ij: The customer rating for menu item i in category j (j = 1, 2, ..., M).
5. C_ij: The cost of improving menu item i in category j.
6. S_j: The customer satisfaction index for service quality factor j.
7. D_j: The cost of improving service quality factor j.
8. B: The budget allocated for improvements.

Decision Variables:

1. x_i: The binary decision variable for menu item i (1 if menu item i is selected, 0 otherwise).
2. y_j: The binary decision variable for service quality factor j (1 if service quality factor j is improved, 0 otherwise).

Objective Function: Maximize $Z = \Sigma(P\_i * x\_i) + \Sigma(S\_j * y\_j)$
Subject to the following constraints:

1. Menu improvement budget constraint: $\Sigma(C\_ij * x\_i) <= B1$ where B1 is the budget allocated for menu improvements.
2. Service quality improvement budget constraint: $\Sigma(D\_j * y\_j) <= B2$ where B2 is the budget allocated for service quality improvements.
3. Total budget constraint: $B1 + B2 <= B$
4. Binary constraints for decision variables: $x\_i \in \{0, 1\}$ for all i = 1, 2, ..., N $y\_j \in \{0, 1\}$ for all j = 1, 2, ..., M

This mixed-integer linear programming (MILP) model can be solved using an optimization solver to find the optimal combination of menu items and service quality factors to improve customer satisfaction within the given budget constraints. The restaurant can then use this information to make data-driven decisions that enhance customer focus and increase their overall satisfaction.

Lean Transformation

A lean transformation is a process of improving organizational efficiency by eliminating waste and increasing value for customers. This approach originated in manufacturing, particularly in the Toyota Production System, but it has since been applied to various industries and functions, including healthcare, software development, and service operations.

A lean transformation typically involves the following steps:

1. Define value: Identify the value that customers expect and are willing to pay for.
2. Map the value stream: Map out the processes involved in creating and delivering the product or service, and identify areas of waste and inefficiency.
3. Create flow: Design processes that minimize interruptions, delays, and bottlenecks, and create a smooth flow of work.
4. Establish pull: Produce only what customers demand, when they demand it, to avoid overproduction and excess inventory.
5. Seek perfection: Continuously improve processes to eliminate waste, improve quality, and reduce costs.

To successfully implement a lean transformation, it is important to have leadership commitment, employee engagement, and a culture of continuous improvement. Training and development programs may also be necessary to build the necessary skills and knowledge among employees.

The Leanness Equation

To create a mathematical model of lean, we can start by defining variables that quantify the level of activity (A) and waste (W) in a process. We can then create an equation to represent the lean index (L) as a function of these variables. Once we have the equation, we can apply it to real-world situations to optimize processes and minimize waste.

1. Define the variables:

- L(lean): Lean index, a numerical value representing the level of leanness in a process.
- A(activity): Activity index, a numerical value representing the total value-added activities in a process.
- W(waste): Waste index, a numerical value representing the total waste or non-value-added activities in a process.

1. Create the lean equation: **L(lean) = A(activity) - W(waste)**

   Normalize the value-added activities (A) and waste (W) by dividing each variable by the maximum possible value for that variable:

- *A_normalized = A(activity) / A_max*
- *W_normalized = W(waste) / W_max*

   Update the lean equation with the normalized variables:

L_normalized(lean) = A_normalized(always equal 1) - W_normalized

Now, the normalized lean index (L_normalized) will have a value between 0 and 1, with 1 representing a completely lean process with no waste, and 0 representing a process with maximum waste. This normalization allows for better comparison and interpretation of the lean index across different processes and industries.

1. Define additional variables: To make the model more accurate, we can include additional variables that represent different types of waste, such as:

- T(time_waste): The amount of time wasted during the process.
- M(material_waste): The amount of wasted materials during the process.
- E(energy_waste): The amount of wasted energy during the process.

1. Update the lean equation: **L(lean) = A(activity) - (T(time_waste) + M(material_waste) + E(energy_waste))**
2. Normalize the variables: To make the lean index more interpretable, normalize the variables to have values between 0 and 1. This can be done by dividing each variable by the maximum possible value for that variable.
   - *A_normalized = A(activity) / A_max or unity*
   - *T_normalized = T(time_waste) / T_max*
   - *M_normalized = M(material_waste) / M_max*
   - *E_normalized = E(energy_waste) / E_max*

   Now, update the lean equation with the normalized variables:

   L(lean) = A_normalized - (T_normalized + M_normalized + E_normalized)

   With this updated equation, the lean index (L) will also have a value between 0 and 1, with 1 representing a completely lean process with no waste, and 0 representing a process with maximum waste. This normalization allows for better comparison and interpretation of the lean index across different processes and industries.

3. Apply the model: To successfully apply the model, follow these steps:

a) Identify and measure the value-added activities (A) and different types of waste (T, M, E) in the process you want to optimize.

b) Calculate the lean index (L) using the updated lean equation.

c) Analyze the results and identify areas where waste can be reduced or eliminated. Focus on the highest waste contributors first.

d) Implement changes to reduce waste, such as process improvements, automation, or employee training.

e) Continuously monitor the process, measure the variables, and update the lean index to track progress and ensure ongoing improvements.

Remember that the mathematical model is a simplified representation of a complex process. In practice, you might need to consider additional factors or adapt the model to your specific industry or organization. However, this model provides a starting point for understanding and applying lean principles to optimize processes and minimize waste.

Let's consider a manufacturing process in a factory that produces wooden chairs as a practical example to apply the lean equation.

1. Identify and measure value-added activities (A) and different types of waste (T, M, E) in the process:

- A(activity): The value-added activities include cutting wood, assembling the chair parts, sanding, and finishing. A normalized A is always equal to 1 or unity.

- T(time_waste): Inefficient production scheduling causes workers to wait for 2 hours each day for materials or instructions.
- M(material_waste): Poor cutting techniques and inaccurate measurements result in 10% material waste.
- E(energy_waste): Old machinery used in the production process consumes 20% more energy than newer, more efficient models.

1. Collect data and normalize variables:

- Total value-added activities (A) = 8 hours of work per day (480 minutes)
- Time wasted (T) = 2 hours per day (120 minutes)
- Material waste (M) = 10% of total material used (0.10)
- Energy waste (E) = 20% of total energy consumed (0.20)

Normalize variables by dividing each by the maximum possible value for that variable. In this case, assume the maximum value for A is 480 minutes, the maximum value for T is 480 minutes, and the maximum values for M and E are 1 (100% waste).

- Normalized A(activity) = 480 / 480 = 1
- Normalized T(time_waste) = 120 / 480 = 0.25
- Normalized M(material_waste) = 0.10
- Normalized E(energy_waste) = 0.20

1. Calculate the lean index (L) using the updated lean equation:
2.

L(lean) = A(activity) - (T(time_waste) + M(material_waste) + E(energy_waste))

L(lean) = 1 - (0.25 + 0.10 + 0.20) = 1 - 0.55 = 0.45

1. Analyze the results and identify areas for improvement:

The lean index (L) is 0.45, indicating significant room for improvement. The largest waste contributors are time waste (T) and energy waste (E).

1. Implement changes to reduce waste:

- Improve production scheduling to minimize waiting times, reducing time waste (T).
- Provide training to workers on cutting techniques and accurate measurements to reduce material waste (M).
- Upgrade to newer, more energy-efficient machinery to reduce energy waste (E).

1. Continuously monitor the process:

Track progress by measuring the variables and updating the lean index over time. As you implement changes, the lean index (L) should increase, indicating a more efficient and less wasteful production process.

You can use the leanness equation (L = A - W) to assess personal performance. In this context, "A" represents your productive activities, and "W" represents waste or non-value-added activities. The goal is to maximize leanness (L) by increasing productive activities and minimizing waste.

Here's how you can use the leanness equation for personal performance assessment:

1. Identify productive activities (A): Make a list of the activities that contribute to your personal or professional goals. These activities should directly contribute to your growth, well-being, or performance. Examples include:

- Completing important tasks at work
- Learning new skills

- Exercising
- Networking

1. Identify waste or non-value-added activities (W): List activities that do not contribute to your goals or are counterproductive. These activities might consume time and resources without providing any real value. Examples include:

- Procrastination
- Unnecessary meetings
- Excessive social media usage
- Multitasking

1. Analyze your daily routine: Analyze your daily routine and allocate time spent on productive activities (A) and waste activities (W). To make this process easier, consider using a time-tracking tool or maintaining a daily activity log.
2. Calculate your leanness (L) score: Using the leanness equation ($L = A - W$), subtract the time spent on waste activities (W) from the time spent on productive activities (A) to get your leanness score.
3. Interpret your leanness score: A positive leanness score indicates that you are spending more time on productive activities than on waste activities, whereas a negative score suggests that waste activities consume more of your time. The higher your leanness score, the more efficient your personal performance.
4. Develop strategies for improvement: Identify areas where you can reduce waste activities and increase productive activities. This might involve setting clear priorities, improving time management, or implementing habits that promote focus and productivity.
5. Monitor progress and adjust as needed: Continuously track your leanness score over time and make adjustments to your habits and routines as needed. This will help you maintain a high level

of personal performance and ensure that you're making the most of your time and resources.

By using the leanness equation to assess personal performance, you can gain valuable insights into how your daily activities align with your goals and identify areas for improvement. With this information, you can develop strategies to increase your productivity, efficiency, and overall personal performance.

Sigma Level

Sigma level, also known as process sigma, is a measure of process capability and performance in Six Sigma methodology. It represents how well a process meets customer requirements and expectations by quantifying the number of defects per million opportunities (DPMO). A higher sigma level indicates a more capable and less variable process, resulting in fewer defects and increased customer satisfaction.

The sigma levels are based on standard deviations from the mean of a normal distribution. Each sigma level corresponds to a specific DPMO value, which represents the number of defects you can expect per million opportunities. The table below shows the relationship between sigma levels and DPMO:

- 1 Sigma: 690,000 DPMO (69% defect-free)
- 2 Sigma: 308,000 DPMO (93.2% defect-free)
- 3 Sigma: 66,800 DPMO (99.379% defect-free)
- 4 Sigma: 6,210 DPMO (99.9937% defect-free)
- 5 Sigma: 233 DPMO (99.999943% defect-free)
- 6 Sigma: 3.4 DPMO (99.999966% defect-free)

To calculate the sigma level of a process, follow these steps:

1. Determine the total number of opportunities for defects in the process. An opportunity is a specific event or step where a defect can occur.

2. Count the number of defects that actually occurred during the process.
3. Calculate the defect rate by dividing the number of defects by the total number of opportunities.
4. Convert the defect rate to DPMO by multiplying it by 1,000,000.
5. Use a Z-table or a sigma conversion tool to determine the corresponding sigma level for the calculated DPMO value.

It's important to note that achieving a Six Sigma level of quality (3.4 DPMO) is considered the gold standard for many industries. However, the target sigma level for a particular process or product may vary depending on industry requirements and customer expectations.

Here's an example in a table format that demonstrates the sigma levels, corresponding DPMO, and defect-free percentages for a hypothetical manufacturing process:

Sigma Level	Defects per Million Opportunities (DPMO)	Defect-Free Percentage
1	690,000	69%
2	308,000	93.2%
3	66,800	99.379%
4	6,210	99.9937%
5	233	99.999943%
6	3.4	99.999966%

Let's consider a real-life example:

Suppose a company manufactures electronic circuit boards. The company has identified 5 opportunities for defects per circuit board produced. Over the course of one month, they produce 10,000 circuit boards and find 800 defects.

To calculate the sigma level of the manufacturing process, we can use the following formula:

Sigma Level = (Total Opportunities - Total Defects) / (Total Opportunities * Number of Units) * 6

1. First, calculate the total opportunities for defects in the month: Total Opportunities = Opportunities per Circuit Board * Number of Circuit Boards Total Opportunities = 5 * 10,000 Total Opportunities = 50,000
2. Next, determine the total defects, which is already given as 800.
1. Now, apply the formula to calculate the sigma level:

Sigma Level = (50,000 - 800) / (50,000 * 10,000) * 6 Sigma Level = (49,200) / (500,000,000) * 6 Sigma Level ≈ 0.0000984 * 6 Sigma Level ≈ 0.0005904

To convert the sigma level to a standard Z-score, multiply by the standard normal deviate, which is approximately 3.4:

Z-score ≈ 0.0005904 * 3.4 Z-score ≈ 2.007

The manufacturing process has a sigma level of approximately 2.007, which indicates there is room for improvement in terms of reducing defects in the process. A higher sigma level (closer to 6) would represent a process with fewer defects and higher quality.

Serving

It is possible to attain success in one's personal life as well as one's professional life by adhering to the age-old maxim known as the Golden Rule, which states, "Treat others as you would like to be treated." The potency of this rule can be increased even further by combining it with the idea that quantum states can be entangled with one another.

In quantum physics, the concept of quantum entanglement refers to a situation in which two particles become coupled in such a way that the state of one particle affects the state of the other particle, despite the fact that these particles are physically separated from one another. This idea may be applied to human relationships and interactions, which are situations in which our actions and thoughts can influence and impact the lives of other people in a significant way.

By treating others with respect and compassion and adhering to the Golden Rule, we are able to generate positive energy and vibrations that can have an effect on those in our immediate environment. In turn, this can lead to enhanced connections as well as increased prospects for success. When we think positively and act generously toward other people, we not only help ourselves but also the others in our immediate environment. This has the effect of creating a ripple effect of positive energy and influence.

In everyday language, this translates to being conscious of our ideas, words, and deeds and giving thought to the effect that they may have on other people. Even in trying circumstances, this requires maintaining a compassionate and understanding demeanor toward other people as well as treating them with justice and respect.

Individuals can harness the power of positive energy and connections to accomplish great things in their lives if they apply the concepts of quantum entanglement to the Golden Rule. This will allow them to achieve greater success. This strategy has the potential to result in stronger connections, a positive reputation, and increased chances for both personal and professional success.

The use of the Golden Rule in conjunction with the theory of quantum entanglement can be a potent instrument for achieving one's goals. By adhering to this principle and maintaining awareness of our thoughts, words, and deeds, individuals have the ability to generate positive energy and form connections that have the potential to result in wonderful developments in their life.

Additionally, attend to the requirements of those who are located in your immediate environment. This can be accomplished by engaging in acts of kindness, taking part in volunteer work, or simply focusing on the needs of those who are located in our immediate environment. When we go out of our way to assist other individuals, not only do we attract positive energy to ourselves, but we also set off a domino effect of generosity and abundance that spreads throughout the entire world.

Pay attention to your own personal development. Education, introspection, and simply taking stock of one's life are all useful strategies for achieving this objective in an efficient manner. You will be in a better position to help other people and to bring success into your own life if you focus your attention and energy on developing yourself rather than on trying to better the lives of others.

Becoming a good servant is one of the most important steps you can take to bring more success and happiness into your life. This is one of the most important steps you can take. Remember that the key to being successful in life is to focus on one's own personal growth and development while also serving the needs of others. This is the only way to achieve lasting happiness.

Combining Ignorance and Confidence for Success

There's a fine line between naiveté and confidence that needs to be walked in order to achieve success in life. Ignorance, here, is a lack of information about or familiarity with the topic at hand. Confidence, on the other hand, is the conviction that one can accomplish one's goals and the bravery to do so despite the danger of failure. Combining these two seemingly opposite characteristics can lead to extraordinary achievement.

The Influence of Ignorance

There are two ways in which ignorance can serve as an effective strategy for achieving one's goals. First, it encourages people to look at a problem from a different angle and be more open to new information. This openness to new ideas and points of view is a direct result of an absence of biases and preconceptions. Second, being uninformed might make you feel liberated. To take risks and explore new things without worrying about making mistakes, people need not be experts in everything.

Confidence

Having faith in oneself and one's abilities is equally essential. It gives people the fortitude to strive after their dreams despite the fact that they may not succeed. As an added bonus, having confidence can help you overcome the doubt and insecurity that can result from being uninformed. When people believe in their own abilities, they are more likely to try new things and pursue exciting chances.

Incorporating Both naiveté and self-confidence

Understanding the advantages and disadvantages of both naiveté and self-confidence is crucial for successfully harnessing their combined power. Naiveté can spark innovative solutions, but it may also result in mistakes and misinterpretations. On the other hand, confidence can fuel courage in the face of challenges, but it can also lead to losing sight of reality and reckless behavior. Striking the right balance between these two qualities is essential.

The fusion of naiveté and self-confidence offers numerous practical applications. Businesses can leverage this strategy in various areas, such as product innovation and market expansion. For personal growth, it can be instrumental in confronting fears and pursuing passions. The key is to find the sweet spot between the excitement of inexperience and the stability of self-assurance.

Blending naiveté and self-confidence can be a powerful combination. By embracing both qualities, individuals can capitalize on their strengths and mitigate their weaknesses, ultimately achieving their objectives and leading fulfilling lives. Whether in business, personal development, or other endeavors, the fusion of naiveté and confidence can lead to remarkable accomplishments.

Chapter 21: Ideation

Idea Generation Techniques

Idea generation, also known as brainstorming or ideation, is the process of creating, developing, and communicating new ideas. It's an essential part of innovation and problem-solving. There are various methods and techniques that can help facilitate idea generation. Some of the most effective methods include:

1. Brainstorming: This is the most well-known idea generation technique. It involves gathering a group of people and encouraging them to share their thoughts and ideas freely without any judgment. The key to successful brainstorming is creating an open and supportive environment where everyone feels comfortable sharing their ideas.
2. Mind Mapping: Mind mapping is a visual technique that helps organize thoughts and ideas in a hierarchical structure. It starts with a central concept and expands outward with branches representing related ideas or subtopics. This method helps stimulate creative thinking and can uncover connections between seemingly unrelated concepts.

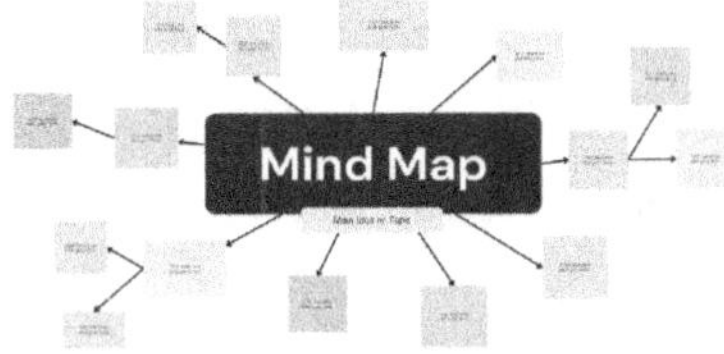

3. SCAMPER: SCAMPER is an acronym for Substitute, Combine, Adapt, Modify, Put to another use, Eliminate, and Reverse. This technique encourages you to think about a problem or idea from different perspectives, prompting you to find innovative solutions. It can be applied to products, services, processes, or any other area where innovation is needed. Here's a brief explanation of each element of the SCAMPER method:

Substitute: Consider replacing a part of your idea or product with something else. Think about what components can be swapped out or replaced with something different to bring a fresh perspective or enhance functionality.

Example: If you're developing a new type of chair, you might substitute traditional wooden legs with metal ones for added durability and modern design.

Combine: Explore ways to merge different ideas, concepts, or features to create something new and unique. Look for synergies between existing elements to enhance value or improve the overall experience.

Example: Combining a smartphone and a camera to create a high-quality camera phone.

Adapt: Modify an existing idea, product, or process to fit a new context or purpose. Examine how other industries or fields have solved similar problems and adapt their solutions to your situation.

Example: Adapting the concept of a drive-through window from fast-food restaurants for use in pharmacies or banks.

Modify: Alter or change a specific aspect of your idea or product to improve it or create new possibilities. This could involve changing the size, shape, color, material, or other attributes. Example: Modifying the design of a water bottle to include an integrated filter, allowing users to fill it

4. The Six Thinking Hats: Developed by Edward de Bono, this method involves wearing six different "hats" representing different thinking styles (White, Red, Black, Yellow, Green, and Blue). By adopting these different thinking styles, participants can approach a problem or idea from various angles,

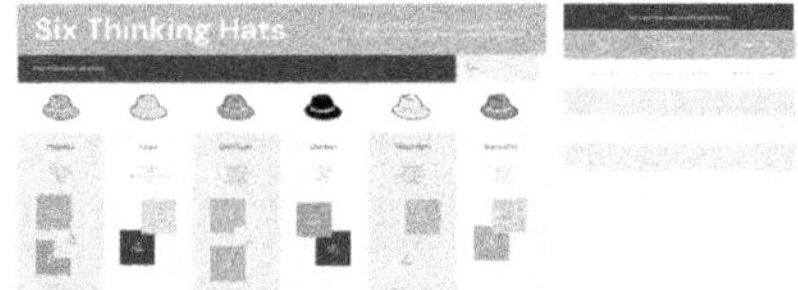

Manifesting a Business with Law of Attraction and SMART Goals

The Law of Attraction is a principle that states that we attract into our lives what we focus on and believe in. This principle can be applied to the process of generating and refining business ideas. By focusing on positive outcomes and visualizing success, entrepreneurs can attract the resources and opportunities they need to make their business a reality.

To use the Law of Attraction in business, it's important to set clear and specific goals. One way to do this is through the use of SMART goals. SMART stands for Specific, Measurable, Achievable, Relevant, and Time-bound. SMART goals help entrepreneurs create a well-defined plan of action that is both realistic and achievable.

To use the Law of Attraction for generating business ideas, individuals should focus their thoughts and emotions on the types of businesses they would like to start and imagine themselves being successful in those businesses. This visualization process can help individuals to attract and generate ideas that align with their passions, interests, and goals.

SMART Goals

Specific, Measurable, Attainable, Relevant, and Time-bound (SMART) Goals is a framework for defining and establishing objectives that meet these criteria. When it comes to launching a company, SMART Goals can be used to hone in on what's most important, eliminate distractions, and map out a path to profitability.

Individuals can benefit from using SMART Goals by first determining what they hope to accomplish and then checking that their goal is SMART (specific, measurable, attainable, relevant, and timely). An individual might plan to open a business selling handmade jewelry and aim to make $50,000 in the first year.

With its emphasis on specific, measurable, achievable, relevant, and timely goals, the SMART Goals framework can be a powerful instrument for honing and clarifying business concepts.

The Law of Attraction and SMART Goals are powerful tools that can help individuals generate and refine ideas for starting a business, which requires a great idea and a well-defined plan for success. Using these strategies, one can draw in and generate ideas that are congruent with their values, interests, and objectives, and craft a clear path to fulfillment.

Manifesting a Business Idea	Law of Attraction	SMART Goals
Step 1	Visualize your business idea: Focus on your vision and imagine it becoming a reality.	Specific: Clearly define your business idea and its purpose.
Step 2	Positivity: Maintain a positive mindset and believe in the success of your idea.	Measurable: Set tangible benchmarks to track progress.
Step 3	Affirmations: Use positive statements to reinforce your belief in the idea.	Attainable: Ensure your business idea is realistic and achievable.

Step 4	Gratitude: Practice gratitude for the opportunities and resources available.	Relevant: Align the idea with your values and passions.
Step 5	Take inspired action: Follow your intuition and seize opportunities that arise.	Time-bound: Set a timeline for achieving your business goals.

Case Study: Using SMART Goals to Improve Sales Performance

Company X, a growing technology firm, has been struggling with stagnant sales figures. The sales team has been working hard but lacks direction and a clear target to aim for. Company X's management decides to implement the SMART goal-setting framework to improve the sales team's performance and boost overall revenue.

Objective

The objective is to increase the sales team's performance by setting and achieving clear, specific, and measurable goals using the SMART framework.

Implementation

1. Specific: Management identified the need to increase sales figures, so they set a specific target for the sales team: "Increase the number of new customers by 20%."

2. Measurable: To track progress, the sales team was asked to record the number of new customers they acquired each month. This allowed management to measure the team's performance against their goal.

3. Achievable: Company X had previously identified untapped markets with potential clients, making the 20% increase a realistic and achievable target. They provided additional training and

resources to the sales team to ensure they were well-equipped to meet this goal.

4. Relevant: Increasing the number of new customers directly contributes to the company's overall growth, making it a relevant goal aligned with the company's long-term objectives.
5. Time-bound: Management set a deadline for achieving the 20% increase in new customers, giving the sales team six months to meet the target.

Monitoring and Adjusting

Monthly progress meetings were scheduled to review the sales team's performance and ensure they were on track to achieve the goal. These meetings allowed management to identify any challenges or obstacles the team faced and make adjustments as necessary. For instance, after three months, it became apparent that some team members were struggling to reach their individual targets. Management decided to provide additional support, such as personalized coaching and mentoring, to help these employees improve their performance.

Results

By the end of the six-month period, the sales team successfully increased the number of new customers by 22%, exceeding the original target. The use of SMART goals provided a clear direction and measurable objectives for the team to work towards. The monthly progress meetings helped keep the team focused and allowed for adjustments to be made as needed, ensuring the team's success.

This case study demonstrates the power of using SMART goals to improve performance in a professional setting. By setting specific, measurable, achievable, relevant, and time-bound goals, Company X's sales team was able to meet and exceed their target, contributing to the overall growth of the company.

JET Goals for Accelerated Success

Even though SMART goals are a tried-and-true way to set effective goals, there are other methods that can help people reach their goals even faster. Let's look at JET goals, which are a way to set goals that focuses on justification, examination, and deadlines. By using JET goals, you can get to where you want to be more quickly and efficiently.

Understanding JET Goals

JET is an acronym that stands for Justifiable, Examinable, and Timeline. This framework emphasizes the importance of creating goals that are grounded in reason, open to scrutiny, and accompanied by a clear timeline. Let's break down each component:

1. Justifiable: Your goal should have a strong rationale behind it, clearly explaining why it is worth pursuing. A justifiable goal aligns with your values, motivations, and overall vision.
2. Examinable: Your goal should be subject to ongoing analysis and evaluation. Regularly examining your progress allows you to identify challenges, make adjustments, and optimize your approach to achieve your goal more quickly.
3. Timeline: Setting a clear timeline for your goal helps maintain focus, urgency, and momentum. This is crucial for accelerating your progress and achieving success in a shorter timeframe.

Crafting JET Goals

Now that we understand the components of JET goals, let's explore how to create them:

1. Start with a broad objective: Identify a general area of improvement or a desired outcome, such as "I want to advance in my career."
2. Make it justifiable: Develop a strong rationale for pursuing your goal. For example, "I want to advance in my career to increase my earning potential and have a greater impact on my organization."
3. Ensure it's examinable: Establish key performance indicators (KPIs) that allow you to evaluate your progress, such as "successfully completing projects" or "receiving positive performance evaluations."
4. Set a timeline: Determine a realistic yet ambitious deadline for achieving your goal, like "I will be promoted within the next 12 months."

Applying JET Goals to Different Areas of Life

JET goals can be applied to various aspects of your life, including career, personal development, relationships, and health. Here are some examples:

- Career: "I will secure a higher-paying job within my field in the next six months by enhancing my skills through online courses and networking events."
- Personal Development: "I will become fluent in Spanish within the next year by taking weekly lessons and practicing daily with a language partner."
- Relationships: "I will deepen my connection with my friends by organizing a monthly get-together for the next six months."
- Health: "I will run a 10K race in under 50 minutes within the next four months by following a structured training plan and maintaining a healthy diet."

Monitoring and Adjusting Your JET Goals

Frequent examination of your JET goals is essential for accelerated success. Schedule regular check-ins to assess your progress, identify potential setbacks, and make necessary adjustments. This iterative approach helps you optimize your strategy and reach your goals more quickly.

JET goals offer an alternative framework for those looking to achieve success in a shorter timeframe. By focusing on justifiable, examinable goals with a clear timeline, you can work more efficiently and effectively toward your desired outcomes. With regular monitoring and adjustments, JET goals can help you make rapid progress in all areas of your life.

SMART and JET Goals Relationship

Criteria	SMART Goals	JET Goals
Acronym	Specific, Measurable, Achievable, Relevant, Time-bound	Justifiable, Examinable, Timeline
Purpose	Creating clear, actionable goals that lead to success	Achieving desired outcomes more efficiently and expediently
Focus	Specificity, measurability, attainability, relevance, and deadlines	Rationale, ongoing analysis, and clear timelines
Applications	Career, personal development, relationships, health	Career, personal development, relationships, health
Monitoring	Regular review and adjustment of goals as needed	Frequent examination and adjustment for accelerated success
Outcome	Effective goal-setting that drives consistent progress and motivation	Optimized strategy for rapid progress towards desired goals

Case Study: Selim's Baby Soap Business Using the JET Framework

Selim is an aspiring entrepreneur who wants to build a successful baby soap business. He understands the importance of setting clear and achievable goals and decides to use the JET framework to guide his journey.

Justifiable:

Selim's goal of creating a baby soap business is justifiable for several reasons:

- He has identified a demand for high-quality, natural, and eco-friendly baby soaps in the market.
- Selim is passionate about providing safe and gentle products for babies and their parents.
- He believes that his business aligns with his values, motivations, and overall vision for a healthier, more environmentally conscious world.

Examinable:

To ensure his goal is examinable, Selim establishes a system for ongoing analysis and evaluation:

- He sets up key performance indicators (KPIs) to track his progress, such as sales growth, customer satisfaction, and market share.
- Selim regularly reviews customer feedback, market trends, and competitor analysis to identify challenges and make adjustments to his products and strategies.
- He uses this information to optimize his approach, ensuring that his baby soap business remains competitive and successful.

Timeline:

Selim sets a clear timeline for his baby soap business goal:

- He outlines a detailed business plan with specific milestones and deadlines, such as finalizing the product formulation, securing suppliers, launching the product, and achieving specific sales targets.
- Selim's timeline also includes intermediate goals, such as developing a brand identity, building an online presence, and establishing retail partnerships.
- He maintains focus, urgency, and momentum by regularly revisiting his timeline and adjusting it as necessary to ensure that he is on track to achieve his goal.

Outcome:

By applying the JET framework, Selim successfully creates a thriving baby soap business. His justifiable goal, coupled with ongoing examination and a clear timeline, helps him navigate challenges, optimize his approach, and achieve success in a shorter timeframe. As a result, Selim's baby soap business gains a strong reputation for providing high-quality, natural, and eco-friendly products, ultimately contributing to a healthier and more sustainable world for both babies and their parents.

The I.D.E.A.S Method to Achieve Any Goal

Use the I.D.E.A.S. technique to make positive changes in your life. This remarkable five-step plan is intended to launch you toward your goals and turn your dreams into actionable reality. Let's explore the exciting journey towards a future full of possibilities and long-lasting positive change. The incredible I.D.E.A.S. method can help you turn your dreams into reality.

The I.D.E.A.S method is a powerful tool for setting and achieving your goals in life. By following these five steps, you can turn your dreams into reality and make lasting change in your life.

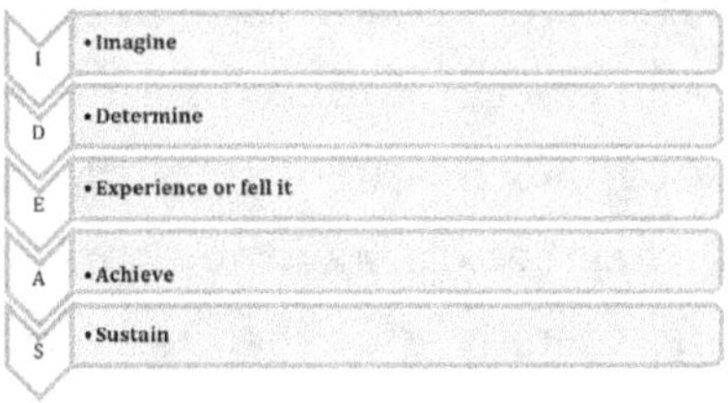

I - Imagine (Clarify Your Goal)

The first step in the I.D.E.A.S method is to imagine your goal clearly. Take the time to think about what it is that you truly want and write it down in detail. What will your life look like when you have achieved this goal? How will you feel? By visualizing your goal in this way, you are creating a roadmap to guide you towards its attainment.

D - Determine (Effort to Make it Possible)

Next, determine what effort will be required to make your goal a reality. This may involve breaking it down into smaller, more manageable steps. Consider what resources you will need, and what obstacles you may face along the way. Make a plan for how you will overcome these challenges and keep moving forward towards your goal.

E - Experience (Assume You Have It)

The third step is to experience your goal as if you have already achieved it. This means that you should act as if it is already a part of your life. Visualize yourself enjoying the benefits of your goal, and think about how it has changed your life for the better. This will help to create a sense of urgency and motivation to work towards making it a reality.

A – Achieve/Action

With a clear vision of your goal and a plan in place, it's time to start taking action. This is the stage where you put your plan into action and start making progress towards your goal. Remember, progress is key - every step forward, no matter how small, is a step closer to achieving your goal.

S – Sustain

Finally, it is important to sustain your progress. This means that you must maintain your focus and commitment to your goal, even when the going gets tough. Celebrate your successes along the way and don't be discouraged by setbacks. Stay the course, and eventually, you will reach your goal and sustain it for the long term.

The I.D.E.A.S method provides a structured and effective approach to achieving any goal. By following these five steps, you can turn your dreams into reality and create lasting change in your life. So, clarify your goal, determine the effort required, experience it as if you have it, achieve it, and sustain it.

Case Study: Karim's E-bike Assembling Shop Using the I.D.E.A.S. Technique

Karim dreams of building a successful e-bike assembling shop, catering to the growing demand for eco-friendly transportation. To turn his dream into reality, Karim decides to use the I.D.E.A.S. technique to make positive changes in his life and launch his business.

Imagine:

Karim starts by visualizing his dream e-bike assembling shop. He pictures a well-equipped workshop with skilled technicians, a wide variety of e-bike models, and a strong customer base. Karim envisions his business as a leader in the e-bike industry, known for its quality products and excellent customer service.

Determine:

Next, Karim determines the necessary steps to achieve his dream. He identifies key milestones, such as developing a business plan, securing funding, finding a suitable location, sourcing e-bike components, hiring skilled technicians, and marketing his business. Karim sets realistic goals and deadlines for each milestone to ensure steady progress.

Experience (Feel it):

Karim immerses himself in the e-bike industry to gain first-hand experience. He visits e-bike shops, attends industry events, and connects with other professionals in the field. By experiencing the e-bike world, Karim gains valuable insights and a deeper understanding of his target market's needs and preferences.

Achieve:

Karim diligently works towards achieving his goals. He develops a solid business plan, secures funding, and finds a suitable location for his shop. He also builds relationships with suppliers to source high-quality e-bike components and hires skilled technicians to assemble the bikes. Karim invests in marketing and promotional efforts to create awareness and attract customers.

Sustain:

With his e-bike assembling shop up and running, Karim focuses on sustaining the business's success. He monitors key performance indicators (KPIs), such as sales, customer satisfaction, and market share. Karim continuously improves his products and services, based on customer feedback and industry trends, to ensure his business remains competitive.

Outcome:

By following the I.D.E.A.S. technique, Karim successfully turns his dream of building an e-bike assembling shop into a reality. His imagination, determination, hands-on experience, achievement focus, and commitment to sustainability help him create a thriving business that contributes to a greener, more eco-friendly future. Karim's e-bike assembling shop becomes a popular destination for customers seeking high-quality, sustainable transportation options, fulfilling his dream and making a lasting positive change in his life.

Chapter 22: Delegation

Delegating Tasks for Success using SWOT Analysis and RACI Model

Success in any endeavor is highly dependent on competent delegation of responsibility. Having the ability to focus on one's strengths and delegate those that are less well suited to others frees up time and energy for more important endeavors. In this chapter, we'll look at how to effectively delegate tasks in a business using tools like the SWOT Analysis and the RACI Model.

The SWOT Analysis is a technique for analyzing a project's advantages, disadvantages, prospects, and dangers. Success in an endeavor can be predicted using this method, and a plan of action can be formulated to deal with the most significant threats and opportunities.

By evaluating each team member's strengths and weaknesses, a SWOT Analysis can help determine which responsibilities are best left to which individuals. Once you have this data, you can design a delegation strategy that plays to everyone's strengths while minimizing anyone's weaknesses.

A member of the team who excels at keeping things organized might be a good fit for project management responsibilities. Tasks that require expertise that a team member lacks may be better handled by another member.

RACI Model

Assigning tasks and duties in a project or business venture can be done using the RACI Model. Responsible, Accountable, Consulted, and Informed is the abbreviation for these four terms. Using this model, you can make sure that everyone on the team knows their place in the delegation process and that responsibilities are clearly defined.

A RACI matrix or responsibility chart is used by Six Sigma teams to identify which people, teams, or departments have various types of connections or responsibilities to a process. The aim is for Six Sigma teams to understand who actually acts on or within the process, who needs to be informed about the process, who is ultimately accountable for the process, and who might offer valuable information about the process.

• **Responsible**(R) – the person or team who actually does the work or is fully in charge of the current activity. Example an employee

• **Accountable** (A)– the supervisor of that shift or the person R reports to.

• **Consult or consulted**(C) – is someone who knows the job because they performed a preceding task to make way for the current task or they have performed a similar task before. On some occasions, the C could be referred to as a SME (subject matter expert).

• **Inform (I)** – is a person who is waiting for this job or the current activity to be done to allow him/her to perform their work (a task after the current job).

Determining what jobs and obligations need to be assigned to whom is the first step in applying the RACI Model. The results of the SWOT Analysis will help them decide which team member is best suited to carry out each task. This method ensures that no one on the team is unclear about their responsibilities during the delegation process.

Both the SWOT Analysis and the RACI Model are powerful resources that can assist individuals in delegating responsibilities effectively, which is a critical factor in the success of any endeavor. These methods help people make the most of their team members' abilities, mitigate their weaknesses, and guarantee that everyone on the team understands their responsibilities during delegation. Successful ventures are led by people who know how to delegate tasks so that others can focus on what they do best while they save time and money

Task	Responsible	Accountable	Consulted	Informed
Develop marketing plan	Marketing team	Marketing Manager	Sales team, Product team	Executive team
Conduct market research	Market Research team	Marketing Manager	Sales team, Product team	Executive team
Design marketing materials	Creative team	Marketing Manager	Marketing team, Product team	Executive team
Create content	Content team	Marketing Manager	Sales team, Product team	Executive team

Execute marketing campaign	Marketing team	Marketing Manager	Sales team, Product team, Creative team	Executive team

In this example, the RACI table outlines the responsibilities and roles for a marketing project. The tasks include developing a marketing plan, conducting market research, designing marketing materials, creating content, and executing a marketing campaign. The RACI table assigns a role for each task, identifying who is responsible, accountable, consulted, and informed.

For example, the marketing team is responsible for developing the marketing plan, while the Marketing Manager is accountable for ensuring its success. The Sales team and Product team are consulted for input and feedback. The Executive team is informed of the progress and outcomes of the project.

By using a RACI table, teams can ensure that everyone understands their role and responsibilities in the project. This helps to increase accountability, improve communication, and ensure the project's success.

EX2. RACI Matrix for an online store

	Employee 1	Employee 2	Employee 3	Shift Supervisor
Take order	R	I		A
package		R	I	A
Ship	I		R	A

In many organizations, the RACI (Responsible, Accountable, Consulted, Informed) matrix is a commonly used tool to clarify roles and responsibilities for projects or tasks. However, some have updated this matrix to include an "S" for "Support." In this updated version of the RASCI matrix, the "S" stands for "Support," which can be used to identify the tools or resources needed to complete a job or task.

When planning a project or task, it's important to consider not only who is responsible for completing each step but also what tools or resources they will need to do so effectively. By adding the "S" to the RACI matrix, teams can more easily identify these tools or resources and ensure they are available when needed.

Here's an example of how the RASCI matrix with the "S" for "Support" can be used in a project:

Task	Responsible	Accountable	Support	Consulted	Informed
Develop Website	Web Designer	Project Manager	Graphic Designer, Front-End Developer	Marketing Team, IT	Stakeholders
Write Content	Content Writer	Project Manager	SEO Research Tool, Copy Editor	Marketing Team	Stakeholders
Plan Social Media	Marketing Manager	Project Manager	Social Media Scheduler	Web Designer, Content Writer	Stakeholders

In this example, the "Support" column identifies the tools or resources needed for each task. For example, the "Develop Website" task requires the support of a graphic designer and front-end developer to provide necessary design elements, and the "Write Content" task needs an SEO research tool and copy editor to ensure that the content is optimized and free of errors.

By using the RASCI matrix with the "S" for "Support," teams can ensure that they have the necessary tools and resources to complete their tasks effectively, making for a smoother and more efficient project overall.

The DELEGATE Framework - A New Task Delegating Tool

Effective delegation is an essential skill for leaders and managers, as it empowers employees, enhances productivity, and fosters a culture of responsibility and accountability. The DELEGATE framework is a new task delegating tool designed to help managers and leaders make informed decisions about assigning tasks to their team members.

THE DELEGATE FRAMEWORK

DELEGATE stands for Define, Evaluate, List, Engage, Guide, Assign, Track, and Evaluate. This framework guides leaders and managers through a systematic process of task delegation, ensuring optimal utilization of team resources and skills.

Define

Clearly define the task to be delegated, including its objectives, expected outcomes, and deadlines. Providing a clear and concise description of the task will minimize misunderstandings and ensure that the team member understands their responsibilities.

Evaluate

Evaluate the skills, competencies, and workload of your team members. Identify those who have the necessary expertise and capacity to complete the task effectively and efficiently.

List

Create a list of potential candidates for the task based on your evaluation. Rank them in order of suitability and availability to ensure that the best-suited team member is assigned the task.

Engage

Engage with the chosen team member(s) and discuss the task in detail. Ensure they understand the objectives, expectations, and deadlines, and provide any necessary resources or support.

Guide

Provide guidance and direction to the team member as needed. Encourage them to ask questions and offer feedback, while also empowering them to make decisions and solve problems independently.

Assign

Formally assign the task to the chosen team member, ensuring that they have a clear understanding of their responsibilities and expectations.

Track

Monitor the progress of the delegated task regularly, offering support and feedback when necessary. Tracking the task's progress ensures that it stays on schedule and helps identify potential issues or obstacles early on.

Evaluate

Once the task is completed, evaluate the team member's performance and provide constructive feedback. Recognize their efforts and successes, and discuss areas for improvement or development. This final evaluation helps to reinforce learning and promotes continuous improvement.

Implementing the DELEGATE Framework

To implement the DELEGATE framework, managers and leaders can follow these steps:

1. Define the task to be delegated.
2. Evaluate the skills, competencies, and workload of team members.
3. List potential candidates for the task.
4. Engage with the chosen team member(s) and discuss the task.

5. Guide the team member throughout the task, providing support as needed.
6. Assign the task formally to the chosen team member.
7. Track the progress of the task and offer support when necessary.
8. Evaluate the team member's performance and provide feedback.

The DELEGATE framework offers a systematic approach to task delegation, helping managers and leaders make informed decisions about assigning tasks to their team members. By following the DELEGATE framework, organizations can enhance productivity, empower employees, and foster a culture of responsibility and accountability.

Here's an example of using the DELEGATE framework to delegate a task:

EX1. Imagine you are a marketing manager who needs to delegate the creation of a new promotional video for your company's latest product launch.

1. Define: Clearly define the task as creating a promotional video, highlighting the product's features and benefits. Specify the deadline, video length, target audience, and any specific branding guidelines.
2. Evaluate: Assess your team's skills, competencies, and current workload. Consider team members with experience in video editing, scriptwriting, and project management.
3. List: Create a list of potential candidates based on their skills, expertise, and availability. Rank them in order of suitability for the task.
4. Engage: Discuss the task with the chosen team member(s), ensuring they understand the objectives, expectations, and deadlines. Provide them with any necessary resources, such as video editing software, product information, and branding materials.
5. Guide: Offer guidance and direction throughout the project, addressing any questions or concerns. Encourage the team

member(s) to make decisions and solve problems independently but remain available for support as needed.

6. Assign: Formally assign the task to the chosen team member(s), ensuring they have a clear understanding of their responsibilities and expectations.

7. Track: Monitor the progress of the video creation regularly. Schedule check-ins or status updates to ensure the project is on track and to address any potential issues or obstacles early on.

8. Evaluate: Once the promotional video is completed, review the team member's performance. Provide constructive feedback on their work, recognizing their successes and discussing any areas for improvement. This evaluation process helps reinforce learning and promotes continuous growth and development.

By following the DELEGATE framework, the marketing manager can effectively delegate the task of creating a promotional video, ensuring optimal utilization of team resources and skills, while also fostering a culture of responsibility and accountability.

EX2.

Step	Acronym	Description	Example
1	D	Define: Clearly outline the task to be delegated, its objectives, and expected outcomes.	Task: Design a new company logo; Objective: Increase brand recognition; Deadline: 3 weeks.

2	E	Evaluate: Assess the task's complexity, required skill set, and available resources.	Complexity: Moderate; Skill set: Graphic design; Resources: Design software, team members.
3	L	List: Create a list of potential team members who possess the necessary skills and experience.	Jane (Graphic Designer), Mike (Creative Director), Susan (Marketing Specialist)
4	E	Engage: Communicate with the selected team members and discuss their roles and responsibilities.	Meet with Jane, Mike, and Susan to discuss their roles, expectations, and collaboration.
5	G	Guide: Provide guidance, support, and resources to help the team members accomplish the task.	Offer design guidelines, access to design software, and regular check-ins for support.

6	A	Assign: Formally assign the task to the chosen team members, ensuring clarity of expectations.	Assign Jane as the lead designer, Mike as creative consultant, and Susan as marketing input.
7	T	Track: Monitor the progress of the delegated task and address any issues or concerns that arise.	Check in weekly to review progress, address concerns, and provide necessary guidance.
8	E	Evaluate: Review the completed task, provide feedback, and identify areas for improvement.	Assess the final logo design, give feedback, and discuss possible improvements for future projects.

This matrix, complete with examples, helps ensure a comprehensive and effective delegation process, leading to enhanced team performance and project success.

Chapter 23: Forecasting

Projecting Business Outcome using the Law of Attraction, Intuition and Forecasting

An essential part of running a successful business is being able to predict its future performance. Individuals can gain a more thorough understanding of the potential outcome of their venture and make educated decisions by employing the Law of Attraction, intuition, and forecasting. This chapter will discuss how to use these methods to predict business outcomes and succeed.

According to the Law of Attraction, similar things are drawn to one another. That's why it's so important to direct one's thoughts and energy toward good, attainable goals; doing so will attract those things to one's life. When applied to business, the Law of Attraction can bring about desired outcomes simply by visualizing and working toward them.

People can manifest their goals and dreams into reality through the power of positive thinking and affirmations. Because of this, people can more accurately predict the future of their company and keep their spirits up during trying times.

The individual's intuition is a potent tool for gaining insight into the future of a business venture. One's intuition can help them gain insight into their inner workings and guide them toward more rational decision-making. In the context of running a business, intuition can be used to foresee and evaluate possible outcomes of a venture. Business owners and decision makers can benefit from tuning into their inner guidance system by increasing their awareness of the implications of their actions.

FORECASTING

It is the practice of making predictions about the future by analyzing and extrapolating from existing information and trends. The purpose of forecasting in a business setting is to help anticipate and plan for potential outcomes of a venture so that decisions can be made with confidence.

Trend analysis, time series analysis, and regression analysis are all examples of forecasting methods that can be used to make predictions about the future and spot potential threats and opportunities. A person's ability to foresee and act upon an endeavor's potential outcomes is greatly enhanced by the application of forecasting methods.

Success in business hinges on being able to predict how things will turn out, and individuals can improve their chances of doing so through practiced use of the Law of Attraction, intuitive reasoning, and strategic planning. Individuals can better understand their businesses and the outcomes of their decisions by focusing on positive outcomes, listening to their intuition, and employing forecasting techniques. Individuals can attract success and prosperity with the help of these tools and techniques, and get the results they want from their business endeavor.

Prediction Models

Prediction models are used to forecast outcomes or trends based on historical data and various factors that influence the phenomenon being studied. Here are a few common prediction models used in different fields:

1. Linear Regression: Linear regression is a simple predictive modeling technique that establishes the relationship between two variables (independent and dependent) using a straight line. It's often used in sales forecasting, economics, and social science research.
2. Logistic Regression: Logistic regression is used to predict the probability of an event occurring based on input features. This model is especially useful when predicting binary outcomes, such as whether a customer will make a purchase or not.
3. Time Series Forecasting: Time series forecasting models analyze historical time-based data to identify patterns and trends, and make future predictions. Examples include the Autoregressive Integrated Moving Average (ARIMA) and Exponential Smoothing State Space Model (ETS).
4. Decision Trees: Decision trees are predictive models that use a tree-like structure to represent decisions and possible outcomes. They are particularly useful for classification and regression tasks, and can be easily visualized and interpreted.
5. Random Forest: Random forest is an ensemble learning method that combines multiple decision trees to improve prediction accuracy and prevent overfitting. It's widely used in various fields, including finance, healthcare, and marketing.
6. Support Vector Machines (SVM): SVM is a supervised learning model used for classification and regression tasks. It works

by finding the best hyperplane that separates data points into different classes, maximizing the margin between the

Enhancing Forecasting Using Lean Six Sigma: A Case Study

A manufacturing company is struggling with inaccurate demand forecasting, leading to stockouts, overstock situations, and high levels of waste. The company decides to apply Lean Six Sigma principles to enhance their forecasting process, reduce waste, and improve overall efficiency.

Step 1: Define the Problem The company identifies the key problem: Inaccurate demand forecasting is causing inefficiencies and waste in production, inventory management, and overall supply chain operations.

Step 2: Measure the Current Process The company collects historical data on demand forecasts, actual demand, production levels, and inventory management. Key metrics are identified to measure the performance of the forecasting process, such as mean absolute percentage error (MAPE), forecast accuracy, and inventory turnover.

Step 3: Analyze the Data Using Lean Six Sigma analytical tools, such as root cause analysis, the company identifies the main causes of inaccurate forecasting:

- Insufficient historical data: The forecasting model is based on a limited amount of historical data, leading to inaccurate predictions.

- Lack of collaboration: There is limited collaboration between different departments, such as sales, marketing, and production, which hampers the forecasting process.
- Overreliance on qualitative judgment: The company relies heavily on qualitative judgment, rather than data-driven methods, for forecasting.

Step 4: Improve the Process The company implements improvements based on the analysis:

- Enhance data collection: Collect and integrate more historical data into the forecasting model, including data from external sources such as market trends and seasonal factors.
- Increase collaboration: Establish cross-functional teams to share information and insights between departments, fostering a collaborative environment for better forecasting.
- Implement data-driven forecasting methods: Adopt advanced forecasting techniques, such as time series analysis and machine learning algorithms, to improve forecast accuracy.

Step 5: Control and Monitor The company establishes control measures to maintain the improvements and monitor the forecasting process:

- Regularly update the forecasting model with the latest data and continuously fine-tune the algorithms.
- Implement key performance indicators (KPIs) to monitor the forecasting process and identify areas for improvement.
- Hold regular cross-functional meetings to review forecasts, share insights, and ensure continuous collaboration.

Step 6: Evaluate Results The company evaluates the results of the enhanced forecasting process, which include:

- Improved forecast accuracy: The MAPE and other forecast accuracy metrics show significant improvement.
- Reduction in stockouts and overstock situations: Better forecasting leads to more efficient inventory management, reducing waste.
- Enhanced production planning: With more accurate forecasts, production planning becomes more efficient, and the company can better align its resources with demand.

Through the application of Lean Six Sigma principles, the company successfully enhances its demand forecasting process, resulting in reduced waste, improved efficiency, and better overall supply chain performance.

Chapter 24: Crisis Management

Companies and other institutions in the modern world need to be flexible enough to adapt to the unexpected. Natural disasters, technological failures, and internal conflicts are just some of the potential causes of a crisis. Managing a crisis well is essential for mitigating its effects and ensuring the continued existence of an organization.

Using crisis technique to manage crisis

The CRISIS MANAGEMENT framework is a comprehensive approach for businesses facing a crisis situation. The process consists of six steps: Contain, Resolve, Implement, Standardize, Improve, and Sustain.

Contain: In this step, you focus on containing the crisis situation. This includes taking immediate action to stop the crisis from spreading and prevent further damage.

Resolve: In this step, you focus on resolving the risk management aspect of the crisis. This includes identifying the root cause of the crisis, assessing the potential impact, and developing a plan to mitigate risks.

Implement: In this step, you focus on implementing the solution to the crisis. This includes executing the crisis management plan, communicating with stakeholders, and monitoring the situation to ensure the crisis is contained.

Standardize: In this step, you focus on standardizing crisis management procedures to ensure that similar situations can be handled efficiently in the future.

Improve: In this step, you focus on continuous improvement of crisis management procedures. This includes regularly reviewing and updating crisis management plans, conducting drills and simulations, and seeking feedback from stakeholders.

Sustain: In this step, you focus on sustaining the improvements made during the crisis management process. This includes maintaining updated procedures and plans, and continuously monitoring for potential crisis situations.

Implementing the CRISIS MANAGEMENT framework requires a commitment to preparedness and a focus on continuous improvement. To get started, establish clear crisis management procedures and plans, and regularly review and update these plans to ensure they are current. During a crisis situation, focus on containing the situation, resolving risk management issues, implementing solutions, standardizing procedures, improving processes, and sustaining the improvements made.

The CRISIS MANAGEMENT framework provides a comprehensive approach for businesses facing a crisis situation. By following the steps of containing, resolving, implementing, standardizing, improving, and sustaining, businesses can effectively manage crises, minimize damage, and ensure their continued success. Stay prepared, stay focused, and never stop seeking ways to improve your crisis management processes.

Case Study: Bread Baking Business Using the Crisis Management Framework

A successful bread baking business encounters a crisis when it discovers that a batch of bread has been contaminated with a foreign substance. The company must act quickly to contain the situation, resolve the issue, and prevent damage to its reputation and customer base. The business owner decides to use the Crisis Management framework to guide their response.

Contain:

The business owner immediately recalls the contaminated batch of bread, halting its distribution to prevent further damage. They also inform customers and stakeholders about the situation and the measures being taken to address the issue.

Resolve:

The business owner investigates the root cause of the contamination and discovers a faulty cleaning procedure in the bakery. They assess the potential impact of the contamination and develop a plan to mitigate risks. This includes enhancing cleaning procedures, retraining staff, and implementing additional quality control measures.

Implement:

The business owner executes the crisis management plan by implementing the improved cleaning procedures, retraining staff, and introducing additional quality control measures. They also communicate with customers and stakeholders, keeping them informed about the actions taken to ensure the safety and quality of their products.

Standardize:

The business owner standardizes the new crisis management procedures, ensuring that similar situations can be handled efficiently in the future. They document the updated procedures and incorporate them into their standard operating procedures (SOPs) and employee training programs.

Improve:

The business owner focuses on continuously improving their crisis management procedures. They regularly review and update their crisis management plan, conduct drills and simulations to test their response, and seek feedback from stakeholders to identify areas for further improvement.

Sustain:

The business owner is committed to sustaining the improvements made during the crisis management process. They maintain updated procedures and plans, continuously monitor for potential crisis situations, and ensure that employees remain well-trained and vigilant.

Outcome:

By using the Crisis Management framework, the bread baking business successfully navigates the contamination crisis. The swift and effective response helps to contain the issue, resolve the root cause, and implement improvements to prevent future occurrences. As a result, the business maintains its reputation for high-quality products, retains its customer base, and becomes more resilient in the face of future crises.

Managing Business Crisis using Pareto Analysis and DMAIC

In today's fast-paced business environment, companies face numerous challenges and crisis that can harm their operations, reputation, and bottom line. The most critical crisis may include financial problems, supply chain disruptions, regulatory changes, and technological failures. To manage these crises effectively, companies must have a structured approach to identifying and resolving the root causes of the problem.

Pareto Analysis is a tool that can help companies prioritize the most significant problems that need to be addressed in a crisis. It is based on the Pareto Principle, which states that 80% of the effects come from 20% of the causes. In a business crisis, Pareto Analysis can help identify the 20% of the problems that are causing 80% of the impact.

By using Pareto Analysis, companies can allocate their resources more effectively, as they will know which problems require the most attention. This tool can also help companies identify patterns and trends in their data and provide insights into the root causes of the crisis.

DMAIC is a problem-solving methodology used in Six Sigma, a quality improvement framework. DMAIC stands for Define, Measure, Analyze, Improve, and Control, and it is a systematic approach to problem-solving that can help companies effectively manage business crises.

Define: The first step in the DMAIC process is to define the problem. This involves identifying the specific issue causing the crisis and clarifying the desired outcome.

Measure: In this step, companies gather data and quantify the problem to get a clear understanding of the extent and impact of the crisis.

Analyze: Using the data collected in the previous step, companies analyze the problem to determine the root cause. This may involve using tools such as Pareto Analysis, cause and effect diagrams, or hypothesis testing.

Improve: In this step, companies develop and implement solutions to resolve the root cause of the crisis. The solution must be both effective and sustainable to ensure that the problem does not reoccur.

Control: The final step in the DMAIC process is to control the solution to ensure that the problem does not reoccur. This may involve monitoring the process and putting in place controls to prevent the problem from happening again in the future.

By combining Pareto Analysis and DMAIC, companies can effectively manage business crises and resolve the root causes of the problem. This structured approach to problem-solving helps companies prioritize the most significant problems and allocate resources effectively, resulting in a more efficient and effective resolution to the crisis.

Managing career crisis using VSM and GAP analysis

In today's competitive job market, individuals may face career crises that can harm their employment status, income, and future career prospects. These crises may include job loss, limited job opportunities, skill obsolescence, or changes in the job market. To manage these career crises effectively, individuals must have a structured approach to identifying and resolving the root causes of the problem.

VSM (Value Stream Mapping):

Value Stream Mapping (VSM) is a tool used in Lean methodology to identify and eliminate waste in business processes. In the context of a career crisis, VSM can be used to analyze an individual's current career path and identify areas of improvement.

VSM involves creating a visual representation of an individual's current career path, including their skills, experience, education, and job history. This allows individuals to see their strengths and weaknesses, identify opportunities for improvement, and determine their value proposition to the job market.

GAP Analysis

GAP Analysis is a tool used to compare an individual's current state to their desired state. In the context of a career crisis, GAP Analysis can help individuals determine the gap between their current skills and experience and what is required for their desired job or career path.

By using GAP Analysis, individuals can identify the skills they need to acquire or improve and develop a plan to close the gap. This tool can also help individuals determine if they need to change their career path or if they need to take additional education or training to achieve their desired state.

Steps to conduct GAP Analysis:

Define the desired state: Determine the ideal job or career path you want to pursue.

Analyze the current state: Evaluate your current skills, experience, education, and job history to determine where you stand in relation to your desired state.

Determine the gap: Compare your current state to your desired state to identify the gap between the two.

Develop a plan: Based on the gap analysis, develop a plan to close the gap, including acquiring new skills, seeking additional education or training, or changing your career path.

Implement the plan: Put the plan into action, taking the necessary steps to close the gap and achieve your desired state.

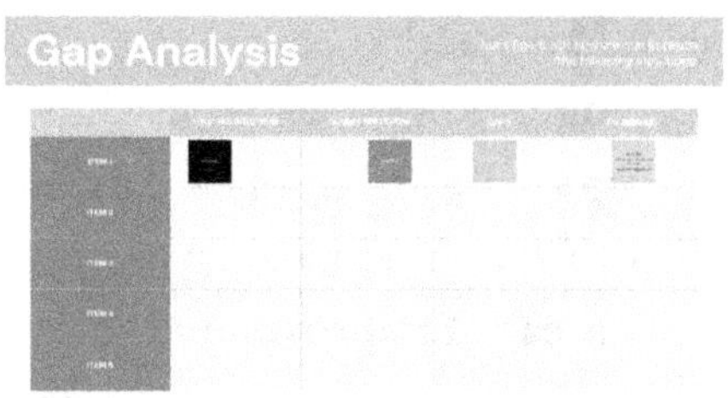

By using VSM and GAP Analysis, individuals can effectively manage their career crises and resolve the root causes of the problem. This structured approach to career development helps individuals identify their strengths and weaknesses, determine their value proposition to the job market, and develop a plan to close the gap and achieve their desired career path.

Overcoming Stagnation

Overcoming Stagnation in Life through the Law of Attraction, Bottleneck Analysis, and 5W2H Action Plan

Lifelong stagnation is frustrating because it prevents people from developing their full potential. The Law of Attraction, Bottleneck Analysis, and the 5W2H Action Plan are all potent methods for breaking through to a new level of productivity and success.

The Law of Attraction is the idea that like attracts like, and that individuals can attract positive experiences and outcomes into their lives by focusing on their thoughts and emotions.

Steps to apply the Law of Attraction:

Clarify goals: Clearly define what you want to achieve.

Visualize: Visualize yourself achieving your goals and imagine the positive emotions that come with it.

Affirmations: Use affirmations to reinforce positive thoughts and beliefs.

Take action: Take consistent and aligned action towards your goals.

Stay positive: Stay focused on positive thoughts and emotions and let go of negative beliefs and habits that may be holding you back.

Bottleneck Analysis is a technique for pinpointing the source of a process's slowdown so that it can be resolved. This approach can be employed in the realm of personal growth to pinpoint the roadblocks that have resulted in a standstill.

Steps for Bottleneck Analysis:

Identify the goal: Clearly define what you want to achieve.

Analyze the process: Break down the process into smaller parts and examine each part to identify any limitations or bottlenecks.

Prioritize: Prioritize the bottlenecks and focus on eliminating the most critical one first.

Take action: Take action to eliminate the bottleneck, whether it be through learning a new skill, seeking support from others, or making changes in habits or behavior.

Continuously evaluate: Continuously evaluate the process and make adjustments as necessary to ensure progress towards the goal.

The 5W2H Action Plan is a tool that helps individuals plan and execute actions to achieve their goals. The 5W2H stands for What, Why, Where, Who, When, How, and How Much.

Steps for creating a 5W2H Action Plan:

What: Clearly define the goal and the action to be taken.

Why: Identify the reasons why the goal is important.

Where: Determine the location where the action will take place.

Who: Identify the individuals involved in the action.

When: Set a timeline for when the action will be taken.

How: Identify the steps required to complete the action.

How Much: Establish the resources (time, money, etc.) required to complete the action.

Overcoming stagnation in life requires a combination of focus, planning, and action. The Law of Attraction, Bottleneck Analysis, and 5W2H Action Plan provide a framework for individuals to identify and eliminate limitations, clarify goals, and take aligned action towards their desired outcomes. By using these tools, individuals can overcome stagnation and achieve their full potential.

Reviving a Dying Business: Using the Law of Attraction and 5S

Reviving a failing company is difficult but not impossible. Businesses can reverse their luck by employing the 5S approach and the concepts of the Law of Attraction.

By keeping your mental and emotional energy directed on your goals, the Law of Attraction suggests that those things will eventually manifest in your life. If you want to see success in your business, you need to envision that success and actively pursue it.

The 5S approach is an approach to process improvement that emphasizes maintaining a neat and orderly workplace. Sort, simplify, sweep, standardize, and sustain are the 5S steps. Businesses can become more productive and waste-free by adopting these five practices.

The 5S technique and the Law of Attraction working together can revive a failing company. Businesses can generate success-attracting good energy by concentrating on desired results and maintaining a tidy, productive office.

Step 1: Sort

The first step in the 5S method is to sort through your business operations and identify areas that can be improved. This might involve streamlining processes, eliminating unnecessary procedures, and focusing on the activities that are most critical to your business. By focusing on what is important, you can create a more efficient and effective work environment.

Step 2: Simplify or set in order

The second step in the 5S method is to simplify your operations. This might involve reducing the number of suppliers you work with, cutting back on inventory, or streamlining your distribution channels. By simplifying your operations, you can reduce waste and increase efficiency, making it easier for your business to thrive.

Step 3: Sweep or shining

The third step in the 5S method is to sweep your workspace, both physically and metaphorically. This means creating a clean and organized work environment, as well as removing negative thoughts and emotions from your business. By focusing on positivity and creating a positive energy, you can attract success and revitalize your business.

Step 4: Standardize

The fourth step in the 5S method is to standardize your operations. This might involve creating standard operating procedures, implementing a quality management system, or using technology to automate processes. By standardizing your operations, you can ensure that your business is running efficiently and effectively, and that your processes are consistent and reliable.

Step 5: Sustain

The final step in the 5S method is to sustain the improvements you have made. This means continually monitoring your operations, making changes as needed, and staying focused on your goals. By sustaining your improvements, you can ensure that your business remains successful and continues to thrive.

By combining the Law of Attraction with the 5S method, businesses can revive a dying business and achieve success once again. By focusing on positive outcomes and creating a clean and efficient work environment, businesses can attract success and revitalize their operations. By following the five steps of the 5S method and sustaining their improvements, businesses can ensure that they remain competitive and continue to thrive in the long term.

Reviving a Dead Business: Using Value Stream Mapping (VSM)

Resurrecting a dormant company may appear impossible without the proper resources and methods, but it is doable with the right approach. Value Stream Mapping (VSM) is one such tool, since it is a process improvement strategy that may help firms find and reduce waste, boost efficiency, and resurrect their operations.

The value stream map (VSM) is a pictorial representation of the procedures carried out by a company. Its purpose is to map out a strategy for reducing waste, increasing efficiency, and capitalizing on potential improvements. Using VSM, firms can get an in-depth look at their operations, zero in on problem areas, and formulate a strategy to turn things around.

Step 1: Identify Current State

To use VSM to bring back an old company from the dead, you must first assess its current condition. For this purpose, you may wish to perform a process analysis, compile data on your operations, and develop a graphical depiction of your processes. In order to make progress, you must first take stock of where you are now.

Step 2: Analyze Current State

If you want to use VSM to bring life back to a dormant company, step two is to assess where you are now and pinpoint where you can make improvements. Finding ways to improve efficiency, cut down on waste, and simplify operations are all possibilities. Analyzing your current situation might help you learn more about your business's inner workings and determine what adjustments need to be made to bring it back from the brink.

Step 3: Create a Future State

Developing a vision for the company's future is the third phase in adopting VSM to bring a dormant enterprise back to life. This could mean coming up with brand-new methods, automating existing ones, or cutting down on unnecessary activity. In this stage, you will envision how your company will function after it has been revitalized and figure out what needs to be done to get there.

Step 4: Develop an Implementation Plan

Creating a strategy for putting VSM into action is the fourth step in resurrecting a failing company. Making a plan, finding the right materials, and figuring out how much money you need to spend are all possible next steps. The purpose of this stage is to guarantee that your company has a well-defined strategy for reviving its activities.

Step 5: Implement Changes

Putting into action the modifications you've identified is the final step in using VSM to bring back a dormant firm. Changing your supply chain or rearranging your office are also examples of how you can improve your operations. You can start revitalizing your company and making it more efficient and productive by adopting the adjustments you've identified.

Value Stream Mapping (VSM) is a tool that can be used to bring a failing company back to life. Businesses can revitalize their operations by developing a plan to eliminate waste and inefficiency. Businesses can guarantee their long-term success by adhering to the five steps of VSM and executing the improvements you've identified.

Chapter 25: Project Management

Project management is the practice of initiating, planning, executing, controlling, and closing projects to achieve specific goals within a specified time frame. It involves the application of knowledge, skills, tools, and techniques to manage and control various aspects of a project, including scope, time, cost, quality, human resources, communications, risk, procurement, and stakeholders.

There are several key concepts and components of project management:

1. Project life cycle: A project typically goes through a series of phases, from initiation to closure. The project life cycle provides a structure for managing the project and ensures that all necessary steps are taken in a logical order.

2. Project management processes: These processes provide a systematic approach to managing projects and include processes for initiating, planning, executing, monitoring and controlling, and closing a project.

3. Project management methodologies: Several methodologies can be used to manage projects, such as Waterfall, Agile, Scrum, Kanban, Lean, and PRINCE2. Each methodology has its own set of principles, processes, and practices, and the choice of methodology depends on the nature of the project and the preferences of the project team.

4. Project management tools: A variety of tools and software applications can help project managers plan, track, and control projects. Some popular project management tools include Microsoft Project, Trello, Asana, Basecamp, and Smartsheet.

5. Project management knowledge areas: The Project Management Institute (PMI) has identified ten knowledge areas that are essential for effective project management: integration, scope, time, cost, quality, human resources, communications, risk, procurement, and stakeholder management.

6. Project manager: A project manager is responsible for leading the project team, ensuring that the project objectives are met, and making decisions throughout the project life cycle. The project manager must have strong leadership, communication, and problem-solving skills, as well as a thorough understanding of project management principles and practices.

7. Project team: A project team consists of individuals with various skills and expertise who work together to achieve the project goals. The team may include members from different departments or organizations, depending on the nature of the project.

8. Project stakeholders: Stakeholders are individuals or groups who have an interest in the outcome of the project. They may include project team members, customers, suppliers, management, and other interested parties. Effective communication and stakeholder engagement are critical for the success of a project.

9. Project risk management: Projects often involve risks and uncertainties that can impact the project's success. Identifying, analyzing, and managing risks is a crucial part of project management to minimize potential negative impacts on the project's objectives.

10. Project performance measurement: Monitoring and controlling the progress of a project is essential to ensure that it stays on track and within budget. Key performance indicators (KPIs) can be used to measure various aspects of project performance, such as schedule variance, cost variance, and quality metrics.

Project management is a critical discipline for organizations that need to deliver projects on time, within budget, and with the desired level of quality. Effective project management requires a combination of knowledge, skills, tools, and techniques to plan, execute, and control projects successfully.

Project crashing

It is a technique used in project management to shorten the duration of a project by expediting or accelerating certain tasks or activities. This is typically done when a project is behind schedule or when there is a need to meet a specific deadline. Project crashing often involves allocating additional resources, such as personnel, equipment, or funds, to critical tasks. However, it is essential to weigh the benefits of reduced project duration against the increased costs and potential risks associated with crashing.

Example:

Consider a simple project consisting of five tasks (A, B, C, D, and E) with the following durations, dependencies, and costs:

Task	Duration	Predecessor	Normal Cost	Crash Cost	Crash Time
A	5 days	-	$2,000	$3,000	3 days
B	3 days	A	$1,500	$2,000	2 days
C	4 days	A	$1,800	$2,500	3 days
D	2 days	B, C	$1,200	$1,600	1 day
E	6 days	D	$2,500	$3,500	4 days

From the table, we can determine the critical path and project duration, along with the total costs under normal and crash conditions.

1. Identify the critical path:

- A → B → D → E
- A → C → D → E

1. Calculate the project duration for both paths:

- A → B → D → E = 5 days (A) + 3 days (B) + 2 days (D) + 6 days (E) = 16 days
- A → C → D → E = 5 days (A) + 4 days (C) + 2 days (D) + 6 days (E) = 17 days

The critical path is the one with the longest duration: A → C → D → E (17 days).

1. Calculate the total normal cost:

- $2,000 (A) + $1,500 (B) + $1,800 (C) + $1,200 (D) + $2,500 (E) = $9,000

1. Calculate the total crash cost:

- $3,000 (A) + $2,000 (B) + $2,500 (C) + $1,600 (D) + $3,500 (E) = $12,600

1. Determine the crash time for the critical path:

- 3 days (A) + 3 days (C) + 1 day (D) + 4 days (E) = 11 days

In summary, the project's critical path is A → C → D → E, with a normal duration of 17 days and a total normal cost of $9,000. If the project is accelerated (crashed), the duration will be reduced to 11 days, and the total crash cost will be $12,600.

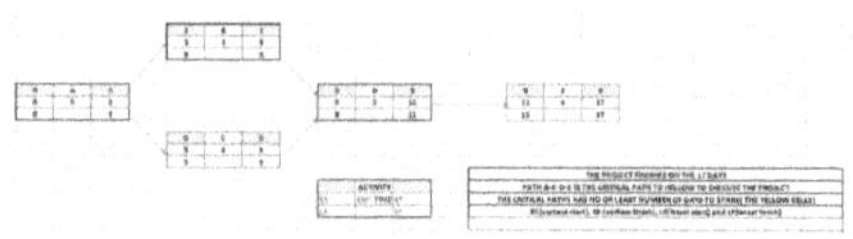

Project optimization

Consider a project management scenario where a company has three ongoing projects (P1, P2, P3) and three available employees (E1, E2, E3). The goal is to allocate the employees to the projects to maximize the total productivity while taking into account the productivity of each employee on each project.

Let the productivity of each employee on each project be represented by the following table:

P1 P2 P3

E1 5 4 6

E2 3 7 5

E3 4 6 8

For example, employee E1's productivity is 5 on project P1, 4 on project P2, and 6 on project P3.

Let's define the decision variables as follows:

- x_{ij}: The fraction of employee i's time allocated to project j, where $i = \{1, 2, 3\}$ and $j = \{1, 2, 3\}$.

Our objective is to maximize the total productivity:

Maximize $Z = 5x_{11} + 4x_{12} + 6x_{13} + 3x_{21} + 7x_{22} + 5x_{23} + 4x_{31} + 6x_{32} + 8x_{33}$

Subject to the following constraints:

1. Each employee's time should be fully allocated: $x_{11} + x_{12} + x_{13} = 1$ $x_{21} + x_{22} + x_{23} = 1$ $x_{31} + x_{32} + x_{33} = 1$

2. Each project should receive at least a specific fraction of an employee's time (e.g., 50%): x11 + x21 + x31 >= 0.5 x12 + x22 + x32 >= 0.5 x13 + x23 + x33 >= 0.5

3. Non-negativity constraints for all decision variables: xij >= 0 for all i = {1, 2, 3} and j = {1, 2, 3}

This linear programming model can be solved using an optimization solver to find the optimal allocation of employees' time to the projects that maximizes the total productivity while satisfying the constraints.

The DRIVE Method for Production and Industrial Project Management

Project management is a critical component of success in the production and industrial sector. Effective project management involves planning, execution, and monitoring projects to ensure they are completed on time, within budget, and to the required quality standards. The DRIVE Method is a proven and effective approach for project management in the production and industrial sector, based on five key principles: Define, Rehearse, Improve, Verify, and Execute.

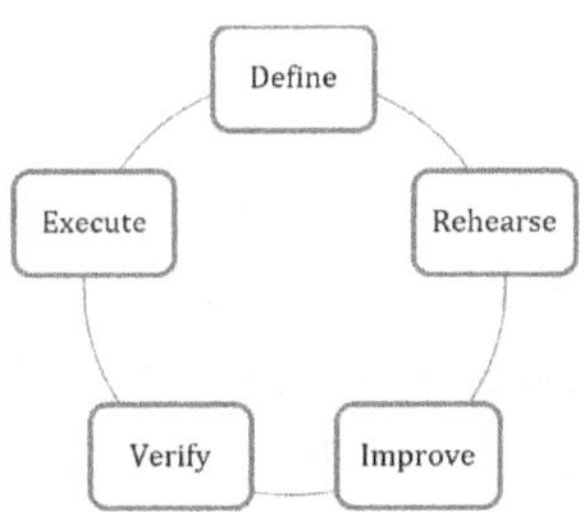

D - Define

The first step in the DRIVE Method is to define your project. This involves clearly defining the scope of the project, establishing project goals and objectives, and determining the resources required to complete the project. By having a clear understanding of your project, you can ensure that everyone involved is on the same page and working towards the same goals.

R - Rehearse

Rehearsing is an important part of the DRIVE Method, as it helps you to prepare for the project. This could involve creating project schedules, testing project processes, and running simulations to identify potential problems. By doing this, you can be better equipped to handle any challenges that may arise as you work on the project.

I - Improve

Improving processes and practices is a key aspect of the DRIVE Method, as it helps you to increase efficiency and quality. This could involve streamlining processes, incorporating new technologies, or seeking feedback to identify areas for improvement. By doing this, you can ensure that your project is running smoothly and efficiently.

V - Verify

Verifying your progress is an important step in the DRIVE Method, as it helps you to assess your progress and make any necessary adjustments. This could involve setting project milestones, tracking progress, and conducting regular progress reviews. By doing this, you can ensure that the project is on track and that any issues are identified and addressed early on.

E - Execute

The final step in the DRIVE Method is to execute the project. This involves putting plans into action, allocating resources, and monitoring progress to ensure the project is completed on time, within budget, and to the required quality standards. By executing the project effectively, you can ensure that the project is completed successfully and that all stakeholders are satisfied with the outcome.

The DRIVE Method is a powerful tool for project management in the production and industrial sector. By following these five steps, you can ensure that your projects are completed on time, within budget, and to the required quality standards. So, start by defining your project, rehearsing for success, improving processes and practices, verifying your progress, and executing the project.

Case Study: Increasing Customer Size Project Using the DRIVE Method

A marketing manager at a manufacturing company is tasked by her boss to increase the customer size for the next quarter. To achieve this goal, she decides to use the DRIVE Method, a proven project management approach that focuses on defining, rehearsing, improving, verifying, and executing projects in the production and industrial sector.

Define:

The marketing manager starts by defining the project's objectives, scope, and timeline. She sets a clear goal of increasing the customer size by 20% for the next quarter. To achieve this, she identifies key tasks such as market research, customer segmentation, creating targeted marketing campaigns, and setting up a system to track and measure results.

Rehearse:

The marketing manager conducts a thorough rehearsal of the project plan, identifying potential bottlenecks, risks, and opportunities. She gathers input from team members, stakeholders, and experts to ensure that the project plan is comprehensive and feasible. During the rehearsal phase, she adjusts the plan as needed, addressing any gaps or weaknesses.

Improve:

With a solid project plan in place, the marketing manager focuses on continuous improvement. She uses feedback from the rehearsal phase to refine the marketing strategies, streamline processes, and optimize resources. Additionally, she implements a feedback loop with her team, encouraging them to share their ideas and suggestions for improving the project's execution.

Verify:

Before the project's execution, the marketing manager verifies that all elements of the project plan are in place and ready for implementation. She checks that the necessary resources, such as budget, staff, and tools, are available and that the team is fully prepared and committed to achieving the project's objectives.

Execute:

Finally, the marketing manager executes the project plan, launching targeted marketing campaigns, tracking progress, and monitoring results. She maintains open communication with her team and stakeholders, keeping them informed about the project's status and addressing any challenges that arise during the execution phase.

Outcome:

By using the DRIVE Method, the marketing manager successfully increases the customer size by 20% for the next quarter. The thorough planning, rehearsal, continuous improvement, verification, and execution of the project ensure that the marketing campaigns are effective and well-targeted, leading to an expanded customer base and increased revenue for the company. As a result, the marketing manager's boss is impressed with her ability to manage the project effectively and achieve the desired outcome, positioning her as a valuable asset to the organization.

Project Management Using DMAIC

Project management is the process of organizing and coordinating resources to achieve specific goals and objectives. One approach to project management is the DMAIC method, which stands for Define, Measure, Analyze, Improve, and Control. This method is commonly used in Six Sigma, a data-driven approach to process improvement.

Define: The first step in the DMAIC method is to clearly define the project goal and objectives. This includes identifying the problem or opportunity to be addressed, defining the scope of the project, and establishing the criteria for success.

Measure: Once the project goal and objectives have been defined, the next step is to measure the current performance of the process. This may involve collecting data, conducting surveys, and gathering other relevant information to determine the current state of the process.

Analyze: The third step is to analyze the data and information collected in the measure phase. This may involve identifying trends, causes and effects, and other relevant factors that are impacting the performance of the process.

Improve: Based on the analysis, the next step is to identify and implement improvements to the process. This may involve making changes to the process, introducing new technologies or methods, and engaging with stakeholders to ensure that the improvements are sustainable and effective.

Control: The final step is to establish a system of control to ensure that the improvements are sustained over time. This may involve implementing performance metrics, monitoring systems, and regular assessments to ensure that the process continues to meet the project goals and objectives.

In conclusion, the DMAIC method provides a structured and systematic approach to project management, and can be used to improve processes and achieve specific goals and objectives. By following the five steps of Define, Measure, Analyze, Improve, and Control, project managers can ensure that projects are planned, executed, and monitored effectively, leading to successful outcomes and improved results.

BASICS method

One approach to project management is the **BASICS method**, which stands for Baseline, Access, Suggest, Implementation, Check, and Sustain. This method provides a simple and straightforward approach to managing projects.

Baseline: The first step in the BASICS method is to set a baseline. This involves establishing the current state of the process or project, and determining the starting point for the project. This may involve collecting data, conducting surveys, and gathering other relevant information.

Access: The second step is to access the situation and analyze the information gathered in the baseline step. This may involve identifying trends, causes and effects, and other relevant factors that are impacting the performance of the process.

Suggest: Based on the analysis, the next step is to suggest solutions to address the problems or opportunities identified. This may involve making changes to the process, introducing new technologies or methods, and engaging with stakeholders to ensure that the solutions are sustainable and effective.

Implementation: The fourth step is to implement the solutions suggested in the previous step. This involves executing the tasks and activities required to address the problems or opportunities.

Check: The fifth step is to check the results of the implementation and evaluate the impact of the changes made. This may involve collecting data, conducting surveys, and gathering other relevant information to determine the effectiveness of the solutions.

Sustain: The final step is to sustain the improvements made and ensure that they are integrated into the process over the long term. This may involve implementing performance metrics, monitoring systems, and regular assessments to ensure that the process continues to meet the project goals and objectives.

The BASICS method provides a simple and straightforward approach to project management and can be used to effectively manage projects and achieve successful outcomes. By following the six steps of Baseline, Access, Suggest, Implementation, Check, and Sustain, project managers can ensure that projects are planned, executed, and completed in a timely and effective manner, leading to improved results and outcomes.

Lean Transformation Project in a Furniture Manufacturer Using the BASICS Method

A furniture manufacturer is facing issues with production efficiency, waste, and long lead times. The company decided to undertake a lean transformation project to streamline their processes, eliminate waste, and improve overall performance. They choose to use the BASICS method for project management.

Baseline:

The project team starts by setting a baseline, documenting the current state of the production process. They collect data on key performance indicators (KPIs), such as lead times, production efficiency, defect rates, and waste. This information serves as the starting point for the project and helps to identify areas requiring improvement.

Access:

The project team analyzes the baseline data to identify trends and factors impacting the production process. They find that excessive inventory, poor communication, and inadequate training are contributing to inefficiencies and waste. The team also identifies opportunities for improvement, such as implementing just-in-time production, improving employee training, and enhancing communication among departments.

Suggest:

Based on their analysis, the project team suggests solutions to address the identified problems and opportunities. These include implementing a just-in-time inventory system, developing a comprehensive employee training program, and creating a cross-functional communication plan to improve collaboration among departments.

Implementation:

The project team begins implementing the suggested solutions. They work closely with employees and stakeholders to ensure buy-in and support. The just-in-time inventory system is put in place, reducing inventory costs and waste. The comprehensive training program is developed and rolled out, improving employee skills and reducing defects. Lastly, the cross-functional communication plan is executed, enhancing collaboration and reducing lead times.

Check:

The project team checks the results of their implementation by gathering data and evaluating the impact of the changes. They compare the new KPIs against the baseline data and find significant improvements in lead times, production efficiency, and waste reduction.

Sustain:

The final step in the BASICS method is to sustain the improvements made. The project team implements performance metrics and monitoring systems to ensure the process continues to meet project goals and objectives. They also schedule regular assessments to identify any potential areas for further improvement and maintain the lean transformation.

Outcome:

By using the BASICS method for project management, the furniture manufacturer successfully transforms their production process and achieves a lean operation. As a result, they experience reduced lead times, improved production efficiency, and decreased waste. The company's overall performance and competitiveness in the market are enhanced, leading to higher customer satisfaction and increased profitability.

The Creation Egg Technique for Innovation

Innovation is essential for the success of any organization, driving growth and ensuring competitiveness in an ever-changing market landscape. Many techniques have been developed to spur creativity and generate new ideas. One such approach, the Creation Egg Technique, offers a unique way to inspire innovative thinking and cultivate a culture of continuous improvement.

Here is an outline of the steps involved in the Creation Egg Technique, providing examples and insights to help you successfully implement this method in your organization or personal projects. By harnessing the power of the Creation Egg, you can unlock your team's creativity and pave the way for breakthrough innovations.

The Concept of the Creation Egg

The Creation Egg is a metaphorical representation of the innovation process, inspired by the idea of a bird nurturing and hatching its egg. It consists of five stages: Nesting, Warming, Hatching, Fledging, and Soaring. Each stage represents a distinct phase in the innovation journey, with specific goals and activities designed to foster creativity, collaboration, and experimentation.

Stage One: Nesting

In the Nesting stage, the focus is on creating a supportive and stimulating environment for innovation. Encourage your team to think outside the box and explore new ideas by:

- Providing necessary resources, tools, and training
- Establishing clear goals and expectations for innovation
- Fostering open communication and collaboration
- Celebrating successes and learning from failures

Stage Two: Warming

During the Warming stage, ideas are gathered, nurtured, and refined. Key activities include:

- Brainstorming sessions to generate a wide range of ideas
- Gathering input and feedback from stakeholders and customers
- Prioritizing ideas based on their potential impact and feasibility
- Developing initial prototypes or concept models

Stage Three: Hatching

The Hatching stage involves the transformation of ideas into actionable projects. This stage includes:

- Identifying and assigning resources, such as personnel, time, and funding
- Establishing project timelines and milestones
- Creating detailed project plans, outlining tasks and responsibilities
- Launching the project and monitoring progress

Stage Four: Fledging

As projects begin to take shape, the Fledging stage focuses on refining and improving the innovation. Activities in this stage include:

- Gathering feedback from customers, stakeholders, and team members
- Iterating and refining the product or solution based on feedback
- Identifying potential roadblocks and developing contingency plans
- Preparing for market launch, including marketing and distribution strategies

Stage Five: Soaring

In the final stage, the innovation is ready to make a significant impact. The Soaring stage encompasses:

- Launching the product or solution in the market

- Tracking performance metrics and measuring the success of the innovation
- Identifying opportunities for expansion, improvement, or new applications
- Celebrating the team's accomplishments and acknowledging their hard work

The Creation Egg Technique offers a structured, step-by-step approach to fostering innovation in your organization. By understanding and implementing each stage of the Creation Egg, you can create a culture of creativity and continuous improvement, leading to breakthrough innovations that drive growth and success.

As you embark on your innovation journey, remember that the Creation Egg is not a rigid formula, but rather a flexible framework that can be adapted to suit your organization's unique needs and goals. By nurturing and supporting your team's ideas, you can hatch groundbreaking innovations that take your organization to new heights.

Top of Form

The following table presents an example of the Creation Egg Technique applied to the development of a new drug. Each stage is represented, along with the corresponding activities and objectives.

Stage	Activities	Objectives
Nesting	- Establish a clear vision and goal for the new drug development	Create a supportive environment for innovation
	- Allocate resources (personnel, budget, equipment)	Encourage creative thinking

Warming	- Foster open communication and collaboration	
	- Conduct literature review and research on potential targets	Generate, gather, and nurture ideas
	- Brainstorm potential drug compounds	Refine and prioritize ideas based on feasibility
Hatching	- Gather input from experts and stakeholders	Develop initial prototypes or concept models
	- Develop detailed project plans	Transform ideas into actionable projects
	- Assign responsibilities and resources	Establish project timelines and milestones
Fledging	- Set up project monitoring and reporting systems	
	- Conduct preclinical trials	Refine and improve the innovation
	- Iterate and refine drug formulation based on trial results	Gather feedback from stakeholders and experts

Soaring	- Prepare for clinical trials	Identify potential roadblocks and develop plans
	- Conduct clinical trials	Launch and scale the new drug
	- Obtain regulatory approval	Measure the success and impact of the innovation
	- Develop marketing and distribution strategies	Identify opportunities for further improvement
	- Launch the new drug in the market	Celebrate team accomplishments

SPARK Model

The SPARK model, a project management and continuous improvement tool specifically designed for startups. SPARK stands for Strategize, Plan, Act, Refine, and Keep Improving. This model provides a structured approach to help startups identify their goals, develop a plan, implement changes, and monitor results.

1. **Strategize (S):** Start by identifying the startup's goals, objectives, and key performance indicators (KPIs). This stage involves understanding the target market, defining the value proposition, and setting strategic priorities.

Key activities:

- Market research and analysis
- Defining the target audience and customer segments
- Establishing the value proposition and unique selling points
- Setting SMART (Specific, Measurable, Achievable, Relevant, Time-bound) goals and objectives
- Identifying KPIs to measure success

1. **Plan (P):** Develop a detailed plan to achieve the startup's goals and objectives. Break down the plan into smaller tasks, assign responsibilities, and establish a timeline for implementation.

Key activities:

- Creating a business model canvas or a lean startup plan
- Developing a marketing and sales strategy
- Outlining an operational plan, including staffing, supply chain, and facilities
- Financial planning, including budgeting, revenue projections, and funding requirements
- Assigning tasks, responsibilities, and deadlines

1. **Act (A):** Execute the plan, taking action on the identified tasks and activities. Monitor progress and ensure effective communication among team members.

Key activities:

- Implementing the marketing, sales, and operational plans
- Regular progress updates and team meetings
- Addressing obstacles and challenges that arise during implementation
- Ongoing communication and collaboration among team members

1. **Refine (R):** Evaluate the results and performance of the implemented plan. Analyze the data and KPIs to identify areas for improvement or adjustments needed to achieve the startup's goals.

Key activities:

- Collecting and analyzing data on KPIs and performance metrics
- Identifying areas of underperformance or inefficiencies
- Determining root causes and potential solutions for improvement
- Adjusting the plan based on insights and analysis

1. **Keep Improving (K):** Continuously monitor the startup's performance, making ongoing adjustments and improvements as needed. Encourage a culture of continuous learning and improvement within the organization.

Key activities:

- Ongoing monitoring and evaluation of KPIs and performance metrics
- Regularly reviewing and updating the startup's goals, objectives, and strategies
- Encouraging feedback and suggestions for improvement from team members
- Implementing a continuous improvement mindset and culture within the organization

The SPARK model offers a structured approach for startups to set goals, plan, execute, and continuously improve their processes. By following the SPARK model, startups can increase their chances of success, minimize risks, and adapt to the ever-changing business environment.

Case Study: New Tech Startup Creating Software for Local Hotels Using the SPARK Model

A group of ambitious entrepreneurs have identified an opportunity to create software tailored for local hotels, helping them manage their operations more efficiently and enhance guest experiences. To launch their tech startup, they decide to use the SPARK model, a project management tool specifically designed for startups, focusing on strategizing, planning, acting, refining, and continuous improvement.

Strategize:

The founders begin by strategizing their startup's objectives, target market, and value proposition. They identify the key features their software should have to address the unique needs of local hotels, such as room inventory management, guest communication, and revenue optimization. The team also conducts market research to understand the competitive landscape and potential barriers to entry.

Plan:

With a clear strategy in place, the founders create a detailed plan outlining the steps needed to develop the software, including setting milestones and deadlines, allocating resources, and establishing a project governance structure. They also outline their marketing and sales strategy, including pricing, promotion, and customer acquisition channels.

Act:

The founders and their development team start executing the plan. They work diligently to develop the software, while the marketing team focuses on raising awareness about the product among local hotels. The founders actively engage with potential clients, demonstrating the software's features and benefits, and seeking feedback to ensure it meets their needs.

Refine:

As the startup receives feedback from early adopters, the founders refine the software to address any issues or suggestions. They also adjust their marketing and sales strategy based on their learnings from initial customer interactions. The team remains agile and adaptable, making improvements to the software and their approach as needed.

Keep Improving:

The founders are committed to continuous improvement, constantly seeking ways to enhance the software and stay ahead of the competition. They monitor key performance indicators, such as customer satisfaction, user growth, and revenue, to evaluate their progress and make data-driven decisions. The team also keeps an eye on industry trends and innovations, ensuring their software remains relevant and valuable to their target market.

Outcome:

By using the SPARK model, the tech startup successfully launches its software tailored for local hotels. The structured approach allows the team to identify their goals, develop a comprehensive plan, implement changes, and monitor results. As a result, their software gains traction in the market, helping local hotels streamline their operations and enhance guest experiences. The startup's continuous improvement mindset ensures that they remain competitive and responsive to their clients' evolving needs, positioning them for sustained growth and success.

Chapter 26: Total quality in personal life

Total Quality is a management approach that was first developed in the manufacturing industry, but it can also be applied to personal life to improve overall well-being and satisfaction. Total Quality is a customer-focused approach that emphasizes continuous improvement, teamwork, and effective communication. By applying Total Quality principles to personal life, individuals can achieve higher levels of success and happiness.

Total Quality in personal life is based on the following principles:

Customer focus: In personal life, the customer is oneself, and the goal is to meet one's own needs and desires.

Continuous improvement: Personal Total Quality is about continuously improving oneself and one's life, setting new goals and working towards them.

Teamwork: In personal life, teamwork refers to collaborating with others, such as family members or friends, to achieve common goals.

Effective communication: Effective communication is essential for Total Quality in personal life, as it helps individuals understand their own needs and the needs of others.

Increased satisfaction: By applying Total Quality principles to personal life, individuals can achieve higher levels of satisfaction and happiness.

Improved well-being: Total Quality in personal life can lead to improved physical, mental, and emotional well-being.

Better relationships: Effective communication and teamwork are key components of Total Quality in personal life, and they can help improve relationships with others.

Increased success: By continuously improving oneself and one's life, Total Quality in personal life can lead to increased success in both personal and professional life.

Implementing Total Quality in Personal Life

Here are the steps for implementing Total Quality in personal life:

Identify your customers: In personal life, your customers are yourself and those close to you. Identify your own needs and the needs of others.

Set goals: Set clear and specific goals for personal growth and improvement.

Continuously improve: Regularly evaluate your progress and make adjustments as needed to achieve your goals.

Collaborate with others: Collaborate with others, such as family members or friends, to achieve common goals.

Communicate effectively: Effective communication is essential for Total Quality in personal life. Practice active listening and clear communication to improve relationships and understanding.

Total Quality in personal life is a valuable approach for improving overall well-being and satisfaction. By applying Total Quality principles to personal life, individuals can achieve higher levels of success and happiness, improve relationships, and live a more fulfilling life. Total Quality is a continuous journey of self-improvement and growth, and it can lead to a more satisfying and meaningful life.

The 4D Framework for Achieving Your Desires

Ignite your passions and manifest your dreams with the phenomenal 4D framework! This ingenious four-step formula is your secret weapon for turning your desires into reality and living the life you've always envisioned. Embrace the power of Desire, Declare, Decide, and Demand, and embark on an exhilarating journey towards a future brimming with success and fulfillment. Unlock your potential and transform your life with the captivating 4D framework today!

The 4D framework is a simple yet powerful tool designed to help individuals achieve their desires and bring their dreams to life. The framework consists of four steps: Desire, Declare, Decide, and Demand.

Desire: In this step, you focus on identifying what you truly desire and what brings you joy and fulfillment. This includes getting clear on your goals, aspirations, and what you want to achieve in life.

Declare: In this step, you declare your desires to the universe, asking for help and guidance in manifesting your goals. This includes visualization, affirmations, and other methods of communicating your desires to the universe.

Decide: In this step, you decide to make all necessary effort to achieve your desires. This includes taking action, making changes, and pursuing your goals with persistence and determination.

Demand: In this step, you demand or expect results, and believe in the manifestation of your desires. This includes maintaining a positive mindset, focusing on your goals, and remaining confident and optimistic in the face of any challenges or obstacles.

Implementing the 4D framework requires a deep commitment to your desires and a focus on bringing them to life. To get started, focus on identifying what you truly desire and declaring your intentions to the universe. As you take action and make all necessary effort, remain focused on your goals, and demand or expect results.

Step	Description	Actions
Desire	Identifying what you truly desire	- Reflect on your goals, aspirations, and desires - Get clear on what brings you joy and fulfillment
Declare	Communicating your desires to the universe	- Visualize your desired outcome - Use affirmations or positive self-talk to declare your intentions - Create a vision board or other visual representation of your goals
Decide	Making necessary effort to achieve your desires	- Take action towards your goals - Make changes in your life to align with your desires - Pursue your goals with persistence and determination

Demand	Expecting results and maintaining a positive mindset	- Believe in the manifestation of your desires - Maintain a positive attitude and mindset - Focus on your goals and remain confident and optimistic

By implementing the 4D framework, individuals can identify their desires, communicate them to the universe, take action, and remain confident and optimistic in achieving their goals. This framework is a simple yet powerful tool for personal growth and can help individuals manifest their dreams into reality.

The 4D framework is a powerful tool for individuals seeking to bring their desires to life. By following the steps of desire, declare, decide, and demand, individuals can bring their goals into reality and achieve the success and happiness they desire. Stay focused, stay committed, and never stop pursuing your dreams.

Case Study: Achieving Success in the Logistics Business Using the 4D Framework

John, a hardworking and ambitious man, has always dreamt of starting his own logistics business. However, he has faced several challenges and setbacks over the years, causing him to feel discouraged and unsure of how to proceed. John decides to use the 4D framework to reignite his passion, manifest his dream, and achieve success in the logistics industry.

Desire:

John takes time to reflect on his deep-seated desire to build a successful logistics business. He evaluates his motivation, identifies the reasons behind his aspirations, and determines the kind of business he wants to create. He envisions providing high-quality and efficient transportation services for businesses, with a focus on excellent customer service and sustainable practices.

Declare:

Next, John declares his intentions and desires to the universe. He practices visualization, imagining his successful logistics business in vivid detail, from the satisfied clients to the efficient operations. John also incorporates affirmations into his daily routine, repeating positive statements such as "I am a successful logistics business owner" and "My business is thriving and growing."

Decide:

John decides to take action and starts working towards his goal. He conducts thorough research on the logistics industry, understanding market trends, competitors, and potential challenges. John creates a comprehensive business plan, detailing his strategies for marketing, operations, and financial management. He also begins to build a network of industry contacts and potential clients, attending events and participating in online forums to establish his presence in the logistics community.

Demand:

As he works on building his logistics business, John remains confident, optimistic, and focused on his goals. He demands results from himself and expects the universe to support his efforts. He maintains a positive mindset, viewing obstacles as opportunities for growth and learning. John continually seeks ways to improve his services, adapt to the ever-changing market, and remain ahead of the competition.

Outcome:

By following the 4D framework, John is able to manifest his dream of owning a successful logistics business. His unwavering desire, clear intentions, decisive action, and high expectations empower him to overcome challenges and grow his business. As a result, John's logistics company becomes known for its exceptional service, efficient operations, and commitment to sustainability. His dream turns into reality, and he enjoys the success and fulfillment he has always envisioned.

The 4C Approach for Personal Growth

The 4C Approach for Personal Growth is a simple yet powerful framework designed to help individuals achieve self-improvement and personal development. This approach focuses on four key aspects: Clarity, Commitment, Consistency, and Courage.

Clarity:

Clearly define your personal growth goals and objectives. Understand your strengths, weaknesses, values, and passions. Create a vision for your future self and identify specific areas in which you want to improve. By gaining clarity, you can make more informed decisions and set achievable targets for your personal growth journey.

Example: Identify a goal, such as improving communication skills or learning a new language and create a plan to achieve it.

Commitment:

Dedicate yourself to your personal growth goals. Recognize that personal development is a long-term process and requires persistence and dedication. Establish a routine or system that keeps you accountable and ensures you stay on track to achieve your goals.

Example: Allocate time each day or week to work on your personal growth goals, and stick to your schedule.

Consistency:

Strive to maintain regular progress towards your personal growth objectives. Consistent effort, even in small increments, will yield more significant results over time. Develop habits and routines that support your goals and facilitate a steady pace of improvement.

Example: Practice your communication skills or language learning for 30 minutes every day, building a habit that promotes steady progress.

Courage:

Embrace challenges, step out of your comfort zone, and face your fears as you pursue personal growth. Accept that setbacks and failures are a natural part of the growth process and use them as learning opportunities. Be resilient and adaptable in the face of adversity and continue pushing forward.

Example: Attend public speaking events, join a language conversation group, or take on new responsibilities at work to challenge yourself and foster growth.

By implementing the 4C Approach for Personal Growth – Clarity, Commitment, Consistency, and Courage – you can create a structured and effective personal development plan that leads to meaningful and lasting self-improvement.

Case Study: Becoming a Top-Performing Young Graduate Using the 4C Approach for Personal Growth

Sarah, a recent university graduate, has a strong desire to excel in her career and become a top performer in her field. To achieve this, she decides to apply the 4C Approach for Personal Growth, focusing on Clarity, Commitment, Consistency, and Courage.

Clarity:

Sarah spends time reflecting on her strengths, weaknesses, values, and passions. She realizes that she is passionate about marketing and wishes to become an expert in digital marketing strategies. She sets a clear goal to enhance her digital marketing skills by attending online courses and workshops, and by staying up to date with industry trends.

Commitment:

Sarah commits to her personal growth by dedicating time and effort to achieving her goal. She sets aside two hours every evening to study digital marketing and enrolls in a reputable online course. She also subscribes to industry newsletters to stay informed about the latest trends and best practices in her field.

Consistency:

To ensure consistent progress, Sarah develops a routine for her personal growth journey. She practices her newly learned digital marketing skills by creating sample marketing campaigns and analyzing successful case studies. By doing so, she gradually builds a portfolio that demonstrates her expertise and commitment to the field.

Courage:

Sarah understands that to achieve her goal, she must embrace challenges and step out of her comfort zone. She starts attending networking events and conferences, where she can connect with industry professionals and learn from their experiences. She also volunteers to take on digital marketing responsibilities at her workplace, demonstrating her skills and commitment to her manager.

Outcome:

By applying the 4C Approach for Personal Growth, Sarah successfully improves her digital marketing skills and becomes recognized as a top performer in her field. Her dedication, consistency, and willingness to face challenges enable her to excel in her career and achieve her personal growth goals.

The Life PIPE Method for Achieving Success

In the pursuit of success, it is essential to adopt a well-rounded approach that addresses various aspects of our lives. The LIFE PIPE Method is a holistic framework designed to help individuals achieve personal and professional success. The LIFE PIPE method is a simple yet effective tool for setting and achieving your goals in life. By following these four steps, you can turn your aspirations into reality and lead a more fulfilling life.

P - Prospect

The first step in the LIFE PIPE method is to prospect your goal. This means that you need to take the time to identify what it is that you truly want in life. Consider your passions, interests, and values, and think about what kind of life you want to lead. Once you have a clear understanding of your goal, you can move on to the next step.

I - Investigate

Next, it's time to investigate your goal in more detail. This involves researching and gathering information about your goal and exploring different ways to achieve it. Look for resources and people who have already achieved what you want to achieve, and learn from their experiences. This will give you a better understanding of the steps you need to take to achieve your goal.

P - Plan

With a clear understanding of your goal and the steps required to achieve it, it's time to plan your course of action. This involves breaking your goal down into smaller, more manageable steps and creating a roadmap for success. Make sure that your plan is realistic and achievable, and that you have the resources you need to make it a reality.

E - Execute

The final step in the LIFE PIPE method is to execute your plan. This means that you need to take action and start making progress towards your goal. Stay focused, stay committed, and stay the course. Remember, progress is key - every step forward, no matter how small, is a step closer to achieving your goal.

The LIFE PIPE method provides a straightforward and effective approach to achieving success in life. By following these four steps, you can turn your aspirations into reality and lead a more fulfilling life. So, prospect your goal, investigate it, plan your course of action, and execute it.

Case Study: Balancing a Professional Career and a Side Hustle Using the LIFE PIPE Method

Michael, a successful banker, is looking to balance his professional life with his passion for running a retail shop as a side hustle. He decides to apply the LIFE PIPE Method to achieve his goals while maintaining a healthy work-life balance.

P - Prospect: Michael begins by identifying his primary goal - successfully balancing his banking career and his retail shop side hustle. He takes time to understand his passions, interests, and values, and envisions a life where he can excel in both aspects without compromising the other.

I - Investigate: Michael investigates his goal by researching successful individuals who have managed to balance a professional career and a side hustle. He connects with people in similar situations and learns from their experiences. This helps him understand the challenges he may face and the strategies he can adopt to overcome them.

P - Plan: With a better understanding of his goal and the steps required to achieve it, Michael starts planning his course of action. He breaks down his goal into smaller, manageable tasks and creates a roadmap for success. This includes setting aside dedicated time for his retail shop, delegating tasks, and finding ways to improve his time management skills.

E - Execute: Michael begins executing his plan by taking action and making progress toward his goal. He commits to the dedicated time for his retail shop and enlists the help of a trusted friend to assist with day-to-day operations. He also enrolls in a time management course to improve his productivity and efficiency.

Outcome:

By applying the LIFE PIPE Method, Michael successfully balances his professional career and his retail shop side hustle. He experiences growth in both areas without sacrificing his work-life balance. Michael's commitment to his goal, careful planning, and consistent execution enables him to achieve success in both his banking career and retail shop side hustle, leading to a more fulfilling life.

The LIFE Method for Starting Anything

The LIFE method is a powerful tool for starting and achieving anything in life. Whether it's a personal or professional goal, the LIFE method provides a step-by-step approach to help you get started and make lasting change.

L – Learn

The first step in the LIFE method is to learn. This means that you need to gather information and knowledge about the thing you want to start. Read books, attend workshops, and talk to experts in your field. The more you learn, the better equipped you will be to take on the challenge.

I – Improve

Next, it's time to improve your skills and abilities. This involves practicing what you have learned and taking steps to get better. Whether it's through taking classes, seeking feedback, or simply putting in the time and effort, improving your skills will help you achieve your goal with greater ease and confidence.

F – Focus

With the knowledge and skills you have acquired, it's time to focus on what you want to achieve. This means that you need to prioritize your time and energy towards your goal, and eliminate distractions and obstacles that could get in the way. By focusing on your goal, you will be able to make faster progress and achieve better results.

E – Energize

Finally, it is important to stay energized and motivated. This means that you need to find ways to recharge and stay inspired, such as setting aside time for self-care, surrounding yourself with supportive people, and celebrating your successes along the way. A positive and energetic attitude will help you stay motivated and committed to your goal, even when the going gets tough.

The LIFE method provides a simple and effective approach to starting anything in life. By following these four steps, you can turn your aspirations into reality and make lasting change. So, learn about your goal, improve your skills, focus on what you want to achieve, and stay energized.

Case Study: Launching a Successful Business Using the LIFE Method

Emma, an aspiring entrepreneur, dreams of opening her own bakery. To turn her dream into reality, she decides to apply the LIFE Method - Learn, Improve, Focus, and Energize - to her business venture.

L - Learn: Emma starts by gathering information and knowledge about the bakery industry. She reads books on baking techniques, business management, and marketing. She also attends workshops and talks to successful bakery owners to learn from their experiences. Through her research, she gains a better understanding of the market, customer preferences, and the skills required to run a successful bakery.

I - Improve: With the knowledge she has acquired, Emma works on improving her skills and abilities. She enrolls in baking classes to refine her techniques, practices her new skills, and seeks feedback from her instructors and peers. Additionally, she takes courses in business management and marketing to better understand the administrative and promotional aspects of running a bakery.

F - Focus: Armed with the necessary knowledge and skills, Emma focuses on her goal of opening her bakery. She creates a detailed business plan, outlining her vision, target market, product offerings, and financial projections. She also allocates time to source suppliers, scout locations, and develop branding for her bakery. By focusing on her goal, Emma can prioritize her time and energy effectively, ensuring that her bakery gets off to a strong start.

E - Energize: Throughout the process, Emma remains energized and motivated. She sets aside time for self-care, ensuring that she maintains a healthy work-life balance. She also surrounds herself with supportive friends and family, who encourage her along the way. Emma celebrates her successes, no matter how small, which helps her stay inspired and committed to her goal.

Outcome:

By applying the LIFE Method, Emma successfully launches her bakery, attracting a steady flow of customers and earning rave reviews. Her commitment to learning, improving her skills, focusing on her goal, and staying energized leads her to achieve her dream of becoming a successful business owner. Emma's bakery flourishes, and she continues to apply the principles of the LIFE Method to grow and expand her business.

Chapter 27: Demon and Angel

Understanding Your Personal Demon and Using it for Success

Everyone has a personal demon, a negative inner voice that can hold them back from achieving their goals and reaching their full potential. This personal demon can take many forms, such as self-doubt, fear, anxiety, and negativity. However, while it may seem like a hindrance, your personal demon can actually be a powerful tool for success if you learn to understand it and harness its energy in a positive way.

Identifying Your Personal Demon

The first step in using your personal demon for success is to identify it. This inner voice can be subtle and often manifests in the form of negative self-talk, such as "I can't do this," or "I'm not good enough." Pay attention to your thoughts and emotions, and take note of any negative or self-defeating patterns.

Understanding the Root Causes

Once you have identified your personal demon, the next step is to understand its root causes. This could be a past experience or trauma that has shaped your beliefs and self-perception. Understanding the root causes of your personal demon can help you address and overcome them.

Channeling Your Demon's Energy

Your personal demon has a powerful energy that can be harnessed for success. Instead of letting this energy hold you back, try to channel it into a positive force. For example, if your demon is telling you that you're not good enough, use that energy to push yourself harder and prove yourself wrong. Transform your negative thoughts into motivation and turn your personal demon into a personal driving force.

Cultivating a Positive Mindset

In order to use your personal demon for success, you need to cultivate a positive mindset. This involves focusing on your strengths and what you're good at, as well as surrounding yourself with positive and supportive people. Cultivating a positive mindset can help you overcome the negativity of your personal demon and turn it into a source of inspiration and motivation.

Continuously Refining Your Approach

Using your personal demon for success is an ongoing process that requires continuous refinement and improvement. Take the time to reflect on your progress, identify areas where you can improve, and make adjustments to your approach as needed. By continuously refining your approach, you can continually harness the power of your personal demon and turn it into a tool for success.

Your personal demon can be a powerful tool for success if you learn to understand it and harness its energy in a positive way. By identifying, understanding, channeling, cultivating, and continuously refining your approach, you can turn your personal demon into a source of inspiration and motivation and achieve greater success in life.

Achieving Success with the D.E.M.O.N Method

Success is a journey, and like any journey, it requires careful planning and execution. The D.E.M.O.N Method for Success provides a roadmap for individuals to reach their goals and achieve success. This method consists of five key steps, each building on the previous one to help you reach your desired destination.

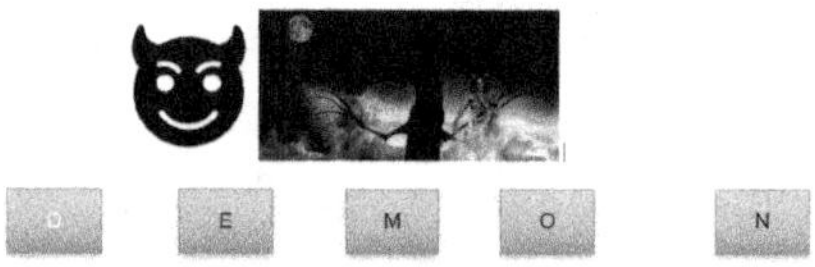

Determine:

The first step of the D.E.M.O.N Method is to determine your goals and what you want to achieve. It is crucial to set clear, specific, and measurable objectives that align with your values and priorities. Write down your goals and make sure they are attainable and realistic. This will help you stay motivated and focused on your journey towards success.

Evaluate:

The second step is to evaluate your current situation, strengths, and weaknesses. Take an honest look at where you are and what you need to change to reach your goals. Identify what resources you have available, what skills you need to acquire, and what obstacles you may face. This information will be invaluable as you map out your plan of action.

Map Out:

The third step is to map out a plan of action to reach your goals. This may include setting milestones, developing a timeline, and creating an action plan. Your plan should be detailed and include specific steps, deadlines, and resources required. This will help you stay on track and make progress towards your goals.

Optimize:

The fourth step is to optimize your plan by continuously improving and refining it. Regularly evaluate your progress and make adjustments as needed. Use feedback and data to refine your approach and make the necessary changes to achieve your goals.

Navigate:

The final step is to navigate the journey towards success by sticking to your plan and making course corrections when necessary. Celebrate your successes and learn from your failures. Stay focused on your goals and stay committed to your plan. Remember that success is a journey, and the D.E.M.O.N Method is a tool to help you reach your destination.

The D.E.M.O.N Method for Success provides a comprehensive and structured approach to achieving success. By following these five steps, you can reach your goals and achieve success in your personal and professional life. Start your journey today and see where the D.E.M.O.N Method can take you.

Case Study: Achieving Enormous Success in the Container Supply Business Using the D.E.M.O.N Method

John, an ambitious entrepreneur, wants to achieve enormous success in the container supply business. He decides to apply the D.E.M.O.N Method for Success to help him reach his goals.

Determine: John starts by determining his goals for the container supply business. He wants to become a leading supplier in the industry, expand his customer base, and increase his annual revenue. He writes down specific, measurable objectives, such as acquiring a certain number of new clients per year and increasing revenue by a set percentage.

Evaluate: John evaluates his current situation, strengths, and weaknesses. He identifies his extensive network of contacts in the industry as a strength, while his limited experience in marketing and sales is a weakness. He also acknowledges the competitive nature of the market and recognizes the need to differentiate his business from competitors.

Map Out: John maps out a detailed plan of action to reach his goals. He sets milestones for client acquisition, sales targets, and revenue growth. His action plan includes strategies to expand his network, improve his marketing and sales skills, and streamline his supply chain. John also creates a timeline for each milestone and allocates resources accordingly.

Optimize: John regularly evaluates his progress and optimizes his plan. He uses feedback from clients and analyzes sales data to identify areas for improvement. As he gains more experience in marketing and sales, he refines his strategies to better target potential clients and close deals. He continually looks for ways to improve his supply chain efficiency and reduce costs.

Navigate: John navigates the journey towards success by staying committed to his plan and making course corrections when necessary. He celebrates his successes, such as securing new clients and increasing revenue, and learns from his failures. As John remains focused on his goals, he successfully grows his container supply business, becoming a leading supplier in the industry.

Outcome:

By applying the D.E.M.O.N Method for Success, John achieves enormous success in the container supply business. His dedication to determining his goals, evaluating his situation, mapping out a plan, optimizing his strategies, and navigating his journey leads to the growth and prosperity of his business. John's container supply business thrives, and he continues to use the D.E.M.O.N Method to set new goals and reach even greater heights.

Personal Angels and How to Receive Informed Messages

Have you ever had a gut feeling about something and it turned out to be true? Or have you received a sudden, clear message in your mind that guided you towards a positive outcome? These could be examples of experiences with your personal angel.

Personal angels are spiritual beings who are assigned to us as our guardians and protectors. They are there to offer us guidance, support, and comfort, and to help us on our life's journey. They communicate with us in many ways, including through intuition, dreams, and sudden messages.

To receive informed messages from your personal angel, it's important to create an open and receptive mindset. Here are some tips to help you do this:

Quiet your mind: Take time each day to meditate or simply sit in quiet contemplation. This will help you focus and clear your mind, making it easier to receive messages from your personal angel.

Pay attention to your intuition: Your intuition is a powerful tool that can guide you towards positive outcomes. Pay attention to the subtle signals it sends you and trust the messages you receive.

Keep a dream journal: Your personal angel may communicate with you through your dreams. Keep a journal next to your bed to record your dreams as soon as you wake up. This will help you to better understand the messages your personal angel is trying to send you.

Ask for guidance: Your personal angel is always there to help you, but it's important to ask for their guidance. Simply close your eyes, take a deep breath, and ask for their help. Then, be open to receiving their messages.

Practice gratitude: Gratitude is a powerful tool that can help you attract positive energy into your life. Practice gratitude by focusing on the things you are thankful for each day. This will help you to stay in a positive, receptive state, making it easier to receive messages from your personal angel.

By following these tips and creating an open, receptive mindset, you can deepen your connection with your personal angel and receive the informed messages they have to offer. Trust in the guidance and support they offer, and have faith that everything is happening for your highest good.

A.N.G.E.L Method for Accurate Prediction

The A.N.G.E.L Method for Accurate Prediction is a systematic approach to making informed predictions about future outcomes. This method is designed to help individuals and organizations make predictions that are based on accurate and relevant information and are continuously improved through learning and feedback.

The method is a systematic approach to improve the accuracy of predictions across various domains, such as finance, business, technology, and social trends. The acronym stands for Analyze, Normalize, Generate, Evaluate, and Learn. This method helps ensure that predictions are based on relevant data, sound reasoning, and continuous learning.

Analyze

Begin by conducting a thorough analysis of the problem or situation for which you want to make a prediction. Identify the key variables, trends, and factors that may influence the outcome. This step involves gathering data from reliable sources, studying historical patterns, and understanding the context in which the prediction will be made.

Normalize

Normalize the data to ensure that the variables are comparable and consistent. This may involve converting raw data into percentages, adjusting for seasonality, or accounting for other factors that may distort the data. Normalization helps prevent errors and biases in the prediction process by ensuring that all relevant information is taken into account in a standardized manner.

Generate

Generate multiple predictive models or hypotheses based on the normalized data. This may involve using statistical techniques, machine learning algorithms, or expert judgment to forecast future outcomes. By considering various models and scenarios, you increase the likelihood of identifying the most accurate and robust prediction.

Evaluate

Evaluate the accuracy and reliability of each prediction model or hypothesis. This may involve comparing the predictions to historical data, assessing the model's performance using standard evaluation metrics, or soliciting feedback from experts in the relevant field. The evaluation process helps identify the strengths and weaknesses of each prediction and provides insights into potential areas for improvement.

Learn

Finally, continuously learn from the prediction process by refining the models, updating the data, and incorporating new information as it becomes available. This ongoing learning process helps ensure that predictions remain accurate and relevant over time, even as conditions change and new trends emerge.

By following the A.N.G.E.L method, individuals and organizations can improve the accuracy of their predictions and make more informed decisions. This systematic approach helps to minimize errors, reduce uncertainty, and support better decision-making in a wide range of domains.

Step	Description	Case Study Example

Background	Context of the problem to be solved.	A telecommunications company wants to predict customer churn more accurately to improve customer retention and reduce marketing costs.
Analyze	Gather historical data and study trends and factors that may influence the outcome.	Data analysts gather data on customer demographics, usage patterns, billing information, previous churn rates, study industry trends, and research factors that influence customer churn in the telecommunications sector.
Normalize	Standardize data to make variables directly comparable, reducing potential errors and biases.	Data analysts normalize data by converting it into consistent units, adjusting for seasonality, and accounting for other factors that may impact customer churn.

Generate	Develop multiple predictive models or hypotheses based on the normalized data.	Data scientists generate multiple predictive models using machine learning algorithms (logistic regression, decision trees, support vector machines) and incorporate expert opinions from the marketing and customer service departments to create additional hypotheses.
Evaluate	Assess the accuracy and reliability of the predictive models or hypotheses.	Models are evaluated against historical data using performance metrics (precision, recall, F1 score) and feedback from experts within the company to refine the models and hypotheses.

Learn	Select the best-performing model, implement it, and continuously monitor and update the model over time.	Based on evaluation, the best-performing model is selected and implemented for predicting customer churn. Data analysts and scientists continuously monitor the model's performance, update it with new data, and regularly review industry trends to ensure the model remains accurate.
Outcome	Results and benefits obtained from implementing the method.	The telecommunications company improves its ability to predict customer churn, enabling it to focus on high-risk customers, resulting in increased customer retention, reduced marketing costs, and a better understanding of factors influencing customer churn for informed decision-making.

Chapter 28: The States

There are an infinite number of states that an individual can experience in their lifetime. These states can be categorized into various dimensions such as health, wealth, social status, and personal growth. Each state can be seen as a unique set of circumstances that a person finds themselves in, and it is important to recognize that each state is temporary and subject to change.

The state of health is one of the most significant states that an individual can experience. Good health is essential to a happy and fulfilling life, and it can provide the energy and vitality needed to achieve one's goals. However, the state of sickness is equally important, as it can teach individuals valuable lessons about self-care, resilience, and the fragility of life.

The state of wealth is another state that many individuals aspire to achieve. Financial stability and abundance can provide individuals with a sense of security and freedom, enabling them to pursue their passions and live a fulfilling life. However, the state of poverty is also significant, as it can teach individuals the value of hard work, resourcefulness, and resilience.

The state of being known or unknown is another dimension of states that individuals can experience. Many people strive to achieve fame, recognition, or a sense of belonging within a community. However, the state of being unknown can also be beneficial, as it can provide individuals with the freedom to pursue their passions without the pressure of public scrutiny.

It is important to recognize that everyone is always in a state, and that these states are subject to change. No matter what state an individual finds themselves in, it is possible to navigate it successfully and learn valuable lessons along the way. By cultivating a growth mindset, practicing self-reflection, and seeking support from others, individuals can navigate the infinite states of being with resilience and grace.

Shifting Your Consciousness to Your Desired State

While it is true that there are an infinite number of states that we can experience in our lives, it is not accurate to say that these states are permanent. In fact, one of the most powerful aspects of being human is our ability to shift our consciousness and create the states that we desire.

The first step in shifting your consciousness to your desired state is to identify what that state is. This requires deep self-reflection and a willingness to be honest with yourself about what you truly want. Once you have identified your desired state, it is important to focus your thoughts and energy on it, and to let go of any limiting beliefs or negative self-talk that may be holding you back.

One effective technique for shifting your consciousness is visualization. Visualization involves imagining yourself in your desired state, and experiencing the feelings and emotions that come with it. By visualizing yourself in your desired state, you are sending a powerful message to your subconscious mind that this state is possible and achievable.

Another powerful technique for shifting your consciousness is affirmations. Affirmations are positive statements that you repeat to yourself, either silently or out loud. By repeating affirmations that are aligned with your desired state, you are programming your mind to focus on the positive aspects of your life and to attract more of what you want.

It is important to remember that shifting your consciousness to your desired state is not a one-time event, but rather an ongoing process. You must continue to focus your thoughts and energy on your desired state, and take action towards achieving it. This may involve making changes to your daily habits, seeking out new opportunities, or developing new skills.

Using 5S to Achieve Your Desired State in Life

As mentioned earlier, there are an infinite number of states that individuals can experience in their lives. These states can be related to health, wealth, social status, and personal growth. By using the 5S methodology, individuals can develop the discipline and structure necessary to achieve their desired state in life.

The first step in using the 5S methodology is to Sort through your thoughts, emotions, and physical environment. This step involves identifying which thoughts, emotions, and possessions are helping you move towards your desired state, and which ones are holding you back. For example, if your desired state is good health, you may need to sort through your diet, exercise routine, and daily habits to identify which ones are supporting your health goals and which ones are hindering them.

The second step in using the 5S methodology is to Set in order your environment and thoughts in a logical and efficient manner. This step can help you create a clear plan for achieving your desired state, and help you identify the steps you need to take to get there. For example, if your desired state is financial stability, you may need to set in order your finances by creating a budget, tracking your expenses, and investing wisely.

The third step in using the 5S methodology is to Shine by cleaning and maintaining your environment and thoughts. This step can help you develop the discipline and commitment necessary to achieve your desired state. By keeping your environment and thoughts clean and organized, you can reduce distractions and stay focused on your goals.

The fourth step in using the 5S methodology is to Standardize your routines and practices. This step can help you stay on track and ensure that you are consistently making progress towards your desired state. For example, if your desired state is personal growth, you may need to standardize your daily routine by setting aside time each day for reading, meditation, and reflection.

The fifth and final step in using the 5S methodology is to Sustain your progress over time. This step involves developing new habits and routines, seeking out support from others, and continuing to monitor your progress towards your desired state. By sustaining your progress over time, you can ensure that you are consistently moving towards your desired state and living the life that you truly want.

The 5S methodology can be a powerful tool for individuals seeking to achieve their desired state in life. By utilizing the five steps of Sort, Set in order, Shine, Standardize, and Sustain, individuals can reduce clutter, create a clear plan, stay focused on their goals, develop new habits and routines, seek out support from others, and achieve sustained progress towards their desired state.

Chapter 29: Investment

Using SWOT Analysis to Start Investing

Investing can be a complex and intimidating process, but with the right tools and techniques, it can be a valuable tool for growing your wealth. One of the most effective methods for assessing your investment opportunities is a SWOT analysis. This chapter will cover how to use the SWOT analysis to make informed investment decisions.

SWOT stands for Strengths, Weaknesses, Opportunities, and Threats. This analysis is a systematic evaluation of your investment portfolio, which can help you identify areas of strength and weakness, as well as opportunities and threats to your investments. By conducting a SWOT analysis, you can gain a comprehensive understanding of the factors that are impacting your investments, and make better investment decisions.

Strengths: This category includes factors that give you an advantage over others, such as access to unique information or resources, strong relationships with key stakeholders, and exceptional skills or expertise. When considering an investment, it is important to identify your strengths and leverage them to maximize your potential for success.

Weaknesses: This category includes factors that may limit your success, such as limited resources, lack of expertise, or a weak competitive position. By identifying your weaknesses, you can take steps to mitigate the impact of these limitations and increase your chances of success.

Opportunities: This category includes factors that may provide you with new opportunities for growth and profitability, such as new markets, changing consumer behaviors, or technological advancements. By recognizing these opportunities, you can take advantage of them to grow your investments and increase your returns.

Threats: This category includes factors that may pose a risk to your investments, such as changes in market conditions, shifts in consumer preferences, or regulatory changes. By recognizing these threats, you can take steps to minimize their impact and protect your investments.

SWOT analysis is a powerful tool for understanding the factors that are impacting your investments, and for making informed investment decisions. By conducting a thorough and systematic analysis of your investment portfolio, you can identify areas of strength and weakness, as well as opportunities and threats. This knowledge will help you make better investment decisions and maximize your returns.

The RAPID Framework - A New Investing Tool

Investing involves making decisions based on an assessment of potential risks, rewards, and market conditions. The RAPID framework is a new investing tool designed to provide a structured approach to evaluating investment opportunities, similar to the SWOT analysis. RAPID stands for Risk, Analysis, Potential, Investment, and Diversification.

The RAPID Framework

The RAPID framework guides investors through a systematic process of evaluating investment opportunities, ensuring a comprehensive and balanced assessment of the factors that influence an investment decision.

Risk

Assess the risk associated with the investment opportunity. Consider factors such as market volatility, credit risk, liquidity risk, and operational risk. Determine your risk tolerance and ensure that the investment aligns with your overall risk profile.

Analysis

Conduct a thorough analysis of the investment opportunity. This may include a review of financial statements, industry trends, competitive landscape, and management quality. Identify any red flags or warning signs that may indicate potential issues or concerns.

Potential

Evaluate the potential rewards and growth prospects of the investment opportunity. Assess factors such as revenue growth, profitability, market share, and innovation potential. Determine whether the investment aligns with your financial goals and desired return on investment (ROI).

Investment

Determine the appropriate amount to invest in the opportunity, based on your risk tolerance, financial goals, and overall investment strategy. Ensure that you have sufficient capital and resources available to support the investment.

Diversification

Consider the role of the investment opportunity within the context of your overall investment portfolio. Ensure that the investment contributes to a well-diversified portfolio, mitigating risk and optimizing potential returns.

Implementing the RAPID Framework

To implement the RAPID framework for evaluating investment opportunities, investors can follow these steps:

1. Assess the risk associated with the investment opportunity.
2. Conduct a thorough analysis of the investment opportunity, including financial, industry, and competitive factors.
3. Evaluate the potential rewards and growth prospects of the investment opportunity.
4. Determine the appropriate amount to invest in the opportunity, based on your risk tolerance and financial goals.
5. Consider the role of the investment opportunity within the context of your overall investment portfolio and ensure proper diversification.

The RAPID framework provides a structured approach to evaluating investment opportunities, helping investors make informed decisions and optimize their investment portfolios. By considering risk, analysis, potential, investment, and diversification, investors can effectively assess investment opportunities and make decisions that align with their financial goals and risk tolerance.

Case Study: Lucy's Investment Decision in the Food Supplying Business Using the RAPID Framework

Lucy, an aspiring investor, is contemplating partnering with her friend in a food supplying business to restaurants. Before making her decision, she decides to apply the RAPID framework to evaluate the investment opportunity systematically.

Risk: Lucy starts by assessing the risks associated with the food supplying business. She considers factors such as market volatility, credit risk, liquidity risk, and operational risk. After researching the industry, Lucy understands that the food supply business can be affected by factors such as fluctuating food prices, changing regulations, and logistical challenges. She determines her risk tolerance and concludes that she is willing to accept moderate risk for potentially higher returns.

Analysis: Lucy conducts a thorough analysis of the investment opportunity, reviewing the financial statements of her friend's business, industry trends, competitive landscape, and management quality. She identifies some potential challenges, such as increasing competition and the need for effective supply chain management. However, she also notes that the business has a strong track record and an experienced management team.

Potential: Lucy evaluates the potential rewards and growth prospects of the food supplying business. She assesses factors such as revenue growth, profitability, market share, and innovation potential. After her analysis, Lucy believes that the business has strong growth potential due to increasing demand for high-quality food supplies and the potential for expansion into new markets.

Investment: Based on her risk tolerance, financial goals, and overall investment strategy, Lucy determines the appropriate amount to invest in the food supplying business. She ensures that she has sufficient capital and resources available to support the investment and is prepared to commit both time and financial resources to the partnership.

Diversification: Lastly, Lucy considers the role of the food supplying business within the context of her overall investment portfolio. She ensures that the investment contributes to a well-diversified portfolio, mitigating risk and optimizing potential returns. Lucy recognizes that the food supplying business complements her other investments, providing a balance between different industries and asset classes.

Outcome:

By applying the RAPID framework, Lucy systematically evaluates the investment opportunity in the food supplying business. Her comprehensive assessment of risk, analysis, potential, investment, and diversification leads her to decide that partnering with her friend in the food supplying business aligns with her risk tolerance, financial goals, and overall investment strategy. As a result, Lucy confidently moves forward with the partnership, contributing to the growth and success of the food supplying business.

Using Value Stream Mapping to Correct Investment Errors

Investing can be a complex and challenging process, and errors can easily occur. In order to achieve success in the world of investing, it is important to identify and correct these errors in a timely and effective manner. One of the most useful tools in this regard is Value Stream Mapping (VSM).

VSM is a visual method for analyzing and improving the flow of value in a business process. It helps to identify areas of waste and inefficiency, and can be used to identify and correct investment errors.

Applying VSM to Investment Errors:

To correct investment errors using VSM, you will need to:

Identify the error: Start by clearly defining the investment error that needs to be corrected. This may involve analyzing past investment decisions, reviewing market trends and performance, or considering other relevant factors.

Map the current process: Create a visual representation of the current investment process, including all relevant inputs, activities, and outputs.

Identify areas of waste and inefficiency: Use the VSM map to identify areas of waste and inefficiency in the investment process. This may include areas where the process is overly complex, where decision-making is slow or unclear, or where resources are being used inefficiently.

Develop a solution: Once the areas of waste and inefficiency have been identified, develop a solution to correct the investment error. This may involve streamlining the process, improving communication and decision-making, or allocating resources more effectively.

Implement the solution: Implement the solution and monitor the results. Use feedback and data to make any necessary improvements to the process.

By using VSM, investors can identify and correct investment errors in a timely and effective manner. By mapping the current process, identifying areas of waste and inefficiency, and implementing solutions, investors can improve their performance and increase their chances of success in the world of investing.

Little's Law

Little's Law is a fundamental principle in queueing theory that relates the average number of items in a queue to the average time it takes for an item to pass through the system. While Little's Law is often applied in operations management and computer science, it can also be useful in finance for analyzing the efficiency of financial processes.

Here's an example of how Little's Law can be applied in finance:

Suppose a bank has an average of 100 customers waiting in line to see a teller at any given time, and it takes an average of 10 minutes for a customer to complete their transaction and leave the bank. We can use Little's Law to calculate the average rate at which customers enter and exit the system, as follows:

Average number of customers in the system (L) = 100 Average time for a customer to complete their transaction and leave (W) = 10 minutes

Using Little's Law, we can calculate the average rate at which customers enter and exit the system as follows:

Average rate of customers entering the system (λ) = L / W = 100 / 10 = 10 customers per minute

This means that, on average, 10 customers enter and leave the bank each minute. This information can be used to identify potential bottlenecks in the system and improve the efficiency of the bank's operations. For example, if the bank wants to reduce the average wait time for customers, they could consider hiring additional tellers to increase the rate at which customers are served and reduce the number of customers waiting in line.

In finance, Little's Law can also be applied to analyze the efficiency of investment portfolios. For example, if an investment firm has an average of 100 securities in their portfolio and it takes an average of 10 days for a security to be sold and replaced with a new one, Little's Law can be used to calculate the average rate at which securities enter and exit the portfolio. This information can be used to optimize the investment process and improve overall portfolio performance.

Case Study: Using Little's Law to Understand Yian's Finance

Yian is a small business owner who runs a clothing store. She has been experiencing long waiting times for her customers, leading to decreased customer satisfaction and lost sales. Yian is looking for ways to improve her store's performance and decides to use Little's Law to understand and optimize her store's finance.

Little's Law:

Little's Law is a mathematical formula that relates the average number of items in a system to the average time they spend in the system. The formula states that the average number of items in a system (N) is equal to the average arrival rate (λ) multiplied by the average time spent in the system (W). In other words, $N = \lambda W$.

Yian calculates her store's average arrival rate to be 10 customers per hour. She also measures the average time her customers spend in her store to be 30 minutes. Using Little's Law, Yian can calculate the average number of customers in her store as:

$N = \lambda W$ = 10 customers/hour * (30 minutes / 60 minutes) = 5 customers

Yian realizes that her store can only accommodate 5 customers at a time before the waiting time starts to increase. To improve her store's performance, Yian decides to implement some changes, such as:

1. Streamlining the checkout process: By introducing a more efficient checkout process, Yian can decrease the average time customers spend in her store, resulting in a lower average number of customers in her store.
2. Increasing the store's capacity: Yian can increase the store's capacity by optimizing the store layout, adding more checkout counters, or expanding the store's physical space. By doing so, Yian can accommodate more customers at a time and reduce waiting times.
3. Managing customer expectations: Yian can communicate with her customers by displaying estimated waiting times or offering a virtual queue system. This way, customers will have a better idea of the waiting time and can plan accordingly.

Results:

After implementing the changes, Yian measures the store's performance and calculates the new average time customers spend in her store to be 20 minutes. Using Little's Law, Yian can calculate the new average number of customers in her store as:

$N = \lambda W = 10$ customers/hour $*$ (20 minutes $/$ 60 minutes) $= 3.33$ customers

Yian's changes have resulted in a lower average number of customers in her store, shorter waiting times, and increased customer satisfaction. Her sales have also improved as a result of reduced waiting times and increased customer satisfaction.

Chapter 30: Inventory Management Using Little's Law

Little's Law is a simple and effective tool for managing inventory levels in a business. It states that the average inventory in a system is equal to the product of the average demand rate and the average lead time.

Inventory management is the process of ensuring that the right amount of inventory is available at the right time and in the right place to meet customer demand. Little's Law can be used to determine the optimal inventory level for a company based on its demand and lead time.

I =RT

I=average inventory eg. How much money you have

R=average throughput, how much money is flowing to you/a time (january)

T=average flow time, how long does it take to spend the money (monthly income)

To use Little's Law, you first need to determine the average demand rate, which is the average number of units sold per day. This can be calculated by dividing the total number of units sold over a certain period of time by the number of days in that period.

Next, you need to determine the average lead time, which is the average time it takes for a company to receive a new shipment of inventory after placing an order. This can be calculated by dividing the total lead time over a certain period of time by the number of orders placed during that period.

Once you have determined the average demand rate and average lead time, you can calculate the average inventory by multiplying the two values. The resulting value is the optimal inventory level for the company, as it will ensure that the company has enough inventory to meet customer demand, but not so much that it is tying up too much capital in inventory.

On cash flow

I=inventory, How much money you have

R=throughput, how much money is flowing to you/a time (january)

T=flow time, how long does it take to spend the money (monthly income)

In conclusion, Little's Law is a useful tool for managing inventory levels in a business. By determining the average demand rate and average lead time, and then calculating the average inventory, a company can ensure that it has the right amount of inventory on hand to meet customer demand while also maximizing its profitability.

Personal Inventory Management Using Little's Law

Little's Law is not just a tool for managing inventory levels in a business; it can also be applied to personal inventory management. Personal inventory refers to the possessions you own, including items such as clothing, electronics, and household goods.

Just as businesses must manage their inventory levels to meet customer demand, you must manage your personal inventory to meet your own needs and wants. Little's Law can help you determine the optimal level of personal inventory to ensure that you have the items you need, while avoiding clutter and overspending.

To use Little's Law for personal inventory management, you first need to determine your average demand rate, which is the average frequency with which you use or purchase items. This can be calculated by dividing the total number of items used or purchased over a certain period of time by the number of days in that period.

Next, you need to determine your average lead time, which is the average time it takes for you to replace an item after it has been used or worn out. This can be calculated by dividing the total lead time over a certain period of time by the number of items that have been replaced during that period.

Once you have determined your average demand rate and average lead time, you can calculate your average personal inventory by multiplying the two values. The resulting value is the optimal level of personal inventory for you, as it will ensure that you have the items you need to meet your demand, without accumulating too much clutter or overspending.

Little's Law can be applied to household budgeting:

Suppose a household has an average of $500 in discretionary spending each month, and it takes an average of 3 months for the household to save up for a $1,500 vacation. We can use Little's Law to calculate the average rate at which the household can save money, as follows:

Average amount of money in the system (L) = $1,500 Average time for the household to save up for a vacation (W) = 3 months

Using Little's Law, we can calculate the average rate at which the household can save money as follows:

Average rate of money entering the system (λ) = L / W = $1,500 / 3 months = $500 per month

This means that, on average, the household needs to save $500 per month to be able to afford $1,500 vacation every three months.

This information can be used to develop a budget and savings plan that aligns with the household's financial goals. For example, the household could consider cutting back on discretionary spending to increase the amount of money they can save each month, or they could consider finding ways to increase their income to meet their savings goals. By using Little's Law to understand the rate at which money enters and exits their budget, households can make informed decisions and develop strategies to save money more effectively.

TIPS Analysis

TIPS Analysis for Inventory Management

Inventory management is a critical aspect of any business or personal inventory system. To ensure that inventory levels are optimized and that customer demand is met, a systematic approach to inventory management is necessary. The TIPS analysis is a tool that can help you effectively manage your inventory.

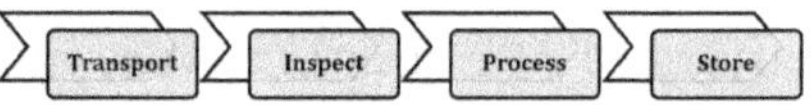

TIPS stands for Transport, Inspect, Process, and Store. These are the four key steps in the inventory management process, and the TIPS analysis provides a structured approach to managing each step.

Transport: The first step in the TIPS analysis is to assess the transportation of inventory. This includes identifying the modes of transportation used, the costs involved, and the time taken to transport inventory. By analyzing the transportation process, you can identify any bottlenecks or inefficiencies and take steps to improve the transportation process, resulting in cost savings and improved customer satisfaction.

Inspect: The next step in the TIPS analysis is to inspect the inventory. This involves checking the quality and quantity of inventory, and verifying that the inventory is in good condition. By regularly inspecting inventory, you can reduce the risk of stock shortages and improve the accuracy of inventory records.

Process: The third step in the TIPS analysis is to assess the process of handling inventory. This includes identifying any steps in the process that can be streamlined or improved, as well as ensuring that the right procedures are in place to handle inventory. By improving the process of handling inventory, you can reduce the risk of damage or loss, and improve the efficiency of the inventory management system.

Store: The final step in the TIPS analysis is to assess the storage of inventory. This includes identifying the types of storage used, the costs involved, and the accessibility of inventory. By analyzing the storage process, you can identify any inefficiencies and take steps to improve the storage process, resulting in cost savings and improved customer satisfaction.

The TIPS analysis is a useful tool for managing inventory levels in a business or personal inventory system. By following the four key steps of transport, inspect, process, and store, you can ensure that your inventory is effectively managed and that customer demand is met. This will result in cost savings, improved customer satisfaction, and increased profitability.

TIPS Analysis Case Study

Criteria	TIPS Analysis Case Study
Background	ABC Electronics, a small retailer, is facing challenges with inventory management, leading to increased costs and decreased customer satisfaction. They decide to apply the TIPS analysis to improve their inventory management process.
Objective	To improve inventory management by implementing the TIPS analysis (Transport, Inspect, Process, and Store), resulting in cost savings, improved customer satisfaction, and increased profitability.
Step 1: Transport	ABC Electronics evaluates their transportation methods, costs, and timeframes. They identify inefficiencies and switch to a more cost-effective and reliable carrier, leading to reduced transportation costs and better on-time deliveries.

Step 2: Inspect	The company implements a regular inspection process for incoming inventory, ensuring quality and quantity checks. This results in fewer stock shortages and improved accuracy of inventory records.
Step 3: Process	ABC Electronics streamlines the inventory handling process by improving staff training and implementing standardized procedures. This reduces the risk of damage or loss and increases the overall efficiency of their inventory management system.
Step 4: Store	The company assesses its storage facilities, costs, and accessibility. They reorganize the storage area, optimizing space usage and improving inventory accessibility, which leads to cost savings and faster order fulfillment.
Results	By implementing the TIPS analysis, ABC Electronics significantly improves its inventory management process, leading to cost savings, enhanced customer satisfaction, and increased profitability.

Conclusion	The TIPS analysis proves to be an effective tool for ABC Electronics, helping them effectively manage their inventory by focusing on the four key steps of transport, inspect, process, and store, ultimately leading to increased efficiency and business success.

ABC Inventory

ABC inventory is a technique used in inventory management to classify items based on their importance and value to the business. This method can help businesses identify which items require more attention and resources for inventory management, as well as which items can be managed more efficiently.

Step 1: Collect data

To begin the ABC inventory analysis, the first step is to collect data on inventory items, such as unit cost, annual demand, and lead time. This data can be obtained from inventory records, purchase orders, and sales reports.

Step 2: Calculate annual usage value

Next, calculate the annual usage value (AUV) for each inventory item by multiplying the unit cost by the annual demand. This value represents the total annual investment in each inventory item.

Step 3: Rank items

Rank inventory items based on their annual usage value, from highest to lowest. Items with the highest annual usage value will be classified as category A, followed by category B and category C items.

Step 4: Determine categories

Determine the categories based on the cumulative percentage of the annual usage value. For example, category A items may represent the top 20% of items with the highest annual usage value, category B may represent the next 30%, and category C may represent the bottom 50%.

Step 5: Manage inventory

Manage inventory for each category based on their importance and value to the business. Category A items should receive the highest priority and may require more attention to ensure sufficient inventory levels and minimize stockouts. Category B items may require less frequent monitoring and ordering, while category C items may require minimal attention and can be managed more efficiently.

By using the ABC inventory method, businesses can identify which items require the most attention and resources for inventory management, as well as which items can be managed more efficiently. This can help businesses optimize their inventory management processes, reduce costs, and improve overall efficiency.

Example of an ABC inventory table:

Item	Annual Demand	Unit Cost	Annual Usage Value	Category
A	1,000 units	$10	$10,000	A
B	500 units	$20	$10,000	A
C	200 units	$10	$2,000	B
D	100 units	$5	$500	C
E	50 units	$5	$250	C
F	25 units	$2	$50	C

In this example, we have six inventory items (A, B, C, D, E, and F) with their respective annual demand and unit cost. Using the ABC inventory method, we can calculate the annual usage value for each item by multiplying the unit cost by the annual demand. We can then rank the items based on their annual usage value and determine their category.

In this example, items A and B have the highest annual usage value and are categorized as category A, representing the top 20% of items. Items C has a moderate annual usage value and is categorized as category B, representing the next 30% of items. Items D, E, and F have the lowest annual usage value and are categorized as category C, representing the bottom 50% of items.

By using this categorization, businesses can prioritize their inventory management efforts, ensuring that items with the highest importance and value are given the most attention and resources. This can help improve inventory control, reduce costs, and improve overall efficiency in the inventory management process.

Chapter 31: Lean Mindset

Adopting a Lean Mentality in Order to Promote Personal and Professional Development

A method of thinking and an approach to life that is influenced by the ideas behind lean manufacturing is referred to as having a "Lean Mindset." This mentality places an emphasis on reducing waste, making constant improvements, and showing respect for other people. Adopting this perspective will allow you to maximize the potential of both your personal and professional lives. This chapter will provide specific methods to help you adopt a lean mindset by delving into the fundamentals of a lean mindset and examining the major components of a lean mindset.

The Fundamentals of Having a "Lean Mindset"

In order to develop a "Lean Mindset," you must first understand and accept the following fundamental ideas:

Eliminating waste is streamlining your life by determining which routines or activities do not offer value and then eliminating them.

Constant improvement (Kaizen)

Make a commitment to continuous personal and professional development by engaging in activities such as contemplation, learning, and experimentation.

Respect for people means cultivating empathy, open communication, and support for the development of others in order to encourage collaboration and mutually beneficial success.

Using a Lean Thinking Approach into Your Everyday Lives

Employ the principles of lean manufacturing to both your personal and professional life by adhering to the following guidelines:

Eliminating Waste

Determine what it is in your life that you want to accomplish as well as the things that are essential to you, and then prioritize them.

You should examine the things you do on a daily basis, including your activities, habits, and routines, to identify the ones that are not contributing to the achievement of your goals and values.

Get rid of or cut back on activities that are a waste of time and replace them with those that are more helpful and productive.

Constant Improvement (Kaizen)

Reflecting on your routines, habits, and decisions on a regular basis might help you identify areas in which you could make changes or improvements.

Create a sense of progress and success by establishing a series of manageable sub-goals that will contribute to the achievement of your larger objectives.

Have a growth attitude, which means you should look at mistakes and losses as chances to improve your strategy and learn new things.

To get fresh understanding and viewpoints, it is beneficial to solicit the feedback of mentors, peers, or specialists.

Regard for Other Individuals

Self-compassion can be developed through the practice of accepting one's own fallibility and approaching oneself with kindness and understanding.

Increase your capacity for empathy by paying attention to what other people have to say and making an effort to comprehend their experiences, ideas, and points of view.

Create an environment that encourages collaboration and achievement by providing support and encouragement to the development of others.

Speak in an open and honest manner, so developing good relationships and building trust between you and others.

Adopting a "Lean Mindset" is a potent strategy for optimizing one's life and achieving one's personal and professional goals in a more time- and resource-effective manner. You will be able to remove waste, continuously improve, and cultivate a culture of respect and collaboration if you apply the concepts of lean manufacturing to your own experiences and adapt them to the context of lean manufacturing. You will be well on your path to better success and fulfillment if you internalize these ideas and incorporate them into your day-to-day life.

Lean Six Sigma Matrix (LSSM)

The Lean Six Sigma Matrix (LSSM), a comprehensive tool that combines the principles and methodologies of Lean and Six Sigma to help organizations streamline processes, reduce waste, and improve quality. The LSSM consists of four main components: Process understanding, Waste Reduction, Quality Control, and Continuous Improvement. Each component includes a set of tools and techniques to help organizations achieve their objectives.

The Lean Six Sigma Matrix (LSSM), also known as the PWQC cycle, serves as a comprehensive framework for organizational improvement. The cycle consists of four key components: Process understanding (P), Waste Reduction (W), Quality Control (Q), and Continuous Improvement (C). The principle in utilizing this matrix is to understand the process (P) thoroughly, identify areas of waste, implement quality control measures and enhance continuous improvement. The PWQC cycle serves as a reminder of the main areas to focus on when applying Lean Six Sigma principles in an organization."

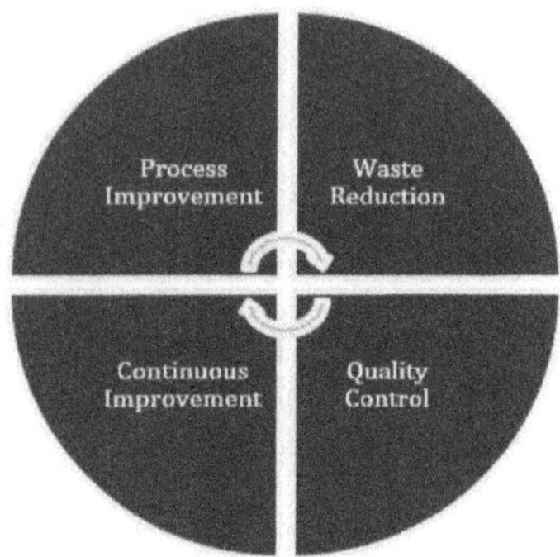

Process understanding: This component focuses on streamlining processes, reducing cycle times, and enhancing overall efficiency. The LSSM recommends the following tools for process improvement:

- Value Stream Mapping (VSM): Identify process bottlenecks and inefficiencies by visualizing the flow of materials and information.
- SIPOC Diagram: Map the Suppliers, Inputs, Process, Outputs, and Customers to gain a high-level understanding of the process.
- Process Flow Diagrams: Create detailed visual representations of individual processes to identify improvement opportunities.

Waste Reduction: This component targets the elimination of waste, including overproduction, waiting, transportation, inventory, motion, over-processing, and defects. The LSSM suggests the following tools for waste reduction:

- 5S Methodology: Sort, Set in order, Shine, Standardize, and Sustain to organize the workplace and eliminate waste.
- Kanban System: Implement a visual management system to control inventory and reduce overproduction.
- Poka-Yoke: Design error-proofing mechanisms to prevent defects and minimize rework.

Quality Control: This component emphasizes the importance of maintaining high-quality products and services. The LSSM proposes the following tools for quality control:

- Control Charts: Monitor process performance over time to identify variations and maintain quality standards.
- Design of Experiments (DOE): Plan and execute experiments to optimize processes and minimize variability.
- Failure Modes and Effects Analysis (FMEA): Assess potential failure modes and their effects on the system to prioritize risk mitigation efforts.

Continuous Improvement: This component encourages organizations to continuously refine their processes and operations. The LSSM recommends the following tools for continuous improvement:

- DMAIC Methodology: Define, Measure, Analyze, Improve, and Control for structured problem-solving and process improvement.
- PDCA Cycle: Plan, Do, Check, and Act to promote iterative learning and continuous improvement.
- Kaizen Events: Organize focused workshops to identify and implement rapid improvements in specific areas.

To use the Lean Six Sigma Matrix, start by assessing your organization's current processes, waste levels, and quality standards. Next, choose the most appropriate tools and techniques from each component and implement them in a systematic manner. Monitor progress and adjust your approach as needed to achieve continuous improvement and operational excellence. By combining the principles of Lean and Six Sigma, the LSSM offers a comprehensive framework for enhancing organizational performance.

Case Study: Improving Customer Service using the Lean Six Sigma Matrix (LSSM)

A large retail chain has been receiving customer complaints about long wait times at checkout lines and poor customer service. The management team decides to use the Lean Six Sigma Matrix (LSSM) to address these issues and improve customer satisfaction.

Application of LSSM

The management team identifies the Process Improvement (P) component of the LSSM as the first area to address. They analyze the checkout process and identify areas for improvement, such as optimizing staffing levels and improving employee training. The team uses tools such as process mapping, flowcharting, and value stream analysis to identify areas of inefficiency.

Next, they move on to the Waste Reduction (W) component of the LSSM. They identify areas of waste, such as excess inventory and unused equipment, and develop a plan to eliminate them. They use tools such as 5S and visual management to organize the checkout area and reduce waste.

The Quality Control (Q) component of the LSSM is then addressed. The team implements quality control measures such as standardized operating procedures and employee training to ensure consistency in the checkout process. They use tools such as control charts and statistical process control to monitor and improve quality.

Finally, the Continuous Improvement (C) component of the LSSM is implemented. The team sets up a system to gather customer feedback and uses tools such as Pareto charts and root cause analysis to identify areas for further improvement.

Results

After implementing the LSSM, the retail chain experiences significant improvements in customer satisfaction. Wait times at checkout lines are reduced, and customers report a higher level of satisfaction with the quality of service. The retail chain also experiences cost savings from the reduction in waste and more efficient use of resources. By implementing the Lean Six Sigma Matrix, the retail chain is able to improve its overall performance and maintain a competitive advantage in the market.

Personal "Spaghetti Diagram" for Increased Efficiency and Effectiveness

A graphic representation of the flow of people, materials, or information during a process is referred to as a "Spaghetti Diagram." A Spaghetti Diagram is a tool that can be utilized in the context of personal productivity to uncover inefficiencies and chances for development in one's day-to-day routines, habits, and responsibilities. This section will introduce the idea of a personal Spaghetti Diagram, discuss the advantages of using such a diagram, and provide a detailed walkthrough on how to make one for yourself.

You may benefit from creating your own personal Spaghetti Diagram by:

Imagine your typical activities and patterns of behavior for a day to get an accurate picture of how you spend your time and resources.

Find wasteful patterns, such as frequent back-and-forth motions, multitasking, or excessive reliance on specific tools or resources, and then eliminate them.

Find areas where you may make improvements, which will enable you to enhance the efficiency of your everyday tasks and raise your level of output.

Help you become more self-aware by encouraging regular reflection on your behaviors and the patterns you follow.

Developing Your Own Spaghetti Diagram

Specify the Boundaries of the Project.

First things first, figure out the boundaries of your Spaghetti Diagram. Choose a particular facet of your life or a time span that you wish to investigate, such as your typical morning routine, workday, or weekly schedule.

Make a list of the things to be done.

Make a list of all of the routine actions and responsibilities that fall under the purview of the chosen scope. Be as specific as you possibly can, including the order in which the tasks will be performed and how long each one will take.

Choose a Method of Representation to Use.

Choose a means to graphically portray the activities and responsibilities you have. You can use traditional materials such as paper and a pen, post-it notes, or digital ones such as software for flowcharts or presentation programs. Make sure that the strategy you chose will not restrict your ability to quickly move and reorganize the components.

Please doodle the diagram.

Begin by sketching the actual or virtual setting in which the duties will be carried out, such as your house, office, or the numerous sites you will be traveling to throughout the day. The following step is to assign a form, symbol, or text label to each individual activity or task. After that, you should describe the flow of your tasks by connecting these elements with lines or arrows to show how they are completed. It should end up looking like a tangled web or "spaghetti," which is meant to represent how complicated your routines are.

Investigate the Schematic

Do an analysis of your own personal Spaghetti Diagram to identify patterns, inefficiencies, and potential growth opportunities. Consider questions such as:

Are there any moves or activities that are performed again and over again that aren't necessary?

Do you spend an inordinate amount of time on certain responsibilities or pursuits?

Is it possible to restructure or combine the duties in order to reduce the amount of movement or other distractions?

Is there a tool, a resource, or a strategy that you might use that would make your work more efficient?

Implement Improvements

Create and put into action plans to improve your day-to-day routines and behaviors, using the findings of your study as a guide. This can require you to reorganize your office, learn some new strategies for managing your time, or delegate some of your responsibilities. Maintain a steady commitment to refining your strategy in light of new information and experience.

Your own personal Spaghetti Diagram is a powerful tool that can help you visualize and improve your daily routines, habits, and activities. You may increase both your productivity and your overall well-being by locating areas in which you can make improvements and detecting inefficiencies. You can cultivate more self-awareness and be motivated to engage in continual self-improvement by regularly updating and evaluating your Spaghetti Diagram. This can assist you in achieving greater success in a variety of facets of your life.

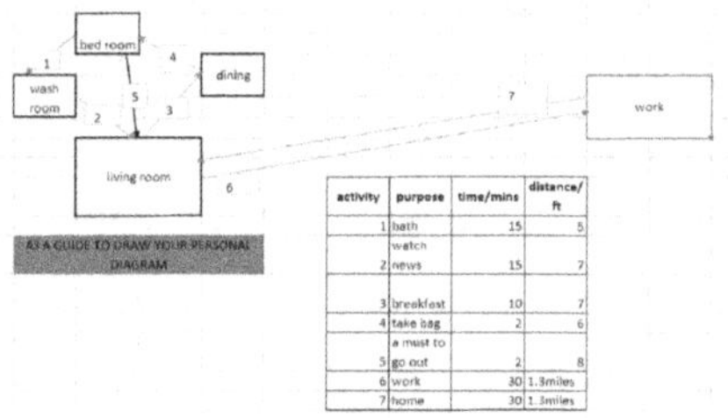

activity	purpose	time/mins	distance/ft
1	bath	15	5
2	watch news	15	7
3	breakfast	10	7
4	take bag	2	6
5	a must to go out	2	8
6	work	30	1.3miles
7	home	30	1.3miles

Personal Checklist for Success

A personal checklist for success is a tool that can help individuals stay on track and focus on their goals. Here is a checklist that outlines key actions and behaviors that can contribute to personal success:

Self-Reflection

- Regularly take time to reflect on personal strengths, weaknesses, and areas for improvement.
- Set clear, realistic, and measurable goals.
- Identify personal values and align actions and behaviors accordingly.
- Practice self-care to maintain physical, mental, and emotional well-being.

Skill Development

- Continuously seek opportunities to learn and develop new skills.
- Build a strong network of mentors, coaches, and peers to provide guidance and support.
- Take risks and embrace challenges as opportunities for growth and learning.
- Seek feedback and act on it to improve performance and outcomes.

Action and Persistence

- Prioritize and manage time effectively to achieve goals and meet deadlines.
- Break down large goals into smaller, manageable steps.
- Embrace failure as a learning opportunity and persevere through setbacks and obstacles.
- Celebrate successes and use them as motivation to continue pushing forward.

Relationship Building

- Build and maintain strong, positive relationships with family, friends, and colleagues.
- Practice active listening and effective communication skills.
- Collaborate with others and seek diverse perspectives and experiences.
- Give back to the community through volunteering and philanthropy.

Category	Actions/Behaviors
Self-Reflection	- Regularly reflect on personal strengths, weaknesses, and areas for improvement. - Set clear, realistic, and measurable goals. - Identify personal values and align actions and behaviors accordingly. - Practice self-care to maintain physical, mental, and emotional well-being.

Skill Development	- Continuously seek opportunities to learn and develop new skills. - Build a strong network of mentors, coaches, and peers to provide guidance and support. - Take risks and embrace challenges as opportunities for growth and learning. - Seek feedback and act on it to improve performance and outcomes.
Action and Persistence	- Prioritize and manage time effectively to achieve goals and meet deadlines. - Break down large goals into smaller, manageable steps. - Embrace failure as a learning opportunity and persevere through setbacks and obstacles. - Celebrate successes and use them as motivation to continue pushing forward.
Relationship Building	- Build and maintain strong, positive relationships with family, friends, and colleagues. - Practice active listening and effective communication skills. - Collaborate with others and seek diverse perspectives and experiences. - Give back to the community through volunteering and philanthropy.

Using this table, individuals can easily refer to the different categories and associated actions and behaviors that contribute to personal success. By checking off items as they are completed, individuals can track their progress and ensure they are taking actionable steps towards achieving their goals.

The ROPE of Upliftment

The ROPE of Upliftment is a four-step approach to personal and professional growth and success. By following these steps, you can turn your aspirations into reality and reach your full potential.

R – Recount

The first step in the ROPE of Upliftment is to recount your shortfalls. This means taking an honest look at the areas in your life where you have fallen short and identifying the reasons why. This could be anything from a lack of confidence to a lack of resources, to poor decision making. By acknowledging your shortfalls, you can begin to work on overcoming them.

O – Open

The next step is to open yourself to new opinions and opportunities. This means being willing to listen to others and consider different perspectives, as well as actively seeking out new opportunities for growth and success. Whether it's through networking, taking classes, or seeking out new experiences, opening yourself to new ideas and opportunities will help you grow and succeed in ways you never thought possible.

P – Plan

With a clear understanding of your shortfalls and a willingness to embrace new ideas and opportunities, it's time to plan for success. This means setting specific, measurable, and achievable goals for your personal and professional growth. This could be anything from improving your public speaking skills, to advancing in your career, to starting a new business.

E – Execute

Finally, it's time to execute your plan. This means taking the necessary steps to achieve your goals and realizing your full potential. Whether it's through hard work, perseverance, or seeking out the right resources, executing your plan is the key to achieving your aspirations and reaching your full potential.

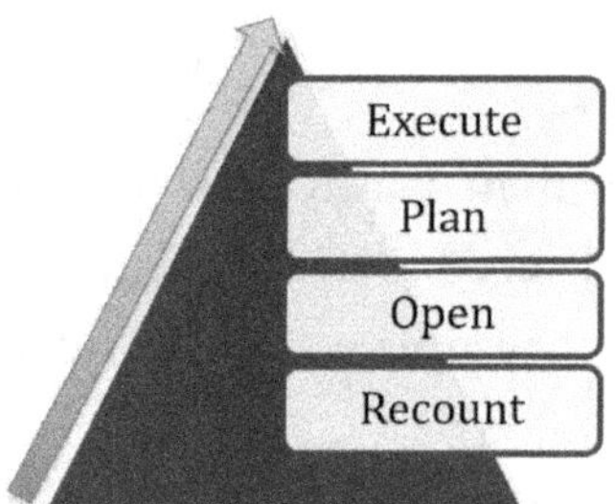

The ROPE of Upliftment provides a powerful and effective approach to personal and professional growth and success. By following these four steps, you can turn your aspirations into reality and reach your full potential. So, recount your shortfalls, open yourself to new opinions and opportunities, plan for success, and execute your plan.

Case Study: Mathew and the ROPE of Upliftment

Mathew is a 28-year-old professional who has been feeling stuck in his career. Despite his efforts to advance and take on new responsibilities, he has hit a plateau and is unsure of how to move forward. He feels unfulfilled and frustrated and is looking for a way to achieve his goals and reach his full potential.

After doing some research, Mathew comes across the ROPE of Upliftment, a four-step approach to personal and professional growth and success. Intrigued by the methodology, Mathew decides to give it a try and begins to implement the steps in his daily life.

Step 1: Recount

Mathew starts by taking an honest look at his shortfalls. He acknowledges that he lacks confidence in his abilities and tends to shy away from taking risks. He also realizes that he has been too comfortable in his current position and has not been proactive in seeking out new opportunities for growth and development.

Step 2: Open

With a better understanding of his shortfalls, Mathew opens himself up to new opinions and opportunities. He seeks out advice from mentors and colleagues, and actively looks for ways to broaden his skill set and knowledge base. He starts attending industry events, taking online courses, and reading books on personal and professional development.

Step 3: Plan

With a newfound confidence and a willingness to try new things, Mathew sets specific, measurable, and achievable goals for his career. He decides to take on a leadership role in his current job and starts working towards a promotion. He also begins to explore other career paths that align with his interests and skills and creates a plan for how to achieve these goals.

Step 4: Execute

Finally, Mathew puts his plan into action. He takes on new responsibilities at work and works hard to prove his abilities and value to the company. He also applies for new jobs and interviews with companies that align with his career goals. Through hard work and perseverance, Mathew achieves his goals and is offered a new job in a leadership role that aligns with his interests and values.

The ROPE of Upliftment was a powerful tool for Mathew to achieve his personal and professional goals. By taking an honest look at his shortcomings, opening himself up to new opportunities and ideas, planning for success, and executing his plan, Mathew was able to achieve his aspirations and reach his full potential. The ROPE of Upliftment can be a useful approach for anyone looking to improve their personal and professional lives.

The P.R.A.Y Method for Solving Problems

Prayer is a deeply personal and significant practice for many individuals and religious communities around the world. It is a deliberate form of communication that involves expressing one's hopes, fears, and desires to a higher power or object of worship. Through prayer, individuals seek to establish a connection with their deity or deified ancestor, and to form a relationship with them. Whether it is a prayer of supplication or intercession, the act of prayer is a powerful way to express faith, gratitude, and reverence for a higher power.

Problems are an inevitable part of life, but they don't have to hold you back. With the P.R.A.Y Method, you can overcome any obstacle and achieve your desired outcomes. This method is based on four key principles: Plan, Reprogram, Attract, and Yield.

P - Plan

The first step in the P.R.A.Y Method is to plan what you want. This means clearly defining the outcome you desire and setting specific, measurable, and achievable goals. Having a clear understanding of what you want will help you stay focused and motivated as you work towards your desired outcome.

R - Reprogram

The next step is to reprogram your subconscious mind and feelings. This means shifting your thoughts and emotions to align with the outcome you desire. By doing this, you can create a positive and empowered mindset that will help you overcome any obstacle and achieve your goals.

A - Attract

With your subconscious mind and feelings aligned with your desired outcome, it's time to attract the resources and support you need to achieve your goals. This means reaching out to others, seeking out opportunities, and building relationships that will help you succeed.

Y - Yield

Finally, it's time to yield the results you desire. This means taking consistent and persistent action towards your goals and being open to new opportunities as they arise. By doing this, you can bring your vision to life and achieve the outcomes you desire.

The P.R.A.Y Method provides a powerful approach to solving problems and achieving your desired outcomes. By following these four steps, you can overcome any obstacle and turn your aspirations into reality. So, plan what you want, reprogram your subconscious mind and feelings, attract the resources and support you need, and yield the results you desire.

PRAY Case Study

Madam X is a business owner who has been struggling to attract new clients to her consulting firm. She has tried various marketing strategies but hasn't seen any significant results. Feeling frustrated, she turns to the P.R.A.Y Method to overcome this obstacle and achieve her desired outcome.

Plan

Madam X starts by clearly defining the outcome she desires, which is to attract more clients to her consulting firm. She sets specific, measurable, and achievable goals, such as increasing her online visibility and networking with potential clients.

Reprogram

Madam X recognizes that her mindset is critical to her success. She begins to reprogram her subconscious mind and emotions by visualizing her desired outcome and affirming positive thoughts and beliefs about herself and her consulting services.

Attract

Madam X takes action to attract the resources and support she needs to achieve her goals. She reaches out to her professional network, attends networking events, and engages with potential clients on social media. She also invests in online marketing strategies to increase her firm's visibility.

Yield

By consistently taking action towards her goals and staying open to new opportunities, Madam X begins to yield the results she desires. She attracts new clients to her consulting firm, and her business begins to grow. She continues to use the P.R.A.Y Method to overcome other obstacles and achieve her desired outcomes, both personally and professionally.

The FOCUS Method for Good Performance

To perform at your best, it is crucial to have a clear focus and stay on track. The FOCUS Method is a simple and effective way to improve your performance and achieve your goals. This method is based on five key principles: Formulate, Operate, Consult, Upgrade, and Sustain.

F - Formulate

The first step in the FOCUS Method is to formulate your goals and objectives. This means taking the time to define what you want to achieve and setting specific, measurable, and achievable targets. Having a clear understanding of what you want will help you stay focused and motivated as you work towards your desired outcome.

O - Operate

The next step is to operate and test your ideas. This means putting your plans into action and evaluating their effectiveness. By doing this, you can identify any weaknesses or areas for improvement and refine your approach accordingly.

C - Consult

Consulting with others can be a valuable part of improving your performance. This means seeking feedback from others, learning from their experiences, and building relationships that will support your success.

U - Upgrade

Once you have evaluated your performance and received feedback, it's time to upgrade and make improvements. This means taking action to address any weaknesses, build upon your strengths, and continually improve your performance.

S - Sustain

Finally, it's important to sustain your focus and momentum. This means staying committed to your goals and consistently taking actions that will bring you closer to your desired outcome. By doing this, you can ensure that your performance remains at its best over time.

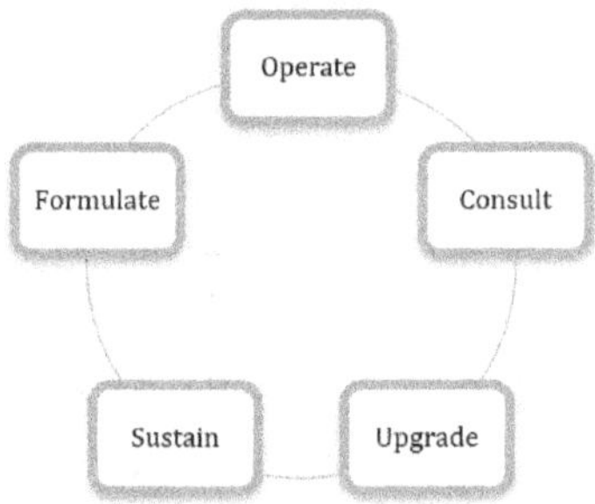

The FOCUS Method provides a practical approach to improving your performance and achieving your goals. By following these five steps, you can stay focused and motivated, build upon your strengths, and continually improve your results. So, formulate your goals, operate and test your ideas, consult with others, upgrade and make improvements, and sustain your focus and momentum.

Case Study: Achieving the Dream of Becoming a CEO using the FOCUS Method

An aspiring young lady named Karen dreams of becoming the CEO of her own company one day. She has a clear vision of what she wants to achieve, but she knows that it will take hard work and dedication to make her dream a reality. To help her stay on track and improve her performance, she decides to apply the FOCUS Method to her career development journey.

Formulate

Karen starts by formulating her goals and objectives. She identifies her strengths and weaknesses, and sets specific, measurable, and achievable targets. Her goals include improving her leadership skills, building her network, and gaining more experience in her industry.

Operate

Karen puts her plans into action by seeking out leadership opportunities in her current job, taking courses to enhance her skills, and attending industry events to build her network. She evaluates her performance regularly and makes adjustments as needed.

Consult

Karen actively seeks feedback from her colleagues, mentors, and other industry experts. She learns from their experiences and insights, and uses this knowledge to improve her approach.

Upgrade

Karen takes the feedback she receives and uses it to make improvements. She addresses her weaknesses, builds upon her strengths, and continually looks for ways to improve her performance.

Sustain

Karen remains committed to her goals and consistently takes action to achieve them. She stays focused and motivated and celebrates her successes along the way.

Through the FOCUS Method, Karen has been able to improve her performance, build her skills and network, and move closer to achieving her dream of becoming a CEO. By staying focused and committed to her goals, she has been able to overcome obstacles and make steady progress towards her desired outcome.

Using the SELF Method for New Opportunities

In our rapidly changing world, fresh opportunities emerge continuously, making it difficult to stay on top of them. However, adopting the right strategy can help you capitalize on these prospects and reach your objectives. The SELF Method offers an uncomplicated and efficient means of pinpointing and grasping new opportunities. This method hinges on four essential principles: See, Evaluate, Learn, and Focus.

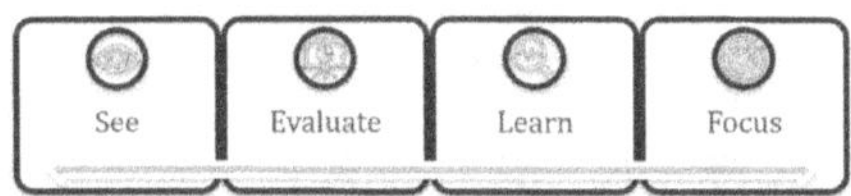

S – See

The first step in the SELF Method is to see the opportunities that are available to you. This means being proactive in your search and taking the time to understand what's available in your field. This could involve researching new trends, networking with others in your industry, and exploring new avenues for growth.

E – Evaluate

Once you have identified potential opportunities, it's important to evaluate them to determine their potential for success. This means considering factors such as your skills, resources, and goals, and assessing whether an opportunity is the right fit for you.

L – Learn

Learning is an important part of any new opportunity, and the SELF Method encourages you to embrace this process. This could involve learning new skills, gaining knowledge, and seeking out new experiences. By doing this, you can build upon your strengths and develop the skills and knowledge you need to succeed.

F – Focus

Finally, it's important to focus on your goals and stay on track. This means setting priorities, staying organized, and committing to the process. By doing this, you can ensure that you stay motivated and focused on achieving your desired outcome.

The SELF Method is a powerful tool for identifying and seizing new opportunities. By following these four steps, you can stay proactive, evaluate opportunities, learn and grow, and stay focused on your goals. So, start by seeing the opportunities available to you, evaluate their potential for success, embrace the learning process, and stay focused on your goals.

Case Study: John's Journey to Discovering New Opportunities Using the SELF Method

John had been working in the marketing industry for a few years and was looking for ways to grow his career. He had heard about the SELF Method and decided to give it a try.

S - See:

John started by researching new trends in the marketing industry. He subscribed to newsletters, read blogs, and attended conferences to gain a better understanding of the latest developments. He also reached out to his colleagues and contacts in the industry to see if they knew of any new opportunities.

E - Evaluate:

After identifying potential opportunities, John evaluated them based on his skills, resources, and goals. He realized that he wanted to focus on the digital marketing space and found a few new opportunities that aligned with his interests.

L - Learn:

John knew that he needed to learn new skills to excel in the digital marketing space. He took online courses, attended workshops, and sought out mentorship from experts in the field. He also attended networking events to meet new people and gain insights into the industry.

F - Focus:

Finally, John narrowed down his options and decided to focus on a specific opportunity in the digital marketing space. He set specific goals, created a plan, and stayed organized to ensure that he remained on track. He worked hard and remained committed to the process, which eventually led to his success. He secured a new job in the digital marketing space and was excited about the fresh opportunities that lay ahead.

Overall, John found that the SELF Method was a great way to identify and capitalize on new opportunities in his career. By following the principles of seeing, evaluating, learning, and focusing, he was able to take his career to the next level and achieve his desired outcomes.

Mastering a Skill: The M.A.S.T.E.R. Method

Learning a new skill can be challenging, but with the right approach, anyone can achieve mastery. The M.A.S.T.E.R. method is a framework for developing the necessary mindset, habits, and techniques for mastering a skill. In this chapter, we will explore each component of the M.A.S.T.E.R. method and how it contributes to achieving success.

M - Motivation

Motivation is the driving force behind mastering a skill. Without a strong desire and drive to succeed, it's easy to give up when faced with challenges and setbacks. To develop motivation, start by identifying why you want to master the skill. What are the benefits? How will it enhance your life or career? Write down your reasons and refer to them when your motivation wavers. Additionally, surround yourself with sources of inspiration and encouragement, such as successful practitioners of the skill or supportive mentors.

A - Attitude

A positive and growth mindset is essential for overcoming challenges and setbacks in the process of mastering a skill. Instead of viewing failures or setbacks as evidence of a lack of ability, adopt a growth mindset that views challenges as opportunities for learning and improvement. A positive attitude also involves focusing on the progress made, no matter how small, rather than solely on the final outcome.

S - Study

Continuous learning and studying of the skill are necessary to improve and achieve mastery. To study effectively, break down the skill into its component parts and focus on mastering one element at a time. Utilize a range of resources, such as books, online courses, and tutorials, to gain knowledge and insights. Additionally, seek out opportunities to practice the skill in a safe and supportive environment.

T - Training

Consistent practice and training of the skill is essential for improvement and mastery. Training should be deliberate and focused, with a clear understanding of what needs to be improved and how it will be achieved. Set achievable goals for each training session and track progress over time. It is also important to challenge oneself with increasingly difficult tasks to continually push beyond current skill levels.

E - Expert guidance

Receiving guidance and mentorship from an expert in the field can accelerate the learning and mastery process. Seek out experienced practitioners or mentors who can offer insights and feedback on your progress. They can provide targeted training and guidance, help identify areas for improvement, and provide motivation and encouragement.

R - Reflection

Reflecting on the learning process and identifying areas for improvement is necessary for growth and continued progress. Regularly evaluate progress and identify areas for improvement, and adjust training and study plans accordingly. It is also important to celebrate achievements and milestones along the way, as a way to maintain motivation and positivity.

Mastering a skill takes time, effort, and dedication, but by focusing on the M.A.S.T.E.R. method, success can be achieved. Motivation, attitude, study, training, expert guidance, and reflection are all critical components of this approach. By adopting this method, anyone can develop the necessary mindset, habits, and techniques for mastering a skill and achieving success.

Case Study: Using the M.A.S.T.E.R. Method to Master Guitar Playing

John is a 25-year-old college graduate who has always been passionate about music. He has been playing the guitar for a few years but feels stuck in his progress and wants to take his skills to the next level. John has heard about the M.A.S.T.E.R. method and decides to apply it to his guitar playing to achieve mastery.

M - Motivation

John starts by identifying his motivation for mastering the guitar. He writes down his reasons, including wanting to play in a band, write his own songs, and express himself creatively through music. He also surrounds himself with inspiring musicians and sets up a practice space in his home to stay motivated.

A - Attitude

John adopts a growth mindset and views challenges as opportunities for learning and improvement. He focuses on his progress, no matter how small, and avoids getting discouraged by setbacks. He also sets realistic expectations for himself and acknowledges that mastery takes time and effort.

S - Study

John breaks down guitar playing into its component parts, such as chord progressions, scales, and fingerpicking techniques. He utilizes a range of resources, including online courses, guitar tutorials, and music theory books. John also practices regularly, setting aside time each day to study and play the guitar.

T - Training

John practices deliberately, focusing on what he needs to improve and setting achievable goals for each practice session. He starts with easier songs and gradually increases the difficulty level as he improves. John also challenges himself with new techniques and songs that push him beyond his current skill level.

E - Expert guidance

John seeks out an experienced guitar player in his community who is willing to provide guidance and feedback on his progress. His mentor helps him identify areas for improvement, provides targeted training, and encourages him to push himself beyond his comfort zone.

R - Reflection

John regularly reflects on his progress and adjusts his training and study plans accordingly. He celebrates his achievements and milestones along the way, such as playing a difficult song or mastering a new technique. John also takes note of areas for improvement and seeks feedback from his mentor to continually grow and improve.

Results

Using the M.A.S.T.E.R. method, John sees significant improvement in his guitar playing within a few months. He feels more confident in his abilities and has started playing with other musicians in his community. John continues to practice and study guitar using the M.A.S.T.E.R. method, knowing that mastery is an ongoing process that requires dedication and effort.

Achieving Your Goals with the S.T.A.R.T Framework

When it comes to achieving your goals, it can be difficult to know where to begin. That's where the S.T.A.R.T framework comes in. This acronym can be used as a guide for setting and achieving your goals, whether they're personal or professional. Let's take a closer look at each step of the S.T.A.R.T framework and how it can help you achieve success.

Set a Specific Goal

The first step of the S.T.A.R.T framework is to set a specific goal. This means defining what you want to achieve and being as specific as possible. For example, instead of setting a goal to "get in better shape," you could set a specific goal to "run a 5K race in 6 months." By setting a specific goal, you give yourself a clear target to work towards and a way to measure your progress.

Take Action

Once you have your goal in mind, it's time to take action. This means breaking down your goal into smaller, more manageable steps and taking consistent action towards each step. For example, if your goal is to run a 5K race in 6 months, you could break down your training plan into weekly goals and daily tasks, such as running a certain distance or incorporating strength training into your routine. Taking action consistently is crucial to achieving your goals.

Assess Progress

Regularly assessing your progress towards your goal is the third step of the S.T.A.R.T framework. This means tracking your progress, celebrating your successes, and identifying areas where you need to improve. By regularly assessing your progress, you can stay on track and make any necessary adjustments to your plan.

Readjust as Needed

If you find that you're not making the progress you want, or if circumstances change, be willing to readjust your plan. This means being flexible and adaptable as needed. For example, if you get injured while training for your 5K race, you may need to adjust your training plan and focus on recovery before continuing your training. By being willing to readjust your plan, you can stay on track towards your goal even in the face of challenges.

Time Management

The final step of the S.T.A.R.T framework is time management. This means making sure to manage your time effectively so that you can make progress towards your goal consistently. Set deadlines for yourself and prioritize your tasks accordingly. For example, if you have a deadline to submit a report for work, prioritize your time to ensure that you're making progress towards that deadline every day. Effective time management is key to achieving your goals.

The S.T.A.R.T framework is a powerful tool for achieving your goals. By setting a specific goal, taking action, assessing progress, readjusting as needed, and managing your time effectively, you can achieve success in any area of your life. Remember to be patient and persistent in your pursuit of your goals, and the S.T.A.R.T framework can help guide you towards the finish line.

Case Study: Nathalie's Candle Business with START Goal Frame

Nathalie runs a successful candle business and has set a specific goal of increasing her average order size from 400 to 1000 candles per order. She wants to achieve this within the next 6 months.

Step 1: Set a Specific

Goal Nathalie has set a specific goal of increasing her average order size from 400 to 1000 candles per order within the next 6 months. This gives her a clear target to work towards and a way to measure her progress.

Step 2: Take Action

Nathalie breaks down her goal into smaller, more manageable steps. She starts by analyzing her current sales data to understand why her customers are buying only 400 candles per order on average. She discovers that most of her customers are buying candles for personal use and may not need more than 400 candles at once. Nathalie decides to target businesses and organizations that may need larger quantities of candles for events, gifts, or promotions. She creates a marketing campaign targeting businesses and starts networking with event planners, wedding coordinators, and corporate gift suppliers.

Step 3: Assess Progress

Nathalie regularly assesses her progress by tracking her sales data and analyzing her marketing campaign's effectiveness. She celebrates her successes by acknowledging every new business customer she acquires and every large order she receives. She also identifies areas where she needs to improve, such as improving her customer service to cater to the needs of businesses and offering more customized packaging options.

Step 4: Readjust as Needed

Nathalie understands that circumstances can change and is willing to readjust her plan as needed. She realizes that some businesses may require customized scents or packaging options that she doesn't offer yet. Nathalie researches her competitors and starts collaborating with local artists and designers to create new packaging options and custom scents that cater to businesses' needs.

Step 5: Time Management

Nathalie manages her time effectively by setting deadlines for herself and prioritizing her tasks accordingly. She sets specific days and times to network with potential business customers, work on her marketing campaign, and develop new product lines. She also delegates some of her routine tasks to her assistant to free up more time for strategic planning and execution.

After six months of consistent effort, Nathalie has achieved her goal of increasing her average order size from 400 to 1000 candles per order. She has acquired several new business customers and has expanded her product line to include custom scents and packaging options. Nathalie's successful use of the S.T.A.R.T framework has enabled her to achieve her specific goal and grow her candle business to the next level.

Applying Tesla's Magic Numbers (3-6-9)

As proposed by one of the 20th century's most talented inventors and thinkers, Nikola Tesla, the Tesla Code 3-6-9 is predicated on the premise that these numbers carry special meaning and potential for tapping into universal energy.

Though the numerical sequence known as Tesla's 369 code fundamentally symbolizes energy, frequency, and vibration, its applications extend far beyond these concepts. Intriguingly, these numbers can be harnessed and utilized in a myriad of ways, permeating various aspects of our daily life. The potential inherent within these numbers is not merely confined to the realms of science and mathematics, but rather, it presents opportunities for us to apply them creatively and strategically across multiple facets of our existence. Here, you'll learn how to use the Tesla Code 3-6-9 to reach your full potential, enhance your creativity, and succeed in a wide range of endeavors.

Appreciate the Importance of the Numbers 3-6-9

It was Nikola Tesla's firm belief that the numbers 3, 6, and 9 held the answers to unlocking the mysteries of the cosmos. Knowing the value of these numbers and the patterns they form is the first step in using them effectively.

GOAL SETTING IS MORE EFFECTIVE WHEN YOU USE THE 3-6-9 RULE.

Using the 3-6-9 rule can help you set and accomplish both professional and private objectives.

a) Choose three overarching aims that represent your short-, medium-, and long-term ambitions.

b) Create a road map to success by breaking each core goal down into six attainable sub-goals or milestones.

Every ninth day, week, or month, depending on the nature of your goals, you should assess your progress and adapt your approach.

ENCOURAGE INNOVATIVE THINKING AND RESOURCEFUL PROBLEM-SOLVING

Use the magic of 3-6-9 to spark your imagination and encourage original ideas.

a) Schedule three distinct periods of time during the day to think creatively.

b) Break down large, intractable issues into six smaller, more manageable chunks.

c) On the ninth day, evaluate your efforts to be inventive and problem-solving and consider whether or not a change in approach might be beneficial.

DEVELOP A DEVELOPMENT MINDSET BY FOLLOWING THE 3-6-9 RULE

A more robust and developed individual is one who has adopted a "3-6-9" mentality.

a) Develop a set of three guiding ideals or concepts that serve as the foundation for your daily decisions and actions.

b) Focus on developing six aspects of yourself, including your physical, mental, emotional, spiritual, social, and financial well.

c) Evaluate your progress toward personal development goals every ninth week and make course corrections or new resolutions as needed.

CREATE A MUTUALLY BENEFICIAL 3-6-9 SYSTEM

Put yourself in a position to succeed by surrounding yourself with like-minded people who want to see you succeed.

As a first step, find two more people who share your interests and can help you along the way by providing encouragement, advice, and company.

b) Add six people who can serve as mentors, role models, or specialists in your profession to your network.

c) Establish rapport with nine more people who come from different walks of life and gain from their perspectives and insights.

The Tesla Code of 3 6 9 is a secret formula for success, creativity, and fulfillment. You'll be better prepared to deal with the obstacles and seize the chances that come your way if you take the time to internalize the meaning of these figures and use them in your goal setting, problem-solving, personal development, and networking efforts.

Case Study: John's Career Development Plan with the Tesla code

John is a recent college graduate who has just started his first job at a marketing firm. He wants to excel in his career and move up the ranks quickly. However, he's not sure how to set goals that will help him achieve his ambitions. That's when he learns about the 3-6-9 rule and decides to apply it to his career development plan.

Step 1: Choose Three Overarching Aims

John's short-term aim is to gain experience in various areas of marketing. His medium-term goal is to become a team leader, and his long-term goal is to become a marketing director.

Step 2: Create a Road Map to Success

To achieve his short-term aim, John breaks it down into six attainable sub-goals, such as attending marketing conferences, taking online courses, and working on different marketing projects. Similarly, to achieve his medium-term goal, he breaks it down into six sub-goals, such as improving his leadership skills, building relationships with team members, and taking on additional responsibilities. For his long-term goal, John sets six sub-goals that include gaining experience in various marketing fields, building a network, and staying current on industry trends.

Step 3: Assess Progress and Adapt

John decides to assess his progress every ninth week. At the end of each period, he reviews his progress towards each of his sub-goals and makes adjustments to his plan if necessary. For example, if he realizes that he's not gaining the experience he needs in a particular area of marketing, he adjusts his plan to include more projects or tasks related to that area.

Results

John's career development plan using the 3-6-9 rule has been successful. He has gained valuable experience in various areas of marketing, taken on additional responsibilities, and built strong relationships with his team members. He has also attended marketing conferences and taken online courses, which have helped him stay up to date on industry trends. As a result, John has been promoted to team leader and is well on his way to achieving his long-term goal of becoming a marketing director.

The 3-6-9 rule is an effective framework for goal setting that can be applied to both professional and personal objectives. By breaking goals down into achievable sub-goals and assessing progress regularly, individuals can stay on track towards their long-term ambitions while also achieving smaller milestones along the way. John's career development plan is a great example of how the 3-6-9 rule can be used to achieve success.

The Life PLUG Method for Achieving Anything

Achieving your goals and dreams can be a challenging journey, but with the right approach, it can also be an exciting and fulfilling one. The LIFE PLUG Method is a simple and effective way to help you reach your goals and achieve anything you desire. It is based on four key principles: Plan, Learn, Upgrade, and Get it Done.

P - Plan

The first step in the LIFE PLUG Method is to plan. This means setting clear and specific goals, identifying the steps you need to take to achieve them, and creating a roadmap to success. By having a clear plan, you can stay organized and focused on your goals.

L - Learn

Learning is an important part of achieving your goals, and the LIFE PLUG Method encourages you to embrace this process. This could involve learning new skills, gaining knowledge, and seeking out new experiences. By doing this, you can build upon your strengths and develop the skills and knowledge you need to succeed.

U - Upgrade

Upgrading yourself is an important part of the LIFE PLUG Method. This means continuously improving your skills, knowledge, and abilities, and seeking out new opportunities for growth. By doing this, you can stay at the forefront of your industry and ensure that you are always making progress towards your goals.

G - Get it Done

The final step in the LIFE PLUG Method is to get it done. This means taking action, staying focused, and committing to the process. By doing this, you can turn your plans into reality and achieve your goals.

The LIFE PLUG Method is a powerful tool for achieving your goals and dreams. By following these four steps, you can stay organized, learn and grow, continuously improve, and turn your plans into reality. So, start by setting clear and specific goals, embrace the learning process, upgrade yourself, and get it done.

Case Study: Alexia's Shop Expansion using the LIFE PLUG Method

Alexia is a successful shop owner who dreams of expanding her business by opening branches all over the city. She wants to use the LIFE PLUG Method to achieve this goal.

Plan

The first step in the LIFE PLUG Method is to plan. Alexia sets clear and specific goals for her business expansion, which include opening three new branches within the next three years. She identifies the steps she needs to take to achieve these goals, such as finding suitable locations, hiring staff, and ensuring a steady supply of inventory. She creates a roadmap to success by breaking down each core goal into smaller, more attainable sub-goals, with deadlines for each step.

Learn

Alexia understands that learning is essential for achieving her goals, so she embarks on a journey of continuous learning. She attends seminars and workshops related to business management and retailing, reads business books and articles, and seeks advice from successful entrepreneurs. By doing this, she gains the knowledge and skills she needs to make informed decisions and stay ahead of the competition.

Upgrade

Alexia also recognizes the importance of upgrading herself to keep up with the fast-paced and ever-changing retail industry. She invests in upgrading her skills by attending training sessions on new retail technology and marketing strategies, and she also keeps up with the latest trends in fashion and design. By doing this, she ensures that her business stays relevant and competitive.

Get it Done.

The final step in the LIFE PLUG Method is to get it done. Alexia takes action and commits to the process of expanding her business. She stays focused on her goals, even during challenging times, and makes the necessary adjustments to her plan as needed. She hires a reliable team to help her with the expansion process and oversees the opening of each new branch. As a result of her hard work and dedication, Alexia successfully opens three new branches within three years, achieving her goal of expanding her business.

Using the LIFE PLUG Method, Alexia was able to plan, learn, upgrade, and get it done to achieve her dream of expanding her business. By following the principles of this method, she was able to stay organized, focused, and committed to her goals, which ultimately led to her success.

The DRIVE Method for Success and Productivity

Success and productivity are key factors in achieving our goals and living a fulfilling life. The DRIVE Method is a simple and effective way to help you stay motivated, focused, and productive as you work towards your goals. It is based on five key principles: Define, Rehearse, Improve, Verify, and Execute.

D - Define

The first step in the DRIVE Method is to define your goals. This means taking the time to understand what you want to achieve, why it's important to you, and what steps you need to take to get there. By having a clear understanding of your goals, you can stay focused and motivated as you work towards them.

R - Rehearse

Rehearsing is an important part of the DRIVE Method, as it helps you to prepare for success. This could involve visualizing your goals, practicing new skills, and preparing for potential challenges. By doing this, you can be better equipped to handle any obstacles that may arise as you work towards your goals.

I - Improve

Improving yourself is a key aspect of the DRIVE Method, as it helps you to grow and develop as you work towards your goals. This could involve seeking out new experiences, learning new skills, or seeking feedback to help you improve. By doing this, you can stay focused and motivated as you work towards your goals.

V - Verify

Verifying your progress is an important step in the DRIVE Method, as it helps you to assess your progress and make any necessary adjustments. This could involve setting milestones, tracking your progress, and seeking feedback from others. By doing this, you can ensure that you are making progress towards your goals and staying on track.

E - Execute

The final step in the DRIVE Method is to execute. This means taking action, staying focused, and committing to the process. By doing this, you can turn your plans into reality and achieve your goals.

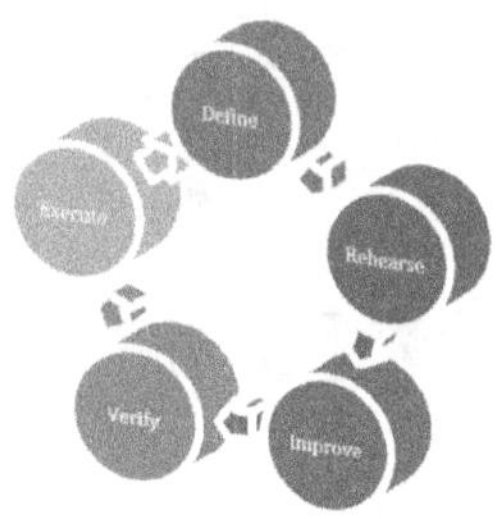

The DRIVE Method is a powerful tool for success and productivity. By following these five steps, you can stay motivated, focused, and productive as you work towards your goals. So, start by defining your goals, rehearsing for success, improving yourself, verifying your progress, and executing your plans.

Case Study: Struggling Engineer Improves Productivity with the DRIVE Method

Michael is a young engineer who has been struggling to stay productive and motivated in his job. Despite his best efforts, he often finds himself feeling overwhelmed and unsure of how to move forward with his projects. His managers have expressed concerns about his productivity, and he knows he needs to make some changes in order to succeed.

After doing some research, Michael discovers the DRIVE Method and decides to give it a try. He starts by defining his goals, both personal and professional, and creating a plan for achieving them. He breaks down his larger goals into smaller, more manageable tasks and creates a schedule for completing them.

Next, Michael starts rehearsing his tasks and practicing new skills. He seeks out feedback from his colleagues and supervisors to help him improve and adjust his approach as necessary. He also starts seeking out new learning opportunities, attending training sessions and conferences to stay up to date with the latest trends and technologies in his field.

As Michael works towards his goals, he frequently verifies his progress and adjusts his approach as needed. He sets milestones and tracks his progress, seeking feedback from others to help him stay on track. He celebrates his successes along the way and learns from his failures, using them as opportunities for growth and improvement.

Finally, Michael executes his plans with focus and determination. He stays committed to his goals, even when faced with challenges and setbacks. By using the DRIVE Method, he is able to stay motivated, focused, and productive, ultimately achieving his goals and earning the respect and recognition of his colleagues and supervisors.

In the end, Michael credits the DRIVE Method with helping him to turn his career around. By defining his goals, rehearsing his tasks, improving his skills, verifying his progress, and executing with focus and determination, he was able to achieve the success he had always dreamed of.

The R.O.A.D Cycle for Success

The R.O.A.D cycle is a framework for continuous improvement and personal growth. The four stages of the cycle, Reflect, Observe, Analyze, and Decide, provide a structured approach for examining experiences and making informed decisions for the future. By consistently following this cycle, individuals can identify areas for growth and make meaningful changes in their lives to achieve their goals.

Reflect: In this stage, individuals take the time to reflect on their past experiences and thoughts. This step involves evaluating previous actions, considering the impact they had, and exploring the emotions and motivations behind them. Reflecting on experiences can provide valuable insights and help individuals gain a deeper understanding of themselves.

Observe: The observation stage involves paying attention to the world around you. This step involves actively seeking out new experiences and gathering information to gain a broader perspective on the world. Observing the world can provide new insights and help individuals understand the context in which they operate.

Analyze: The analyze stage involves breaking down information gathered from the reflect and observe stages to gain a deeper understanding of the situation. This step requires critical thinking and the ability to evaluate information objectively. Analysis can help individuals identify patterns and make connections that might not have been apparent before.

Decide: The final stage of the R.O.A.D cycle involves making informed decisions based on the insights gained from the reflect, observe, and analyze stages. This step requires individuals to take action and make changes in their lives based on the information they have gathered. Decisions made in this stage should be aligned with individual goals and values.

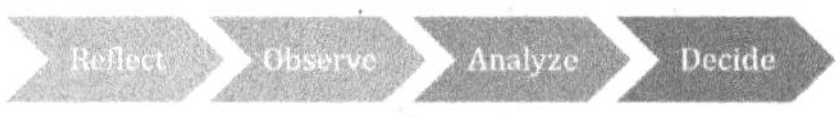

The R.O.A.D cycle is a powerful tool for personal growth and development. By consistently following the cycle, individuals can gain a deeper understanding of themselves and the world and make informed decisions that lead to a fulfilling and successful life.

Case Study: Overcoming Fear and Starting a Dream Business with the R.O.A.D Cycle

Lili had always dreamed of starting her own business, but she was too afraid to take the first step. She was unsure of what business to start, how to market it, and how to handle the financial aspects of it. Despite her fears, Lili decided to use the R.O.A.D cycle to help her overcome her doubts and start her dream business.

Reflect

Lili started by reflecting on her past experiences and thoughts. She asked herself what her passions were, what she enjoyed doing, and what she was good at. She also reflected on her fears and doubts about starting a business. Through this process, she gained a better understanding of herself and what she wanted to achieve.

Observe

The observation stage involved Lili actively seeking out new experiences and gathering information about the business world. She read books and articles about entrepreneurship, attended workshops and networking events, and talked to other business owners. By doing this, she gained a broader perspective on the business world and learned about the challenges and rewards of starting a business.

Analyze

In the analyze stage, Lili broke down the information she had gathered from the reflect and observe stages. She evaluated the strengths and weaknesses of her business idea, identified potential opportunities and threats in the market, and evaluated her financial situation. By doing this, she was able to develop a business plan that was aligned with her goals and values.

Decide

Finally, Lili made an informed decision to start her dream business. She took action and made changes in her life based on the insights she gained from the reflect, observe, and analyze stages. She created a business plan, secured financing, and launched her business. While she faced some challenges along the way, Lili remained focused and determined, using the R.O.A.D cycle to continuously improve and grow her business.

In the end, Lili credits the R.O.A.D cycle with helping her to overcome her fears and start her dream business. By reflecting on her past experiences and thoughts, observing the world around her, analyzing information objectively, and making informed decisions, she was able to turn her dream into a reality. Today, Lili is a successful business owner who is passionate about her work and grateful for the tools she used to get there.

The P.I.P.E Cycle for Production Success

The P.I.P.E cycle is a framework for managing and improving production processes. The four stages of the cycle, Preparation, Implementation, Performance, and Evaluation, provide a structured approach for ensuring consistent and effective production outcomes. By consistently following this cycle, organizations can improve their production processes and achieve their goals.

Preparation: In this stage, organizations lay the foundation for effective production by planning and organizing the process. This step involves defining the goals and objectives of the production process, identifying the resources needed, and developing a plan to ensure smooth implementation. Preparation is a crucial step in ensuring the success of the production process.

Implementation: The implementation stage involves putting the plan into action. This step involves the actual execution of the production process and requires the coordination of various resources and activities. Proper implementation is crucial in ensuring that the production process is carried out effectively and efficiently.

Performance: The performance stage involves monitoring the production process to ensure that it is operating as planned. This step involves collecting data, tracking progress, and making adjustments to the process as necessary. Performance monitoring is essential in ensuring that the production process is producing the desired results.

Evaluation: The final stage of the P.I.P.E cycle involves evaluating the production process to identify areas for improvement. This step involves analyzing the results of the production process, assessing the impact of the process on the organization, and determining areas for improvement. Evaluation is crucial in ensuring that the production process is consistently delivering the desired results.

The P.I.P.E cycle is a powerful tool for improving production processes. By consistently following the cycle, organizations can identify areas for improvement, make informed decisions, and take action to achieve their goals. By following the P.I.P.E cycle, organizations can ensure the success of their production processes and achieve their production goals.

Production PIPE Case study

Paul is the production manager of a wood products manufacturing company. His team is responsible for creating high-quality wood products, but they have been struggling with consistency in their production process. Paul decides to implement the P.I.P.E cycle to improve their production process.

Preparation

Paul starts by defining the goals and objectives of the production process. He identifies the resources needed, including materials, equipment, and manpower. He then develops a plan to ensure smooth implementation, which includes setting up a schedule for production, assigning tasks to team members, and providing training where necessary.

Implementation

The team puts the plan into action, with Paul overseeing the process. The team works together to ensure the smooth running of the production process. The team adheres to the schedule, and any issues that arise are addressed promptly.

Performance

Paul monitors the production process closely to ensure that it is operating as planned. He collects data on the production process, including the number of products produced, the time taken, and the quality of the products. He tracks progress and makes adjustments to the process as necessary.

Evaluation

After implementing the production process for a period, Paul evaluates the results. He analyzes the data collected and assesses the impact of the process on the organization. He then determines areas for improvement and creates a plan to address these areas.

By following the P.I.P.E cycle, Paul is able to improve the production process of the wood products manufacturing company. He identifies areas for improvement, makes informed decisions, and takes action to achieve the production goals. The implementation of the P.I.P.E cycle has resulted in a more efficient and effective production process, leading to increased productivity, profitability, and customer satisfaction.

RIDE For Resolving a Failure of Dream/Product

The RIDE method is a powerful tool that can help you overcome the obstacles that are preventing you from achieving your dream or realizing your product's potential. This method consists of four key steps, each of which can help you take your dream or product to the next level:

Redevelop/Re-design (R) - The first step in the RIDE method is to take a step back and re-examine your dream or product. Ask yourself what you can do differently to overcome the challenges that you are facing. Consider changing the design of your product, or the approach that you are taking to achieve your dream. This step is all about being creative and finding new solutions to old problems.

Inspect (I) - The second step in the RIDE method is to inspect your dream or product in detail. Take the time to look at each aspect of your dream or product and determine what is working well and what is not. This step is about being honest with yourself and acknowledging what needs to be improved.

Deploy (D) - The third step in the RIDE method is to put your newly developed or redesigned dream or product into action. This step is about taking the lessons that you have learned and using them to make your dream or product a reality. This is where you will put your plans into action and make your dream or product a tangible reality.

Examine (E) - The final step in the RIDE method is to examine the results of your efforts. Take the time to evaluate what worked well and what did not. Use this information to make further improvements to your dream or product. This step is all about continuous improvement and never being satisfied with mediocrity.

The RIDE method is a powerful tool that can help you overcome the obstacles that are preventing you from achieving your dream or realizing your product's potential. By following the four steps of this method, you can take your dream or product to the next level and achieve the success that you are looking for.

Case study for Jesse's failed shower gel product using the RIDE method.

Jesse Kimi had a dream of creating a unique and all-natural shower gel product. She spent months developing the formula and packaging, and was excited to bring her product to market. However, after a few months of sales, Jesse realized that her product was not selling as well as she had hoped. Customers complained about the scent and the packaging, and sales were declining. Jesse decided to use the RIDE method to address the issues with her product:

Redevelop/Re-design (R): Jesse realized that she needed to make some changes to her product to address the customer complaints. She decided to redevelop the formula and create new packaging that was more appealing to customers.

Inspect (I): Jesse took a closer look at the aspects of her product that were not working well. She realized that the scent was too strong and the packaging was not eye-catching enough. She also realized that the price was too high for the value that customers were receiving.

Deploy (D): Jesse put her newly redesigned product into action by creating a new formula with a milder scent, and designing new packaging that was more attractive to customers. She also lowered the price to make it more affordable for customers.

Examine (E): After a few months of selling her new and improved product, Jesse examined the results of her efforts. She saw that her sales had increased significantly and that customers were responding positively to her new product. She also realized that she needed to continue to make improvements to her product to keep up with customer demand.

By using the RIDE method, Jesse was able to identify the issues with her product and make the necessary changes to improve it. She was able to turn her failing product into a successful one by continuously improving and never being satisfied with mediocrity.

Bottleneck Analysis of Personal Activities

Bottleneck analysis is a process used to identify areas in a system where the flow of work is slowed down or impeded, often due to a limited resource or constraint. This approach can be applied to personal activities to identify areas where productivity is being hindered and to find ways to optimize the flow of work.

To conduct a bottleneck analysis of personal activities, follow these steps:

1. Identify the activities you regularly engage in: List all the tasks and activities you regularly engage in, such as work tasks, household chores, and personal projects.
2. Estimate the time required for each activity: Estimate the amount of time it takes to complete each activity.
3. Determine the dependencies between activities: Determine which activities are dependent on other activities and cannot be started until the previous activity is completed.
4. Identify potential bottlenecks: Look for activities that take longer than expected, have many dependencies, or require a significant amount of resources.
5. Analyze the bottlenecks: Identify the root causes of the bottlenecks and find ways to eliminate or reduce them.
6. Optimize the flow of work: Implement changes to optimize the flow of work and increase productivity.

Here's an example of a bottleneck analysis table for personal activities:

Activity	Time Required	Dependencies	Potential Bottlenecks	Root Causes	Solutions
Write report	2 hours	Must complete research first	Difficulty finding relevant research articles	Poor search terms	Refine search terms, ask for help from colleagues
Clean the kitchen	30 minutes	None	Dishes pile up quickly	Lack of dishwasher	Invest in a dishwasher, do dishes more frequently
Complete project proposal	4 hours	Requires input from team members	Team members are slow to respond	Busy schedules	Set clear deadlines, follow up with team members
Exercise	1 hour	None	Lack of motivation	Boredom	Try new exercises, find a workout buddy

In this example, the table lists several activities, their time requirements, dependencies, potential bottlenecks, root causes of the bottlenecks, and potential solutions. By analyzing each activity in this way, individuals can identify areas where productivity is being hindered and find ways to optimize the flow of work. This approach can help individuals to work more efficiently and effectively, and achieve their goals and objectives more quickly.

Criteria	Bottleneck Analysis Case Study (with Calculations)
Background	XYZ Manufacturing, a growing company, is experiencing production delays and struggling to meet customer demands. They decide to conduct a bottleneck analysis to identify and address the causes of these delays.
Objective	To identify and eliminate bottlenecks in the production process, resulting in increased efficiency, reduced lead times, and improved customer satisfaction.
Step 1: Identification	XYZ Manufacturing maps their production process, collects data on the time taken for each step, and calculates process capacity (units/ hour) for each machine:

Machine A: 60 units/hour Machine B: 45 units/hour (Bottleneck) Machine C: 80 units/hour Machine D: 70 units/hour

Machine B is identified as the bottleneck with the lowest process capacity.

Step 2: Analysis | The company performs a root cause analysis and finds that Machine B is outdated and improperly maintained, leading to reduced performance and increased downtime. The machine's utilization rate is 95%, while other machines' utilization rates are below 85%.

Step 3: Intervention | XYZ Manufacturing invests in upgrading Machine B, increasing its process capacity to 70 units/hour. They also implement a preventive maintenance schedule to minimize breakdowns and cross-train employees to operate the machines, reducing dependency on a few individuals.

Step 4: Monitoring | The company establishes key performance indicators (KPIs) to monitor the efficiency and throughput of the bottleneck machine. They measure the new utilization rates:

Machine A: 70% Machine B: 85% (Bottleneck, improved) Machine C: 75% Machine D: 65%

Continuous tracking and reviewing of the data ensure ongoing improvement.

Results | The bottleneck analysis leads to significant improvements in production efficiency and a reduction in lead times. With the increased process capacity of Machine B, the overall production output increases, and XYZ Manufacturing can now meet the growing demand for their products.

Conclusion | The bottleneck analysis proves to be a valuable tool for XYZ Manufacturing, helping them identify and address production bottlenecks, resulting in a more efficient production process and increased customer satisfaction. Calculations show the improvements in process capacity and utilization rates. |

Chapter 32: Soul

Unlocking the Power of the Soul Self

The soul self, also known as the inner self or the universe within, is a powerful force that can influence our thoughts, emotions, and actions. It is the source of our intuition, creativity, and inner peace. Understanding and tapping into the power of the soul self can lead to profound personal growth and fulfillment.

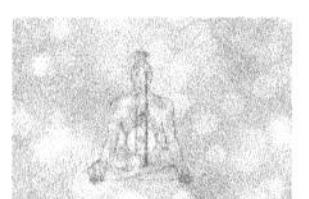

To unlock the power of the soul self, it is important to start by cultivating self-awareness. This involves taking the time to reflect on your thoughts, emotions, and behaviors, and understanding the underlying motivations and desires that drive them. By becoming more self-aware, you can start to identify patterns and habits that may be holding you back, and work towards breaking free from them.

Next, it is important to develop a spiritual practice that allows you to connect with the soul self. This could be meditation, journaling, or any other activity that helps you quiet the mind and connect with your inner self. It is important to make time for this practice regularly, so that you can maintain a connection with the soul self and continue to develop its power.

Once you have established a connection with the soul self, you can start to harness its power to help you achieve your goals. By trusting your intuition and allowing your inner voice to guide you, you can tap into a well of creativity and inspiration that can help you find new solutions and ideas.

Finally, it is important to maintain a positive relationship with the soul self by taking care of your mental and emotional well-being. This could involve practicing self-care, seeking out supportive relationships, and making time for activities that bring you joy and fulfillment.

In conclusion, unlocking the power of the soul self is a journey of self-discovery and personal growth. By cultivating self-awareness, developing a spiritual practice, trusting your intuition, and taking care of your mental and emotional well-being, you can tap into the power of the universe within and live a more fulfilling life.

The Soul Diet: A Path to Achieving Your Goals

Embark on an extraordinary journey of self-discovery and transformation with 'The Soul Diet: A Path to Achieving Your Goals.' Savor the delectable wisdom, nourish your deepest desires, and satisfy your cravings for success with this life-changing recipe for personal growth. Unleash your inner power, unlock your limitless potential, and create a radiant, thriving life that truly feeds your soul!

The Soul Diet is a four-step process for harnessing the power of your inner self to achieve your goals. By following these four steps, you can tap into the infinite potential of the universe within and bring your desires to life.

Step 1: Desire

The first step in the Soul Diet is to clearly define what it is that you desire. This could be a specific goal, a change you want to make in your life, or a feeling you want to experience. Whatever it is, it should be something that resonates deeply with your soul and aligns with your values and purpose.

Step 2: Imagine

Once you have a clear desire, the next step is to imagine what it would be like to have it. Close your eyes and allow yourself to fully experience the feelings and emotions that come with having your desire fulfilled. Imagine yourself living in a world where your desire has already become a reality. This visualization will help to imprint the image of your desire on your subconscious mind and make it more real in your mind.

Step 3: Expect

The third step in the Soul Diet is to expect that your desire will come to fruition. Trust that the universe is conspiring in your favor and that you are capable of making your dreams a reality. This step is about building confidence and courage, and strengthening your faith in your ability to bring your desires to life.

Step 4: Thankful

Finally, the fourth step in the Soul Diet is to be thankful for the manifestation of your desire. Express gratitude for the opportunities and experiences that are already present in your life, and acknowledge the abundance that already exists. By focusing on gratitude and positivity, you will attract more abundance and good into your life, and be better positioned to receive your desire when it arrives.

The Soul Diet is a powerful tool for achieving your goals and fulfilling your desires. By following these four steps and tapping into the power of the universe within, you can create the life you want and live with purpose, passion, and joy.

Steps	Description

Desire	Clearly define what it is that you desire, aligning with your values and purpose.
Imagine	Visualize yourself living in a world where your desire has already become a reality, imprinting the image on your subconscious mind.
Expect	Trust that the universe is conspiring in your favor and have confidence and courage in your ability to make your dreams a reality.
Thankful	Express gratitude for the opportunities and experiences present in your life, and acknowledge the abundance that already exists. Focus on positivity and attract more abundance and good into your life.

SOUL DIET Case Study

John, a college student, was struggling with anxiety and stress. He wanted to find a way to manage his mental health and feel more at ease. He decided to try the Soul Diet to help him achieve his goal.

Step 1: Desire John defined his desire as feeling calm and at ease. He wanted to be able to manage his anxiety and stress in a healthy way.

Step 2: Imagine John closed his eyes and visualized himself in a peaceful environment, surrounded by nature. He imagined himself feeling calm and relaxed, with a sense of inner peace.

Step 3: Expect John began to trust that the universe was working in his favor and that he was capable of managing his anxiety and stress. He built up his confidence and started to believe that he could achieve his desire.

Step 4: Thankful John expressed gratitude for the good things in his life, such as his supportive friends and family. He focused on the positives and looked for opportunities to be thankful for every day.

By following the Soul Diet, John was able to manage his anxiety and stress and feel more at ease. He used the visualization techniques he learned to calm his mind and focus on positivity. The Soul Diet helped John achieve his desired outcome, leading to a more fulfilling and happy life.

Chapter 33: Supply and Demand

Solving Supply and Demand Problems

Supply and demand are the basic forces that drive the economy. When supply and demand are balanced, the market operates efficiently and prices remain stable. However, when supply and demand are not in balance, market imbalances can occur, leading to problems such as surplus or shortage of goods, price fluctuations, and other economic challenges. In order to effectively solve supply and demand problems, it is important to understand the root cause of the problem and take appropriate action.

Identifying the Problem: The first step in solving supply and demand problems is to identify the root cause of the problem. This may involve analyzing market trends, consumer behavior, and the production process. It may also involve gathering data on supply and demand to better understand the market imbalances.

Evaluating Alternatives: Once the problem has been identified, the next step is to evaluate potential solutions. This may involve analyzing the potential impact of different solutions on the market, considering the costs and benefits of each option, and determining the feasibility of each solution.

Implementing Solutions: The final step in solving supply and demand problems is to implement the chosen solution. This may involve adjusting production processes, changing pricing strategies, or implementing new marketing campaigns. It is important to monitor the results of the solution and make adjustments as necessary.

Continuous Improvement: Solving supply and demand problems is an ongoing process. It is important to continuously monitor market trends, consumer behavior, and production processes in order to identify potential problems early and take appropriate action. By continuously improving the supply and demand balance, organizations can ensure the success of their business.

In conclusion, solving supply and demand problems requires a systematic approach that involves identifying the problem, evaluating alternatives, implementing solutions, and continuously improving the supply and demand balance. By taking a proactive approach to supply and demand management, organizations can ensure the success of their business and stay ahead of potential market imbalances.

The Law of Supply and Demand

The Law of Supply and Demand is a fundamental economic principle that governs the way markets function. It describes the relationship between the quantity of a product or service that producers are willing to supply and the quantity that consumers are willing to purchase at different price levels. The interaction between supply and demand determines the market price and the quantity of goods and services exchanged in a market.

Demand:

Demand refers to the quantity of a product or service that consumers are willing and able to purchase at a given price level. The Law of Demand states that, all other factors being equal, the quantity demanded of a good or service decreases as its price increases, and vice versa. This inverse relationship between price and quantity demanded is represented by the downward-sloping demand curve.

Factors that can influence demand include:

- Consumer preferences
- Income levels
- Prices of substitute and complementary goods
- Market expectations
- Population size and demographic factors

Supply:

Supply refers to the quantity of a product or service that producers are willing and able to bring to the market at a given price level. The Law of Supply states that, all other factors being equal, the quantity supplied of a good or service increases as its price increases, and vice versa. This direct relationship between price and quantity supplied is represented by the upward-sloping supply curve.

Factors that can influence supply include:

- Production costs
- Technological advancements
- Prices of related goods in production
- Market expectations
- Government policies (taxes, subsidies, regulations)

The Law of Supply and Demand maintains that the market will eventually reach an equilibrium point, where the quantity demanded equals the quantity supplied at a specific price level. At this equilibrium price, there is no shortage or surplus of the product or service, and both producers and consumers are satisfied with the market outcome.

When there is a change in one or more factors affecting supply or demand, it can lead to a shift in the supply and demand curves, resulting in a new equilibrium price and quantity. These shifts can cause price fluctuations and changes in the availability of goods and services in the market. Understanding the Law of Supply and Demand is essential for making informed decisions about production, pricing, and consumption in various economic contexts.

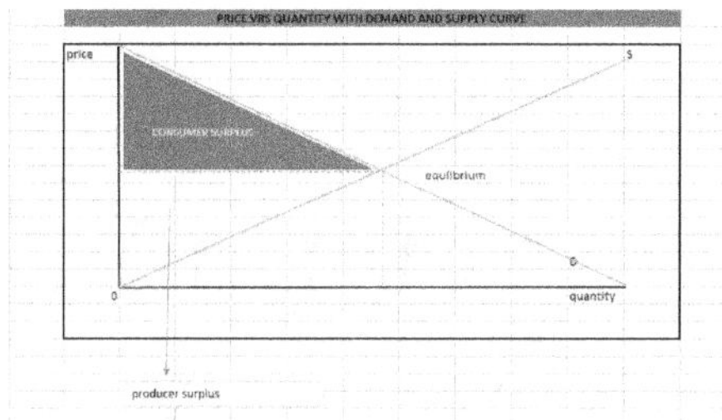

When we go to the store, we usually pay a price for what we want to buy. But sometimes we are willing to pay more for it than what we actually have to pay. That extra value we get is called consumer surplus. On the other hand, the producers of the things we buy also have a minimum price they want to sell it for. When they sell it for more than their minimum price, they get producer surplus. Both of these things help show how well the market is working, and when everyone gets the right price, it is the most efficient.

MARGINAL COST AND MARGINAL REVENUE

Marginal cost is how much more it costs to make one more thing. Marginal revenue is how much more money you get when you sell one more thing. It's important for businesses to know these things so they can decide how much to make and how much to charge. They want to make sure they make the most money they can.

Case Study: AX Toy Company

AX Toy Company produces a popular children's toy, the "Super Bouncy Ball." The company currently sells 10,000 Super Bouncy Balls per month at a price of $2 per ball. AX's production manager, Bob, is interested in determining the profit-maximizing level of output for the Super Bouncy Ball.

Bob knows that the cost of producing the first 10,000 Super Bouncy Balls is $10,000 per month. However, he also knows that the cost of producing each additional Super Bouncy Ball increases due to the need for additional labor and materials.

To determine the marginal cost of producing an additional Super Bouncy Ball, Bob looks at the cost of producing the 10,001st ball. He finds that the cost of producing this additional ball is $1.50. This means that the marginal cost of producing an additional ball is $1.50.

Next, Bob wants to calculate the marginal revenue of selling an additional Super Bouncy Ball. He knows that the current price of a Super Bouncy Ball is $2, so the marginal revenue of selling an additional ball will also be $2.

Finally, Bob needs to compare the marginal cost and marginal revenue to determine the profit-maximizing level of output. If the marginal revenue is greater than the marginal cost, then AX should produce and sell additional Super Bouncy Balls, as doing so will increase profits. However, if the marginal cost is greater than the marginal revenue, then producing additional Super Bouncy Balls will decrease profits.

In this case, the marginal revenue of selling an additional Super Bouncy Ball is $2, which is greater than the marginal cost of producing an additional ball, which is $1.50. Therefore, AX should produce and sell additional Super Bouncy Balls until the marginal revenue equals the marginal cost, which is the profit-maximizing level of output.

Profit-Maximizing Level of Output.

The profit-maximizing level of output is the production level at which a business earns the highest possible profit. It is determined by finding the point at which marginal revenue equals marginal cost. At this level, the business is producing the optimal quantity of goods or services that generate the highest profit.

For example, if a company produces widgets and sells them for $10 each, they may find that the cost to produce each widget (including materials, labor, and overhead) is $5. If they sell 100 widgets, their total revenue will be $1,000 (100 widgets x $10 each), and their total cost will be $500 (100 widgets x $5 each). This means their profit is $500.

However, if they increase production to 150 widgets, their total revenue will be $1,500 (150 widgets x $10 each), but their total cost will be $750 (150 widgets x $5 each). This means their profit is only $750 - $500 = $250.

In this scenario, the profit-maximizing level of output is 100 widgets, as this is the point at which the business earns the highest profit. Beyond this level, the cost of producing additional units (marginal cost) exceeds the revenue generated by selling those units (marginal revenue), resulting in lower profits.

Case Study: Profit Maximization for a Customized T-Shirt Company

Jane was recently hired as the new production manager at Custom-Tee, a company that specializes in producing customized t-shirts. CustomTee operates in an imperfectly competitive market, meaning it faces a downward-sloping demand curve.

Jane is responsible for determining the optimal production level to maximize the company's profit.

Production Costs: CustomTee incurs both fixed and variable costs in its production process. Fixed costs, such as rent and equipment, total $10,000 per month, while variable costs increase with production. The variable cost per t-shirt is $3 for the first 100 t-shirts, $4 for the next 100, and $5 for any additional t-shirts beyond 200.

Demand and Revenue: CustomTee has conducted a market analysis and determined that the demand for its customized t-shirts can be represented by the following equation:

Price (P) = 20 - 0.01 * Quantity (Q)

To calculate marginal revenue (MR), Jane needs to find the first derivative of the total revenue function with respect to quantity (Q). Total revenue (TR) is calculated as:

TR = P * Q = (20 - 0.01Q) * Q

Taking the first derivative with respect to Q, Jane gets:

MR = d(TR)/dQ = 20 - 0.02Q

Marginal Cost (MC): Jane calculates the marginal cost (MC) at different production levels:

- For the first 100 t-shirts, MC = $3
- For the next 100 t-shirts (101-200), MC = $4
- For any additional t-shirts (201+), MC = $5

Profit Maximization: To find the profit-maximizing production level, Jane needs to equate MC to MR and solve for Q. She does this for each MC range:

1. MC = $3 (first 100 t-shirts) MR = 20 - 0.02Q = 3 Q = (20 - 3) / 0.02 = 850

   Since 850 is beyond the range of the first 100 t-shirts, this is not the profit-maximizing level for this range.
2. MC = $4 (next 100 t-shirts) MR = 20 - 0.02Q = 4 Q = (20 - 4) / 0.02 = 800

Since 800 is within the range of the second MC level (101-200), this is the profit-maximizing quantity.

To maximize profit, Jane should advise CustomTee to produce 800 customized t-shirts per month. This production level ensures that the marginal cost of producing an additional t-shirt is equal to the marginal revenue gained from selling it, resulting in optimal profit.

Solving Supply and Demand Problems using the PDCA Cycle

The PDCA cycle is a continuous improvement framework that can be used to solve supply and demand problems in a systematic and efficient manner. The four stages of the PDCA cycle, Plan, Do, Check, and Act, provide a structured approach for continuously improving supply and demand balance and achieving business success.

Plan: The first stage of the PDCA cycle involves planning the solution to the supply and demand problem. This stage involves gathering data, analyzing the market and consumer trends, and identifying the root cause of the problem. Based on the data and analysis, a plan of action can be developed to address the problem and improve the supply and demand balance.

Do: The next stage is to put the plan into action. This involves implementing the solution and making any necessary adjustments to the production process, pricing strategy, or marketing campaigns.

Check: The third stage of the PDCA cycle is to monitor the results of the solution and check for effectiveness. This stage involves collecting data, tracking progress, and measuring the impact of the solution on the market and the business.

Act: The final stage of the PDCA cycle is to take action based on the results of the check. If the solution is effective, it can be continued and improved upon. If the solution is not effective, it can be modified or a new solution can be developed and implemented.

By following the PDCA cycle, organizations can continuously improve their supply and demand balance and achieve their business goals. The PDCA cycle provides a structured approach for identifying and solving supply and demand problems, ensuring the success of the business and staying ahead of potential market imbalances.

The PDCA cycle is a powerful tool for solving supply and demand problems. By consistently following the cycle, organizations can continuously improve their supply and demand balance, achieve their business goals, and ensure the success of their business.

Applying Supply and Demand Principles: By understanding the basic principles of supply and demand, we can make more informed decisions in our personal lives. For example, we can choose to purchase goods and services when the supply is high and the demand is low, taking advantage of lower prices. We can also plan our spending and investments based on our income and the demand for the goods and services we need.

Understanding the principles of supply and demand can help us make better financial decisions and improve our personal finances. By staying informed about market trends and consumer behavior, we can ensure that we are making smart choices that will benefit us in the long run.

Takt Time: Balancing Supply and Demand for Optimal Efficiency

In the world of manufacturing and production, striking the perfect balance between supply and demand is crucial for success. Takt time, a concept originating from the German word "Taktzeit," meaning cycle time, is a powerful tool that helps organizations align their production rates with customer demand. By understanding and effectively implementing takt time, businesses can optimize their processes, reduce waste, and ultimately, achieve greater efficiency.

Understanding Takt Time:

Takt time is a metric that represents the available production time divided by customer demand. Essentially, it is the maximum amount of time a product should take to be manufactured to meet customer requirements. By calculating takt time, organizations can establish a consistent production rhythm that matches the rate of demand, ensuring products are produced efficiently without overburdening resources or creating excess inventory.

Formula:

Takt Time = (Available Production Time) / (Customer Demand)

Advantages of Implementing Takt Time:

Implementing takt time in production processes offers several benefits:

a. Aligning supply with demand: Takt time helps organizations avoid overproduction and underproduction, ensuring they meet customer demand without accumulating excess inventory.

b. Increased efficiency: By creating a consistent production pace, organizations can optimize resource allocation and reduce waste, resulting in improved efficiency and cost savings.

c. Enhanced quality: A well-paced production process reduces the likelihood of errors and defects, leading to higher product quality.

d. Improved predictability: Takt time allows businesses to better forecast their production capabilities, making it easier to plan and make informed decisions.

Implementing Takt Time in Your Organization:

To effectively integrate takt time into your production process, follow these steps:

a. Calculate takt time: Use the formula mentioned above to determine the optimal production rate based on your available production time and customer demand.

b. Analyze current processes: Evaluate your existing production processes to identify bottlenecks, inefficiencies, and areas for improvement.

c. Adjust production processes: Modify your production processes to align with the calculated takt time, focusing on resource allocation, workflow, and pacing.

d. Monitor and review: Continuously monitor your production performance, and make adjustments as needed to maintain alignment with takt time.

Takt time is a valuable tool that helps organizations balance supply and demand for optimal efficiency. By understanding and applying this concept, businesses can enhance their production processes, reduce waste, and better meet customer needs. Embrace the power of takt time and unlock the full potential of your organization's production capabilities.

Cycle Time: Boosting Efficiency and Meeting Customer Demand

In today's competitive market, optimizing production processes to meet customer demand is crucial for businesses. One valuable tool for achieving this is cycle time, which measures the time it takes to complete a specific task or process in a production system. By understanding and effectively managing cycle time, organizations can enhance efficiency, reduce lead times, and better align their production rates with customer demand.

Understanding Cycle Time:

Cycle time is the time duration between the start and completion of a single unit of output in a production process. It is an essential metric for determining the efficiency of a manufacturing process and can be used to identify areas for improvement. By monitoring and optimizing cycle time, businesses can ensure that they are producing goods at a pace that aligns with customer demand while minimizing waste and excess inventory.

Advantages of Monitoring Cycle Time:

Monitoring and managing cycle time in production processes offer several benefits:

a. Aligning supply with demand: By optimizing cycle times, organizations can better align their production rates with customer demand, avoiding overproduction or underproduction.

b. Improved efficiency: Shortening cycle times can result in a more streamlined production process, leading to increased efficiency and cost savings.

c. Enhanced quality: Faster cycle times can help identify and eliminate bottlenecks or inefficiencies, leading to improved product quality and reduced defects.

d. Better decision-making: Understanding cycle times allows businesses to make informed decisions regarding resource allocation, capacity planning, and process improvements.

Implementing Cycle Time Management in Your Organization:

To effectively integrate cycle time management into your production process, follow these steps:

a. Measure existing cycle times: Identify key production processes and tasks, and measure the time it takes to complete each task from start to finish.

b. Analyze current processes: Evaluate your existing production processes to identify bottlenecks, inefficiencies, and areas for improvement that may be impacting cycle times.

c. Implement process improvements: Develop and execute strategies to optimize cycle times, such as reducing setup times, streamlining workflows, and implementing lean manufacturing techniques.

d. Monitor and review: Continuously track cycle times and adjust your production processes as needed to maintain optimal efficiency and alignment with customer demand.

Cycle time is an essential metric for organizations aiming to balance supply and demand, boost efficiency, and enhance product quality. By understanding and managing cycle time, businesses can optimize their production processes to meet customer needs while minimizing waste and costs. Embrace the power of cycle time management and unlock your organization's full potential in production efficiency.

Chapter 34: Magnetism

Applying Personal Magnetism for Success

Personal magnetism is the aura of charisma and confidence that attracts people towards you. It is the combination of qualities that make you stand out, both in your personal and professional life. When you have strong personal magnetism, you exude a powerful energy that draws people to you, and you are able to influence and persuade them to your point of view. Here are some tips on how to apply personal magnetism for success.

Develop a positive attitude: A positive attitude is the cornerstone of personal magnetism. When you have a positive outlook on life, people are naturally drawn towards you. Your positive energy is contagious and it makes others feel good when they are around you.

Be confident: Confidence is key when it comes to personal magnetism. When you are confident in yourself, you exude an aura of power and self-assurance that makes others trust and respect you. To develop confidence, practice positive self-talk, set achievable goals, and surround yourself with supportive people.

Be charismatic: Charisma is the ability to connect with others and make them feel comfortable. To be charismatic, listen to others actively, show genuine interest in what they have to say, and be positive and upbeat.

Show empathy: Empathy is the ability to understand and share the feelings of others. When you are able to connect with others on an emotional level, they feel seen and heard, and this creates a strong bond between you.

Be a good communicator: Effective communication is a key component of personal magnetism. When you are able to express your thoughts and ideas clearly, people are more likely to listen and respond positively.

Be adaptable: Personal magnetism requires you to be adaptable to different situations and people. When you are able to adjust your communication style to suit different people, you are able to build strong relationships with a diverse group of people.

Practice body language: Nonverbal cues, such as body language, can have a significant impact on how others perceive you. To exude personal magnetism, practice good posture, make eye contact, and use open and confident body language.

Personal magnetism is a powerful tool that can help you succeed in both your personal and professional life. By developing a positive attitude, being confident, charismatic, empathetic, a good communicator, adaptable, and practicing body language, you can attract people to you and influence them to your point of view. With time and effort, you can become a magnetic and successful individual.

Building Personal Magnetism for Attraction Using the 5W2H Method

The 5W2H method is a problem-solving technique that can be used to build personal magnetism and attract positive energy into your life. The 5W2H stands for "What, Why, Where, When, Who, How, and How Much." By using this method, you can identify your goals and the steps needed to achieve them, creating a clear path towards building personal magnetism.

Here's how to use the 5W2H method to build personal magnetism:

What: Define your goal of building personal magnetism. What specifically do you want to achieve, and why is it important to you?

Why: Identify the reasons why you want to build personal magnetism. What will it bring to your life? How will it help you to achieve your other goals?

Where: Think about where you want to build your personal magnetism. Will you focus on your professional life, your personal relationships, or both?

When: Determine when you want to start building your personal magnetism, and set a deadline for achieving your goal.

Who: Consider who can help you build your personal magnetism. Who are the people in your life who will support you and encourage you? Who can you turn to for advice and guidance?

How: Determine the steps you need to take to build your personal magnetism. Some strategies may include practicing self-confidence, being kind and compassionate, and being authentic and genuine in your interactions with others.

How much: Establish how much time, effort, and resources you are willing to put into building your personal magnetism. This will help you stay motivated and focused on your goal.

By using the 5W2H method, you can build a clear and actionable plan for building personal magnetism and attracting positive energy into your life. Remember, it's a process and it may take time, but with patience and persistence, you can achieve your goal and enjoy the benefits of having strong personal magnetism.

Sex Transmutation

Sex transmutation is a concept popularized by Napoleon Hill in his book, "Think and Grow Rich." It refers to the idea that a person can harness the creative energy generated through sexual desire and redirect it towards other aspects of their life, such as their work or personal goals. According to Hill, when this energy is properly channeled and focused, it can lead to increased productivity and success.

The concept of sex transmutation is based on the idea that sexuality is one of the most powerful and primitive instincts in human nature. When harnessed and directed towards a specific goal, this energy can drive a person to achieve great things.

To practice sex transmutation, it is important to understand the difference between healthy and unhealthy sexual desires. Unhealthy desires can be distracting and disruptive to a person's life, while healthy desires can be channeled into a powerful force for growth and achievement.

To effectively transmute sexual energy, it is necessary to redirect this energy towards a specific goal. This can be achieved through visualization, meditation, and other mental exercises that help to focus and direct this energy. It is important to remember that this process requires discipline and focus, as it can be easy to get sidetracked by other distractions.

It is also important to understand that sex transmutation is not about suppressing or denying one's sexual desires. Rather, it is about transforming these desires into a positive force that drives personal growth and success.

Sex transmutation is a powerful tool for personal development and success. By harnessing the creative energy generated through healthy sexual desires and redirecting it towards a specific goal, individuals can tap into a powerful force for growth and achievement. However, it is important to approach this process with discipline, focus, and an understanding of the difference between healthy and unhealthy desires.

Mastering Sex Transmutation Using the PDCA Cycle

The PDCA cycle, also known as the Deming Cycle or the Plan-Do-Check-Act cycle, is a continuous improvement methodology that can be applied to many areas of life, including mastering sex transmutation. The cycle consists of four steps: Plan, Do, Check, and Act.

Plan: In the first step, you need to identify the goal you want to achieve through sex transmutation. This could be a specific personal or professional goal, or a more general desire for personal growth and success. Next, you need to determine how you will redirect your sexual energy towards this goal. This could involve visualization exercises, meditation, or other mental techniques for directing your focus and energy.

Do: Once you have a plan in place, it's time to put it into action. Start by redirecting your sexual energy towards your goal and focus your thoughts and actions towards its achievement. Make this a daily practice and be persistent in your efforts.

Check: Regularly assess your progress towards your goal and reflect on what is working and what is not. Take note of any obstacles or challenges that arise and determine how you can overcome them.

Act: Based on your reflection and analysis, make any necessary changes to your plan and continue to put it into action. Repeat the cycle as needed until you have achieved your goal.

By using the PDCA cycle to master sex transmutation, you can ensure that you are continually making progress towards your goal and making any necessary adjustments along the way. This process requires discipline and focus, but by sticking to it, you can tap into the powerful energy generated through healthy sexual desires and use it to drive personal growth and success.

The PDCA cycle is a useful tool for mastering sex transmutation and harnessing the power of sexual energy to achieve personal and professional goals. By following the cycle of Plan, Do, Check, and Act, individuals can direct this energy towards their desired outcomes and achieve great things in their lives.

The Power of Enthusiasm: A Key to Success

Enthusiasm is a powerful force that can drive individuals towards success in all aspects of life. It is a positive and energetic feeling of excitement and inspiration that can be contagious and motivating to those around you. Enthusiasm is often described as a spark that ignites passion and motivation, leading individuals to take action and achieve their goals.

In the world of business and entrepreneurship, enthusiasm can play a crucial role in determining success. Research has shown that individuals who approach their work with enthusiasm and passion are more likely to be successful than those who lack this energy and drive. Enthusiasm can give individuals a greater power to overcome challenges and push through difficulties, helping them to achieve their goals and reach new heights of success.

There are several key benefits of having enthusiasm in the workplace, including:

1. Increased Motivation: Enthusiasm is a powerful motivator, providing individuals with the energy and drive to pursue their goals and overcome obstacles. When individuals approach their work with excitement and passion, they are more likely to stay focused, work harder, and achieve their objectives.

2. Improved Relationships: Enthusiasm is contagious, and individuals who exude this energy and positivity are often more

approachable and likable. In the workplace, this can lead to improved relationships with colleagues, clients, and customers, as well as better teamwork and collaboration.

3. Enhanced Creativity: Enthusiasm can also enhance an individual's creativity, leading to new and innovative ideas and solutions. When individuals approach their work with excitement and passion, they are more likely to think outside the box and find new and creative ways to solve problems and achieve their goals.

4. Better Decision-Making: Enthusiasm can also lead to improved decision-making, as individuals who approach their work with excitement and passion are more likely to take calculated risks and pursue new opportunities. This can result in greater success and growth in their careers and businesses.

5. Increased Productivity: Finally, enthusiasm can lead to increased productivity, as individuals who approach their work with energy and drive are more likely to complete tasks and achieve their goals in a timely manner.

Enthusiasm is a powerful force that can drive individuals towards success in all aspects of life, including business and entrepreneurship. By approaching their work with excitement and passion, individuals can increase their motivation, improve their relationships, enhance their creativity, make better decisions, and increase their productivity. Ultimately, this can lead to greater success and fulfillment in their personal and professional lives.

Self-Control and Sexual Intelligence

Sexual intelligence is the ability to understand and manage one's own sexuality in a healthy and positive way. One of the key components of sexual intelligence is self-control. In this chapter, we will explore how self-control plays a crucial role in developing sexual intelligence and how to cultivate it.

Understanding Self-Control

Self-control is the ability to regulate your own behavior, emotions, and thoughts in the face of temptation or desire. It involves delaying gratification and making conscious choices that align with your long-term goals and values. In terms of sexuality, self-control means being able to resist impulsive sexual behavior and instead choose to engage in sexual activities that are safe, consensual, and respectful.

The Importance of Self-Control in Sexual Intelligence

Self-control is a vital component of sexual intelligence. It allows individuals to make informed decisions about their sexual behavior and avoid engaging in risky or harmful activities. Without self-control, people may engage in behaviors that put their physical and emotional health at risk, such as having unprotected sex or engaging in sexual activities with multiple partners.

Additionally, self-control is essential for building healthy and respectful relationships. When individuals have self-control, they are better able to communicate their sexual desires and boundaries, listen to and respect their partners' desires and boundaries, and make choices that are mutually beneficial for both partners.

Cultivating Self-Control

Developing self-control is a lifelong process that requires practice and discipline. Here are some tips for cultivating self-control in the context of sexual intelligence:

a. Develop a healthy relationship with sex

One of the first steps in cultivating self-control is developing a healthy relationship with sex. This means taking the time to understand your own sexual desires and values, as well as learning about safe and respectful sexual practices. Educate yourself about the risks and benefits of different sexual behaviors, and make informed decisions that align with your values.

b. Identify triggers

Identifying the triggers that lead to impulsive sexual behavior can help individuals develop self-control. This might involve recognizing situations or feelings that trigger sexual desires or identifying patterns of behavior that lead to risky sexual activities. Once identified, individuals can develop strategies for avoiding these triggers or managing them in a healthy way.

c. Practice mindfulness

Practicing mindfulness can help individuals develop self-awareness and self-control. Mindfulness involves paying attention to the present moment without judgment. When individuals practice mindfulness, they are better able to identify their thoughts and emotions, and make conscious choices about their behavior.

d. Set goals

Setting goals for sexual behavior can help individuals develop self-control. For example, individuals might set a goal to only engage in sexual activities that are safe, consensual, and respectful. By setting clear goals, individuals can hold themselves accountable for their behavior and work towards building healthy and positive sexual relationships.

self-control is an essential component of sexual intelligence. Developing self-control involves cultivating a healthy relationship with sex, identifying triggers, practicing mindfulness, and setting clear goals for sexual behavior. By building self-control, individuals can make informed decisions about their sexual behavior, build healthy relationships, and maintain physical and emotional well-being.

Chapter 35: Case Studies

Building a Real Estate Business Using the Law of Attraction

The Law of Attraction is a concept that states that we can attract positive outcomes into our lives by focusing on positive thoughts and feelings. This principle can be applied to building a successful real estate business, allowing individuals to manifest their desired outcomes and create the business of their dreams.

The Basics of the Law of Attraction

The Law of Attraction states that we attract what we focus on, both consciously and unconsciously. When we focus on positive thoughts and feelings, we attract positive experiences and outcomes into our lives. Conversely, when we focus on negative thoughts and feelings, we attract negative experiences and outcomes.

To use the Law of Attraction in building a real estate business, it is important to focus on positive thoughts and feelings related to success, abundance, and prosperity. This can include visualizing a successful business, feeling gratitude for the abundance in one's life, and focusing on the positive aspects of the real estate industry.

Applying the Law of Attraction in Real Estate

Visualization: Visualize your real estate business as a successful and thriving enterprise. Imagine yourself closing deals, building relationships with clients, and experiencing financial success. This visualization will help to attract positive experiences and outcomes into your life.

Gratitude: Express gratitude for the abundance in your life, including your current clients and opportunities for growth. Focusing on gratitude can help to attract more abundance into your life and business.

Positive Affirmations: Use positive affirmations to reinforce your beliefs about your business and your ability to succeed. For example, you can affirm "I am a successful real estate agent, and I attract abundance and prosperity into my life."

Surround Yourself with Positive People: Surround yourself with positive and supportive people who believe in your vision and goals. This can include clients, colleagues, and friends who support your business and encourage you to succeed.

Take Action: While visualization and positive affirmations are important, they must be accompanied by action to be effective. Take steps to build your business, such as networking, marketing, and building relationships with clients.

The Law of Attraction can be a powerful tool in building a successful real estate business. By focusing on positive thoughts and feelings, visualizing success, expressing gratitude, surrounding yourself with positive people, and taking action, individuals can attract the abundance and prosperity they desire into their lives and businesses. With persistence and determination, the Law of Attraction can help individuals build the real estate business of their dreams.

Improving Real Estate Business Using the DMAIC Method

The DMAIC (Define, Measure, Analyze, Improve, Control) method is a systematic approach used to improve processes and solve problems. It is commonly used in the field of quality management, and can be applied to a wide range of industries, including real estate. By using the DMAIC method, real estate businesses can improve their processes and increase efficiency, ultimately leading to improved results.

The DMAIC Method: A Step-by-Step Approach

Define: Identify the problem or opportunity for improvement in the real estate business. This can be a specific issue, such as a low conversion rate for leads, or a general desire to increase efficiency in a certain area of the business.

Measure: Gather data and establish a baseline for the problem or opportunity for improvement. This may involve collecting data on conversion rates, response times, or any other relevant metrics.

Analyze: Analyze the data collected in the previous step to identify the root cause of the problem or opportunity for improvement. This may involve using tools such as cause-and-effect diagrams or process flow charts to identify areas for improvement.

Improve: Based on the analysis, develop and implement solutions to improve the process or resolve the problem. This may involve changing processes, implementing new technology, or making other changes to improve efficiency and results.

Control: Establish a system for monitoring and controlling the improvements made to ensure they remain effective over time. This may involve regularly collecting and analyzing data, and making any necessary adjustments to maintain the desired level of performance.

Examples of Improving Real Estate Business Using the DMAIC Method

Improving Lead Conversion Rates: A real estate business may want to improve its lead conversion rates, which is the percentage of leads that result in a sale. By using the DMAIC method, the business can identify the root cause of the low conversion rate and make changes to improve the process and increase efficiency.

Improving Response Time: A real estate business may want to improve its response time, which is the time it takes to respond to a customer inquiry. By using the DMAIC method, the business can identify the root cause of the slow response time and make changes to improve the process and increase efficiency.

Improving Marketing Efforts: A real estate business may want to improve its marketing efforts, such as increasing the number of leads generated from a particular marketing campaign. By using the DMAIC method, the business can identify the root cause of the low lead generation and make changes to improve the marketing process and increase efficiency.

The DMAIC method is a powerful tool for improving real estate businesses. By following the step-by-step approach of Define, Measure, Analyze, Improve, and Control, businesses can identify areas for improvement and make changes to increase efficiency and achieve better results. Whether it's improving lead conversion rates, response time, or marketing efforts, the DMAIC method can help real estate businesses to achieve their goals and succeed in a competitive market.

Improving Real Estate Business Using SWOT Analysis

SWOT analysis is a strategic planning tool used to evaluate the Strengths, Weaknesses, Opportunities, and Threats (SWOT) of a business. In the real estate industry, SWOT analysis can be a valuable tool for improving business performance and identifying areas for growth. By considering each of the four elements of the SWOT analysis, real estate businesses can gain a comprehensive understanding of their strengths and weaknesses, as well as the opportunities and threats that exist in the market.

Conducting a SWOT Analysis for Your Real Estate Business

Strengths: Identify the unique strengths and advantages that your real estate business has in comparison to your competitors. This could include a strong brand, a large network of contacts, or a deep understanding of the local real estate market.

Weaknesses: Identify areas where your real estate business may be vulnerable or at a disadvantage when compared to your competitors. This could include a lack of resources, an outdated website, or a limited understanding of market trends.

Opportunities: Consider the external factors that could create new opportunities for your real estate business. This could include changes in consumer preferences, new technologies, or a growing market for a particular type of property.

Threats: Identify external factors that could pose a threat to your real estate business, such as economic downturns, changes in regulations, or increased competition.

Using the Results of Your SWOT Analysis to Improve Your Business

Once you have completed your SWOT analysis, you can use the results to make informed decisions about improving your real estate business. Here are a few examples of how the results of a SWOT analysis can be used:

Leveraging Strengths: If your real estate business has a strong brand, you can use this to your advantage by investing in marketing efforts to reach a wider audience and attract more clients.

Addressing Weaknesses: If your real estate business has a limited understanding of market trends, you can invest in market research and analysis to gain a deeper understanding of the local real estate market and make informed decisions.

Taking Advantage of Opportunities: If new technologies are emerging in the real estate market, you can invest in these technologies to stay ahead of your competitors and improve your business.

Mitigating Threats: If your real estate business is vulnerable to economic downturns, you can invest in financial planning and risk management strategies to mitigate the impact of these threats.

SWOT analysis is a valuable tool for real estate businesses looking to improve their performance and achieve their goals. By considering the four elements of the SWOT analysis, businesses can gain a comprehensive understanding of their strengths and weaknesses, as well as the opportunities and threats that exist in the market. By using the results of their SWOT analysis to make informed decisions, real estate businesses can improve their processes, increase efficiency, and achieve better results.

Applying the PDCA Cycle to Improve Real Estate Business Performance

The PDCA (Plan-Do-Check-Act) cycle is a continuous improvement method that can be applied to a wide range of business processes, including those in the real estate industry. The PDCA cycle provides a structured approach to making improvements, allowing businesses to achieve their goals and remain competitive in an ever-changing market.

Step 1: Plan

The first step in the PDCA cycle is to plan the improvement process. This involves defining the problem or opportunity for improvement, as well as setting specific goals and objectives for the process. In the real estate industry, this might involve identifying areas where the business is underperforming, or opportunities for growth that could be pursued.

Step 2: Do

The second step in the PDCA cycle is to take action and implement the planned improvements. This may involve making changes to processes, procedures, or systems within the real estate business, or developing new strategies to achieve the goals and objectives set in the planning phase.

Step 3: Check

The third step in the PDCA cycle is to check the results of the changes made in the previous step. This may involve collecting data and measuring the impact of the changes on the business, as well as evaluating whether the goals and objectives set in the planning phase have been met. In the real estate industry, this might involve tracking sales and revenue, customer satisfaction, and other key metrics.

Step 4: Act

The final step in the PDCA cycle is to take action based on the results of the check phase. If the changes made in the previous step have been successful, they should be continued and improved upon. If the changes have not been successful, the process should be re-evaluated, and new changes should be made to improve the results.

Examples of How the PDCA Cycle Can Be Applied to Real Estate Businesses

Improving Customer Satisfaction: If a real estate business is experiencing low levels of customer satisfaction, they can use the PDCA cycle to identify the problem, make changes to improve the customer experience, and track the results of these changes over time.

Streamlining Processes: If a real estate business is experiencing inefficiencies in their processes, they can use the PDCA cycle to identify the root cause of the inefficiencies, make changes to streamline the processes, and evaluate the results of these changes over time.

Expanding the Business: If a real estate business is looking to expand into new markets, they can use the PDCA cycle to plan the expansion, implement the expansion strategies, track the results of the expansion, and make changes as needed to achieve their goals.

The PDCA cycle is a valuable tool for real estate businesses looking to improve their performance and achieve their goals. By following the four steps of the PDCA cycle, businesses can make informed decisions about changes to their processes and systems, track the results of these changes, and continuously improve their performance over time. By applying the PDCA cycle to their operations, real estate businesses can stay ahead of their competitors, respond to changing market conditions, and achieve long-term success.

Lean Life at Home

Your home should be a sanctuary, a place where you can relax and recharge after a long day. Embracing a lean life at home means creating a living environment that fosters balance, efficiency, and sustainability. In this part, we will explore three essential components of a lean life at home: decluttering your living space, creating efficient home systems, and adopting sustainable living practices.

DECLUTTERING YOUR LIVING SPACE

Decluttering your living space is a crucial step in creating a more harmonious and stress-free home environment. By eliminating excess items and organizing your belongings, you can increase your focus, mental clarity, and overall well-being.

The Benefits of Decluttering

- Increased focus and mental clarity
- Reduced stress and anxiety
- Easier maintenance and cleaning

THE KONMARI METHOD

The KonMari Method revolves around the concept of only keeping items that "spark joy" and discarding those that do not. By focusing on the emotional connection, we have with our belongings, this method aims to create a more harmonious and purposeful living space.

The Six Basic Rules of the KonMari Method

Commit to tidying up

Make a firm decision to declutter and organize your entire home, dedicating the necessary time and effort.

Imagine your ideal lifestyle

Visualize the kind of living space and lifestyle you want to achieve after decluttering, using this as motivation throughout the process.

Finish discarding first

Before organizing, sort through all items and decide what to keep or discard. This ensures you're only organizing items that truly spark joy.

Tidy by category, not location

Instead of decluttering room by room, sort items by category (e.g., clothing, books, papers). This approach provides a clearer perspective on the volume of each category in your home.

Follow the right order

Kondo recommends decluttering in a specific order: clothing, books, papers, komono (miscellaneous items), and sentimental items. This order helps build momentum and decision-making skills.

Ask yourself if the item sparks joy

Hold each item in your hands and ask yourself if it sparks joy. If it does, keep it; if not, thank the item for its service and let it go.

THE FOUR-BOX METHOD

Decluttering can be a daunting task, especially if you have a lot of items to sort through. The four-box method is a simple and effective way to declutter your living space and make decisions about what to keep, donate, trash, or relocate.

Create Four Boxes

The first step in the four-box method is to create four boxes or designated areas to sort your items. These boxes can be actual boxes or labeled areas in your living space. The four boxes should be labeled: keep, donate, trash, and relocate.

Sort Your Items

Once you have your boxes or designated areas, it's time to start sorting your items. Begin in one area of your living space, such as a closet or dresser, and go through each item one by one. Ask yourself if the item is something you want to keep, donate, trash, or relocate.

Keep Box

The keep box is for items that you want to keep and continue to use. These are items that you use frequently, have sentimental value, or are essential to your daily life. Be mindful not to keep items just because you think you might need them someday. Only keep items that you truly value and will use.

Donate Box

The donate box is for items that are still in good condition but no longer serve a purpose in your life. These items can be donated to a local charity or thrift store. Not only will you be decluttering your living space, but you'll also be giving back to your community.

Trash Box

The trash box is for items that are no longer usable or in poor condition. These items should be disposed of properly, either by recycling or throwing them away. Be sure to check with your local recycling guidelines for proper disposal of certain materials.

Relocate Box

The relocate box is for items that belong in another area of your living space. These items should be moved to their proper location immediately after sorting. This box can prevent items from piling up in the wrong place and creating more clutter.

EMBRACING 5S TO ELIMINATE CLUTTER

Every one of us is guilty of hoarding and clinging to possessions we no longer use. Cluttered homes can be stressful, impacting residents' emotional well-being as well as their ability to go about their daily lives. To help you declutter, organize, and keep your home stress-free, we present the idea of "Lean Living at Home," which is based on the 5S methodology used in Lean Manufacturing.

Seiri (Sort)

The first order of business in adopting a Lean Lifestyle at Home is to do a thorough inventory of all of your personal possessions. First, divide your stuff into three distinct piles:

a) Necessities: Things you can't live without, like the clothes on your back or the appliances in your kitchen.

b) Infrequently used but necessary; examples include seasonal attire, holiday decorations, and tools.

c) Unnecessary pile consists of things you no longer need or use, or that are broken or out of date.

After you've sifted through your stuff, it's time to get rid of the unused goods. Depending on their condition, you can either donate, sell, or recycle them. It's important to keep in mind that clearing up clutter and unneeded belongings can feel great.

Seiton (Set in Order)

In the second phase, "Put in Order," you'll give everything a home. If you keep your home or office neat and tidy, you'll save time and energy in your day-to-day activities.

To straighten out your house:

Put things in order of how often you use them, a. Put things you use often within easy reach, and put things you don't use often in places you have to go to further afield to get to.

Clearly label your storage areas so that it's quicker and simpler to retrieve your belongings.

Make use of storage solutions like shelves, drawers, and containers to maintain order in your home.

Seiso (Shine)

If you keep your house tidy, you'll have a more pleasant experience there. Maintaining a clean and clutter-free home with routine cleaning and upkeep is an excellent way to improve the quality of one's life.

So that Seiso can be used:

Dedicate time every week to clean every room in your house, including the dusting, vacuuming, and mopping.

In order to get more use out of your furniture, gadgets, and home appliances, you need keep them clean and perform routine maintenance on them.

Motivate family members to pitch in with keeping the home tidy.

Seiketsu (Standardize)

The first three steps of Lean Living at Home can only be maintained with the support of standardization. You can keep your home neat and tidy by instituting rules and rituals.

Towards a more standardized dwelling:

Have a plan and a checklist to keep your home tidy and organized.

Figure out who does what around the house and what they're responsible for.

Assess the efficiency of your home's current system and make any necessary changes on a regular basis.

Shitsuke (Sustain)

The last phase consists of sticking to your newfound routine and maintaining your progress through discipline and determination. This calls for persistent work and the formation of new routines.

In order to live frugally at home:

After using an item,

a) make a concerted attempt to return it to its proper storage location.

c) Do a regular inventory of your possessions and donate or sell anything that is no longer useful to you.

c) Urge everyone living there to stick to the routines and expectations you've set.

The 5S approach can be used to build a more peaceful, orderly, and productive family life. Your happiness, efficiency, and satisfaction with life are all likely to rise as you adopt the practices outlined in Lean Living at Home.

5S Step	Description	Example

Sort	Remove unnecessary items and keep only what's needed	Donate or sell clothes that haven't been worn in a year
Set in order	Organize items in a logical and efficient manner	Store cooking utensils near the stove
Shine	Clean and maintain the area	Wipe down countertops and sweep the floor
Standardize	Establish a consistent way of doing things	Always put items back in their designated place
Sustain	Continuously maintain the organized and clean space	Regularly declutter and donate or sell unwanted items

This table provides a brief overview of each step of the 5S methodology and gives an example of how it can be applied in a home setting to eliminate clutter and create a more organized and efficient living space.

Implementing Six Sigma in the Distribution Industry/ Supply Chain

The distribution industry plays a critical role in enabling businesses to recoup their investments and generate profits. A well-planned distribution strategy ensures that products reach the right customers through the right channels. In this competitive landscape, it's essential to continually improve efficiency, reduce costs, and enhance customer satisfaction. This case study discusses how implementing Six Sigma, a data-driven methodology for process improvement, can help achieve these goals in the distribution industry.

Understanding Six Sigma in Distribution

Six Sigma is a systematic approach to identifying and eliminating defects and inefficiencies in processes, aiming for near-perfect results. In the distribution industry, it can be applied to various aspects, including inventory management, order fulfillment, logistics, and customer service.

a) Define: Set clear objectives and identify the key processes that need improvement within the distribution chain.

b) Measure: Collect data on current performance and establish relevant metrics to track progress.

c) Analyze: Identify the root causes of inefficiencies, bottlenecks, or defects in the distribution processes.

d) Improve: Implement solutions to address the root causes, and monitor their impact on performance.

e) Control: Establish ongoing monitoring and control mechanisms to sustain the improvements and prevent future inefficiencies.

Optimizing Inventory Management

Effective inventory management is crucial for meeting customer demand while minimizing costs. Six Sigma can help optimize inventory levels and reduce excess stock, stockouts, and obsolescence.

a) Analyze demand patterns and forecast accuracy to better predict customer needs.

b) Implement inventory control mechanisms, such as just-in-time (JIT) or vendor-managed inventory (VMI), to minimize stock levels while maintaining service levels.

c) Use root cause analysis to identify and address issues leading to stock discrepancies, such as inaccurate data entry or procedural errors.

Streamlining Order Fulfillment

Efficient order fulfillment is essential for customer satisfaction and timely product delivery. Six Sigma can be employed to enhance the accuracy and speed of order processing, picking, packing, and shipping.

a) Analyze the order fulfillment process to identify inefficiencies and potential areas for improvement.

b) Implement solutions, such as automation or process standardization, to reduce errors and cycle times.

c) Monitor key performance indicators (KPIs) to track progress and ensure continuous improvement.

Enhancing Logistics and Transportation

Logistics and transportation play a vital role in delivering products to customers promptly and cost-effectively. Six Sigma can help optimize routes, reduce transportation costs, and improve delivery times.

a) Collect and analyze data on transportation costs, delivery times, and service levels.

b) Optimize routing and scheduling to minimize transportation costs and delivery times.

c) Implement real-time tracking and performance monitoring to ensure timely deliveries and address issues proactively.

Improving Customer Service

Excellent customer service is crucial for retaining customers and maintaining a positive brand reputation. Six Sigma can help enhance communication, responsiveness, and issue resolution in the customer service process.

a) Identify and prioritize customer pain points and areas for improvement.

b) Standardize customer service processes and implement best practices for communication and issue resolution.

c) Monitor customer satisfaction levels and use feedback to drive continuous improvement.

By implementing Six Sigma in the distribution industry, companies can optimize their operations, reduce costs, and improve customer satisfaction. Through a systematic approach to process improvement, Six Sigma enables businesses to identify and address inefficiencies and defects, ultimately leading to enhanced performance and long-term success.

Six Sigma Application in Warehouse Operations

Warehouses play a crucial role in the retail industry, ensuring smooth operations and timely delivery of products to customers. Efficient warehouse management is vital for maintaining customer satisfaction and optimizing costs. This case study discusses how applying Six Sigma, a data-driven methodology for process improvement, can help enhance warehouse operations and overcome the complexities of managing inventory and order fulfillment.

Understanding Six Sigma in Warehouse Operations

Six Sigma focuses on identifying and eliminating defects and inefficiencies in processes, aiming for near-perfect results. In warehouse operations, it can be applied to various aspects, including inventory management, order fulfillment, space utilization, and workforce management.

a) Define: Set clear objectives and identify the key processes in warehouse operations that need improvement.

b) Measure: Collect data on current performance and establish relevant metrics to track progress.

c) Analyze: Identify the root causes of inefficiencies, bottlenecks, or defects in warehouse processes.

d) Improve: Implement solutions to address the root causes and monitor their impact on performance.

e) Control: Establish ongoing monitoring and control mechanisms to sustain improvements and prevent future inefficiencies.

Optimizing Inventory Management

Effective inventory management is essential for meeting customer demand while minimizing costs. Six Sigma can help optimize inventory levels and reduce excess stock, stockouts, and obsolescence.

a) Analyze demand patterns and forecast accuracy to better predict customer needs and determine optimal stock levels.

b) Implement inventory control mechanisms, such as cycle counting and real-time inventory tracking, to minimize discrepancies and improve accuracy.

c) Use root cause analysis to identify and address issues leading to stock discrepancies or inefficiencies in the inventory management process.

Enhancing Order Fulfillment

Efficient order fulfillment is critical for customer satisfaction and timely product delivery. Six Sigma can be employed to improve the accuracy and speed of order processing, picking, packing, and shipping.

a) Analyze the order fulfillment process to identify inefficiencies and potential areas for improvement.

b) Implement solutions, such as automation, process standardization, or improved warehouse layouts, to reduce errors and cycle times.

c) Monitor key performance indicators (KPIs) to track progress and ensure continuous improvement in order fulfillment.

Maximizing Space Utilization

Optimal space utilization is crucial for reducing costs and increasing the efficiency of warehouse operations. Six Sigma can help identify opportunities to optimize warehouse layouts and storage systems.

a) Collect and analyze data on warehouse space usage, including product dimensions, storage locations, and material handling equipment.

b) Implement solutions, such as reconfiguring warehouse layouts, using vertical space, or adopting advanced storage systems, to optimize space utilization.

c) Monitor space usage and make adjustments as needed to accommodate changes in inventory levels or product mix.

Improving Workforce Management

Effective workforce management is essential for maintaining productivity and minimizing labor costs. Six Sigma can help enhance workforce planning, training, and performance monitoring.

a) Analyze workforce requirements, productivity levels, and skill sets to determine optimal staffing levels and allocation of tasks.

b) Implement standardized training programs and continuous improvement initiatives to enhance employee skills and productivity.

c) Monitor employee performance and provide feedback to drive continuous improvement and maintain high levels of efficiency.

By implementing Six Sigma in warehouse operations, companies can optimize their processes, reduce costs, and improve customer satisfaction. Through a systematic approach to process improvement, Six Sigma enables businesses to identify and address inefficiencies and defects, ultimately leading to enhanced warehouse performance and long-term success.

Six Sigma Application in E-Commerce

E-commerce has revolutionized the way businesses operate, offering an extensive range of products and services to customers worldwide. To remain competitive, e-commerce businesses must continually optimize their processes, including shipping logistics, product offerings, and customer tracking. This case study discusses how applying Six Sigma, a data-driven methodology for process improvement, can help enhance various aspects of e-commerce operations and drive success.

Understanding Six Sigma in E-commerce

Six Sigma focuses on identifying and eliminating defects and inefficiencies in processes, aiming for near-perfect results. In e-commerce, it can be applied to various aspects, such as shipping and logistics, product offerings, and customer tracking and analytics.

a) Define: Set clear objectives and identify the key processes in e-commerce operations that need improvement.

b) Measure: Collect data on current performance and establish relevant metrics to track progress.

c) Analyze: Identify the root causes of inefficiencies, bottlenecks, or defects in e-commerce processes.

d) Improve: Implement solutions to address the root causes and monitor their impact on performance.

e) Control: Establish ongoing monitoring and control mechanisms to sustain improvements and prevent future inefficiencies.

Optimizing Shipping and Shipping-Related Logistics

Efficient shipping and logistics processes are vital for e-commerce businesses to ensure timely delivery of products and maintain customer satisfaction. Six Sigma can help optimize shipping operations and reduce costs.

a) Analyze shipping processes to identify inefficiencies, delays, and potential areas for improvement.

b) Implement solutions, such as carrier selection, shipping route optimization, and order consolidation, to reduce shipping costs and improve delivery times.

c) Monitor shipping performance metrics, such as on-time delivery rates and shipping costs, to track progress and ensure continuous improvement.

Enhancing the Scope of Products Offered

A diverse and appealing product offering is essential for attracting and retaining customers in the competitive e-commerce landscape. Six Sigma can help businesses identify gaps in their product offerings and optimize their product mix.

a) Collect and analyze data on customer preferences, sales trends, and market demand to identify opportunities for expanding product offerings.

b) Implement data-driven strategies, such as targeted promotions, product bundling, and personalized recommendations, to enhance the customer experience and drive sales.

c) Monitor product performance metrics, such as sales volume, customer reviews, and return rates, to continuously improve the product mix and identify areas for further expansion.

Improving the Ability to Track How Purchases Originate

Understanding customer behavior and tracking the origin of purchases is crucial for e-commerce businesses to optimize marketing efforts and enhance the customer experience. Six Sigma can help businesses improve their tracking and analytics capabilities.

a) Analyze current tracking methods and identify potential gaps or inaccuracies in capturing customer data and purchase origins.

b) Implement solutions, such as integrating advanced tracking tools, using cookies and tracking pixels, and refining attribution models, to improve the accuracy and granularity of purchase origin data.

c) Monitor customer behavior metrics, such as conversion rates, click-through rates, and bounce rates, to inform marketing strategies and drive continuous improvement.

By implementing Six Sigma in e-commerce operations, businesses can optimize their processes, reduce costs, and improve customer satisfaction. Through a systematic approach to process improvement, Six Sigma enables e-commerce companies to identify and address inefficiencies and defects, ultimately leading to enhanced performance and long-term success. Applying Six Sigma principles to shipping logistics, product offerings, and customer tracking can help e-commerce businesses thrive in the competitive digital marketplace.

Six Sigma Application in the Retail Industry

The retail industry is characterized by constant change, fierce competition, and the need for excellent customer service. To stay ahead, retail businesses must continually optimize their processes, including inventory management, scheduling, and employee productivity. This case study discusses how applying Six Sigma, a data-driven methodology for process improvement, can help enhance various aspects of retail operations and drive success.

Understanding Six Sigma in Retail

Six Sigma focuses on identifying and eliminating defects and inefficiencies in processes, aiming for near-perfect results. In the retail industry, it can be applied to various aspects, such as inventory management, scheduling, and employee productivity.

a) Define: Set clear objectives and identify the key processes in retail operations that need improvement.

b) Measure: Collect data on current performance and establish relevant metrics to track progress.

c) Analyze: Identify the root causes of inefficiencies, bottlenecks, or defects in retail processes.

d) Improve: Implement solutions to address the root causes and monitor their impact on performance.

e) Control: Establish ongoing monitoring and control mechanisms to sustain improvements and prevent future inefficiencies.

Enhancing Inventory Management

Effective inventory management is crucial for meeting customer demand while minimizing costs. Six Sigma can help optimize inventory levels and reduce excess stock, stockouts, and obsolescence.

a) Analyze demand patterns and forecast accuracy to better predict customer needs and determine optimal stock levels.

b) Implement inventory control mechanisms, such as just-in-time (JIT) or vendor-managed inventory (VMI), to minimize stock levels while maintaining service levels.

c) Use root cause analysis to identify and address issues leading to stock discrepancies, such as inaccurate data entry or procedural errors.

Optimizing Scheduling

Efficient scheduling is essential for maintaining smooth retail operations and ensuring adequate staffing during peak times. Six Sigma can help optimize scheduling processes and reduce labor costs.

a) Collect and analyze data on store traffic patterns, sales trends, and employee productivity to determine optimal staffing levels and shift allocations.

b) Implement data-driven scheduling tools and strategies to create more accurate and flexible schedules that account for fluctuations in customer demand.

c) Monitor key performance indicators (KPIs) related to scheduling, such as labor costs and customer wait times, to track progress and ensure continuous improvement.

Improving Employee Productivity

High employee productivity is vital for retail businesses to maintain excellent customer service and achieve sales targets. Six Sigma can help enhance workforce performance through training, process improvement, and performance monitoring.

a) Analyze employee performance data, skill sets, and training needs to identify opportunities for improvement.

b) Implement standardized training programs and continuous improvement initiatives to enhance employee skills and productivity.

c) Monitor employee performance and provide feedback to drive continuous improvement and maintain high levels of efficiency.

By implementing Six Sigma in the retail industry, businesses can optimize their processes, reduce costs, and improve customer satisfaction. Through a systematic approach to process improvement, Six Sigma enables retail businesses to identify and address inefficiencies and defects, ultimately leading to enhanced performance and long-term success. Applying Six Sigma principles to inventory management, scheduling, and employee productivity can help retail businesses thrive in the competitive marketplace.

Life Hack from Animals' Strategy

The Lion Hunting Method: A Proven Plan of Action for Realizing Your Dreams

The lion is a powerful representation of leadership and bravery because of its reputation as the jungle's top predator. Lions are able to adapt to and even control their habitats thanks to their specialized hunting techniques. Lessons applicable to reaching any objective can be gleaned from the lion hunting strategy. In this chapter, we'll break down the main parts of the lion hunting plan and show you how to put them to use to achieve your goals.

Determine Your Objectives Specifically

You need to identify your prey as precisely as a lion does if you want to succeed. Having a clear target in mind helps with concentration, inspiration, and fulfillment.

First, you need to zero in on what it is you want to get out of this whole endeavor.

Aim for detail: b) Define the objective precisely, using numbers and other quantifiable measures.

Deadlines should be established c) Create a deadline for yourself to keep the pressure and motivation high.

Formulate Strategies and Plans

To successfully capture their prey, lions must first formulate elaborate plans that take into account not only the environment, but also the timing and the prey's behavior. In a similar vein, you need a well-thought-out strategy that takes into account your available assets, any necessary restraints, and any potential roadblocks on the path to success.

a) Figure out what you have at your disposal; list the equipment, abilities, and information you'll need to do the task.

Evaluate possible roadblocks (point b) Have contingency plans to deal with any obstacles you encounter.

Create a strategy: c) Convert your long-term objective into a series of shorter, more attainable objectives, then plan out the order in which you will complete each objective.

Strengthen your capacity for patience and perseverance.

Lions are incredibly patient and persistent predators that stalk their prey until the perfect moment presents itself. Realizing that your efforts may not immediately pay off requires you to practice patience and perseverance.

a) Don't give up: Keep working toward your goal despite experiencing setbacks.

b) Take failures in stride, realizing the lessons they can teach you about how to go forward and enhance your performance.

c) Strengthen your capacity for recovery and perseverance in the face of setbacks.

Team up

Lions frequently team up to hunt, capitalizing on each member of the pride's unique set of skills to maximize the odds of success. The same holds true for improving your odds of success: coordinating with others.

a) Create a community of people who believe in you and your goals, or who can offer advice, inspiration, and help.

b) Assign duties to others so that you can concentrate on your most important work.

c) Promote teamwork through inspiring trust, open dialogue, and coordinated efforts among members.

Use Your Chances

When the moment is right, a lion will pounce on his prey. If you want to succeed, you have to be able to seize chances when they present themselves.

a) Take the initiative and look for ways to further your progress that are consistent with your aims.

If new opportunities present themselves, be flexible enough to change your approach.

c) Have a growth mentality; see setbacks as chances to learn and improve; and persevere to reach your goals.

The tactics used by lion hunters provide lessons applicable to obtaining success in any endeavor. Maximize your chances of success by establishing specific objectives, preparing and strategizing accordingly, practicing patience and tenacity, fostering teamwork, and seizing opportunities when they present themselves. If you take on the lion's mindset and use these guidelines in your personal and professional life, you'll be well-prepared to achieve your goals and realize your dreams.

How to Optimize Like an Ant

Although they are very little, ants have incredible abilities that can instruct us on how to maximize productivity. Ants, thanks to their remarkable capacities for cooperation, problem-solving, and ingenuity, are able to adapt and prosper in a wide range of habitats. we'll look at what we can learn from ants and how we may use their optimization techniques in our own lives, both at work and at home.

Collaboration and clear communication are essential for success.

Ants share information and work together to achieve their goals, which allows them to overcome obstacles and make the most of their efforts as a group.

Lesson

- Create open lines of communication to guarantee that everyone is on the same page with their obligations.
- Create a setting where people are comfortable working together by rewarding people for their efforts to build on the skills of others and contribute to a common goal.
- In order to make sure that everyone on the team is working toward the same end, it is important to establish mutually agreeable goals and align individual and team objectives.

Capacity for Change and Adaptation

Ants are remarkable in their ability to adapt to new circumstances. If you want the best results, you have to be able to roll with the punches and adjust to new circumstances.

Lesson

- Assume a growth mindset and look at transitions positively.
- Foster a growth mentality, in which you view setbacks and new experiences as opportunities to progress rather than as things to be avoided.
- Be flexible in your approach; be ready to make changes to your strategies and tactics to meet your objectives.

Managing Assets Efficiently

Ants are experts at managing their resources, allocating their time, energy, and food in a way that ensures the greatest possible success for the colony as a whole.

Lesson

a) Set priorities: Figure out what needs to be done, and do it first.

b) Master time management skills in order to make the most of each day.

c) Maximize impact while minimizing waste by allocating resources such as money, people, and tools in the most efficient way possible.

Tenacity and Stamina

Ants are tough little bugs who keep on trucking' no matter what life throws their way, displaying incredible grit and persistence in the process.

Lesson

a) Grow your "grit": Practice staying motivated and determined in the face of adversity.

b) Grow from your mistakes, rather than letting them deter you.

c) Don't give up: Keep working toward your goals despite encountering setbacks.

Constant Refinement and Development

In order to succeed, ant colonies are continually gathering information and adjusting their tactics based on what they've learned. You need to be dedicated to lifelong education and development if you want to achieve your full potential.

Lesson

a) Consistently ask for people's opinions so you may learn where you can make changes for the better.

b) Take up the practice of lifelong learning; that is, make it a priority to expand your horizons and acquire new information and expertise over the course of your lifetime.

c) The third step is to think about what you've learned: Check in on your progress toward your objectives on a regular basis, and figure out what you can do to make it better.

The ant can teach us a lot about optimization and efficiency, both of which have practical applications in our daily lives. You may maximize your performance and reach your objectives if you embrace qualities like good communication and teamwork, flexibility, efficient resource management, persistence, and ongoing education. If you take a cue from the ant and apply its astonishing techniques to your own life, you will be well-prepared to deal with the trials and triumphs that lie ahead.

Project Management Skills from Bees and Termites

Insects like bees and termites are known to exhibit exceptional project management skills. These species display impressive levels of organization, efficiency, and teamwork in a variety of settings, including the construction of complex structures and the management of enormous colonies. We may improve our own project management abilities and that of our businesses and organizations by looking to the ways in which insects like bees and termites operate as models.

Separation of Duties

Each member of a colony of either bees or termites has a specific job to do that helps the colony as a whole.

Application

- For starters, make sure everyone on the team knows what they're supposed to be doing and how they can help with the project.
- Play to everyone's strengths by making sure everyone on the team is using their talents to their full potential.
- Foster teamwork by laying the groundwork for successful communication and cooperation between team members.

The Art of Conveying Information

In order to communicate information, coordinate their actions, and keep the peace within their colonies, bees and termites use complex ways of communication.

Application

a) Provide a safe space where team members can freely express their thoughts and receive constructive criticism.

b) Report both successes and failures: Keep everyone in the loop on the project's progress, both good and bad.

b) Make use of effective methods of communication: Keep everyone informed and involved through the use of a variety of tools and methods such as meetings, emails, and project management software.

Making Changes During the Process

Termites, like bees, can modify their tactics in light of new knowledge and shifting circumstances.

Application

a) Establish a project plan that may be modified as needed to account for changes in priorities or unanticipated events.

b) Keep an eye on development and make changes as required: Maintain a consistent schedule of project reviews, using the results to inform any necessary course corrections in strategy or tactics.

c) Foster creative thinking and problem-solving skills: Foster a mindset where innovation and flexibility are valued, and give your team members the freedom to come up with their own answers to problems.

Managing Assets Efficiently

Both bees and termites are masters of resource management, making the most of their available time, food, and labor.

Application

a) Establish priorities, based on how important each activity and resource is to the completion of the project.

b) Maximize resource efficiency by using tools and techniques like critical route analysis and resource leveling to distribute resources in the most effective way possible.

c) Keep an eye on how hard your resources are working by keeping tabs on their usage and performance and adjusting as needed to get the best possible results.

Evolving and Educating Without Stopping

As they gain more experience, both bees and termites modify their habits to become more productive.

Application

- Review and reflect on past project performance to find ways to enhance future efforts.
- Promote a mindset of lifelong learning by encouraging team members to proactively expand their base of technical knowledge, practice effective methods, and share what they've learned with others.
- Take note of both your triumphs and your blunders: Examine the good and bad results of the project to learn anything that can be used in the future.

The project management lessons that can be learned from bees and termites include the importance of having a defined set of roles and responsibilities, maintaining open lines of communication, being flexible in your approach, using your resources efficiently, and never stopping to rest on your laurels. With these methods, you may improve your project management abilities, leading to more fulfillment in your life and career. Study the lives of these incredible insects and apply the lessons you learn to your own work, and you'll be prepared to deal with whatever obstacles and possibilities may come your way.

Partnership to Achieve Goals: A Lesson from the Wolf and the Ravens

This unexpected friendship between wolves and ravens in the wild exemplifies the efficacy of working together toward a similar objective. Both species prosper as a result of their symbiotic relationship, which allows them to share resources and increase their chances of survival. We can learn a lot about how to work well with others and build strong teams by studying the relationship between wolves and ravens.

Value the Contributions of Others

Wolves and ravens team up because they know there is strength in numbers. Similarly, we need to see the benefits of working together if we are to develop fruitful alliances.

a) Find possible collaborators; look for people and groups who have similar objectives, philosophies, and interests.

b) Consider the qualities of potential partners and how they might be complemented by your own. This will allow you to form a more powerful and fruitful relationship.

c) Create win-win conditions by making sure everyone participating in the partnership benefits from it. This will foster trust and loyalty in the partnership over the long haul.

Build Mutual Trust and Efficacy in Discussion

The relationship between wolves and ravens only works when both species are able to open up and trust one another. We need to encourage straightforward dialogue and build trust with our partners if we're going to forge lasting collaborations.

a) Be transparent and aligned with your collaborators by regularly sharing your progress, expectations, and worries.

b) Establish a solid foundation of trust by being reliable, honest, and respectful at all times.

c) Deal with differences maturely and respectfully, working collaboratively to find solutions that satisfy everyone involved.

Get the Most out of Your Partnership by Capitalizing on Your Partners' Strengths

The wolf and the raven make a formidable team since they each contribute something special to the alliance and help increase its chances of success. We need to play to each other's strengths if we want to establish productive collaborations.

a) Appreciate and value one another's strengths: Understand and respect the special skills and knowledge that each collaborator brings to the table.

b) Delegate duties as needed: Make the most of your time and effort by dividing up duties according to who is best suited to do them based on your partners' individual skills and experience.

c) Urge partners to help and support one another, which will increase the worth of the partnership and encourage further collaboration.

Together, Evolve and Expand

Because of their shared flexibility and willingness to adjust to new circumstances, wolves and ravens have found great success as a working alliance. Cooperation succeeds when both participants are able to bend and grow with the circumstances.

a) Be adaptable; use new circumstances and difficulties as opportunities to grow and improve your relationship.

b) Improve by learning from one another; foster the exchange of information, expertise, and insight.

c) The third step is to assess and make necessary changes. Ensure the partnership's continuous success and alignment with agreed goals by regularly evaluating its progress and making adjustments as appropriate.

Raise a Glass to Our Successes

The cooperation of the wolf and the raven is an example of the benefits of working together toward a common objective. In order to keep our bonds of friendship strong, we must acknowledge and appreciate our joint achievements.

a) Celebrate successes: Honor the accomplishments of all parties involved.

b) Recognize and thank all participants: It is important that everyone involved in the collaboration feels appreciated.

c) Forge deeper ties by commemorating joint achievements; doing so will serve to underline the partnership's worth and encourage the two parties to work together and develop further.

Wolves and ravens work together to great effect because they share a same purpose and know how to support one other in the pursuit of that goal. We may form great partnerships in our personal and professional lives by appreciating the value of teamwork, working to improve our communication and trust with one another, playing to our respective strengths, learning from one another, and rejoicing in our joint accomplishments. Take to heart the advice of the wolf and the ravens, and use their guiding principles in your own partnerships, and you will be well-prepared to succeed in your endeavors via the combined effort of your team members.

The Power of Silence: What the Owl's Silent Flight Can Teach Us About Life

We often forget how important silence is in the busy world we live in. The owl, which is known for flying almost silently, is a powerful example of how silence can help us. By thinking about what we can learn from the owl's silent flight, we can understand the power of silence better and use it in our personal and professional lives to get the most out of it.

Improve your ability to observe and listen

The owl can watch and listen for prey without being seen or heard because it can fly quietly. Silence can help us become better observers and listeners in the same way.

a) Practice active listening. Instead of just waiting for your turn to talk, focus on really hearing and understanding what other people are saying.

b) Give your full attention to the task or conversation at hand. Get rid of any distractions that might get in the way.

c) Develop empathy: When we really listen and watch, we can better understand and feel what other people are feeling and see things from their point of view.

Encourage people to think and be aware.

Silence gives the owl a chance to think and plan what it will do next. Accepting quiet times can help us become more self-aware and mindful.

a) Set aside quiet time: Give yourself regular times to be alone and think to improve your mental health.

b) Practice mindfulness: Pay attention to the here and now and accept your thoughts and feelings without judging them.

c) Keeping a journal: writing down your thoughts and experiences helps you think about yourself and grow as a person.

Help you make better decisions and solve problems

The owl's quiet flight lets it think about its options and choose the best one. Silence can help us think about what we've learned and make better choices for ourselves.

a) Take a moment to think before acting. Before making important decisions, take a moment of silence to think about your options and possible outcomes.

b) Weigh the pros and cons. Think about the possible pros and cons of each choice so you can make an informed decision.

c) Enjoy your alone time. Use quiet and alone time to think critically and creatively about problems and opportunities.

Make your relationships stronger.

The owl can build trust with its surroundings because it is quiet. Accepting silence can help us connect with people more deeply and make our relationships stronger.

a) Prioritize quality over quantity. Instead of talking all the time, focus on conversations that matter.

b) Be respectful: Give other people time and space to say what they think and feel.

c) Practice being vulnerable. Use times of silence as chances to share and connect more deeply.

Reduce stress and improve your health.

The owl's quiet flight lets it move through its environment with as little noise as possible. Adding silence to our lives can help us feel less stressed and better about ourselves.

a) Use relaxation techniques: Take deep breaths, meditate, or do other exercises to help you calm down and concentrate.

b) Make a peaceful environment: Reduce the amount of noise and distractions around you to create a calm atmosphere.

c) Make self-care a top priority. Include quiet time in your self-care routine to help your emotional and mental health.

The owl's silent flight shows us how important silence can be in our lives. We can use the power of silence to improve our personal and professional lives by getting better at observing and listening, encouraging reflection and mindfulness, making better decisions and solving problems, building stronger relationships, and lowering stress. If you learn from the owl and make quiet time a part of your daily routine, you'll be able to handle the complicated parts of life with grace and wisdom.

Defeat to Victory: The Eagle's Lesson in Resilience

Eagles, which are renowned for their power and resilience, undergo a process of regeneration as they age, discarding their old, weak feathers in favor of new, stronger ones. This astounding metamorphosis is a potent allegory for how we, too, may welcome and benefit from personal growth and change. By dissecting the eagle's resurgence, we can learn how to revitalize ourselves when we're up against hardship.

Recognize the Importance of Altering Your Ways

In the same way that an eagle knows when a feather is too old and must be replaced, we too must be able to identify when it is time for a change.

a) Being in tune with yourself: Take stock of your current state of physical, mental, and emotional health on a regular basis to pinpoint any potential problem areas.

b) If you want things to improve, you have to accept the truth about where you are now and make peace with the idea that something has to shift.

c) Ask for input: Talk to reliable people for honest assessments of your strengths and places for improvement, or get advice from people in your life who have been there and know what they're talking about.

The old must go so that the new can come.

Eagles are known to shed their feathers in order to grow new, improved ones. The same is true for our own lives; in order to leave room for development and reinvention, we must release outmoded practices, ideas, and connections.

If you want to make progress, there are several things you can do to free yourself from bad influences.

- Recognize and remove yourself from unhealthy relationships and environments.
- Contemplate on the ways in which you may be limiting yourself by accepting false ideas about who you are and what you're capable of, and then actively work to dispel those notions.
- Make room for development; get rid of all the unnecessary things in your life, both material and mental, to make room for progress.
  Accept the Need for Change
  The eagle doesn't turn into an eagle overnight; the process takes time and perseverance. Take on the process of reinvention of yourself with the same dogged resolve.
- Create reasonable, attainable, and progressive objectives to direct your progress toward revitalization.
- Keep at it: Persevere in the pursuit of your objectives despite encountering challenges.
- Accept that positive transformation is a slow process and give yourself time and room to evolve at your own speed.

Be kind to yourself on all levels.

The eagle's new feathers make it stronger and more agile than ever. In our quest for regeneration, it is crucial that we take care of our bodies, minds, and hearts.

a) Make taking care of yourself a top priority; this includes activities like exercising, eating right, and getting enough sleep.

b) Develop a habit of being in the present moment by engaging in contemplative practices like meditation, writing, or yoga.

c) Get help: If you feel like you need it, talk to a therapist, a mentor, or a member of a support group for advice.

Commemorate Your Progress and Change

Think of the eagle's triumphant flight after getting new feathers as a metaphor for your own personal journey toward regeneration, and reward yourself for the steps you've already taken along the way.

a) Think about what you have accomplished so far; consider the steps you have taken and the results you have seen.

b) Inspire others with your story: Discuss your personal growth and development by detailing your journey.

c) Take pride in your renewed vitality; use the insight and fortitude you've attained on your path to self-improvement to boldly pursue new chances.

Through the process of losing its old feathers and replacing them with new, stronger ones, the eagle teaches us valuable lessons about adapting to change and revitalizing ourselves. We can experience our own resurrection and emerge stronger and more resilient if we recognize the need for change, let go of the old, embrace the process of renewal, nurture our body, mind, and soul, and celebrate our progress and transformation. Adopt the eagle's perspective and you'll flourish.

The Cleverness of the Snake: A Lesson for Life

Snakes are known for being smart and able to change, so they have been used as symbols of wisdom, change, and resourcefulness in many cultures for a long time. By thinking about what we can learn from the snake's cleverness, we can figure out how to handle the complicated parts of our own lives with intelligence, flexibility, and strength.

Ability to change and be flexible

Snakes are adaptable and flexible because they can move gracefully through their environment. In the same way, we must learn to change with the times and be open to new ways of doing things.

a) Embrace change: Be open to the changes that life brings and be willing to accept and adapt to them.

b) Be resourceful: Use the tools you have and try to think of creative ways to solve problems.

c) Keep a growth mindset: see problems as chances to get better and grow as a person.

Time and Patience

Snakes are known for being patient. They wait until the right time to strike. This ability to wait and watch teaches us that timing is important and that we should take advantage of opportunities when they come up.

a) Be patient: Train yourself to be able to wait calmly until the right time to act.

b) Observe and judge: Before making a decision, carefully judge the situation and gather information.

c) Seize opportunities: When they come up, look for them and make the most of them.

Snakes rely on their instincts to find their way around and stay away from danger. We can learn from them to trust our own instincts and make decisions based on what our hearts tell us.

a) Trust your gut: When making decisions, pay attention to how you feel in your gut.

b) Get to know yourself. Think about your feelings, thoughts, and experiences to learn more about your instincts and intuition.

c) Balance intuition and logic. To make well-rounded decisions, use both your intuitive insights and your logical analysis.

Getting back up and starting over

Snakes are known for being able to shed their skin, which is a sign of change and rebirth. Their ability to keep going shows us how important it is to accept change and start over when we need to.

a) Embrace change: Think of personal growth and change as important parts of life.

b) Deal with problems: Build resilience by facing problems head-on and learning from them.

c) Reinvent yourself: Know when it's time to let go of old habits, beliefs, or situations and start on a new, more fulfilling path.

Wisdom and Common Sense

Snakes' cleverness is a sign of deep wisdom and good judgment. By having these traits, we can make better decisions and move through our lives with more wisdom.

a) Seek knowledge: Keep learning and improving yourself throughout your life to learn more about the world around you.

b) Develop discernment: learn to tell the difference between truth and lies and have the sense to know when to act.

c) Think about what you've done: Think about what you've done often and use what you've learned in the future.

The snake's cleverness can teach us a lot about how to be flexible, patient, wise, resilient, and intuitive. By embracing these traits and putting them to use in our own lives, we can handle life's challenges and unknowns with more ease, intelligence, and strength. Accept the snake's wisdom and let its cleverness guide you on your journey of personal growth and change.

The Wisdom of the Hyenas: There Is Strength in Numbers

Misunderstood and underestimated as a species, hyenas teach us valuable lessons about the value of working together. Hyenas are social animals that form big groups, termed clans, in which they hunt, defend their territory, and raise their young. Thinking about hyenas and how they work together to accomplish their goals can teach us a lot about the value of cooperation and togetherness in our own lives.

Working Together Can-Do Wonders

Hyenas band together to kill bigger animals and protect themselves from predators. Their collective productivity will increase if they can learn to complement one another.

a) Value collaboration and the contributions of others; acknowledge that success is more likely when people work together.

b) Capitalize on the distinct abilities, points of view, and experiences of all team members.

c) Promote open communication by stressing the importance of honest and respectful dialogue within the team.

Connection and Helping Hands

Hyenas form tight-knit families that look out for one another. Likewise, we have the ability to form communities of mutual aid that will aid in our development and enable us to weather any storms that may come our way.

a) Make an effort to develop your network by maintaining positive ties with people in your life, such as those you've just met or those who have guided you in the past.

b) Be there for others when they need help, and be willing to accept aid yourself when it's offered.

d) Instill a feeling of community: Create a welcoming environment and acknowledge everyone's accomplishments.

We All Carry the Load

Hunting, defending the territory, and caring for the young are all tasks that are divided up among the members of a hyena clan. This demonstrates the value of delegating work to different people so that more substantial goals can be met.

When working in a team, it's important to a) delegate tasks to team members who are the most qualified to complete them, and b) utilize the team's collective skills and strengths.

Decisions should be made in a way that allows for input from all parties, so that everyone feels like they contributed.

Keep yourself and others accountable for completing duties and obligations to which they have been allocated.

Ability to improvise and find a solution

Hyenas are adaptable creatures that can make do with a wide range of habitats and diets. This versatility should serve as a reminder to us to maintain a similar disposition toward our own situations.

a) Have a flexible mindset, so that you can readily accept and adjust to novel situations and opportunities.

b) Be on the lookout for original answers; as you grow in ingenuity, try out some new approaches to old challenges.

b) Get wisdom via experience; use what you've learnt to evolve and adapt to changing circumstances.

Endurance and Fortitude

Hyenas show resiliency and perseverance despite confronting several obstacles in their natural habitat. In spite of hardships, they are able to persevere thanks to their large population.

a) Keep your chin up: In spite of any difficulties, you must keep your eye on the prize.

b) Develop a strong mental and emotional constitution via experience with and acceptance of disappointments.

Recognize and honor the accomplishments of both yourself and your community members to keep spirits high and motivation high.

Hyenas teach us about the benefits of working together, having a strong social network, taking turns, dividing and conquering, and being flexible and resilient. To overcome obstacles and reach our goals, we need to work together, and by adopting these principles we may tap into the strength of togetherness. Take a cue from hyenas and find safety in numbers while also making genuine connections with those around you; that's how you'll succeed.

Profiting from Waste: A Life Lesson from Vulture

Vultures, renowned for their capacity to flourish in circumstances that appear unsuitable, serve as a compelling example of resourcefulness and adaptation. These extraordinary birds serve as nature's garbage collectors, devouring animal carcasses and limiting the spread of illness. By exploring the life lessons we can glean from vultures and their capacity to profit from garbage, we may gain a better understanding of how to utilize our resources and seize chances despite difficult circumstances.

Innovativeness and Effectiveness

Vultures excel at maximizing the use of available resources, finding sustenance in what others may consider waste. This demonstrates the significance of resourcefulness and efficiency in our own lives.

a) Maximize resources: Seek innovative ways to utilize the resources at your disposal in an efficient manner.

b) Minimize waste: Strive for efficiency by minimizing waste and saving resources in your daily life.

c) Accept frugality: Adopt a thrifty lifestyle, prioritizing needs over desires, and finding value in simplicity.

Adaptability and Hardiness

Vultures are extremely adaptive, able to thrive in a variety of settings and conditions. Its adaptation reminds us to remain adaptable and resilient in our own lives.

a) Be adaptable: Accept new difficulties and possibilities, adjusting your strategy as necessary.

b) Build mental and emotional resilience by learning from setbacks and persisting in the face of adversity

b) Grow as a result of experience: Utilize the lessons acquired from prior experiences in order to adapt and develop in response to new challenges.

Seizing Opportunity

Vultures are opportunistic eaters that take advantage of food sources when they become available. This demonstrates the necessity of grasping opportunities when they present themselves.

a) Be vigilant and prepared: Maintain awareness of your surroundings and be ready to act when opportunities present themselves.

b) Take measured risks Assess prospective opportunities and take calculated risks to accomplish your objectives.

c) Embrace the unorthodox: Be receptive to unorthodox routes and strategies that may lead to success.

Environmental Sustainability and Awareness

By recycling nutrients and avoiding the spread of illnesses, vultures serve a critical role in maintaining ecological balance. Their contribution to the ecosystem teaches us the significance of environmental consciousness and sustainability.

a) Employ eco-friendly behaviors and activities in your daily life to lessen your environmental effect.

b) Promote conservation: Advocate for and support local and worldwide conservation activities.

c) Educate others: Disseminate information and promote awareness about environmental issues and sustainable practices.

Turning Obstacles into Opportunity

By obtaining food in ostensibly unfavorable circumstances, vultures exhibit the power of changing obstacles into opportunities. This ability to profit from garbage can motivate us to adopt a similar mentality towards our own issues.

a) Reframe obstacles as opportunities for personal growth and development.

b) Use hardship to gain new abilities, knowledge, and resiliency.

c) Identify hidden chances: In challenging situations, look for hidden possibilities and be prepared to act when they show themselves.

The life lessons we may learn from vultures, such as resourcefulness, adaptation, seizing opportunities, and sustainability, can motivate us to make the most of our circumstances and attain our objectives. By adopting the vultures' intelligence and their capacity to benefit from garbage, we may cultivate a mindset of resilience and resourcefulness, enabling us to prosper even in difficult circumstances. Let the extraordinary flexibility of the vulture guide you on your path to personal growth and achievement.

Learning from Elephants: Incorporating Their Traits into Your Own Development

Elephants are well-known for their massive stature, sharp minds, and close-knit communities. They model a wide range of traits that might motivate us to work on ourselves and our connections with others. Elephants are fascinating creatures, and by studying them, we can gain insight into how to improve our own lives.

Elephant and Empathy: Two Sides of the Same Coin

Elephants show high levels of emotional intelligence and empathy by looking out for members of their herd and grieving the deaths of loved ones.

a) Work on your EQ by learning to identify and assess your own and others' emotional states, as well as those of the people around you.

b) Strive for genuine emotional and cognitive understanding of other people by putting yourself in their shoes.

c) Be there for those you care about by providing emotional support and comfort when circumstances are tough.

Close-knit communities and cherished traditions

Elephants create tight relationships with their families, which they use to care for and defend one another.

a) Take the time to cultivate meaningful relationships with those closest to you.

b) Put family first: Recognize the value of your loved ones and do everything you can to spend quality time with them.

c) Create a safety net: Surround yourself with loving, encouraging, and encouraging friends and family members.

Learning and Remembering

Elephants can recall names, faces, and even entire landscapes for long periods of time.

a) Boost your memory by using memory-boosting strategies like mental imagery, mental association, and repeated exposure.

b) Gain wisdom through introspection and application of past events when making present and future choices and moves.

c) Have a growth mindset and a thirst for knowledge by actively seeking out new information and experiences throughout your life.

Sharing Information and Working Together

Elephants have refined methods of communicating with one another, employing a wide range of sounds and body language to exchange information and coordinate behavior.

- Improve your ability to convey your thoughts and emotions via both spoken and nonverbal means.
- Value teamwork and mutual support as you work with others toward a common objective
- Be a good listener and recognize the value of other people's input and work to create a climate where people feel comfortable talking to one another and sharing their views.

The matriarchs of elephant herds provide leadership and make important decisions for the herd's well-being and survival.

a) Hone your leadership chops by learning to shoulder more responsibility, inspire those around you, and make well-informed choices.

b) Use your best judgment; make decisions after giving due consideration to all relevant factors.

c) Set a good example by being trustworthy, responsible, and knowledgeable in whatever you do.

Capacity for Recovery and Change

Elephants are highly resilient and adaptable animals, able to flourish despite facing many obstacles in their natural habitats.

a) Encourage resiliency; this means bolstering one's capacity to bounce back from mental and emotional failures by reflecting on and gaining wisdom from past experiences of struggle.

b) Have a flexible and open mindset, ready to make adjustments to your strategy as needed to deal with setbacks and take advantage of opportunities.

c) Take cues from nature; be inspired by the tenacity and versatility of the natural world and model your own behavior after it.

Emotional intelligence, strong social attachments, memory and learning, communication, leadership, and resilience are just some of the elephant-like traits that can help us improve our relationships, develop as people, and achieve our goals in life. Use the knowledge of these incredible animals to better yourself and gain insight into the world around you.

Harnessing the Power of the Tiger: Strength and Determination Lessons

Tigers, renowned for their power, dexterity, and solitary nature, evoke reverence and awe. These magnificent creatures exemplify attributes such as strength, resiliency, and adaptability that can be utilized to promote our own development and success. By observing and studying the tiger's characteristics, we may apply these lessons to our own life and overcome obstacles with grace and resolve.

Fortitude and Courage

Tigers are fearsome predators that rely on their power and bravery to hunt and defend their territories.

a) Build inner strength: Develop mental and emotional resiliency, so equipping yourself to confront obstacles and adversity.

b) Embrace courage: Confront your concerns and take calculated chances, extending outside your comfort zone in pursuit of achievement and growth.

c) Take a stand for yourself: Confidently assert your rights and opinions, defending your principles and boundaries when appropriate.

Focus and Resoluteness

Tigers stalk their prey with extreme concentration and determination, using patience and accuracy to achieve their objectives.

a) Improve your capacity to concentrate by minimizing distractions and keeping totally committed to your duties and objectives.

b) Develop determination: Pursue your goals with uncompromising devotion, persisting despite hurdles and failures.

c) Create SMART (specific, measurable, attainable, relevant, and time-bound) goals, which provide a clear road map for success.

Flexibleness and Resourcefulness

Tigers are extremely versatile animals, able to thrive in a variety of situations and make the most of available resources.

a) Embrace adaptability: Be receptive to change and adaptable, modifying your approach as necessary to overcome obstacles and capture opportunities.

b) Be resourceful: Use your imagination and problem-solving skills to find unique solutions while maximizing the available resources.

b) Learn from experience: Reflect on past experiences and use them to educate future actions and more effectively adapt to new situations.

Self-Reliance and Independence

Tigers are solitary creatures who rely on their abilities and instincts to flourish in the wild.

a) Develop independence by accepting responsibility for your decisions, actions, and personal development.

b) Rely on your instincts: Use your inner wisdom to aid you in making decisions and navigating obstacles by listening to your intuition.

c) Gain independence: Get the skills and information necessary to handle your personal, professional, and financial well-being with confidence.

Covertness and Patience

Tigers are masters of stealth, using patience and camouflage to sneak up on their prey unobserved before pounce.

a) Exercise patience: Develop the capacity to remain patient in stressful or difficult situations, rejecting the impulse to act rashly.

b) Be strategic: Before acting, plan your actions thoroughly, taking into account probable outcomes and repercussions.

c) Exercising restraint: Recognize when to hold back and wait for the appropriate chance before striking with accuracy and intent.

By harnessing the power of the tiger and adopting characteristics such as ferocity, concentration, adaptability, independence, and stealth, we can boost our personal development and attain success in a variety of areas. The journey towards self-improvement, resiliency, and tenacity can be aided by the insight of these amazing creatures. Always strive for greatness and self-discovery, embodying the spirit of the tiger as you tackle adversities with elegance and tenacity and with a commitment to excellence.

How to Conquer Fear with the Persistence of a Honey Badger: How to Get What You Want in Life

Honey badgers are infamous for their resiliency and hardiness despite their diminutive size. Their ability to take on enemies considerably larger than themselves can serve as a lesson in overcoming apprehension and hardship in our own lives. The honey badger's fearlessness can teach us the strength and determination to realize our own dreams.

courage and fearlessness

The honey badger is known for its amazing lack of fear in the face of danger.

a) Get fearless by facing your anxieties head-on, so that you can gain the confidence to take risks when necessary.

b) Have an attitude of boldness; do what needs to be done regardless of whether or not you are sure of the outcome.

c) Conquer self-doubt: Have faith in your skills and believe in your judgment; ignore the negative chatter in your head.

Determination and tenacity

The honey badger has a reputation for being incredibly resilient and determined.

a) Strengthen your persistence by training yourself to persevere no matter how difficult things get.

b) Be steadfast in the face of adversity; keep moving forward toward your goals despite the fact that you may encounter some resistance.

c) Use your setbacks as motivation to push yourself to greater heights, and view failure as a stepping stone to achievement.

Ability to improvise and find a solution

Honey badgers are extremely versatile animals that can prosper in a wide range of ecosystems and come up with novel approaches to old issues.

a) Accept flexibility; have an open mind and be ready to make adjustments to your strategy as needed to meet new obstacles and take advantage of emerging opportunities.

b) Make the most of what you have by being inventive and using your problem-solving talents to come up with original approaches to issues you encounter.

c) Adaptability: hone your capacity to respond successfully to novel circumstances by drawing on your existing store of expertise and experience.

Independence and self-sufficiency

Honey badgers are solitary creatures that rely only on their innate abilities to live in nature.

a) Cultivate independence and self-assurance by taking charge of your own life and being accountable for your actions and development.

b) Follow your gut: When faced with a decision or a difficult situation, rely on your inner wisdom and trust your instincts.

c) Become more self-reliant by arming yourself with the know-how to take charge of your own life on all fronts, including the financial, emotional, and professional ones.

Tackling Difficulties Head-On

Honey badgers are fearless animals who dive headfirst into danger.

- Take on difficulties head-on: When faced with a difficult situation, don't shy away from it; instead, face it with confidence and resolve.
- Increase your capacity for analysis and problem-solving, allowing you to better face and overcome difficulties.
- While independence is crucial, it's also important to know when to ask for assistance in order to triumph over extremely daunting challenges.

Adopting the honey badger's doggedness and lack of apprehension can help us build the bravery, resilience, and resolve to face our anxieties and succeed in the face of adversity. Use this incredible animal as motivation to take on obstacles head-on and realize your full potential. It's important to keep in mind that, just like the honey badger, you're equipped with the intrinsic strength and resourcefulness to overcome any obstacle in your path.

A Life Lesson from the Curiosity of a Cat

As we try to figure out how to get through life, we often look for advice from different places. Surprisingly, the curiosity of a cat can teach us one of the most important lessons we can learn. This section will talk about the life lessons we can learn from cats' natural curiosity and desire to explore, as well as how we can use these lessons in our own lives.

Embrace Curiosity

Cats are natural explorers who are always eager to check out something new, like a new toy, a mysterious box, or a hidden corner. This constant desire to learn helps them understand their surroundings better. In the same way, embracing our curiosity can help us grow as people and improve our minds. By asking questions and looking for new things to do, we learn more and get new ideas that can make our lives better.

Overcome Fear

Cats are known for not being afraid of anything. To satisfy their curiosity, they often take calculated risks. They push themselves by climbing to high places or going through places they have never been before. We can learn from this bravery by getting out of our comfort zones and facing our fears. This can not only lead to new opportunities, but it can also help us feel better about ourselves and make us stronger.

Be Present

Cats are great at living in the present because they pay close attention to what they're doing, whether it's stalking prey or playing with a toy. This ability to be in the moment lets them fully enjoy and enjoy themselves in the moment. As people, we often can't stop thinking about the past or the future, which can cause anxiety or stress. Learning to be here and now, like a cat, can help us feel less stressed and enjoy the beauty of our surroundings.

Adaptability

Cats are very good at getting used to new places and situations. Their desire to find out more drives them to explore, learn, and, in the end, change in response to any challenges they face. We can learn from their ability to change and become more interested in change instead of afraid of it. By doing this, we can learn to be more resilient and better deal with the fact that life is always changing.

Believe your gut.

Cats rely on their instincts a lot, and they use them to find their way around and make decisions. Even though humans are smarter than animals, we can still learn from them how important it is to trust our instincts. When faced with hard choices or situations, it's sometimes important to listen to our inner voice, which can give us important information that our rational mind might miss.

Seeing how curious a cat is can teach us important lessons about being curious, getting over our fears, being in the moment, being flexible, and trusting our instincts. By putting these lessons into practice in our daily lives, we can grow, get ahead, and learn more about the world around us.

Meerkat Security Shift: A Lesson for Life

Meerkats are small mammals that live in the Kalahari Desert in southern Africa. They are in the same family as mongooses. These fascinating creatures have a unique way of organizing their social structure and performing their daily activities, which can teach us valuable life lessons. The meerkats' security shift system is a great example of working as a team, taking responsibility, and staying alert. In this section, we'll look at what we can learn from the meerkat's security shift and how we can use it in our own lives.

Teamwork and Working Together

Meerkats live in big groups called "mobs" or "clans," which are often made up of more than one family. Their ability to stay alive depends on how well everyone works together. When looking for food, one or more meerkats take turns being sentinels and keeping an eye out for possible dangers. This cooperative behavior ensures the safety of the entire group.

Teamwork and cooperation are important for success in many parts of a person's life, from personal relationships to the workplace. Working together, we can accomplish more and overcome challenges that might be insurmountable for an individual acting alone.

Shared Responsibility

In a meerkat mob, everyone takes turns being a sentinel, no matter how old or important they are. This shared responsibility ensures that everyone contributes to the group's well-being and no individual is overly burdened.

Life Lesson: Sharing responsibilities is important if we want to keep our lives in balance and harmony. By dividing up the work and working together, we can make each other's lives easier and reach our goals more quickly.

Be careful and aware

As sentinels, meerkats are very alert and aware of what's going on around them. They stay on high alert for any signs of danger, making sure that their friends who are out hunting are safe. This kind of care is essential for the group to stay alive.

Life Lesson: Being alert and aware can help us spot potential risks and opportunities in our own lives. We can make better decisions, take advantage of opportunities, and avoid problems if we stay aware and pay attention.

Communication

When a meerkat sentinel sees a threat, it sounds an alarm call to warn the rest of the group. The type of call changes depending on the danger, so the meerkats can take the right steps, like hiding or running away. Their survival depends on being able to talk to each other well.

Life Lesson: Being able to talk to people and get things done well is an important skill. We can avoid misunderstandings, solve problems, and work together better if we say what we mean and listen to what others say.

Trust and Reliability

Meerkats rely on their sentinels to keep them safe, trusting that they will alert the group in case of danger. This trust is important for the group to work well and for its members to stay alive.

Lesson for Life: Trust and dependability are important parts of our relationships and communities. By being dependable and trustworthy, we can foster stronger bonds and contribute to the well-being of those around us.

In the end, the meerkat security shift system teaches us important lessons about working as a team, sharing responsibility, being alert, talking to each other, and trusting each other. By following these rules, we can make our relationships stronger, improve our own growth, and do good things for our communities.

A Lesson in Focusing on One's Strengths from Crocodiles

Because of the unique ways in which they have adapted to their environments, crocodiles are not just ancient but also fearsome predators. These distinctions can motivate us by showing us how others have made the most of challenging circumstances and taught them to their advantage. In this study, we'll learn about the crocodile's remarkable adaptations and the science underlying them.

Accepting Our Strengths: The Mighty Jaws

The ferocity of a crocodile's bite is a key adaptation that helps it succeed as a predator. All of this should serve as a reminder of the value of recognizing and honing one's own abilities. Recognizing and honing one's individual strengths makes one more capable, assured, and successful.

The key to realizing your full potential and succeeding in life is to first recognize and then cultivate your unique set of strengths.

Learning to Wait Patiently: Hide and Stride

Crocodiles are experts at hiding in plain sight until the right moment to strike presents itself. This underlines the significance of timing and the virtue of patience. It's wiser to wait for the correct time to act than to leap into an uncertain scenario without proper preparation.

Understand the significance of timing while making choices and seizing opportunities; practice patience.

Quickness and dexterity in adapting to new settings

Crocodiles, despite their bulk, are surprisingly swift and nimble in both the water and on land. Because of this versatility, they are able to survive in many settings and hunt a wide variety of animals. As such, we might take this as a lesson in the importance of developing a wide range of talents and perspectives.

Lesson in life: hone a flexible set of abilities and perspective that will serve you well no matter what comes your way.

Crocodiles' thick, armor-like skin protects them from danger and heals quickly after being damaged or punctured. Having the ability to bounce back from adversity and safeguard one's own well-being are two skills that are essential to our daily survival. Some examples of this might be learning to say "no" and sticking to those limits, putting yourself first, and establishing positive coping techniques.

Takeaway: If you want to succeed in life, you need to develop the ability to bounce back from adversity and strengthen your emotional and mental defenses.

Learning and Improvement Across a Lifetime: Tooth Regeneration

Crocodiles can replace their teeth throughout their lives, giving them a fresh set of tools for hunting and eating during their entire lifespan. This modification is meant to symbolize the value of continuous education and development. The only way to keep ahead of the competition and succeed in our chosen fields is to constantly expand our repertoire of relevant skills and information.

The world is always changing, so it's important to embrace learning and development as a way to stay current and effective.

We can learn from crocodiles' unique strategies how to better value our own abilities, be patient, flexible, open to change, and committed to learning throughout our lives. This knowledge and practice will allow us to maximize our individual strengths and succeed in all aspects of life.

Conclusion

The "Lean Life Solution" offers a comprehensive and practical approach to optimizing various aspects of one's life, drawing inspiration from the lean principles that have proven successful in organizational and industrial contexts. By embracing the lean mindset and employing the tools and techniques presented throughout the book, readers can embark on a transformative journey to minimize waste, streamline processes, and maximize value in their personal and professional lives.

This book has covered a wide range of topics, from enhancing productivity and decision-making to improving relationships and personal well-being. It has provided actionable steps and guidelines for implementing lean principles in everyday life, enabling readers to experience the benefits of a lean lifestyle firsthand.

As we conclude this journey, it is essential to remember that the pursuit of a lean life is an ongoing process, not a one-time event. Continuous improvement and self-reflection are at the core of the lean philosophy, and readers are encouraged to make a lifelong commitment to learning and growth.

The "Lean Life Solution" is more than just a book; it is a roadmap to a more fulfilling, efficient, and purpose-driven life. By embracing the lean principles and fostering a culture of continuous improvement, readers can unlock their full potential and achieve lasting success in all areas of life.

So, as you close the final pages of this book, remember that the real journey is just beginning. Take the lessons you've learned, apply them to your life, and watch as the lean lifestyle propels you towards a happier, more efficient, and more fulfilling existence. Embrace the lean life solution, and let it guide you towards the life you've always envisioned.

www.ingramcontent.com/pod-product-compliance
Lightning Source LLC
Chambersburg PA
CBHW071725150726
47998CB00005B/1501